NORTHERN
CALIFORNIA
BIKING

NORTHERN
CALIFORNIA
BIKING

150 of the Best
Road and Trail Rides

Ann Marie Brown

AVALON
TRAVEL

FOGHORN OUTDOORS:
NORTHERN CALIFORNIA BIKING
150 of the Best Road and Trail Rides

First Edition

Ann Marie Brown

Published by
Avalon Travel Publishing, Inc.
1400 65th Street, Suite 250
Emeryville, CA 94608, USA

Please send all comments, corrections, additions, amendments, and critiques to:

FOGHORN OUTDOORS:
NORTHERN CALIFORNIA BIKING
Avalon Travel Publishing
1400 65th Street
Suite 250
Emeryville, CA 94608

email: atpfeedback@avalonpub.com
website: www.foghorn.com

Printing History
1st edition—November 2003
5 4 3 2 1

ISBN: 1-56691-422-1
ISSN: 1539-9451

Editor: Marisa Solís
Series Manager: Marisa Solís
Copy Editor: Emily Lunceford
Graphics Coordinator: Jane Musser
Production Coordinator: Amber Pirker
Interior Design: Alvaro Villanueva, Amber Pirker
Cover Design: Jacob Goolkasian
Icons: Jacob Goolkasian
Map Editors: Olivia Solís, Naomi Adler Dancis, Mike Morgenfeld
Cartographers: Ben Pease, Kat Kalamaras, Mike Morgenfeld
Indexer: Rachel Kuhn
Profilers: Donald Patterson, Becky Owston, Mike Morgenfeld, Suzanne Service, Naomi Adler Dancis

Front cover photo: © Paul Souders/WorldFoto

Distributed by Publishers Group West

Printed in the United States of America by Worzalla

ABOUT THE AUTHOR

Author of 10 outdoor guidebooks with Avalon Travel Publishing, Ann Marie Brown is a dedicated California outdoorswoman. She bikes, hikes, and camps more than 150 days each year in a dedicated effort to avoid routine, complacency, and getting a real job.

Ann Marie's love of bicycling was founded in her youth. At age 2, she commandeered her older sister's tricycle, pointed it down the steepest

© ANN MARIE BROWN

stretch of her family's driveway, and had her first experience with "road rash." She pedaled her first century tour at age 15, although the ride ended prematurely at mile 82 when her brakes failed on a steep descent in the rain. Fortunately, her bruises quickly healed, and her loving parents chipped in to buy her a new set of wheels. Ann Marie has been falling off one bike or another at regular intervals ever since. (She prefers the term "involuntary dismount.")

Ann Marie's work has appeared in *Sunset, VIA, Smithsonian,* and *California* magazines. As a way of giving back a bit of what she gets from her outdoor experiences, she writes and edits for several environmental groups, including the Sierra Club and National Resources Defense Council.

When not riding or hiking along a California trail, Ann Marie lives on the Northern California coast with her two cats, who also serve as her chief editors.

In addition to *Foghorn Outdoors: Northern California Biking,* Ann Marie's outdoor guidebooks include:

Foghorn Outdoors: 101 Great Hikes of the San Francisco Bay Area
Foghorn Outdoors: California Hiking with Tom Stienstra
Foghorn Outdoors: California Waterfalls
Foghorn Outdoors: Day-Hiking California's National Parks
Foghorn Outdoors: Easy Biking in Northern California
Foghorn Outdoors: Easy Camping in Southern California
Foghorn Outdoors: Easy Hiking in Northern California
Foghorn Outdoors: Easy Hiking in Southern California
Foghorn Outdoors: Southern California Cabins & Cottages

For more information on these titles, visit www.annmariebrown.com.

CONTENTS

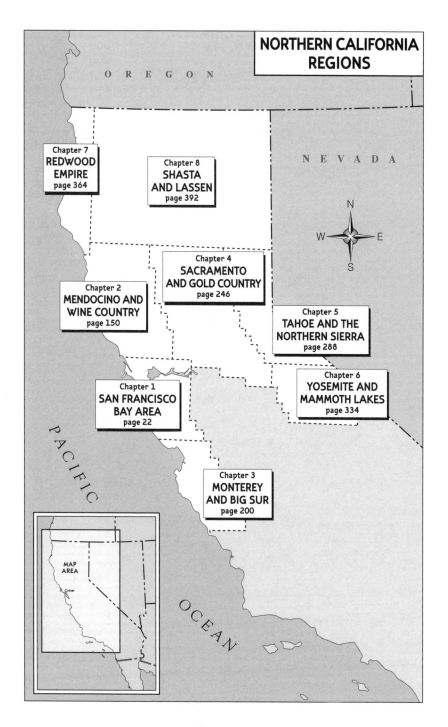

NORTHERN CALIFORNIA
REGIONS

OREGON

NEVADA

Chapter 7
REDWOOD EMPIRE
page 364

Chapter 8
SHASTA AND LASSEN
page 392

N
W E
S

Chapter 4
SACRAMENTO AND GOLD COUNTRY
page 246

Chapter 2
MENDOCINO AND WINE COUNTRY
page 150

Chapter 5
TAHOE AND THE NORTHERN SIERRA
page 288

Chapter 1
SAN FRANCISCO BAY AREA
page 22

Chapter 6
YOSEMITE AND MAMMOTH LAKES
page 334

PACIFIC

Chapter 3
MONTEREY AND BIG SUR
page 200

MAP AREA

OCEAN

OUR COMMITMENT

We are committed to making *Foghorn Outdoors: Northern California Biking* the most accurate and enjoyable guide to mountain biking and road cycling in the nothern part of the state. Each ride has been carefully selected and tested so that we may offer readers the best of a variety of rides in the area. We've also incorporated nearby attractions and stops in each ride. Be aware, however, that with the passing of time, road conditions may have been upgraded (or downgraded), changes in weather may close trails, and featured attractions and bike shops may have moved. With these possibilities in mind, or if you have a specific need or concern, it's best to call the number(s) listed for the ride ahead of time.

If you would like to comment on the book, whether it's to suggest your favorite ride or to let us know about any noteworthy experience—good or bad—that occurred while using *Foghorn Outdoors: Northern California Biking* as your guide, we would appreciate hearing from you. Please address correspondence to:

> *Foghorn Outdoors:*
> *Northern California Biking*
> Avalon Travel Publishing
> 1400 65th Street, Suite 250
> Emeryville, CA 94608
>
> email: atpfeedback@avalonpub.com

If you send us an email, please put "Northern California Biking" in the subject line. Thanks.

HOW TO USE THIS BOOK

Foghorn Outdoors: Northern California Biking is divided into eight chapters: San Francisco Bay Area, Mendocino and Wine Country, Monterey and Big Sur, Sacramento and Gold Country, Tahoe and the Northern Sierra, Yosemite and Mammoth Lakes, The Redwood Empire, and Shasta and Lassen. Although that is a lot of territory to cover in one book, navigating this guide can be done easily in two ways:

1. If you know the general area you want to visit within one of the eight regions, turn to the map at the beginning of that chapter. You can then determine which bike routes are in or near your destination by their corresponding numbers. Opposite the map will be a chapter table of contents listing each route in the chapter by map number and page number. Then turn to the corresponding page for the route you're interested in.

2. If you know the name of the route, or the name of the surrounding geographical area or nearby feature (town, national or state park or forest, lake, etc.), look it up in the index and turn to the corresponding page.

About the Ride Number and Name

Each ride in this book has a number and name. The ride's number allows you to find it easily on the corresponding chapter map. The name is either the actual trail or street name (as listed on signposts and maps) or a name I've given to a series of trails or streets. In these cases, the ride's name is taken from the focal point of the route, usually a geographic landmark, such as the name of a ridge it traverses or destination it reaches.

About the Route Details

Each ride is composed of one or more routes—the physical path that the ride takes. Here is where you'll find key information about the ride in five categories:

type of trail — This section notes the kind of trail surface(s) you'll encounter, plus how much car or other traffic is common along the route. Single-track trails are also noted here. Icons are used to provide at-a-glance information:

 = paved road or bike path; road bikes are appropriate

= dirt road or trail; mountain bikes are appropriate

If both icons appear, the route is a mix of pavement and dirt; these routes are typically traveled by mountain bikes.

difficulty — This rating, from 1 to 5 water bottles (with 1 being the easiest), is determined by the amount of climbing required, the total mileage, and, for mountain bike rides, the trail surface and level of technical skill required. Other factors can also affect the rating, such as high-elevation air or extremely steep grades in sections of the route even when the total elevation gain is not exceptional. Changeable factors like hot weather can also make a relatively easy ride feel like a very difficult ride.

Thus, with a few modifications and adjustments, the scale is generally applied as follows:

— These rides would be suitable for families with young children, novice riders, or those wanting a casual, recreational ride for a little exercise and fresh air. They include both road and mountain bike rides that are nearly level (less than 500 feet of elevation gain) and less than 15 miles. Trail surfaces are smooth.

— These rides are suitable for families with older children and for strong beginners, i.e. novice riders who are physically fit. They include both road and mountain bike rides that have between 500 and 1,200 feet of elevation gain. Mountain bike trails are generally less than 15 miles; paved routes are generally less than 25 miles. Dirt trail surfaces may not be completely smooth, but they do not require any special skills for riding.

— These rides are suitable for road bike riders with solid aerobic fitness, and mountain bike riders with solid aerobic fitness and a moderate amount of experience on dirt trails, including single-track. They include both road and mountain bike rides that have between 1,200 and 2,000 feet of elevation gain. Mountain bike trails are generally less than 15 miles; paved routes are generally 25 to 50 miles. Dirt trail surfaces may require technical skills for riding, such as the ability to ride over and around rough surfaces (rocks, roots, or ruts), descend steep hills, maneuver through tight turns, follow a narrow line with good balance, etc.

— These rides are suitable for road bike riders with excellent aerobic fitness, and mountain bike riders with excellent aerobic fitness and substantial technical skills. They include both road and mountain bike rides that have between 2,000 and 3,500 feet of elevation gain. Mountain bike trails are generally less than 20 miles; paved routes are generally 25 to 50 miles, but with steeper climbs than rides rated 3. Dirt trail surfaces may require superior technical skills to handle steep descents, rocky terrain, etc.

— These are challenging rides for serious road cyclists. They include road rides having more than 3,500 feet of elevation gain. Routes are generally 50 or more miles.

total distance — This section conveys the total *round-trip* distance covered in miles.

riding time — This section conveys the total time it will take to complete the route for an adult with some biking experience in moderate shape. Riding times may vary due to level of experience, weather, and the number and length of any breaks taken.

elevation gain — This section conveys the approximate total elevation *climbed*. For example, if there are two peaks in a route, one with an 850-foot climb and the other with a 1,000-foot climb, the total elevation gain would be 1,850 feet. The measurements were taken using topographic maps and other paper sources. They may not be precise, but should be considered very good estimates.

About the Route Description

This narrative section outlines the less measurable elements of the ride. You'll read my observations about the ride in general, plus first-hand experience with other user groups, route conditions, and any technically difficult spots. How rain, wind, and heat can affect your ride is discussed, along with car traffic and any steep grades. I also describe the scenery and outstanding qualities of each ride.

About the Route Directions

With each ride in this book you'll find a mile-by-mile listing of what to expect along the trail or road. Every major junction or turn is noted in the mileage log and recorded to the nearest tenth of a mile. Please note, however, that determining mileage is an inexact science. One bicycle's cyclometer will often disagree with another bicycle's cyclometer. For example, reducing your tire pressure changes the rolling radius of your wheel, which affects what your cyclometer registers as mileage. Putting more weight on your front tire (such as during a descent) affects your cyclometer's reading. Then there is human error: Where you "zero out" your mileage (or where you start the clock) will have a big impact on your mile-by-mile status. Small diversions from the path (such as riding back 50 yards to check on your riding partner, then turning around and heading back) create noticeable changes in your mileage.

To put it simply, use some perspective when using the mileage logs. If the log notes that a right turn is coming up at mile 4.2 and you can't find it, try riding another quarter mile or so to see if it shows up (or backtrack, to see if you've missed it!). Most importantly, always carry a good map with you.

About the Elevation Profiles

Provided for each ride is an elevation profile, which approximately graphs the hills and dips on the route in height and distance. The scales on each profile are dramatically different, varying from 25-foot to 1,000-foot increments for height (elevation), and varying from a few miles to nearly 100 miles for distance. In addition, not all profiles begin at an elevation of zero feet. For this reason, please pay special attention to the numbers marked on the two axes of the graphs.

About the Maps

Each chapter in this book begins with a map of the region it covers. Every ride's starting point is noted by a number on the map. These points are placed as precisely as possible, but the scale of these maps often makes it difficult to pinpoint a ride's exact starting point. I advise that you purchase a detailed map of the area, especially if it is new to you.

All rides also feature a trail map. However, if the area is new to you, or if you would like maps showing topographic lines, I advise obtaining a more detailed map. If you are riding in a national, state, county, or regional park, obtain a park trail map from the visitor center or entrance station. If you are riding on the road, get a detailed AAA map of the area. Bike and outdoors shops also carry detailed maps.

MAP SYMBOLS

———	Road Route	○	City
······	Unpaved Road Route	○	Town
----	Trail Route	🅟	Trailhead Parking
----	Other Trail	Start	Start of Ride
············	Other Trail (Bikes Prohibited)	▪	Point of Interest
═══	Divided Highway	★	Natural Feature
═══	Primary Road	▲	Mountain
═══	Secondary Road	⚑	State Park
········	Unpaved Road	Λ	Campground
		⍦	Waterfall

Introduction

INTRODUCTION

It used to be that bicyclists fell into two categories: road cyclists and mountain bikers. The former spent a lot of money on bikes that weighed less than a full water bottle and black Spandex tights that fit like a second skin. They joined cycling clubs and milled around with their compatriots at coffee shops on Sunday mornings, drinking lattes and studying road maps before the day's ride.

The latter saw themselves as rebels, riding fat-tire bikes that were often splattered with mud. They wore baggy shorts and hiking boots, and were frequently heard yelling "yahoo" (or something similar) as they cleaned a boulder-lined descent or bunny-hopped over a fallen log. They coined their own phrases, like "eat rocks" and "dual-boing suspension."

At different phases of my life, I have been a card-carrying member of one group or the other. I pedaled century rides on a 19-pound skinny-tire wonder—a jerry-rigged, hand-me-down relic that was coveted by other riders for its all-Campy components. I searched out long and winding country roads and rode them in the good company of friends. In my best moments, I felt like I was a member of the peloton riding in the Tour de France.

Then, after moving to San Francisco and later to Marin County, I switched over to mountain bikes and cruised around the hills and dales of Northern California. I learned the difference between serpentine and granite and schist, and what it feels like to ride on, over, and around those marvelous rocks. I spotted red-tailed hawks and golden eagles, and shared the trails with deer, bears, and bobcats. In my best moments, I felt like I was using a two-wheeled machine to get closer to nature, to travel farther than I could on foot and visit places where automobiles could not go.

It never occurred to me that the twain could ever meet—that my two bicycling selves could shake hands and coexist happily. But somewhere inside a small voice was seeking integration. Why be one thing and not the other? Why not embrace the two biking sports as one? And so this book was born. To me, the beauty of bicycling is its wind-in-the-hair, feeling-like-a-kid-again euphoria, which can be achieved on either road or trail. It is knowing that no matter what ails you in the rest of life—monotonous job, unrequited love, too much housework—all you need do is get on your bike and pedal and everything will feel better.

The 150 rides in this book, plus multiple dozens of options and add-ons, celebrate the all-in-one joy of both road biking and mountain biking. Whether you own both types of bikes or only one or the other, you will find a wealth of rides in these pages that suit your desires and ability level.

Inevitably you'll also discover my personal biases for scenery and serenity. On trail rides, you'll find waterfalls, ocean views, redwood forests, and summit vistas. (I don't enjoy grinding out miles just for the sake of it.) On paved rides, you'll find more of the same, plus wide shoulders and as few cars as possible. (I don't like cars flying by at 60 mph, shaving my legs with hot exhaust.) My guiding rule for choosing bike routes is this: With every ride, on road or trail, I like to return home feeling like I've done something extraordinary with my day.

Happy riding to you.

—*Ann Marie Brown*

"When I see an adult on a bicycle, I do not despair for the future of the human race."

—*H.G. Wells*

BIKING TIPS

Biking Safety

Like the Boy Scout motto says, "you must be prepared." It's easy to set off on a bike ride, especially near your home, carrying nothing except your wallet and keys. We've all done it from time to time. But even on the shortest spin through the neighborhood or local park it's wise to have a few items with you. Some riders carry all of the following items on every ride, some carry only some of the items some of the time. But each of these could prove to be a real lifesaver.

- **A helmet for your head.** They don't call them "brain buckets" for nothing. Don't get on your bike without one; many parks require them and the ones that don't, should. Just as you wear your seat belt when you drive, wear your helmet when you ride. Make sure yours fits properly and strap it on securely.
- **Food and water.** Being hungry or thirsty spoils a good time, and it can also turn into a potentially dangerous situation. Even if you aren't the least bit hungry or thirsty when you start, you will feel completely different after 30 minutes of riding. Always carry at least two water bottles on your bike, and make sure they are full of fresh, clean water when you head out. Add ice on hot days, if you wish. For a two- to three-hour ride, 100 ounces of water is not overkill, especially in summer. Many riders prefer to wear a bladder-style backpack hydration system, which has the extra advantage of providing room to carry a few snacks or car keys. Always bring some form of calories with you, even if it's just a couple of energy bars. If you

Wearing a helmet is important when biking anywhere, including this busy stretch along West Cliff Drive in Santa Cruz.

carry extras to share, you'll be the hero or heroine when you give them to a rider in need.

- **Cycling gloves and cycling shorts.** These make your trip a lot more comfortable. Cycling gloves have padded palms so the nerves in your hands are protected from extensive pressure when you lean your upper body weight on the handlebars. Cycling shorts have chamois or other padding in the saddle area, and it's obvious what that does.

- **A map of the park or roads you are riding.** Sometimes trails and roads are signed, sometimes they're not. Signs get knocked down or disappear with alarming frequency, due to rain, wind, or souvenir hunters. Get a map from the managing agency of the park you're visiting; all their names and phone numbers are listed in this book. For road rides, take along a detailed AAA or other map for the region.

- **A bike repair kit.** How much and which tools to carry is a great subject of debate. At the very least, if you're going to be farther than easy walking distance from your car, carry what you need to fix a flat tire. Great distances are covered quickly on a bike. This is never more apparent than when a tire goes flat 30 minutes into a ride and it takes two hours to walk back. So why walk? Carry a spare tube, a patch kit, tire levers, and a bike pump attached to your bike frame. Make sure you know how to use them.

  Many riders also carry a small set of metric wrenches, allen wrenches, and a couple of screwdrivers, or some type of all-in-one bike tool. These are good for adjusting derailleurs and the angle on your bike seat, making minor repairs, and fidgeting with brake and gear cables. If you're riding on dirt trails, carry extra chain lubricant with you, or at least keep some in your car. Some riders carry a few additional tools, such as a spoke wrench for tightening loose spokes, or a chain tool to fix a broken chain.

- **Extra clothing.** On the trail, weather and temperature conditions can change at any time. It may get windy or start to rain, or you can get too warm as you ride uphill in the sun and then too cold as you ride downhill in the shade. Wear layers. Bring a lightweight jacket and a rain poncho with you. Tie your extra clothes around your waist or put them in a small daypack.

- **Sunglasses and sunscreen.** Wear both. Put on your sunscreen 30 minutes before you go outdoors so it has time to take effect.

- **A bike lock.** It comes in handy if you want to stop for anything. Many of the trails in this book combine a bike ride with a short hike or a visit to a winery, museum, or historic site. If you are planning to stop anywhere, even to use a restroom, a bike lock is valuable. Never leave your bike unlocked and unattended.

- **First-aid kit and emergency money for phone calls.** See the next page for more details.

First Aid and Emergencies

Like most of life, bicycling is a generally safe activity that in the mere bat of an eye can suddenly become unsafe. The unexpected occurs—a rock in the trail, a sudden change in road surface, a misjudgment or momentary lack of attention—and suddenly, you and your bike are sprawled on the ground. Sooner or later it happens to everyone who rides. Usually, you look around nervously to see if anybody saw you, dust yourself off, and get back on your bike. But it's wise to carry a few emergency items just in case your accident is more serious: A few large and small Band-Aids, antibiotic cream, and an Ace bandage can be valuable tools. I also carry a Swiss Army knife, one with several blades, a can opener, and scissors. If I don't need it for first aid, I'll use it for bike repairs or picnics. Finally, it's a good idea to carry matches in a waterproof container and a candle, just in case you ever need to build a fire in a serious emergency.

Some riders carry a cell phone everywhere they go, but be fore-warned that this is not a foolproof emergency device. You won't get cell reception in many areas, particularly in nonurban places. Carry a cell phone if it makes you feel better, but don't expect to rely on it.

Always bring along a few bucks so you can make a phone call from a pay phone, or buy food or drinks for yourself or someone who needs them.

Bike Maintenance

Most bike-related problems won't occur if you do a little upkeep on your machine. Remember to check your tire pressure, seat height, brakes, and shifters before you begin each ride. Lubricate your chain and wipe off the excess lubricant. Make sure all is well before you set out on the trail.

Second- and third-growth redwoods line the lower reaches of Purisima Creek Canyon.

If you are riding often, you should also clean your bike and chain frequently, lubricate cables and derailleurs, tighten bolts, and check your wheels for alignment. Don't wait to have your bike worked on when you bring it into the shop occasionally; learn to perform your own regular maintenance and do it frequently.

Mountain Biking Etiquette

Mountain bikes are great. They give you an alternative to pavement, a way out of the concrete jungle. They guarantee your freedom from auto traffic. They take you into the woods and the wild, to places of natural beauty.

On the other hand, mountain bikes are the cause of a lot of controversy. In the past 15 years, mountain bikers have shown up on trails that were once the exclusive domain of hikers and horseback riders. Some say the peace and quiet has been shattered. Some say that trail surfaces are being ruined by the weight and force of mountain bikes. Some say that mountain bikes are too fast and clumsy to share the trail with other types of users.

Much of the debate can be resolved if bikers follow a few simple rules, and if nonbikers practice a little tolerance. The following are a list of rules for low-impact, "soft cycling." If you obey them, you'll help to give mountain biking the good name it deserves:

1. **Ride only on trails where bikes are permitted.** Obey all signs and trail closures.
2. **Yield to equestrians.** Horses can be badly spooked by bicyclists, so give them plenty of room. If horses are approaching you, stop alongside the trail until they pass. If horses are traveling in your direction and you need to pass them, call out politely to the rider and ask permission. If the horse and rider moves off the trail and the rider tells you it's okay, then pass.
3. **Yield to hikers.** Bikers travel much faster than hikers. Understand that you have the potential to scare the daylights out of hikers as you speed downhill around a curve and overtake them from behind, or race at them head-on. Make sure you give other trail users plenty of room, and keep your speed down when you are near them. If you see a hiker, slow down to a crawl, or even stop.
4. **Be as friendly and polite as possible.** Potential ill will can be eliminated by friendly greetings as you pass: "Hello, beautiful day today . . ." Always say thank you to other trail users for allowing you to pass.
5. **Avoid riding on wet trails.** Bike tires leave ruts in wet soil that accelerate erosion. This makes bikers very unpopular with park managers and other trail users.
6. **Riders going downhill should always yield to riders going uphill on narrow trails.** Get out of their way so they can keep their momentum as they climb.

Mountain Biking Basics

- First-time mountain bike riders are always surprised at how much time they spend walking instead of riding. They walk their bike up steep grades, down steep grades, and in level places where the terrain is too rugged. Mountain bikers frequently have to deal with rocks, boulders, tree roots, sand traps, holes in the ground, stream crossings, eroded trails, and so on. Often the best way to deal with these obstacles is to walk and push your bike.

- If something looks scary, dismount and walk. If you are unsure of your ability to stay in control while heading downhill, or your capacity to keep your balance on a rough surface, dismount and walk. It will save you plenty of Band-Aids.

- Learn to shift gears before you need to. This takes some practice, but you'll soon find that it's easier to shift before you're halfway up the hill and the pedals and chain are under pressure. When you see a hill coming up ahead, downshift.

- Play around with the height of your seat. When the seat is properly adjusted, you will have a slight bend in your knee while your leg is fully extended on the lower of the two pedals.

- Take it easy on the handlebar grips. Many beginners squeeze the daylights out of their handlebars, which leads to hand, arm, shoulder, and upper back discomfort. Grip the handlebars loosely and keep a little bend in your elbows.

- Learn to read the trail ahead of you, especially on downhills. Keep your eyes open for rocks or ruts which can take you by surprise and upset your balance.

- Go slow. As long as you never exceed the speed at which you feel comfortable and in control, you'll be fine. This doesn't mean that

Barker Pass can be ridden on dirt, on pavement, or as a combined loop.

you shouldn't take a few chances, but it's unwise to take chances until you are ready.

- Experienced riders can maneuver their bikes on nearly any terrain. But, remember that good technical ability also means managing one's speed. Especially when riding on trails shared by hikers, dogs, and horses, it's important to use one's brakes wisely. Brake before you enter turns or corners so you can ride through them *without* braking. Braking during a turn or curve causes you to lock up your rear wheel and skid or slide. Sliding lessens your control over the bike and is very destructive to the trail. Ride it; don't slide it, or you'll make yourself very unpopular with people who love trails.

- Use the front brake simultaneously and in combination with the back brake to slow you down. But don't pull too hard on the front brake or you'll go over the handlebars. Remember that 70 percent of your braking force is in your front brake.

- Learn to move your weight back and lift up your front wheel to get it over obstacles, like rocks or bumps. Otherwise, your front wheel can get trapped, causing you to fly over the handlebars. Your back wheel will usually roll over obstacles.

- Lean inside and forward into turns and curves. This keeps your center of gravity over your tires.

- On downhills, get your rear end as far back on the bike as possible—behind the seat and over the back tire if you can.

- When you are approaching a long, steep downhill, stop for a moment and lower your seat. You want to be able to stand in a crouched position without the seat getting in the way.

- Never ride in mud; your tire tracks will encourage erosion. Walk your bike around muddy areas; don't ride around them and create another trail.

Protecting the Outdoors

Take good care of this beautiful land you're riding on. The primary rules are to leave no trace of your visit, to pack out all your trash, and to try not to disturb animal or plant life. But you can go the extra mile and pick up any litter that you see on the trail or road. Carry an extra bag to hold the litter you pick up until you get to a trash receptacle, or just keep an empty pocket for that purpose.

If you have the extra time or energy, you can join a trail organization in your area or spend some time volunteering in your local park. Biking and hiking trails need constant upkeep and maintenance, and most of the work gets done by volunteers. Anything you do to help this lovely planet will be repaid to you, many times over.

BEST BIKE RIDES

Of the hundreds of road and trail rides in this book, here are my favorites in 12 categories:

Best Bike-and-Hike Rides

Fern Canyon Trail Bike & Hike, Mendocino and Wine Country, page 154. It's a short and easy pedal and hike to Russian Gulch Falls, a 36-foot waterfall that drops into a rocky fern grotto in Russian Gulch State Park.

Cone Peak Lookout Bike & Hike, Monterey and Big Sur, page 239. An uphill ride on a dirt road brings you to the steep hiking trail for Cone Peak Lookout, on which you climb 2.5 miles to a historic fire lookout perched at 5,155 feet.

Bear Valley Trail Bike & Hike, San Francisco Bay Area, page 33. This easy, level biking trail in Point Reyes National Seashore accesses a short hike to a coastal overlook at Arch Rock.

Berry Creek Falls Bike & Hike, San Francisco Bay Area, page 143. An 11-mile round-trip bike ride in Big Basin State Park brings you to a short trail to one of the Bay Area's most spectacular waterfalls.

Best Mountain Bike Rides for Families

Bizz Johnson Trail, Shasta and Lassen, page 420. The first 6.7 miles of this 25-mile-long railroad grade are easy pedaling along the scenic Susan River canyon, perfect for any kind of rider.

Quarry Road Trail, Sacramento and Gold County, page 266. The only trail in Auburn State Recreation Area that is suitable for novice mountain bikers, this old road winds along the Middle Fork of the American River.

Sugar Pine Railway, Sacramento and Gold County, page 283. Two stretches of this old railroad grade, one from Lyons Reservoir and one from Fraser Flat near Strawberry, make excellent easy riding for families.

General Creek Loop, Tahoe and the Northern Sierra, page 308. A pretty loop through pine and fir forest starts and ends at General Creek Campground in Sugar Pine Point State Park.

Bear Valley Trail Bike & Hike, San Francisco Bay Area, page 33. This excursion in Point Reyes National Seashore is easy enough for cyclists of any ability, and leads to a spectacular coastal overlook.

Perimeter Trail, San Francisco Bay Area, page 63. This 5.5-mile, nearly level trail circumnavigates Angel Island in the middle of San Francisco Bay, providing outstanding views and some interesting history lessons.

Families should also try any of the Paved Bike Paths listed below.

Best Paved Bike Paths

Monterey Recreation Trail, Monterey and Big Sur, page 221. This 29-mile round-trip trail runs from Marina to Pacific Grove, passing by famous Monterey attractions such as Cannery Row and the Monterey Bay Aquarium.

Truckee River Recreation Trail, Tahoe and the Northern Sierra, page 300. Lake Tahoe has several excellent paved recreation trails, but this pathway along the scenic Truckee River is the best of the lot.

Nimitz Way Trail, San Francisco Bay Area, page 69. Perched on the tip of San Pablo Ridge in Tilden Park, Nimitz Way Trail offers the best views of any paved trail in the East San Francisco Bay.

Sawyer Camp Recreation Trail, San Francisco Bay Area, page 104. This trail in the pristine San Francisco Watershed lands near Hillsborough travels the length of Lower Crystal Springs Reservoir and leads through marshlands to southern San Andreas Lake.

Hammond Trail, Redwood Empire, page 380. A 13-mile out-and-back from Mad River in McKinleyville leads to windswept Clam Beach County Park.

Sacramento River Trail, Shasta and Lassen, page 412. This 10-mile-long, paved path in Redding is the hub of a well-developed trail system in and around town, connecting to sights such as the Turtle Bay Museum and Redding Arboretum.

Eagle Lake Trail, Shasta and Lassen, page 418. Ride your bike on the south shore of Eagle Lake, the second largest natural lake in

© ANN MARIE BROWN

There's no better way to see Yosemite Valley than on the seat of a bike.

California and one of the best spots in Northern California for bird watching.

Yosemite Valley Bike Path, Yosemite and Mammoth Lakes, page 340. The best way to visit car-choked Yosemite Valley is to park your car and ride your bike past its spectacular granite walls and waterfalls.

American River Parkway, Sacramento and Gold County, page 272. This 32.8-mile-long trail is one of the oldest and longest paved recreation trails in the United States.

Best Rides through History:

Masonic Mountain/Chemung Mine, Tahoe and the Northern Sierra, page 328. The Chemung Mine was one of several profitable gold mines near Bridgeport; its stamp mill buildings still stand.

Old Stage Road & Old Railroad Grade to East Peak, San Francisco Bay Area, page 54. Take a ride through Mount Tamalpais history on this eight-mile out-and-back on the old Mount Tamalpais Scenic Railway route, home of the "Crookedest Railroad in the World."

Stewartville & Ridge Trail Loop, San Francisco Bay Area, page 83. Pedal through Black Diamond Mines Regional Preserve, which from 1860 to 1906 was the largest coal mining district in California.

Aptos Creek Fire Road to Sand Point, Monterey and Big Sur, page 212. The old railroad grade in Forest of Nisene Marks State Park was built in 1881 and used to haul out every big redwood tree in Aptos Creek Canyon.

Oak Bottom Channel/ Great Water Ditch, Shasta and Lassen, page 404. An easy, smooth single-track along the edge of Whiskeytown Lake, this trail finishes up at the El Dorado Mine buildings, built in 1885.

Bizz Johnson Trail, Shasta and Lassen, page 420. Where cyclists ride on the Bizz Johnson Trail today, in the early 1900s thundering locomotives

pedaling the historic Old Stage Road from Pantoll to West Point Inn

rumbled through the Susan River canyon, carrying heavy loads of logs and lumber.

Sacramento River Delta, Sacramento and Gold County, page 275. As you pedal along the Delta's blue, flat-water estuaries you can recall the days when paddlewheeler steamboats plied these waters, carrying passengers and goods from Sacramento to San Francisco.

Perimeter Trail, San Francisco Bay Area, page 63. Visit the many remaining buildings on Angel Island, which has had a long and varied history as a military outpost, Russian sea otter hunters' site, and immigrant detention center.

Best Oceanfront Rides:

Old Haul Road/Ten Mile Coastal Trail, Mendocino and Wine Country, page 152. The Old Haul Road in MacKerricher State Park travels right alongside wide open beaches, coastal dunes, and rocky coves north of Fort Bragg.

Wilder Ranch Bluffs Ride, Monterey and Big Sur, page 207. Cruise along the marine terrace at Wilder Ranch State Park and view sea arches and cliffs, a seal rookery, sandy beaches, and a hidden fern cave.

17-Mile Drive, Monterey and Big Sur, page 224. A seven-mile coastal stretch of the 17-Mile Drive is full of jaw-dropping coastal scenery, plus grand mansions and golf courses, too.

Golden Gate Bridge & Marin Headlands Loop, San Francisco Bay Area, page 66. Ride across the Golden Gate Bridge, visit the Point Bonita Lighthouse, and stop at Black Sand and Rodeo Beaches on this remarkable coastal loop route.

Pescadero & San Gregorio Loop, San Francisco Bay Area, page 117. Pedal south on coastal Highway 1 past Pigeon Point Lighthouse and Whaler's Cove, then loop back through the historic towns of Pescadero and San Gregorio.

Coastal Drive, Redwood Empire, page 373. This eight-mile stretch on gravel and pavement in Redwood National Park offers nonstop sweeping views of the ocean.

Best Rides for Wildlife Viewing:

Boggs Lake Loop, Mendocino and Wine Country, page 171. Boggs Lake is a Nature Conservancy–managed preserve where more than 150 bird species, including bald eagles, have been recorded in winter and spring.

Gold Bluffs & Ossagon Trail Loop, Redwood Empire, page 375. Here in Prairie Creek Redwoods State Park is your best chance of sharing the trail with a 1,000-pound Roosevelt elk (or a whole herd of them).

Eagle Lake Trail, Shasta and Lassen, page 418. Eagle Lake, the second largest natural lake in California, is a prime spot for bird watching, particularly for eagles and osprey.

Cyclists head south on Highway 1 with fully loaded panniers.

Davenport to Santa Cruz Loop, Monterey and Big Sur, page 202. In autumn and winter, see the spectacle of thousands of monarch butterflies nesting in the eucalyptus trees at Natural Bridges State Beach.

Lake Almanor Recreation Trail, Shasta and Lassen, page 416. Lake Almanor near Chester boasts the largest summer population of ospreys in California.

Stinson Beach & and Mount Tamalpais Loop, San Francisco Bay Area, page 51. From mid-March to mid-July, see hundreds of pairs of great white egrets nesting in the trees at Bolinas Lagoon Preserve.

Point Reyes Lighthouse, San Francisco Bay Area, page 35. From December to April, spot gray whales from the Point Reyes Lighthouse coastal promontory and observe elephant seals from an overlook at nearby Chimney Rock.

Big Sur to Lucia, Monterey and Big Sur, page 234. Watch for gray whales, dolphins, and sea otters as you pedal down this remarkable stretch of Highway 1 south of Big Sur.

Best Rides with Overnight Camping Options:

Stewart Trail, San Francisco Bay Area, page 38. Pack your panniers and spend the night at Glen or Wildcat Camps on this ride in Point Reyes National Seashore.

Gold Bluffs & Ossagon Trail Loop, Redwood Empire, page 375. A backpacker's camp is found at the end of the Ossagon Trail near the coast, or car campers can set up their tents on Gold Bluffs Beach in Prairie Creek Redwoods State Park.

Little Bald Hills Loop, Redwood Empire, page 371. A primitive camp in Little Bald Hills provides a chance for solitude in a high grassland prairie above the redwood forests.

General Creek Loop & Lost Lake, Tahoe and the Northern Sierra, page 308. An easy loop through a pine and fir forest and a more difficult out-and-back to an alpine lake start and end at General Creek Campground in Sugar Pine Point State Park.

Boulder Creek Loop, Shasta and Lassen, page 406. For a little solitude, try camping along the single-track on Boulder Creek Trail at Whiskeytown Lake.

Lassen Park Road, Shasta and Lassen, page 414. At either end of the scenic Lassen Park Road lie two well-developed park campgrounds: Southwest and Manzanita.

Bizz Johnson Trail, Shasta and Lassen, page 420. If you choose to ride the entire 25 miles of this old railroad grade, you can spend the night at Goumaz Primitive Campground at the halfway point.

Additionally, the vast majority of trails in this book start at or pass by state park or other agency campgrounds. You can ride right from your car campsite at China Camp State Park, MacKerricher State Park, Van Damme State Park, Russian Gulch State Park, Big Basin Redwoods State Park, Yosemite National Park, Big Sur's state park and national forest campgrounds, and many others.

Best Rides to High Overlooks:

Mount St. Helena, Mendocino and Wine Country, page 179. This 12-mile mountain bike ride takes you up a wide dirt road to the 4,343-foot summit of Mount St. Helena, where the vista on clear days expands over 200 miles.

Martis Peak Lookout & Watson Lake, Tahoe and the Northern Sierra, page 298. One of the best views of Lake Tahoe and its environs can be found from the fire lookout tower atop Martis Peak, elevation 8,656 feet.

Mount Diablo, San Francisco Bay Area, page 88. You haven't experienced Mount Diablo's Summit Road until you've ridden it on a bike—all the way to

© ANN MARIE BROWN

Kings Creek and Mount Lassen as seen from Lassen Park Road

standing atop the summit of 4,343-foot Mount St. Helena

the mountain summit at 3,849 feet, where you can see as far as the Sierra Nevada mountains.

Mount Hamilton, San Francisco Bay Area, page 135. Climb to the top of the Bay Area's loftiest peak, Mount Hamilton at 4,209 feet, where astronomers at Lick Observatory keep a watch on the stars.

Glacier Point Road, Yosemite and Mammoth Lakes, page 338. A ride on Yosemite's Glacier Point Road takes you to one of the grandest views in the West—an overlook directly across from Half Dome and Vernal and Nevada Falls.

Best Single-Track:

Soquel Demonstration State Forest, Monterey and Big Sur, page 215. Miles of gnarly single-track in Soquel Forest twist, turn, and pitch steeply uphill and downhill through dense forests of redwoods, tan oaks, and madrones.

Emigrant Trail, Tahoe and the Northern Sierra, page 292. This 15-mile stretch of single-track runs from Stampede Reservoir to Prosser Creek Reservoir, north of Lake Tahoe.

Hole-in-the-Ground Trail, Tahoe and the Northern Sierra, page 295. A loop ride near Soda Springs visits two granite-bound swimming lakes and doles out 10-plus miles of exciting single-track.

Henry Coe State Park, San Francisco Bay Area, pages 21 and 140. It isn't easy riding in this steep, hilly park, but Henry Coe is known to have some of the best single-track in the Bay Area.

Clikapudi, Shasta and Lassen, page 402. A popular 9.7-mile loop at Lake Shasta, the Clikapudi single-track is manageable for riders of almost any ability.

Lower Rock Creek, Yosemite and Mammoth Lakes, page 358. Nearly eight miles of highly technical and sometimes treacherous single-track follow the path of Lower Rock Creek near Tom's Place, south of Mammoth Lakes.

Salmon Falls/Darrington Trail, Sacramento and Gold County, page 268. If you live anywhere near Sacramento, you've probably ridden this challenging single-track on the South Fork of the American River that leads to Folsom Lake.

Pioneer Trail, Sacramento and Gold County, page 258. If you're in or around Nevada City, this is the perfect single-track for getting a dose of the area's wonderful trail system.

Downieville Downhill, Sacramento and Gold County, page 255. Everyone rides these 13 miles of single-track as a shuttle trip—all downhill—making this the most popular single-track in the Sierra Nevada.

Best Rides for Wine Tasting:

Geyserville Winery Loop, Mendocino and Wine Country, page 168. This road ride leads past a half-dozen major wineries in and around the Alexander Valley.

Healdsburg Westside & Eastside Loop, Mendocino and Wine Country, page 176. Visit the historic Hop Kiln Winery and more than a dozen others on this easy ramble that starts and ends in Healdsburg.

Yountville & Silverado Trail, Mendocino and Wine Country, page 192. You'll pass 10 major wineries on this wine country ramble and end your ride at Domain Chandon, the champagne-maker.

Annapolis Road Loop, Mendocino and Wine Country, page 166. Taste the fruits of their sauvignon blanc, pinot noir, and gewürz-traminer grape crop at this out-of-the-way winery near Sea Ranch.

Saratoga to Montebello Road Summit, San Francisco Bay Area, page 129. Weekend wine tasting at Ridge Winery is the reward for the ascent up Montebello Road in the Saratoga area.

Davenport to Santa Cruz Loop, Monterey and Big Sur, page 202. Sample the varietals at the Bonny Doon Winery in the hills above Santa Cruz on this 31-mile road loop.

Best Butt-Kickers on Pavement:

Sonora Pass Road Ride, Tahoe and the Northern Sierra, page 323. If the 3,900 feet of elevation gain from Dardanelle to Sonora Pass isn't enough for you, keep riding to U.S. 395 and then turn back for a 58-mile ride with 6,600 feet of gain.

Lassen Park Road, Shasta and Lassen, page 414. With 4,350 feet of elevation gain, this out-and-back ride through Lassen's volcanic landscape isn't for everybody.

Woodside to Coast Long Loop, San Francisco Bay Area, page 113.

You'll gain 4,900 feet on this 57-mile loop through the San Francisco Peninsula, passing redwoods, grasslands, and coastal scenery.

Cavern to Cavern Loop, Sacramento and Gold County, page 280. This loop between Murphys, Mercer Caverns, and California Caverns has a 3,800-foot elevation gain on quiet backroads that can get mighty hot in summer.

Boonville's Mountain View Road, Mendocino and Wine Country, page 161. The 25-mile-long Mountain View Road runs from Boonville to the Mendocino coast and then back again with a total 5,600-foot elevation gain.

Nacimiento-Fergusson Road to the Mission, Monterey and Big Sur, page 236. This nearly 60-mile ride has a big climb and big descent in both directions, adding up to a total 4,200-foot elevation gain.

Best Rides to Waterfalls:

Feather Falls, Sacramento and Gold County, page 253. A smooth and easy single-track takes you to 640-foot Feather Falls, the sixth highest freefalling waterfall in the continental United States and the fourth highest in California.

Fern Canyon Trail Bike & Hike, Mendocino and Wine Country, page 154. On this easy trip for families, ride a paved path and then hike to Russian Gulch Falls, a 36-foot waterfall in Russian Gulch State Park near Mendocino.

Berry Creek Falls Bike & Hike, San Francisco Bay Area, page 143. This easy-to-moderate bike and hike trip takes you to a 70-foot waterfall in a beautiful redwood forest at Big Basin Redwoods State Park.

Yosemite Valley Bike Path, Yosemite and Mammoth Lakes, page 340. You can practically ride to the base of Lower Yosemite Falls on this bike path in Yosemite Valley.

Gold Bluffs & Ossagon Trail Loop, Redwood Empire, page 375. This loop ride in Prairie Creek Redwoods State Park travels past three tall, narrow waterfalls, including 80-foot-high Gold Dust Falls.

magnificent, 640-foot Feather Falls flooded with spring snowmelt

© ANN MARIE BROWN

CHAPTER 1

San Francisco Bay Area

*W*hether your tastes run to fat tires or skinny tires, Campagnolo or Rockshox, the San Francisco Bay Area is an undisputed mecca for cyclists. Home to thousands of pairs of well-toned legs, closets full of black Lycra shorts, and more than 100 bike shops, the City by the Bay and its surrounding landscape afford a world of opportunities for mountain bikers, road cyclists, and recreational riders of all types, including those pulling Burley trailers or sporting training wheels.

The Bay Area has all the right ingredients for cycling nirvana: hilly back roads, narrow and winding coastal Highway 1, world-famous landmarks like the Golden Gate Bridge, and even Mount Tamalpais, the self-proclaimed birthplace of mountain biking. It was on Mount Tam's steep slopes that Gary Fisher, Joe Breeze, and others held the first formal off-road bike races in the late 1970s. Those first bikes were heavy, clunky, and downright dangerous, but a few years and a few modifications later, mountain bike fever caught on and an industry was born.

Several park agencies around the Bay are particularly friendly to mountain bikers. We're fortunate to have the East Bay Regional Park District, Golden Gate National Recreation Area, and Midpeninsula Open Space District on our side. Even Point Reyes National Seashore allows mountain bikes on many of its trails—a rarity in the national park system. Several state parks do, too: Mount Diablo, Mount Tamalpais, Big Basin Redwoods, Angel Island, McNee Ranch, Portola, Henry Coe, and China Camp. A handful of these parks even allow bikers on some of their single-track trails, not just wide fire roads.

For a tamer ride, the San Francisco Bay Area is nationally recognized for its wealth of paved bike paths, most which began as railroad right-of-ways. Seven of these trails are described in this chapter, varying in length from six to 30 miles.

Then there are the miles of backroads that travel the lesser known regions between the Bay Area's traffic-clogged interstates and highways. For the road cyclist, there are more routes to ride here than one could complete in a lifetime. Set among natural features such as towering redwood forests, teeming bay wetlands, and the rugged coastline south to Waddell Creek and north to the outer reaches of west Marin County, the San Francisco Bay Area is the most wild metropolitan area in the United States. Whether you choose to ride on road or trail, you'll be witness to an urban wilderness like no other.

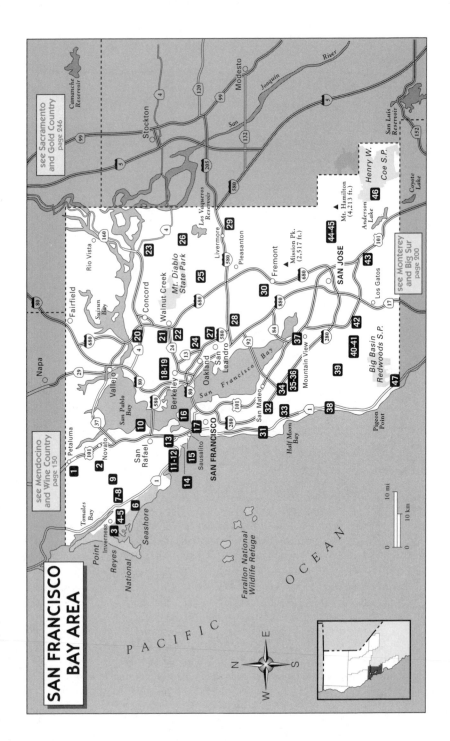

CHAPTER 1
SAN FRANCISCO BAY AREA

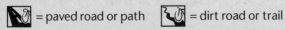 = paved road or path   = dirt road or trail

1. PETALUMA & DILLON BEACH RAMBLE

Petaluma to Dillon Beach, northwest Marin County

Chileno Valley Road is the long, rambling way to get to the coast from Petaluma, but for bicyclists, it's the obvious choice. The road is filled with small ups and downs, multiple curves and twists, and a whole lot of cows standing beside it and sometimes in it. Few motorists bother with this road; they use the more direct Bodega Avenue instead.

Pasture-lined Chileno Valley Road is the rambler's way from Petaluma to the coast.

ROUTE DETAILS

type of trail	paved roads with minimal car traffic
difficulty	🍶🍶🍶
total distance	55.3 miles (or 25- or 27-mile options)
riding time	4 hours
elevation gain	1,800 feet

After a 12.6-mile stint on Chileno Valley's bucolic, pasture-lined thoroughfare, this rambling ride makes a loop through the small towns of Valley Ford, Dillon Beach, and Tomales. This results in a perfect half-day ride with no killer climbs, but with plenty of great scenery, both in the inland hills and on the windswept coast.

Each of these three towns has an interesting history. Valley Ford was a potato-farming community in the 19th century, but in the 1920s the residents took up sheep farming. Little has changed since then; you'll still see plenty of woolly sheep. Dillon Beach has been a seaside resort since 1888, when George Dillon constructed a hotel at the end of the West Marin railroad line, hoping to attract city folk to the local beaches and clamming beds.

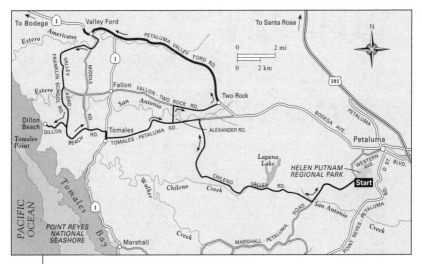

Tomales was a railroad stop in the late 1880s. Today its short main street boasts a general store, a delicious bakery, a café, and a restaurant.

If the mileage on this ride seems intimidating, it is easy enough to cut it into two rides for two separate days: a 25-mile out-and-back on Chileno Valley Road starting from Helen Putnam Regional Park, and a 27-mile loop through Tomales, Dillon Beach, and Valley Ford, starting from any of those towns.

Driving Directions

From U.S. 101 in Petaluma, take the Petaluma Boulevard South exit and drive north two miles. Turn left (west) on Western Avenue and drive 2.2 miles, then turn left on Chileno Valley Road and drive .8 mile to Helen Putnam Regional Park on the left.

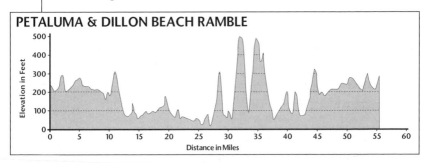

Route Directions for Petaluma & Dillon Beach Ramble

0.0 Park at Helen Putnam Regional Park and ride west on Chileno Valley Road. (Parking is available inside the park or in pullouts along the road.) *Supplies are available in Petaluma.*

3.0 RIGHT to stay on Chileno Valley Road.

12.6 LEFT on Tomales-Petaluma Road.

13.8 RIGHT on Alexander Road.

14.8 RIGHT on Fallon-Two Rock Road.

17.2 LEFT on Petaluma-Valley Ford Road (hamlet of Two Rock).

26.0 LEFT on Valley Ford Estero Road (town of Valley Ford). *Supplies are available.*

31.8 RIGHT on Dillon Beach Road. Ride out and back through Dillon Beach, then TURN AROUND and return to junction with Valley Ford Road. *Supplies are available in Dillon Beach.*

34.6 RIGHT on Dillon Beach Road.

37.2 RIGHT on Shoreline Highway (Highway 1) in town of Tomales. *Supplies are available.*

37.5 LEFT on Tomales-Petaluma Road.

42.7 RIGHT on Chileno Valley Road.

52.3 LEFT to stay on Chileno Valley Road.

55.3 Arrive at starting point.

2. CHEESE COMPANY & TOMALES BAY LOOP

Novato to Marshall, northwest Marin County

This is a ride for the gourmet cyclist. You'll work up an appetite on this 46-mile ride, then satisfy it with barbecued oysters from Tomales Bay and brie and camembert from the Marin French Cheese Company (707/762-6001).

cranking up the start of Marshall-Petaluma Road's demanding two-mile climb

ROUTE DETAILS

type of trail paved roads with minimal car traffic

difficulty 🚴🚴🚴

total distance 46 miles

riding time 3–4 hours

elevation gain 1,800 feet

Although Marin County has many scenic road rides, this is one of the loveliest. It offers a mix of pastoral hills and green, fertile valleys, plus level riding along the edge of Tomales Bay. The bucolic charms of this ride will make you forget you are in the same county (perhaps even the same country) as the busy corridor of U.S. 101 north of the Golden Gate.

Plus, the loop visits two of west Marin's most charming towns: Marshall and Point Reyes Station. Marshall is known for two things: tranquil bay views and shellfish. More than half of California's oyster and shellfish growers lease acreage on the floor of Tomales Bay. To sample the local mollusks, head for either Hog Island or Tomales Bay Oyster Companies.

Point Reyes Station is three-tenths of a mile off the loop. The old railroad town features an eclectic mix of shops and cafés that cater to visitors at nearby Point Reyes National Seashore.

The ride has two major hills you should be warned about. The first is a two-mile brutal stint on Marshall-Petaluma Road. Although the seldom-traveled road is a beauty, with lots of ups, downs, and winding curves, its one major hill is infamous for bringing cyclists to their knees. Know in ad-

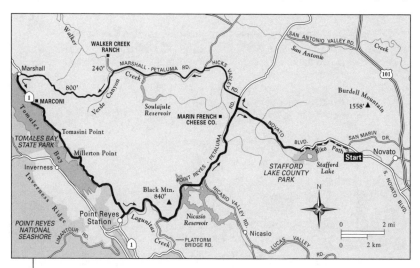

vance that the hardest climbing takes place from mile 15.9 to 17.5, in an area called Three Peaks.

With that ascent accomplished, your reward is a euphoric descent to the coast at Marshall, where after snacking on a half-dozen oysters, you'll enjoy nine miles of gentle pedaling along the edge of Tomales Bay. This is some exquisite water's-edge scenery, and if you're lucky enough to ride it on a weekday, you'll contend with fewer cars on Highway 1.

After your bayside stint, you can opt for a brief side trip into Point Reyes Station, or just head inland for the final leg to the Marin French Cheese Company. On this stretch you'll face the second big hill, about a mile past Nicasio Reservoir. The ascent is sustained over 1.5 miles, but it's not as bad as the Marshall-Petaluma hill because you know a big round of brie is waiting on the other side. Be sure to take the Cheese Company's factory tour so you can learn how the yummy stuff is made. *Bon appétit.*

Driving Directions

From San Rafael, drive north for 10 miles on U.S. 101 and take the San Marin Drive exit. Drive northwest for 2.7 miles to the intersection of San Marin Drive and Novato Boulevard, where the bike path begins.

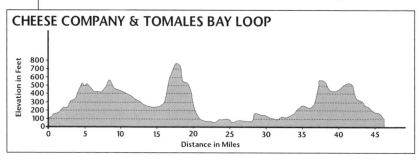

CHEESE COMPANY & TOMALES BAY LOOP

Route Directions for Cheese Company & Tomales Bay Loop

0.0 Park at the intersection of San Marin Drive and Novato Boulevard in Novato, then ride west on the bike path that parallels Novato Boulevard. *Supplies are available in Novato.*

2.5 Pass Stafford Lake County Park on the left; bike trail ends and you ride on Novato Boulevard. *Water is available.*

6.2 RIGHT on Petaluma-Point Reyes Road.

6.7 LEFT on Hicks Valley Road.

9.4 LEFT on Marshall-Petaluma Road.

15.9 Start of steepest climb

17.5 Summit.

20.3 LEFT on Highway 1 in Marshall. *Supplies are available; stop at Tony's Seafood or Hog Island Oyster Company.*

24.3 Tomales Bay Oyster Company on right.

25.1 Tomales Bay State Park/Millerton Point beach and picnic area.

29.2 LEFT on Petaluma-Point Reyes Road. *Or go right to head into town of Point Reyes Station in .3 mile.*

33.1 LEFT at junction with Platform Bridge Road.

33.9 Pass Nicasio Reservoir.

39.3 LEFT into Marin French Cheese Company parking lot. *Tours of the cheese factory are available from 10 A.M. to 4 P.M. daily; supplies are available.*

39.7 RIGHT on Novato Boulevard.

43.5 Pick up bike trail at Stafford Lake County Park.

46.0 Arrive at starting point.

3. ESTERO TRAIL

Point Reyes National Seashore

The Estero Trail is quintessential Point Reyes. It's full of good surprises, including an exemplary display of Douglas iris in spring; a dense Monterey pine forest; ample bird-watching opportunities; nonstop views of estuary, bay, and ocean; and access to a pristine beach and high blufftop overlook. Pack a lunch and binoculars and plan on an unhurried ride to fully enjoy this excursion.

From the parking lot, the trail laterals across a grassy hillside, then rounds a corner and descends into a dense stand of Monterey pines, the tall and aged remains of an old Christmas tree farm and the nesting site of owls and egrets. Shortly the trail opens out to blue, serene Home Bay. A

ROUTE DETAILS

type of trail	dirt road and single-track
difficulty	
total distance	12 miles
riding time	3 hours
elevation gain	1,200 feet

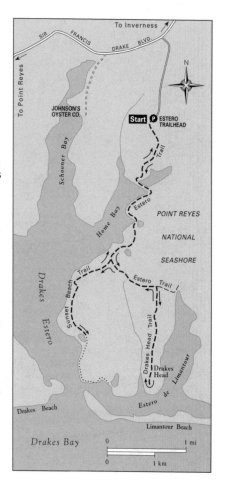

bridge crossing leads you to the first of several short climbs, this one rewarding you with high views of Home Bay's joining with Drakes Estero.

The ride continues parallel to the estero, with nonstop water views. If the tide is out, mud flats and the oyster beds of nearby Johnson's Oyster Farm will be revealed. If the tide is in, you'll see miles of azure water. You'll climb and descend a total of three hills on this trail; the third one has a lone eucalyptus tree growing on its summit.

At 2.5 miles, a sign marks Drakes Head to the left and Sunset Beach straight ahead. Turn left and climb through grasslands and chaparral to a confusing maze of cattle gates and fences (watch for arrow signs along the fence). Drakes Head

Trail continues southward; the path crosses a coastal prairie and ends on a high bluff overlooking the ocean and Limantour Spit, a long, narrow stretch of sand and bluffs.

Returning to the junction, take Sunset Beach Trail. The path levels and in 1.5 miles you are within view of Sunset Beach. A large, quiet pond separates it from you, and the trail becomes mucky and impassable for bike tires. Stash your bike and explore beautiful Sunset Beach on foot.

For more information, contact Point Reyes National Seashore, 415/464-5100.

Driving Directions

From San Francisco, cross the Golden Gate Bridge and drive north on U.S. 101 for 7.5 miles. Take the Sir Francis Drake Boulevard exit west toward San Anselmo, and drive 20 miles to the town of Olema. At Olema, turn right (north) on Highway 1 for about 150 yards, then turn left on Bear Valley Road. Drive 2.2 miles on Bear Valley Road until it joins with Sir Francis Drake Highway. Bear left on Sir Francis Drake and drive 7.6 miles to the left turnoff for the Estero Trailhead. Turn left and drive one mile to the trailhead parking on the right.

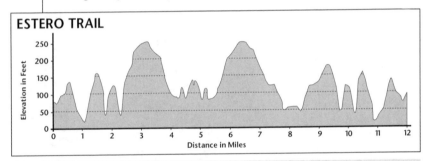

ESTERO TRAIL

Elevation in Feet / *Distance in Miles*

Route Directions for Estero Trail

0.0 Park at Estero Trailhead. *Supplies are available in the town of Inverness on Sir Francis Drake Highway.*

1.1 Bridge across Home Bay.

2.5 LEFT at junction with Drakes Head Trail (Sunset Beach Trail continues straight).

2.8 Maze of cattle gates, fences, and hiker gates; follow the fenceline path signed with arrows.

3.2 RIGHT on Drakes Head Trail; trail becomes indistinct in places—keep heading south toward the bluff's edge.

4.5 Drakes Head overlook. TURN AROUND.

6.5 LEFT on Sunset Beach Trail at previous junction.

8.0 Arrive at edge of pond with Sunset Beach beyond; stash your bike and explore on foot. TURN AROUND.

12.0 Arrive at starting point.

4. BEAR VALLEY TRAIL BIKE & HIKE

Point Reyes National Seashore

Don't forget your bike lock for this easy, scenic ride in Point Reyes National Seashore (415/464-5100). You'll ride for 3.1 miles, then hike almost a mile to the top of Arch Rock, a spectacular coastal overlook. Because of this trail's well-deserved popularity, time your trip for a weekday or an early morning on the weekends. It's more fun to ride if you aren't dodging a crowd of bikers and hikers.

Beginning just past the Bear Valley Visitor Center and Morgan Horse Ranch, the wide dirt trail is simple to follow. Several side trails intersect

ROUTE DETAILS

type of trail   dirt road

difficulty

total distance   6.2 miles (plus 1.8-mile hike)

riding time   2 hours

elevation gain   500 feet

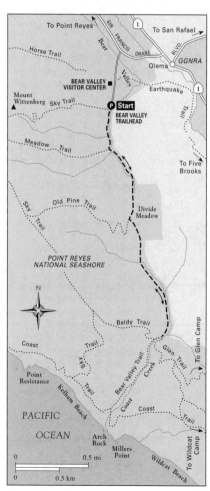

Bear Valley Trail but none are open to bikes. Just stay on the main path and cruise through the shady forest canopy, a dense mix of alders, laurel, fir, and bay. At the midway point, after the only noticeable climb of the ride, you'll reach grassy Divide Meadow, a popular picnic spot. Deer are common.

At 3.1 miles you come to a bike rack and several trail junctions. Lock up your bike and continue on foot to Arch Rock. The trail continues through the woods for .5 mile, following Coast Creek, then suddenly opens out to coastal marshlands. The final steps of the hike are extremely dramatic as you walk along the top of Arch Rock's jagged, jade-green bluff, which juts out over the sea. The wind can howl with tremendous fury out here—quite a surprise after the protected forest trail.

A spur trail leads down the cliffs to the beach; it's worth hiking during low tide when you can crawl through the tunnel of Arch Rock and

the final steps to Arch Rock on the Bear Valley Trail Bike & Hike

explore the beach. Many visitors are content to stay on top of Arch Rock and enjoy the view of the surging waters below. If luck is with you, you'll catch sight of a passing gray whale, or at least a couple sea lions.

Driving Directions

From San Francisco, cross the Golden Gate Bridge and drive north on U.S. 101 for 7.5 miles. Take the Sir Francis Drake Boulevard exit west toward San Anselmo, and drive 20 miles to the town of Olema. At Olema, turn right (north) on Highway 1 for about 150 yards, then turn left on Bear Valley Road. Drive .5 mile, then turn left at the sign for Seashore Headquarters Information. Drive .25 mile and park in the large lot on the left, past the visitor center. Start riding along the park road, heading for the signed Bear Valley Trail.

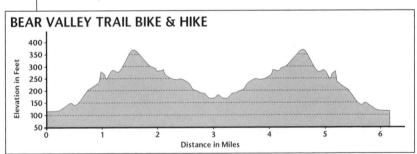

BEAR VALLEY TRAIL BIKE & HIKE

Elevation in Feet / Distance in Miles

Route Directions for Bear Valley Trail Bike & Hike

0.0 Park at Bear Valley Trailhead just past the visitor center. Ride west on the continuation of the park road, which turns to dirt at a wide gate. *Supplies are available less than a mile away in the town of Olema; water is available at the visitor center.*

1.6 Divide Meadow.

3.1 Bike rack and junction with Glen, Baldy, and Bear Valley trails; TURN AROUND. *Lock up your bike and hike .9 mile on Bear Valley Trail to Arch Rock (straight ahead).*

6.2 Arrive at starting point.

5. POINT REYES LIGHTHOUSE

Point Reyes National Seashore

Road cycling in Point Reyes National Seashore (415/464-5100) can be heavenly if the weather gods are on your side. If they aren't, you could face headwinds of 40-plus miles per hour, or fog so thick you miss all the scenery the park has to offer.

A visit to the lighthouse is one highlight of a road ride in Point Reyes.

© ANN MARIE BROWN

ROUTE DETAILS

type of trail paved roads with moderate car traffic

difficulty 🍶🍶🍶🍶🍶
(4 if windy)

total distance 45 miles

riding time 3.5–4.5 hours

elevation gain 1,900 feet

Remember this: Autumn and spring days are the surest bets for clear weather. Winter isn't bad, either, and that's when you have the best chance of spotting migrating whales from the park's shores. This road tour travels to two of the park's best whale-watching spots, the Point Reyes Lighthouse and Chimney Rock, and detours to gastronomic delights at Drake's Beach Cafe (415/669-1297) and Johnson's Oyster Company (415/669-1149).

From the Bear Valley Visitor Center, the route follows Bear Valley Road to Sir Francis Drake Highway and the bayside town of Inverness. Then Sir Francis Drake heads northwest into the park, leaving most of civilization behind with a short-but-steep ascent up and over Inverness Ridge. The ride continues on Sir Francis Drake as it threads through fields of colorful wild radish and acres of cow pastures to the western tip of Point Reyes National Seashore.

At Chimney Rock Trailhead, you can walk a 1.5-mile stretch where more than 60 species of wildflowers bloom on a narrow, windswept headland jutting into Drake's Bay, or look for elephant seals and gray whales in winter or

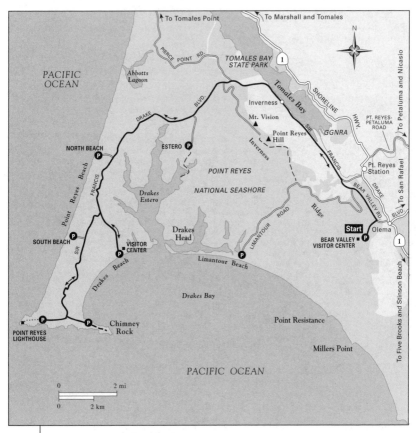

spring. The ride finishes out at Point Reyes Lighthouse, where 300-plus steps descend to this breathtaking coastal promontory. To tour the lighthouse, plan your trip for Thursday through Monday; it's closed year-round on Tuesday and Wednesday.

Driving Directions

From San Francisco, cross the Golden Gate Bridge and drive north on U.S. 101 for 7.5 miles. Take the Sir Francis Drake Boulevard exit west toward San Anselmo, and drive 20 miles to the town of Olema. At Olema, turn right (north) on Highway 1 for about 150 yards, then turn left on Bear Valley Road. Drive .5 mile, then turn left at the sign for Seashore Headquarters Information. Drive .25 mile and park by the visitor center.

POINT REYES LIGHTHOUSE

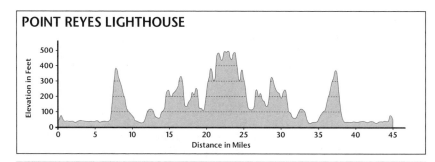

Route Directions for Point Reyes Lighthouse

0.0 Park at Bear Valley Visitor Center, then ride back out the park road the way you came in. *Water is available at the visitor center.*

0.2 LEFT on Bear Valley Road.

1.8 LEFT on Sir Francis Drake Highway.

5.9 Town of Inverness. *Supplies are available.*

7.4 LEFT at Y-junction with Pierce Point Road.

8.7 STRAIGHT at junction with Mount Vision Road.

9.4 STRAIGHT at junction with Estero Trailhead Road.

10.4 Johnson's Oyster Company entrance on left. *If the oyster company is open, stop in for a grown-in-Point Reyes snack.*

13.2 STRAIGHT at junction for North Beach.

15.1 RIGHT at junction with Kenneth C. Patrick Visitor Center and Drake's Beach (save the left fork for your return trip).

19.4 LEFT at access road for Chimney Rock Trailhead.

20.3 Chimney Rock Trailhead. TURN AROUND. *Hike or mountain bike the 1.5-mile Chimney Rock Trail in winter for whale watching and in spring for wildflowers. From December to April, walk a few hundred yards to the Elephant Seal Overlook to see the seals hauled out on Drakes Beach.*

21.2 LEFT on Sir Francis Drake Highway.

21.8 Point Reyes Lighthouse parking lot. TURN AROUND. *Tour the lighthouse and neighboring visitor center.*

26.7 RIGHT for Kenneth C. Patrick Visitor Center and Drake's Beach.

28.3 Drake's Beach parking lot. TURN AROUND. *The visitor center features fascinating exhibits on local history, flora, and fauna. Drake's Beach Cafe serves food every weekend and most weekdays.*

29.9 RIGHT on Sir Francis Drake Highway.

45.0 Arrive at starting point.

6. STEWART TRAIL

Point Reyes National Seashore

Few national parks permit bikes on their trails, and even fewer allow bike-in camping at remote campgrounds. Point Reyes National Seashore (415/464-5100) is a rare exception, and Stewart Trail from Five Brooks Trailhead is your ticket to two backcountry camps in Point Reyes: Glen and Wildcat. Those wishing to bike-backpack can make a reservation and get a permit for one of the camps. Riders looking for a challenging daytime sojourn will also enjoy pedaling Stewart Trail.

ROUTE DETAILS

type of trail 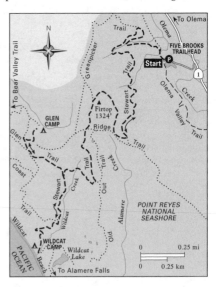 dirt road

difficulty

total distance 13 miles

riding time 2–3 hours

elevation gain 2,300 feet

Be prepared for some climbing; this is an aerobically strenuous ride with a long ascent in both directions of the out-and-back. The initial climb begins a quarter mile from the parking lot and makes a steady 1,200-foot ascent over 3.5 miles to a ridge called Fir Top. The name is apt—the area is completely shaded by Douglas firs. Then Stewart Trail drops steeply toward the ocean, losing all that hard-won elevation, plus another 100 feet. At 5.2 miles is the turnoff for Glen Camp, where some riders spend the night. Stewart Trail continues downhill to the coast and Wildcat Camp. As you descend, be sure to give your brakes a rest now and then by stopping to enjoy occasional peeks at the ocean through the trees. And keep in mind that you'll face this slope in the uphill direction on your way home.

Stewart Trail ends 6.5 miles out at Wildcat Camp. Day visitors and campers alike will want to lock up their wheels and head to the neighboring beach to explore. If you're burning with energy, an option is to hike two miles south on Coast Trail (bikes are not allowed) to visit Alamere Falls, one of the Bay Area's loveliest waterfalls. Water drops 50 feet over a coastal bluff to the sea.

Driving Directions

From San Francisco, cross the Golden Gate Bridge and drive north on U.S. 101 for 7.5 miles. Take the Sir Francis Drake Boulevard exit west toward San Anselmo, and drive 20 miles to the town of Olema. At Olema, turn left (south) on Highway 1 for 3.5 miles to Five Brooks Trailhead on the right.

STEWART TRAIL

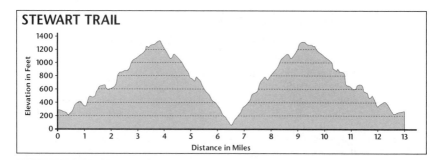

Route Directions for Stewart Trail

0.0 Park at Five Brooks Trailhead. Ride out the paved road past a large pond. *Supplies are available 3.5 miles away in the town of Olema; water is available at the trailhead.*

0.2 RIGHT on wide Stewart Trail.

3.0 RIGHT to stay on Stewart Trail at junction with Ridge Trail.

3.8 Arrive at Fir Top summit at 1,324 feet.

5.2 LEFT to stay on Stewart Trail at junction with Glen Trail (campers staying at Glen Camp turn right here).

6.5 Arrive at Wildcat Camp; TURN AROUND. *Lock up your bike and visit neighboring Wildcat Beach, or take a two-mile hike south on Coast Trail to Alamere Falls.*

13.0 Arrive at starting point.

7. BOLINAS RIDGE LOOP

Golden Gate National Recreation Area near Olema

The first time you ride Bolinas Ridge, you wonder how a trail could go up and down so much without ever leveling out. The path seems to have no pedal-and-cruise sections; you are either climbing up or coasting down the whole way (more of the latter than the former). The ridge's rollercoastering grassland terrain is just plain fun, and scenic to boot: Its high points afford expansive views of Bolinas Lagoon to the south and Tomales Bay to the north. The trail is well-suited for all levels of riders; beginners can go out and back for a few miles while more advanced riders can choose from a variety of loops.

ROUTE DETAILS FOR 7A

(loop with Randall Trail)

type of trail	dirt road
difficulty	
total distance	15 miles (or shorter out-and-back options)
riding time	2 hours
elevation gain	1,000 feet

ROUTE DETAILS FOR 7B

(loop with Bolinas-Fairfax Road)

type of trail	dirt road and paved roads with minimal car traffic
difficulty	
total distance	26 miles
riding time	4 hours
elevation gain	2,200 feet

The key is to start on the Olema side of Bolinas Ridge at the Sir Francis Drake Highway trailhead, rather than on the Mount Tamalpais side at the Bolinas-Fairfax Road trailhead. From the Olema side, less ambitious riders can pedal southward for a handful of miles as the trail climbs moderately. The route carves through open pasturelands until the 5.4-mile mark, where it suddenly enters a thick Douglas fir and redwood forest. Say good-bye to the sun and the views and hello to the refreshing woods. When you've had enough and are ready to turn around and head home, a fun descent awaits.

Meanwhile, those with more energy can continue southeast on Bolinas Ridge and then loop around to Highway 1 on one of two steep downhill routes: Randall Trail at 6.2 miles out or paved Bolinas Fairfax Road at 11.1 miles out. The second half of either loop is an easy cruise northward on mostly level Highway 1 back to Olema. Your car awaits one mile up Sir Francis Drake Highway.

If the idea of riding on pavement insults your mountain biking sensibilities, you can omit a few road miles by riding dirt Olema Valley Trail, which runs parallel to Highway 1 from Dogtown to Five Brooks Trailhead. This is a dry-season option only, however: Olema Valley Trail is notorious for flooding with even the slightest rain.

Note that much of Bolinas Ridge is cattle country, so you'll have to lift your bike over several livestock gates in the first couple miles of trail. Be sure to leave every gate the way you found it, either open or closed.

For more information, contact Golden Gate National Recreation Area, 415/331-1540 or visit their website at www.nps.gov/goga.

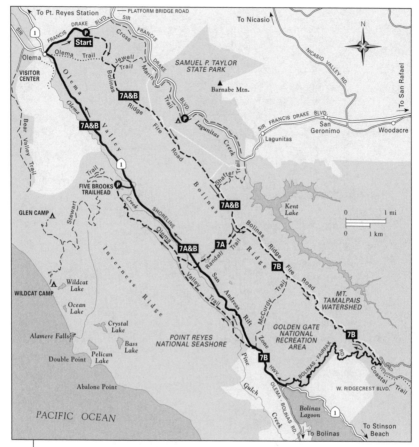

Driving Directions

From San Francisco, cross the Golden Gate Bridge on U.S. 101 and travel north toward San Rafael. Take the Sir Francis Drake Boulevard exit west toward San Anselmo, and drive 19.5 miles to the trailhead for the Bolinas Ridge Trail on the left side of the road. If you reach the town of Olema and Highway 1, you've gone one mile too far.

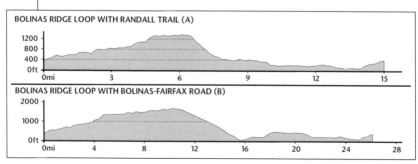

BOLINAS RIDGE LOOP WITH RANDALL TRAIL (A)

BOLINAS RIDGE LOOP WITH BOLINAS-FAIRFAX ROAD (B)

Bolinas Ridge Loop

Route Directions for 7A *(loop with Randall Trail)* **for Bolinas Ridge Loop**

0.0   Park at the Bolinas Ridge trailhead pullout alongside Sir Francis Drake Highway, 1 mile northeast of Olema. Ride uphill and veer left onto the wide dirt road. *Supplies are available in Olema.*

1.4   RIGHT at junction with Jewell Trail to stay on Bolinas Ridge.

5.2   STRAIGHT at junction with Shafter Trail.

6.2   RIGHT at junction with Randall Trail.

7.9   RIGHT at junction with Highway 1.

14.0   RIGHT at junction with Sir Francis Drake in Olema.

15.0   Arrive at starting point.

Route Directions for 7B *(loop with Bolinas-Fairfax Road)*

Follow directions for Ride 7A to the 6.2-mile mark, then continue:

6.2   STRAIGHT at junction with Randall Trail.

7.8   STRAIGHT at junction with McCurdy Trail.

9.4   High point of Bolinas Ridge at 1,700 feet.

11.1   RIGHT at junction with Bolinas Fairfax Road.

15.6   RIGHT at junction with Highway 1.

25.0   RIGHT at junction with Sir Francis Drake in Olema.

26.0   Arrive at starting point.

8. CROSS MARIN TRAIL/ SIR FRANCIS DRAKE BIKEWAY

Samuel P. Taylor State Park near Olema

The Cross Marin Trail/Sir Francis Drake Bikeway is one trail with two names, under two different park jurisdictions. It's called the Cross Marin Trail when it's on Golden Gate National Recreation Area (415/331-1540)

The paved Sir Francis Drake Bikeway is lined with redwood needles.

© ANN MARIE BROWN

ROUTE DETAILS FOR 8A
(bike path only)

type of trail dirt road and paved bike path

difficulty 🍼🍼🍼🍼

total distance 10 miles (6 miles are paved)

riding time 1 hour

elevation gain 350 feet

ROUTE DETAILS FOR 8B
(loop with Bolinas Ridge Trail)

type of trail dirt road and paved bike path

difficulty 🍼🍼🍼

total distance 13.4 miles

riding time 2.5 hours

elevation gain 1,250 feet

land, and the Sir Francis Drake Bikeway when it's on Samuel P. Taylor State Park (415/488-9897 or 415/893-1580) land. Two names, one trail.

The ride offers something for skinny tires and fat tires alike, with three miles of smooth pavement and another two miles of gavel and dirt suitable for mountain bikes. While plenty of people ride out and back on the bike path only (Ride 8A), others make a more strenuous loop by joining with Bolinas Ridge Trail (Ride 8B).

The bike path is an old rail trail, built in 1874 by the North Pacific Coast Railroad. Its first section is heavily wooded as it travels parallel to Papermill Creek, then opens out to a broad meadow. The path then heads back into the trees, entering dense second-growth redwood stands surrounded by prolific sorrel and ferns.

At the state park border your primeval redwood fantasy gets rudely interrupted by campgrounds, restrooms, and other indicators of civilization. Where the paved surface erodes to gravel and dirt past Redwood

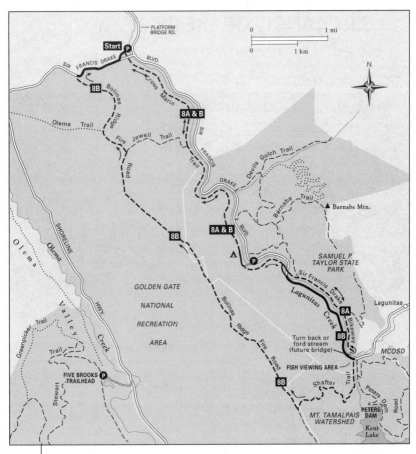

Grove Picnic Area, skinny tires must turn around but mountain bikers continue riding, crossing a footbridge over Sir Francis Drake Highway. The trail ends two miles later at the park boundary, where Shafter Bridge arches over Papermill Creek.

But loop riders won't be discouraged by the abrupt trail ending. If the creek level is low enough, carry your bike across, then climb uphill to Shafter Bridge. (If the stream is too high to ford, backtrack and ride on Sir Francis Drake Highway from the park entrance to Shafter Bridge.) Next comes a gnarly, 1.8-mile winding climb up Shafter Bridge Fire Road that slays even the best of 'em (1,100-foot gain). At the top, a heavenly, mostly downhill cruise on Bolinas Ridge Road awaits. Where the ridge trail ends at Sir Francis Drake Highway, cruise down the paved road back to your car.

Driving Directions

From San Francisco, cross the Golden Gate Bridge on U.S. 101 and drive north for 7.5 miles. Take the Sir Francis Drake Boulevard exit west toward San

Anselmo and drive 18.7 miles to the right turnoff for Platform Bridge Road, located 3.4 miles past the main entrance to Samuel P. Taylor State Park. (If you reach the town of Olema and Highway 1, you have gone 1.8 miles too far.) Turn right on Platform Bridge Road and park in the pullout on the left.

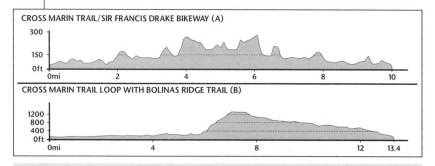

Route Directions for 8A *(bike path only)* for Cross Marin Trail/ Sir Francis Drake Bikeway

0.0 Park at the Platform Bridge Road trailhead. Ride on the paved path leading from the pullout, cross a concrete bridge, go about 50 feet, then turn left on the signed Cross Marin Trail. *Supplies are available in Olema, two miles west.*

1.5 STRAIGHT at junction with Jewell Trail.

2.7 State park camping and picnic areas. *Water is available.*

3.0 Pavement ends; skinny tires must turn around.

3.4 Cross bridge over Sir Francis Drake Highway.

5.0 Trail ends at Papermill Creek and base of Shafter Bridge. TURN AROUND.

10.0 Arrive at starting point.

Route Directions for 8B *(loop with Bolinas Ridge Trail)*

Follow the route directions for 8A to mile 5.0, then continue:

5.0 Ford the stream and climb up to the bridge.

5.2 Take Shafter Bridge Fire Road uphill (road on right side of creek).

7.0 RIGHT on Bolinas Ridge Trail at end of climb.

12.2 RIGHT on paved Sir Francis Drake Highway at end of Bolinas Ridge Trail.

13.3 LEFT on Platform Bridge Road.

13.4 Arrive at starting point.

9. NICASIO RESERVOIR LOOP

Western Marin County

A favorite of Marin County cyclists, this 24.5-mile road ride is an easy-to-moderate loop on mostly level backroads surrounding the small town of Nicasio and its large reservoir. Although these roads see some traffic, especially on nice-weather weekends, most drivers in the area are accustomed to sharing the road with bikes.

ROUTE DETAILS

type of trail   paved roads with moderate car traffic

difficulty

total distance   24.5 miles (or 44.5-mile option)

riding time   2 hours

elevation gain   900 feet

The loop begins in Nicasio, a gentrified country town—the kind of place where almost everybody owns at least one horse. If you prefer, you could easily add on up to 10 miles each way by parking near the junction of Lucas Valley Road and U.S. 101, then riding your bike to Nicasio. (To do so, leave your car on one of the side streets that intersects Lucas Valley Road. The road has a wide shoulder for the first four miles, then no shoulder at all for the next six, but not a lot of traffic, either.)

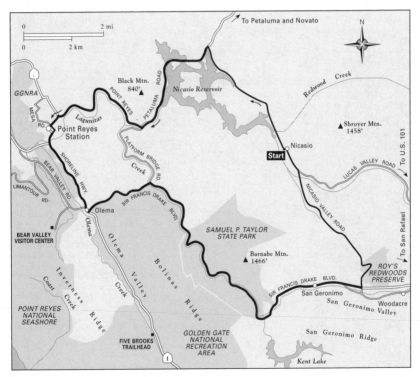

From the town of Nicasio, the loop's first 10 miles on Nicasio Valley Road and Point Reyes-Petaluma Road provide nearly perfect cycling, with a wide shoulder, smooth paved surface, and relatively few cars. The two roads skirt the edge of Nicasio Reservoir, a surprisingly large and pretty lake that is popular year-round for shoreline bass fishing.

Upon reaching Highway 1, you'll ride through Point Reyes Station and Olema—both good stops for coffee, food, and camaraderie with other bikers. Then Sir Francis Drake Boulevard climbs and curves through Samuel P. Taylor State Park and continues gently uphill through a succession of small towns: Lagunitas, Forest Knolls, and San Geronimo. By the golf course in San Geronimo, you'll turn north on Nicasio Valley Road to head back to Nicasio. All in all, this is an easy, low-pressure ride, with plenty of places to stop and enjoy the countryside.

Driving Directions

From San Rafael, drive three miles north on U.S. 101 and take the Lucas Valley Road exit. Drive 10.4 miles west on Lucas Valley Road, then turn right on Nicasio Valley Road. Drive .5 mile and park in the town of Nicasio.

NICASIO RESERVOIR LOOP

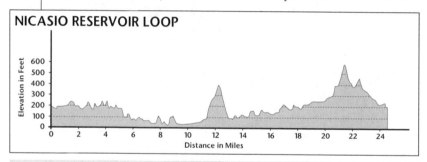

Route Directions for Nicasio Reservoir Loop

0.0   Park in the town of Nicasio and ride north on Nicasio Valley Road. *Supplies are available in Nicasio or San Rafael.*

3.2   LEFT on Point Reyes-Petaluma Road.

6.3   RIGHT to stay on Point Reyes-Petaluma Road.

9.4   LEFT on Shoreline Highway (Highway 1).

9.8   LEFT on Mesa Road through town of Point Reyes Station. *Supplies are available in town.*

10.0   RIGHT to get back on Highway 1.

10.2   STRAIGHT to stay on Highway 1.

12.2   LEFT on Sir Francis Drake Boulevard in Olema. *Supplies are available in Olema.*

17.0   Pass through Samuel P. Taylor State Park.

20.0   LEFT on Nicasio Valley Road by San Geronimo golf course.

24.5   Arrive at starting point.

10. CHINA CAMP LOOPS

China Camp State Park near San Rafael

China Camp State Park (415/456-0766 or 415/893-1580) is a rare bird in the California State Park system. One of only a handful of state parks that allows mountain bikes on single-track trails, China Camp also holds a sce-

High views of San Pablo Bay and Rat Rock can be seen from China Camp's trails.

ROUTE DETAILS FOR 10A
(Shoreline Trail out-and-back)

type of trail — dirt single-track

difficulty —

total distance — 11.2 miles (or 8-mile option)

riding time — 2 hours

elevation gain — 250 feet

ROUTE DETAILS FOR 10B
(Ridge Fire Road and Bay View Loop)

type of trail — dirt road and single-track

difficulty —

total distance — 11.6 miles

riding time — 2 hours

elevation gain — 600 feet

nic location on San Pablo Bay, with blue-water vistas from more than 1,500 shoreline acres. Bikers and hikers generally mind their manners and get along just fine here, although in recent years the park has seen more of the former and less of the latter, especially on weekends. China Camp has slowly evolved into a biker's park.

It's also a historic preserve, showcasing the remains of a Chinese shrimp fishing village from the 19th century, where immigrants netted shrimp from the bay. Don't neglect visiting the historic buildings and experiencing the unique history of this area.

Several rides are possible at China Camp. Beginners should stick to the smooth single-track Shoreline Trail (Ride 10A), while more advanced riders will want to tackle the rutted, steep hills in the backcountry of the park (Ride 10B). The latter ride is a good workout and supplies opportunities to practice your uphill and downhill

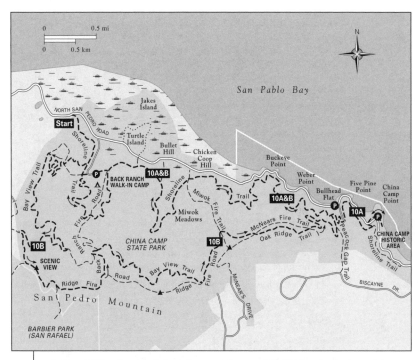

skills—it has plenty of short but steep ones. Highlights include a visit to one of Marin County's best viewpoints, a Nike radar site at 900 feet above the bay; and pedaling on Oak Ridge Trail, a lovely pathway through grasslands and oak woodlands.

Driving Directions

From San Francisco, cross the Golden Gate Bridge and drive north on U.S. 101 for 11 miles to San Rafael. Take the North San Pedro exit and drive east for 3.5 miles to China Camp State Park.

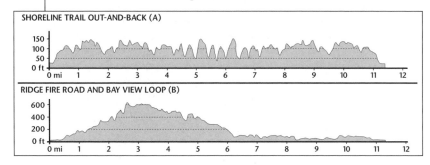

Route Directions for Ride 10A *(Shoreline Trail out-and-back)* for *China Camp Loops*

0.0 Park along the road near Back Ranch Meadows Campground. Follow Shoreline Trail from the right side of the kiosk. *Supplies are available in San Rafael, three miles west. Water is available at the campground.*

0.1 LEFT on Shoreline Trail.

0.2 Ride across the parking lot and continue on Shoreline.

2.6 Miwok Meadows Group Camp; follow the dirt road.

2.9 RIGHT on Shoreline Trail.

4.7 LEFT at Y-junction.

4.8 Cross the paved road and continue on trail.

5.2 LEFT on Village Trail.

5.3 Cross San Pedro Road and follow pavement to China Camp Village.

5.6 China Camp Village. TURN AROUND. (If you want to shorten your ride back, return on paved North San Pedro Road instead of Shoreline Trail for an eight-mile loop.) *Lock up your bike and explore the historic buildings and museum. A snack bar is open on weekends and holidays.*

11.2 Arrive at starting point.

Route Directions for Ride 10B *(Ridge Fire Road and Bay View Loop)*

Follow parking directions for Ride 10A, follow Shoreline Trail from the right side of the kiosk, then continue:

0.1 RIGHT on Bay View Trail.

0.5 RIGHT on fire road, then immediate LEFT back on Bay View Trail.

1.1 LEFT to stay on Bay View Trail.

2.0 RIGHT (hairpin) on trail to Bay Hills Drive.

2.6 LEFT on paved Bay Hills Drive; steep uphill.

3.0 Nike radar base; great views of Marin and San Francisco Bay

3.3 LEFT on Ridge Fire Road.

3.6 LEFT at junction; steep downhill.

3.9 RIGHT on fire road at powerline junction; stay RIGHT on Bay View Trail.

5.2 LEFT at junction with Ridge Fire Road.

5.5 LEFT on Miwok Fire Road for 30 yards, then RIGHT on Oak Ridge Trail.

5.8 Cross fire road to stay on Oak Ridge.

6.2 Cross fire road to stay on Oak Ridge.

6.8 STRAIGHT on Peacock Gap Trail.

6.9 STRAIGHT on Shoreline Trail.

8.7 STRAIGHT on fire road, then RIGHT at restrooms by picnic area to get back on Shoreline Trail.

9.6 LEFT at V-junction.

9.9 LEFT on Shoreline Trail.

10.1 LEFT on Shoreline Trail.

11.6 Arrive at starting point.

11. STINSON BEACH & MOUNT TAMALPAIS LOOP

Mount Tamalpais State Park

A day on less-traveled roads showcases the wonders of Mount Tamalpais, from coast to mountaintop. This ride is a workout, but it's worth it.

From the 2,571-foot summit of Mount Tamalpais' East Peak, southern Marin County comes into full view.

ROUTE DETAILS

type of trail paved roads with moderate car traffic

difficulty

total distance 23.9 miles

riding time 3 hours

elevation gain 2,700 feet

A level four-mile warm-up alongside Bolinas Lagoon on Highway 1 is followed by a circuitous and unrelenting 1,500-foot climb up the historic Bolinas-Fairfax stage road. When at last you reach the top, prepare yourself for one of the Bay Area's most filmed and photographed roads—West Ridgecrest Boulevard on Mount Tamalpais, site of dozens of car commercials and calendar shots. The trees give way to open grassy hillsides, where deer graze and hang gliders take off for a breezy, graceful descent to the ocean below. You'll keep climbing as you travel the ridge, but much more gradually now.

At Rock Springs parking lot and road junction, continue straight for another 2.9 miles to Mount Tamalpais' East Peak at elevation 2,571 feet. The vistas are even better from this summit than what you've seen so far. In addition to the bird's-eye view out to sea, much of Marin County and San Francisco comes into full perspective. East Peak's snack stand is open on weekends to refuel hungry bikers. When you've had your fill of snacks and views, backtrack to the Rock Springs parking lot.

Now it's time for a steep, fast, memorable descent. The traffic will pick

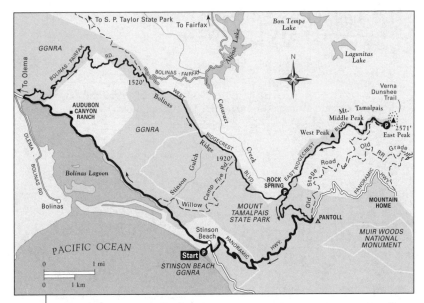

up as you drop to Pantoll ranger station, and it will continue racing downhill to the ocean, but you'll be rolling along just as fast, or maybe faster, than the cars. Since you are riding on aptly named Panoramic Highway, take a break now and then to admire the views of the coast ahead and Mount Tamalpais behind.

With a final screech of brakes, you come to a stop sign at Highway 1. A right turn and you're back at your car in less than half a mile. Hope you brought your swimsuit for a dip in the ocean at Stinson Beach, or your wallet for a well-deserved meal at the beachside hamburger stand.

For more information, contact Mount Tamalpais State Park, 415/388-2070.

Driving Directions

From San Francisco, cross the Golden Gate Bridge and drive north on U.S. 101 for four miles. Take the Mill Valley/Stinson Beach/Highway 1 exit and continue straight for one mile to a stoplight at Shoreline Highway (Highway 1). Turn left on Shoreline Highway and drive 12 miles to Stinson Beach. Turn left at the sign for Stinson Beach parking (Golden Gate National Recreation Area).

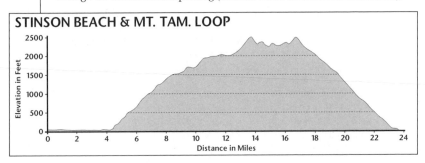

Route Directions for Stinson Beach & Mount Tamalpais Loop

0.0 Park at Stinson Beach parking lot, ride out to Highway 1, and turn left (north). *Supplies are available in town of Stinson Beach.*

1.0 Edge of Bolinas Lagoon; look for hauled-out seals and wide variety of birds.

3.3 Audubon Canyon Ranch. *The ranch, a major great egret nesting site, is open to the public on weekends and holidays from mid-March to mid-July. Walk a .5-mile trail to a viewing platform, then look through sighting scopes into the nests of baby egrets.*

4.3 RIGHT on Bolinas-Fairfax Road (unsigned paved road with open metal gate). Begin 4.4-mile climb.

8.7 RIGHT on West Ridgecrest Boulevard.

12.5 STRAIGHT at Rock Springs parking lot.

15.4 East Peak parking lot; TURN AROUND. *Water and snacks are available. Lock your bike and walk the one-mile Verna Dunshee Trail that circumnavigates the peak.*

18.3 LEFT at Rock Springs parking lot.

19.8 RIGHT on Panoramic Highway at Pantoll junction. *Water is available across the road by the ranger station.*

23.5 RIGHT on Highway 1.

23.9 LEFT into Stinson Beach parking lot; arrive at starting point.

12. OLD STAGE ROAD & OLD RAILROAD GRADE TO EAST PEAK

Mount Tamalpais State Park

Take a ride through Mount Tamalpais history on this eight-mile out-and-back ride to the 2,571-foot East Peak of Mount Tam. Although you could just drive your car on paved roads to the summit, this ride on a stretch of the old Mount Tamalpais Scenic Railway is a much more enjoyable way to get there.

ROUTE DETAILS

type of trail — dirt road

difficulty

total distance 8.0 miles

riding time 1.5 hours

elevation gain 1,100 feet

The railway, known in the early 1900s as the "Crookedest Railroad in the World," carried passengers through 281 turns and curves up the slopes of Mount Tamalpais. The last two miles of this ride trace the train's exact route to the mountain summit, while the first two miles follow the route used by passengers who rode the stagecoach to Stinson Beach and Bolinas. (See Ride 13 in this chapter for more riding on Old Railroad Grade.) The two halves of this ride converge at West Point Inn, as much a popular stopover for cyclists and hikers today as it was for train and stage passengers 100 years ago.

Begin your ride at the large parking area by Pantoll Ranger Station. After a hasty and cautious crossing of Panoramic Highway, mount your bike and ride on paved Old Stage Road. The pavement soon turns to dirt and the views of San Francisco and Marin start to amaze you. Old Stage Road's grade is remarkably gradual as it winds through myriad twists and turns.

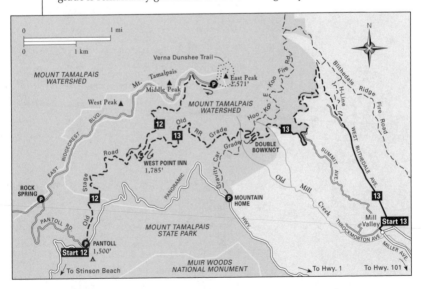

At West Point Inn, fill up your water bottle at an old stone fountain, or buy a glass of lemonade and have a seat on the outside deck, then pick up Old Railroad Grade on the inn's west side and continue uphill to East Peak. This dirt road is steeper, and more rocky, than Old Stage Road. At the trail's end you'll find yourself at the paved East Peak parking lot, enjoying far-reaching views of Marin County, the East Bay, and San Francisco and its bridges. Be sure to walk up the stairs to the Gardner Fire Lookout so you can say you went to the tip-top of the mountain.

If you don't want to ride back the way you came, you can always follow the paved route back to Pantoll: Take Ridgecrest Boulevard 2.9 miles to Rock Spring, then turn left on Pantoll Road and ride 1.5 miles downhill. This is a fun loop if you don't mind some car traffic.

Contact Mount Tamalpais State Park, 415/388-2070, for more information.

Driving Directions

From San Francisco, cross the Golden Gate Bridge and drive north on U.S. 101 for four miles. Take the Mill Valley/Stinson Beach/Highway 1 exit and continue straight for one mile to a stoplight at Shoreline Highway (Highway 1). Turn left on Shoreline Highway and drive 2.5 miles, then turn right on Panoramic Highway. Drive .9 mile to a junction of roads. Continue straight 4.3 miles farther to Pantoll Ranger Station and the parking lot on the left.

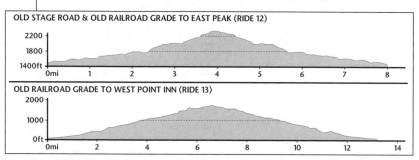

OLD STAGE ROAD & OLD RAILROAD GRADE TO EAST PEAK (RIDE 12)

OLD RAILROAD GRADE TO WEST POINT INN (RIDE 13)

Route Directions for Old Stage Road & Old Railroad Grade to East Peak

0.0 Park by Pantoll Ranger Station, then cross Panoramic Highway to the start of Pantoll Road. On the right is a paved road signed Old Stage Road to East Peak. *Supplies are available in Mill Valley.*

0.1 Begin riding on Old Stage Road.

0.4 Pavement turns to dirt.

2.0 West Point Inn. After enjoying the view, pick up Old Railroad Grade on the left (west) side of the inn. *Water and snacks are available.*

4.0 RIGHT on pavement at East Peak parking lot; TURN AROUND. *A small visitor center, overlook area, and Gardner Lookout are located here. Walk the Verna Dunshee Trail or climb the stairs to the lookout for the best view of the day.*

8.0 Arrive at starting point.

13. OLD RAILROAD GRADE TO WEST POINT INN

Mill Valley to Mount Tamalpais

Beginning in Mill Valley, this popular ride on the slopes of Mount Tamalpais follows the lower route of the "Crookedest Railroad in the World," a major tourist attraction that carried passengers up the mountain in the early 1900s. Your destination is historic West Point Inn (415/388-9955 or 415/646-0702), built in 1904 to serve railway passengers; it's still serving cyclists and hikers today. The inn has small cabins for rent and sells drinks and snacks (closed on Monday). Its water fountain will come in handy after you ride these 6.7 ascending (and dusty in summer) miles.

Mountain bikers use historic West Point Inn as a water and rest stop on the ascent up Mount Tamalpais.

ROUTE DETAILS

type of trail dirt road

difficulty

total distance 13.8 miles (or 17.8-mile option)

riding time 2 hours

elevation gain 1,700 feet

Downtown Mill Valley is Cyclist Central on fair-weather weekends. You'll have to park a mile or so from the start of Old Railroad Grade; there is almost no parking at the trailhead. From downtown, follow West Blithedale Road to the Marin Open Space District gate at the start of the railroad grade. This is your level warm-up; soon you start to climb on a remarkably consistent grade. A highlight on the ride is the "double bowknot," where the Crookedest Railroad curved through a series of tight, gradual switchbacks. You'll know it when you ride it.

This is an excellent ride for mountain bikers who have progressed past the beginner stage but aren't interested (or ready for) very technical riding. It is a solid aerobic and leg workout with only minor challenges from rocks and ruts. Note that if you wish to add a few more miles, Old Railroad Grade continues another two miles from West Point Inn to East Peak (see Ride

12). From there you could retrace your tire treads or loop back on Eldridge Grade, Indian Fire Road, and Hoo Koo E Koo Road. A Mount Tamalpais State Park (415/388-2070) or Marin Municipal Water District (415/945-1195) map gives all the details.

Driving Directions

From San Francisco, cross the Golden Gate Bridge and drive north on U.S. 101 for six miles. Take the Tiburon/Highway 131/East Blithedale Avenue exit, then turn left and drive two miles west on East Blithedale. Turn left on Throckmorton Avenue and drive one block to Miller Avenue in downtown Mill Valley.

For trail map and elevation profile see pages 54–55 (Ride 12—Old Stage Road & Old Railroad Grade to East Peak).

Route Directions for Old Railroad Grade to West Point Inn

0.0 Park near the junction of Miller and Throckmorton Avenues in Mill Valley. Ride north on Throckmorton for one block to its junction with East and West Blithedale Avenues. *Supplies are available in the surrounding blocks.*

0.1 LEFT on West Blithedale.

1.4 RIGHT at gate on dirt Old Railroad Grade.

2.1 LEFT at junction.

3.3 RIGHT on pavement (uphill) where dirt road ends.

3.7 Back on dirt road.

4.4 RIGHT at junction; start of "double bowknot."

6.9 West Point Inn. TURN AROUND or continue 2 miles to East Peak (see route description). *Water and snacks are available.*

13.8 Arrive at starting point.

14. TENNESSEE VALLEY & COYOTE RIDGE

Golden Gate National Recreation Area near Mill Valley

On weekends, the Tennessee Valley Trailhead in Mill Valley is busier than a shopping mall at Christmas. The parking lot is filled with a mix of bikers, walkers, and runners, all wanting to get a piece of the scenery at Tennessee Valley Beach and/or its surrounding ridges and hillsides.

And no wonder; there's something for everyone here. Biking families and novice riders enjoy the easy, wide dirt road that rolls gently out to Tennessee Beach, a black gravel pocket beach framed by jagged bluffs on both sides. Mountain bikers seeking more of a challenge choose from two possible loops: Tennessee Valley and Coyote Ridge to the west, or Miwok and Bobcat to the east. (The latter loop can also be accessed from the Marin Headlands and is described in Ride 15, later in this chapter.)

Those simply following Tennessee Valley Trail to the beach (Ride 14A) will find the path amazingly easy and scenic. Bring a picnic and a bike lock (a bike rack is provided) for the picturesque beach, and be sure to hike up the short trail on the north bluff for a memorable view of the coast.

Those following the Tennessee Valley and Coyote Ridge Loop (Ride 14B) will cut off .5 mile before the beach (or go check it out first while you're here), then make a short but hellacious climb up Coastal Trail. At the summit, catch your breath and enjoy the views, because there's more

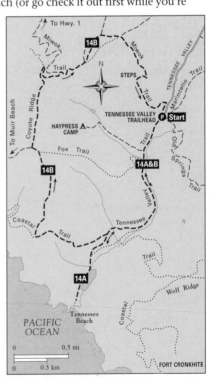

ROUTE DETAILS FOR 14A

(Tennessee Valley Trail to beach)

type of trail   dirt road

difficulty

total distance   3.8 miles

riding time   1 hour

elevation gain   250 feet

ROUTE DETAILS FOR 14B

(Tennessee Valley & Coyote Ridge loop)

type of trail   dirt road and single-track

difficulty

total distance   5.3 miles

riding time   1.5 hours

elevation gain   1,200 feet

climbing ahead on Coyote Ridge Trail. A final downhill stint on Miwok Trail will bring you back to Tennessee Valley Trailhead with some exciting—and surprisingly technical—single-track. (Don't let the railroad-tie stairsteps .5 mile from the end catch you by surprise.) This loop's total mileage is short, but the steep uphills and rutted dirt trails dole out a solid workout. Oh yeah, and the Marin Headlands scenery never disappoints.

For further information, call Golden Gate National Recreation Area, 415/331-1540, or visit www.nps.gov/goga.

Driving Directions

From San Francisco, cross the Golden Gate Bridge and drive north on U.S. 101 for four miles. Take the Mill Valley/Stinson Beach/Highway 1 exit and continue straight for .6 mile to Tennessee Valley Road on the left. Turn left and drive two miles to the trailhead.

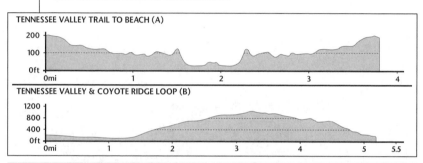

Route Directions for 14A *(Tennessee Valley Trail to beach)* **for Tennessee Valley & Coyote Ridge**

0.0   Park at Tennessee Valley Trailhead and follow the main, wide road south-west. *Supplies are available in Mill Valley, two miles north.*

1.3   STRAIGHT at junction with Coastal Trail.

1.9   Tennessee Beach bike rack. TURN AROUND.

3.8   Arrive at starting point.

Route Directions for 14B *(Tennessee Valley & Coyote Ridge Loop)*

Follow directions for Ride 14A to the 1.3-mile mark, then continue:

1.3   RIGHT at junction with Coastal Trail; hill climb.

1.9   RIGHT at junction.

2.6   LEFT then immediate RIGHT on Coyote Ridge Trail.

3.1   STRAIGHT at two Green Gulch junctions.

3.2   High point and end of climb.

3.4   STRAIGHT on Miwok Trail.

4.2   RIGHT to stay on Miwok Trail.

4.4   STRAIGHT on Miwok at junction with Countryview Road Trail on left.

5.3   Arrive at starting point.

15. MARIN HEADLANDS MIWOK & BOBCAT LOOP

Golden Gate National Recreation Area near Sausalito

Riders can choose from many possible starting points for this loop: the San Francisco or Marin sides of the Golden Gate Bridge, the Tennessee Valley Trailhead in Mill Valley, the Rodeo Avenue exit off U.S. 101 near Sausalito, or Rodeo Beach at the Marin Headlands. I describe starting from the Conzelman parking lot on the northwest side of the Golden Gate Bridge because that allows for the most off-road miles. (Three of the total 14 miles are paved; the rest are wide fire roads and single-track.) Ride this loop any way you like; it's all good.

The coastal hills of the Marin Headlands are lined with chaparral and wildflowers.

ROUTE DETAILS

type of trail dirt road and single-track; paved roads with moderate car traffic

difficulty

total distance 14 miles

riding time 2 hours

elevation gain 2,100 feet

Like the other Marin Headlands loop described in this book (Ride 14B, above), this route offers ocean views, grasslands, wildflowers, and coastal hills. Two significant climbs will get your heart and lungs pumping. One is a 1.5-mile stretch on Miwok Trail from Rodeo Valley up to the top of Wolf Ridge. The other is the 1.5-mile Marincello Trail heading uphill from Tennessee Valley. At least they are memorable: You'll gain some wide blue-water views.

A highlight is Bobcat Trail, which drops through one of the Bay Area's most special places, the Gerbode Valley. This beautiful valley was just barely saved from development in the 1960s, when a community for 20,000 people was planned to be built there. With your first glimpse of Gerbode Valley, you'll grimace at the idea of developers paving over its pristine grasslands. Chalk up a victory for the hawks, bobcats, and butterflies.

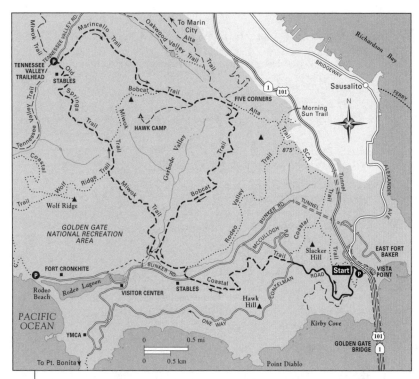

A backpacking camp is found .5 mile off Bobcat Trail; you could turn this ride into an overnight if you wish. Don't overload your mountain bike's panniers, however, or these Headlands hills will be very unforgiving.

For more information, call Golden Gate National Recreation Area, 415/331-1540, or visit www.nps.gov/goga.

Driving Directions

From San Francisco, cross the Golden Gate Bridge on U.S. 101 and take the first exit north of the bridge, Alexander Avenue. Turn left and loop back under the freeway, then turn right on Conzelman Road (signed for Marin Headlands). Park in the lot on the left, 100 feet up the road.

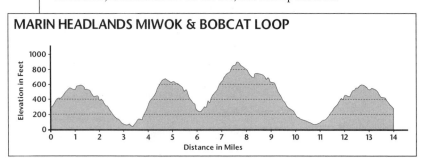

San Francisco Bay Area **61**

Route Directions for Marin Headlands Miwok & Bobcat Loop

0.0   Park at lot at start of Conzelman Road, on the northwest side of the Golden Gate Bridge. Ride out of the parking lot and turn left and uphill on Conzelman. *Supplies are available in Sausalito, two miles away.*

1.3   RIGHT at junction with McCullough Road (paved); then LEFT on signed dirt Coastal Trail.

2.9   STRAIGHT at junction to cross paved Bunker Road.

3.0   LEFT on Rodeo Valley Trail.

3.4   LEFT on Bobcat Trail at Y-junction.

3.5   RIGHT on Miwok Trail; now you're on the loop; steep climb ahead.

4.6   RIGHT to stay on Miwok at junction with Wolf Ridge Trail.

4.9   LEFT on Old Springs Trail (single-track).

6.2   Stables at Tennessee Valley Trailhead. Walk your bike through stables and parking lot and pick up Marincello Trail on right (northeast) edge of lot; prepare to climb.

7.7   LEFT on Bobcat Trail.

8.5   RIGHT to stay on Bobcat at junction with Rodeo and Alta Trails; steep descent into Gerbode Valley begins.

10.5   LEFT on Rodeo Valley Trail at end of loop; backtrack on Rodeo Valley Trail, Coastal Trail, and Conzelman Road to parking lot.

14.0   Arrive at starting point.

16. PERIMETER TRAIL & FIRE ROAD LOOPS

Angel Island State Park

The Perimeter Trail at Angel Island State Park provides 360-degree views from its setting in the middle of the bay, making it arguably the most scenic bike trail in the entire Bay Area. Views change constantly as you pedal, allowing you to see the cities and towns surrounding the bay in an entirely

a bench with a view of the Golden Gate Bridge on Angel Island's Perimeter Trail

ROUTE DETAILS FOR 16A
(Perimeter Trail only)

type of trail dirt road and deteriorating pavement

difficulty

total distance 5.5 miles

riding time 1 hour

elevation gain 600 feet

ROUTE DETAILS FOR 16B
(double loop)

type of trail dirt road and deteriorating pavement

difficulty

total distance 9.6 miles

riding time 2 hours

elevation gain 900 feet

new perspective. One of the best vistas lies on the southeast side of the island, where an open stretch captures the Bay and Golden Gate Bridges, plus Alcatraz Island. The 180-degree scene encompasses the whole sweep of urban skylines from Berkeley to San Francisco to Sausalito.

And the island doles out more than just views. Bikers on the Perimeter Trail can also enjoy two sandy beaches just off the trail, a series of history lessons, and the simple joy of getting to the island—a half-hour ferry cruise from various cities around the Bay.

Perimeter Trail is a partially paved road, with the pavement deteriorating to gravel and dirt in places. True to its name, the trail loops around the island's perimeter, so you can ride your bike in either direction (the route suggested here goes counterclockwise). History lessons are readily available, because Angel Island has had a long and varied history as a military outpost, a Russian sea otter hunters' site, and an immigrant detention

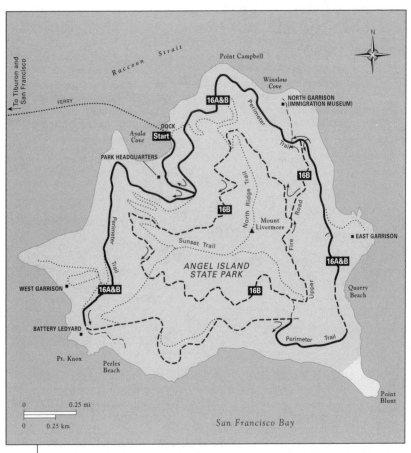

center. Be sure to read the interpretive signs around the island or stop in at the visitor center near Ayala Cove to get more information.

Those seeking a longer ride than the 5.5-mile Perimeter Trail can connect to a loop-within-the-loop, a dirt fire road on the island's interior (Ride 16B). The route suggested here connects the two loops at the fire station on the north side of the island, but you can also connect them via the cutoff for Mount Livermore on the southeast side. Because the upper fire road is situated higher in elevation, it offers even more expansive views than Perimeter Trail.

One note of caution: The wind can blow at Angel Island, and the fog can come in on a moment's notice, so come prepared with an extra jacket, even on sunny days.

For more information, contact Angel Island State Park, 415/435-1915 or 415/893-1580; website: www.angelisland.org.

Driving Directions

Ferry service to Angel Island is available from Tiburon, San Francisco, Oakland/Alameda, and Vallejo. For Tiburon departures, phone the Tiburon Ferry at 415/435-2131. For Oakland or Alameda departures, phone East Bay Ferry at 510/522-3300. For San Francisco departures, phone Blue & Gold Fleet at 415/773-1188. For Vallejo departures, phone Baylink at 707/64-FERRY (707/643-3779).

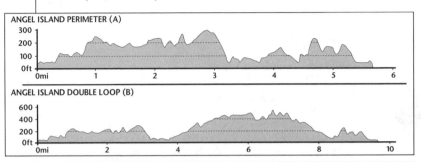

ANGEL ISLAND PERIMETER (A)

ANGEL ISLAND DOUBLE LOOP (B)

Route Directions for 16A *(Perimeter Trail only)* for Perimeter Trail & Fire Road Loops

0.0 Arrive at ferry landing at Ayala Cove. Retrieve your bike from the ferry and ride to your right, past the café and toward the picnic area. *Water, pay phones, restrooms, and rental lockers are available at the ferry landing; food is available at the landing café.*

0.2 LEFT on gravel bike trail by picnic area.

0.5 RIGHT on Perimeter Trail.

1.3 West Garrison and Camp Reynolds.

1.7 Cutoff for road to Perle's Beach; views of San Francisco and Alcatraz from the beach.

2.9 STRAIGHT on Perimeter Trail at junction with Upper Fire Road.

3.5 East Garrison and old military hospital.

3.9 STRAIGHT at junction with Upper Fire Road.

5.0 RIGHT at junction with trail to Ayala Cove.

5.5 Arrive at starting point.

Route Directions for 16B *(double loop)*

Follow directions for Ride 16A to the 3.9-mile mark, then continue:

3.9 LEFT at junction with upper Fire Road at Fire Station.

4.3 RIGHT on Fire Road.

7.7 RIGHT on connecting road back to Perimeter Trail.

8.0 LEFT on Perimeter Trail.

9.1 RIGHT at junction with trail to Ayala Cove.

9.6 Arrive at starting point.

17. GOLDEN GATE BRIDGE & MARIN HEADLANDS LOOP

Golden Gate National Recreation Area near Sausalito

This ride is classic San Francisco, with vista after vista of world-class scenery. A favorite training ride for city riders, it's also perfect for visiting tourists seeking a "real" taste of the City by the Bay and its environs.

ROUTE DETAILS

type of trail paved roads with moderate car traffic

difficulty ▮▮▮▯▯

total distance 15 miles

riding time 1.5–2 hours

elevation gain 1500 feet

Beginning at Fort Point in San Francisco's Presidio, the route crosses the Golden Gate Bridge, then follows Conzelman Road through the Marin Headlands, with frequent jaw-dropping views back toward the mouth of the Golden Gate. A challenging climb up to Hawk Hill (920 feet) is followed by a dizzying descent on cliffside Conzelman Road, which thankfully is one-way in this stretch. Make sure your brakes are working well before you begin the precipitous drop.

At the edge of the headlands, a narrow strip of land curves out to Point Bonita Lighthouse, which can be visited via a one-mile round-trip walk. Time your trip carefully: The 1855-built lighthouse is open only on Saturday, Sunday, and Monday from 12:30 to 3:30 P.M., and is accessed via a 50-foot-long tunnel and 40-yard-long suspension footbridge. Its location is the most dramatic of any lighthouse on the California coast; don't miss seeing it.

Other highlights along the loop include Black Sand Beach, the Marin Headlands Visitor Center, and beautiful Rodeo Beach and Rodeo Lagoon. With all these places to visit, a bike lock is more than a good idea. The trip back includes a ride through a long, lighted tunnel with bike lanes, and then another jaunt across the magnificent Golden Gate Bridge.

Use some caution in crossing the bridge, especially if you ride on a weekday when you must use the east sidewalk (shared with oblivious pedestrians toting video cameras). On weekends, cyclists ride on the west sidewalk while pedestrians use the east sidewalk, so there's less congestion. Either way, keep your speed down and take time to enjoy the view from 225 feet above San Francisco Bay.

For more information, contact Golden Gate National Recreation Area, 415/331-1540; website: nps.gov/goga.

Driving Directions

From the Crissy Field and marina area of San Francisco, take Lincoln Boulevard west toward the Golden Gate Bridge. Turn right just before the bridge entrance into the Battery East parking lot at Fort Point.

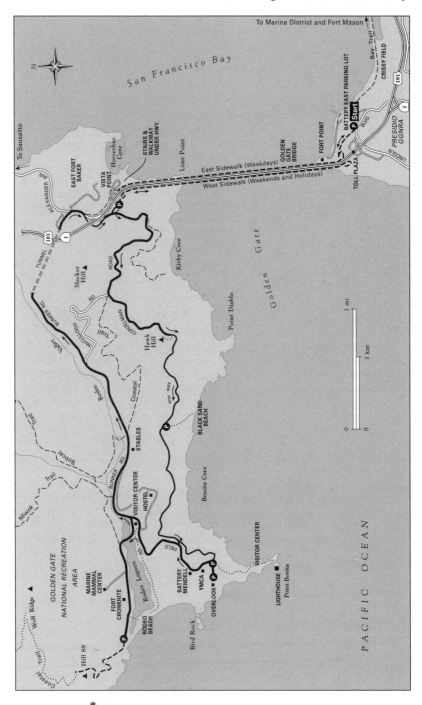

GOLDEN GATE BRIDGE & MARIN HEADLANDS LOOP

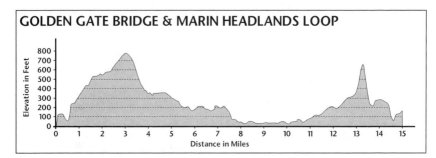

Route Directions for Golden Gate Bridge & Marin Headlands Loop

0.0 Park at the Battery East parking lot at Fort Point on Lincoln Boulevard (east side of the Golden Gate Bridge). At the entrance to the parking lot is a gated, paved road that is signed as a bike route (#202) to get on the bridge. *Water and snacks are available at Bridge Cafe at the bridge entrance (Bridge View Area).*

0.2 Start across the Golden Gate Bridge (ride on west side on weekends and holidays and east side on weekdays; obey all posted instruction signs for cyclists).

1.8 LEFT up hill on Conzelman Road at north (Marin County) side of Golden Gate Bridge. *If you're on the east sidewalk, exit at the Vista Point area and take the stairway underpass under the highway to the start of Conzelman Road. If you're on the west sidewalk, follow the signs for cyclists to the start of Conzelman Road.*

3.5 LEFT at junction with McCullough Road.

4.1 Summit of Hawk Hill; two-way road turns to one-way and descent begins.

5.0 Parking lot for Black Sand Beach on left. *Lock up your bike and hike .5 mile to one of Marin County's most spectacular beaches.*

6.0 STRAIGHT for Point Bonita Lighthouse.

6.5 Lighthouse trailhead. *Lock up your bike and hike .5 mile to the lighthouse.*

6.7 Road ends at Battery Mendell and overlook. TURN AROUND.

7.8 Marin Headlands Visitor Center on left.

8.0 LEFT at junction with Bunker Road.

8.5 LEFT at junction; Marin Mammal Center above to the right.

8.9 Road ends at Rodeo Beach parking lot. TURN AROUND. *Lock up your bike and explore the beach and lagoon trail. Mountain bikers can continue up Coastal Trail (gated road) 1.6 miles from parking lot to top of Hill 88 and spectacular view; a turnaround is required at the top.*

10.0 LEFT at junction of Field Road and Bunker Road.

12.2 Entrance to one-way tunnel. Push button to alert motorists that a cyclist is in the tunnel.

12.7 Exit tunnel and ride uphill.

12.9 RIGHT at stop sign.

13.2 Start of Conzelman Road. Return to proper side of the bridge according to day of the week.

15.0 Arrive at starting point.

18. NIMITZ WAY & WILDCAT CANYON

Tilden and Wildcat Canyon Regional Parks, Berkeley hills

Of all the paved recreation trails in the East Bay, Nimitz Way wins the prize for best views. Perched on the tip of San Pablo Ridge in Tilden Park, the trail serves up nonstop scenery changes. Near its start cyclists survey San Pablo

Wildcat Creek Trail rollercoasters along the bottom of Wildcat Canyon.

© ANN MARIE BROWN

ROUTE DETAILS FOR 18A
(Nimitz Way Trail only)

type of trail	paved bike path
difficulty	🍼🍼🍼🍼
total distance	7.8 miles
riding time	1 hour
elevation gain	450 feet

ROUTE DETAILS FOR 18B
(Nimitz Way & Wildcat Canyon Loop)

type of trail	dirt road and paved bike path
difficulty	🍼🍼🍼🍼🍼
total distance	11.3 miles
riding time	2 hours
elevation gain	800 feet

Reservoir, with Briones Reservoir behind, plus looming Mount Diablo. A few pedal cranks later, San Francisco Bay, the Golden Gate Bridge, and Angel Island come into view. At every turn in the trail, over every hill, you gain a different perspective: The Richmond Bridge appears, the Gold Coast shows up, San Francisco's skyline emerges, and the Brothers Islands steal the scene. On a clear day, the panorama will amaze you.

Nimitz Way is mostly level with only one short hill right before the pavement ends at 3.9 miles. It is well-loved by every kind of rider, including those on tricycles and training wheels, and with good reason. Mountain bikers can use Nimitz Way to connect to dirt trails in Tilden and Wildcat Canyon parks; Ride 18B describes an easy to moderate loop through Wildcat that affords a good workout and more memorable views. Be forewarned that the loop has two very steep downhills, where I've seen riders walking their bikes while simultaneously biting their nails. Hey, at least you don't have to ride *up* those hills.

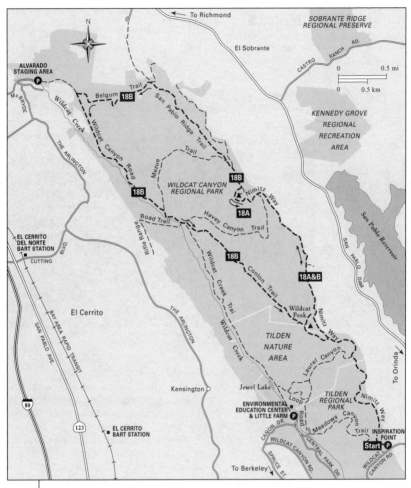

If you're planning on riding in this area on the weekend, get to the Inspiration Point parking lot early. The place is Bike City every Saturday and Sunday, and parking spots are at a premium.

For more information, contact East Bay Regional Park District, 510/562-7275 or 510/635-0135; website: www.ebparks.org.

Driving Directions

From I-580 in Oakland, take Highway 24 east. Go through the Caldecott Tunnel and exit at Orinda. Turn left on Camino Pablo. Drive north for two miles, then turn left on Wildcat Canyon Road. Drive 2.4 miles to the Inspiration Point parking lot.

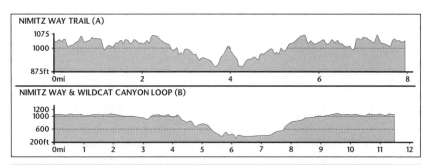

Route Directions for 18A *(Nimitz Way Trail only)* Nimitz Way & Wildcat Canyon

- 0.0   Park at Inspiration Point parking lot and take the well-signed Nimitz Way Trail. *Supplies are available in Berkeley or Orinda.*
- 3.9   End of paved Nimitz Way Trail at gate. TURN AROUND.
- 7.8   Arrive at starting point.

Route Directions for 18B *(Nimitz Way & Wildcat Canyon loop)*

Follow the route directions for 18A to mile 3.9, then continue:

- 3.9   Go through gate at end of Nimitz Way to join dirt San Pablo Ridge Trail; ignore trails branching right and left.
- 5.2   LEFT on Belgum Trail; steep descent.
- 6.1   LEFT on Wildcat Creek Trail. *Water is available .5 mile to the right on Wildcat Creek Trail (Alvarado Staging Area).*
- 7.7   STRAIGHT at junction with Mezue Trail on left.
- 7.9   LEFT at junction with Havey Canyon Trail then immediate RIGHT on Conlon Trail.
- 9.9   RIGHT on paved Nimitz Way.
- 11.3   Arrive at starting point.

19. SKYLINE LOOP

Berkeley and Oakland hills

You can't call yourself a road cyclist in the San Francisco Bay Area until you've ridden the Skyline Loop in the East Bay hills. On a clear day, the loop's far-reaching views of San Francisco Bay, the cities of the East Bay, and Mount Diablo will knock your socks off. The route has just enough hills to provide a workout, but none are so steep that they are out of the range of possibility for most riders. Plus, the roads have surprisingly little traffic, except for Moraga Way, which has a wide shoulder. All this and you can easily start the ride from Orinda, Moraga, Berkeley, or at one of several parks on Skyline Boulevard.

Far-reaching views of San Francisco Bay and East Bay cities are seen from the Skyline Loop.

ROUTE DETAILS

type of trail paved roads with moderate car traffic

difficulty 🏋🏋🏋

total distance 28.5 miles (or 23-mile option)

riding time 2 hours

elevation gain 2,000 feet

I describe the loop starting from the Inspiration Point parking lot at Tilden Regional Park, a popular gathering place for cyclists on weekends and a great place to find a riding partner. (Get there early to procure a parking spot.) This trailhead choice means you begin your ride with a twisty descent and end with a twisty climb on Wildcat Canyon Road. But the ride has a multitude of climbs and descents, so you might as well get in the spirit right away.

The major hills are on Pinehurst Road, Skyline Boulevard, and Grizzly Peak Road. (The latter two roads are where you gain most of your bay views.) You also face a steep descent on South Park Drive, just after you pass the miniature steam train at Tilden Park, where families pay a couple bucks to go for a 12-minute, open-air train tour. Keep your speed down as you descend on this moderately busy park road. Not just to avoid cars, but also to avoid California newts: The cute brown and orange salamanders cross the road by the thousands each year during

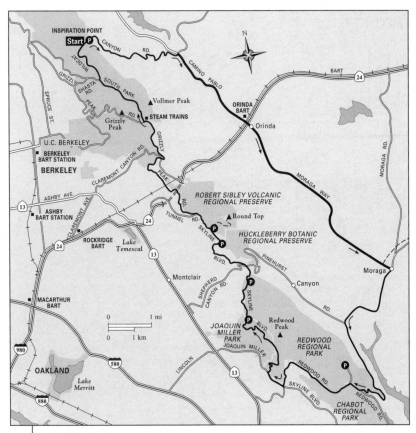

the rainy season. During the peak newt migration, South Park Drive is closed to cars, but open to cyclists.

Besides Tilden, this loop passes by two other East Bay Regional Parks: Redwood Regional and Robert Sibley. Redwood is a popular spot for mountain biking and hiking; Sibley has Round Top Peak, the remains of an ancient volcano.

For riders short on time, note the shortcut at mile 10.9 on Pinehurst Road. Turning right instead of left on Pinehurst will cut 5.5 miles off the loop, but you'll face a steep climb up to Skyline Boulevard. The Pinehurst shortcut does have charms, however: The road sees almost no car traffic, is lined with redwoods, and passes by the tiny hamlet of Canyon, with its one-room schoolhouse and post office. You may ask yourself, is this the East Bay?

Driving Directions

From I-580 in Oakland, take Highway 24 east. Go through the Caldecott Tunnel and exit at Orinda. Turn left on Camino Pablo. Drive north for two miles, then turn left on Wildcat Canyon Road. Drive 2.4 miles to Inspiration Point parking lot.

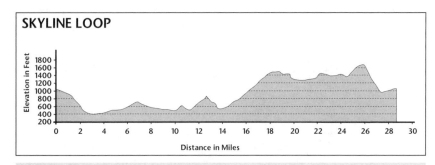

SKYLINE LOOP

Route Directions for Skyline Loop

0.0   Park at Inspiration Point parking lot. Turn left out of the lot and head downhill on Wildcat Canyon Road. *Supplies are available in Berkeley or Orinda.*

2.4   RIGHT on Camino Pablo Road.

4.5   Cross under Highway 24; Camino Pablo becomes Moraga Way.

4.6   Arrive in Orinda. *Supplies are available.*

9.1   RIGHT on Canyon Road. *Supplies are available at the shopping center.*

10.9   LEFT on Pinehurst Road. *You can cut 5.5 miles off the loop by turning right on Pinehurst Road here. After a steep climb, you'll rejoin the route at mile 20.4, below, where you'll go straight onto Skyline.*

13.8   RIGHT on Redwood Road.

16.2   RIGHT on Skyline Boulevard.

16.8   RIGHT to stay on Skyline Boulevard at Joaquin Miller Road.

19.9   Redwood Regional Park Skyline gate. *Water is available.*

20.4   LEFT to stay on Skyline Boulevard at Pinehurst Road.

21.9   Robert Sibley Regional Preserve. *Water is available.*

22.0   RIGHT on Grizzly Peak Road.

24.4   STRAIGHT to stay on Grizzly Peak Road.

25.6   Tilden Regional Park's miniature steam train. *Water is available.*

25.8   RIGHT on South Park Road.

27.3   RIGHT on Wildcat Canyon Road.

28.5   Arrive at starting point.

20. CARQUINEZ STRAIT LOOP

Martinez to Crockett

The northeastern arm of the conglomeration of waterways that constitute the bay and river delta, Carquinez Strait forms the narrow passageway between San Pablo and Suisun Bays. It's the meeting place of the Sacramento and San Joaquin Rivers, where they join together to flow to the Pacific Ocean through the Golden Gate.

Grasses and weeds push up through the broken pavement on this stretch of Carquinez Scenic Drive, which has been closed to cars since 1982.

ROUTE DETAILS

type of trail	paved roads with minimal car traffic
difficulty	🍶🍶🍶🍶🍶
total distance	18.5 miles
riding time	1.5–2 hours
elevation gain	1,200 feet

Hundreds of thousands of king salmon once passed through here on their way to the Sacramento and San Joaquin Rivers to spawn. Native Americans lived off their abundance for centuries. In the 1800s, white settlers set up commercial fishing operations and canneries along the strait; king salmon ruled the economy of this area. Today, the only salmon you'll find in the towns of Martinez and Crockett are on dinner plates in the nicer restaurants, but it's fascinating to recall the area's history as you ride this road tour between the two towns.

Due to events in more recent history, one portion of this road loop is closed to cars. A landslide in 1982 washed out a 1.7-mile-long section of Carquinez Scenic Drive. There's still enough road left for cyclists, but watch for broken pavement, gravel, and rocks. It's easy to get distracted by the views overlooking Carquinez Strait, a wide expanse of blue waterway punctuated by the journeying of ships, large and small. As Carquinez Scenic Drive twists and turns, you gain changing views of the Carquinez Bridge and the towns of Benecia and Vallejo.

Most of the climbing is accomplished in the first five miles of this ride (600-foot gain). The rest of the loop's "ups" are short, 200-foot-or-less climbs. There's also an exhilarating downhill on Crockett Boulevard into Crockett.

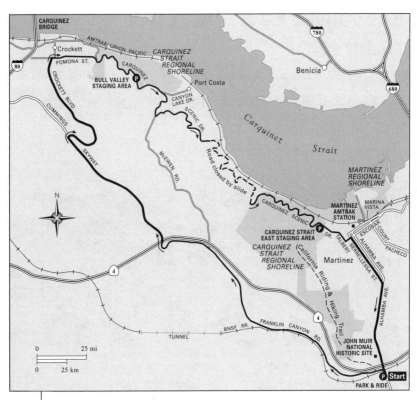

For more views of the waterway, you might want to stop at Carquinez Strait Regional Shoreline just outside of Crockett and hike the one-mile Carquinez Overlook Loop Trail.

Driving Directions

From Walnut Creek, take I-680 north for six miles to Highway 4. Turn west on Highway 4 and drive three miles; take the Alhambra Avenue exit and drive south to the Park and Ride lot on the right.

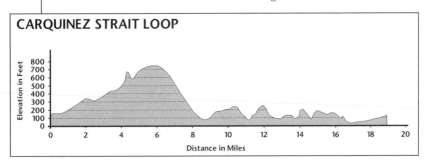

Route Directions for Carquinez Strait Loop

0.0 Park at the Park and Ride lot at the junction of Alhambra Avenue and Franklin Canyon Road. Ride west on Franklin Canyon Road. *Supplies are available in Walnut Creek, Concord, or Martinez.*

4.4 RIGHT on Cummings Skyway.

6.5 RIGHT on Crockett Boulevard.

8.5 RIGHT on Pomona Street into downtown Crockett; Pomona Street becomes Carquinez Scenic Drive just outside of town. *Supplies are available in downtown Crockett.*

10.3 Carquinez Regional Strait Shoreline on the left (Bull Valley Staging Area). *You can lock up your bike and hike the one-mile Carquinez Overlook Loop Trail.*

12.5 Road closure; ride around the gate.

14.2 Road is open to cars again.

16.4 RIGHT on Talbart Street.

16.5 LEFT on Escobar Street.

16.6 RIGHT on Berrellessa Street (becomes Alhambra Avenue).

18.5 Arrive at starting point.

21. BRIONES CREST LOOP

West of Walnut Creek and south of Martinez

Briones Regional Park is nearly 6,000 acres of grasslands and oaks that was once part of Rancho San Felipe, a Spanish land grant. In the mid 1800s, it was an important fruit-growing region. Today it's the grassy home of graz-

Briones Regional Park contains nearly 6,000 acres of rolling grassland hills.

ROUTE DETAILS FOR RIDE 21A
(single loop)

type of trail	dirt road and single-track
difficulty	▮▮▯▯▯
total distance	8 miles
riding time	1.5 hours
elevation gain	1,200 feet

ROUTE DETAILS FOR RIDE 21B
(double loop)

type of trail	dirt road and single-track
difficulty	▮▮▮▯▯
total distance	13.5 miles
riding time	2 hours
elevation gain	1,800 feet

ing cows and frequently visited by mountain bikers, dog walkers, hikers, and horseback riders.

The park is well known for its sunny exposure, numerous dirt roads, and large expanse of open grasslands. Bordered on three sides by freeways—Highway 4, I-680, and Highway 2—it's an oasis of open space in a heavily urbanized area.

Because of an absence of shade in the park, summer is not the best time for riding here. It can be as hot as Hades on August afternoons, although quite pleasant in winter, spring, and fall. Note that cows roam the Briones pasturelands, so you must pass through a number of cattle gates. And those same cows are notorious for rutting the heck out of the ranch roads, so expect a lot of bumps, especially on the downhills.

Briones Crest Loop is the most popular

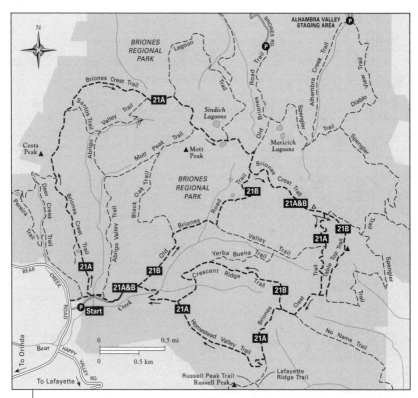

ride at this park for mountain bikers. I've written it as a double loop that can be split up into two rides. The first half mile on wide single-track is a grunt of a climb (three short hills with a total 400-foot elevation gain), but beyond that, the remaining hills are more moderate. Most of the ride is on wide ranch roads, which lend themselves to some fun downhills. The final descent on Crescent Ridge Trail (Ride 21B only) is memorably steep.

Don't forget to pause for a moment at mile 4.3, where you pass Briones Peak, the highest point in the park at 1,483 feet. The hilltop affords great views of mighty Mount Diablo.

For more information, contact East Bay Regional Park District, 510/635-0135 or 510/562-7275; website: www.ebparks.org.

Driving Directions

From I-580 in Oakland, take Highway 24 east. Go through the Caldecott Tunnel and exit at Orinda. Turn left on Camino Pablo and drive north for two miles. Turn right on Bear Creek Road and drive 4.4 miles, then turn right into Briones Regional Park/Bear Creek Staging Area entrance. Turn left just past the kiosk and park in the lower parking lot.

Briones Crest Loop

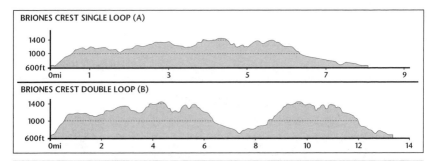

Route Directions for 21A *(single loop)* for Briones Crest Loop

0.0   Park at the lower parking lot at the Bear Creek Staging Area. The trailhead is at the end of the parking lot on the left. Follow Briones Crest Trail. *Water is available at the trailhead.*

0.1   RIGHT at Y-junction on to Briones Crest Trail.

0.5   End of the climb; trail widens and levels out.

1.1   STRAIGHT on Briones Crest Trail at junction with Deer Creek Trail. Stay straight on Briones Crest Trail at next four junctions.

3.3   Pass by Sindicich Lagoons (ranch ponds).

3.5   RIGHT on Old Briones Road.

3.6   LEFT on Briones Crest Trail.

4.3   Briones Peak, elevation 1,483 feet.

4.4   RIGHT to stay on Briones Crest Trail.

4.8   STRAIGHT on Briones Crest Trail.

5.7   STRAIGHT on Briones Crest Trail.

6.2   RIGHT on Homestead Valley Trail.

7.7   LEFT on Old Briones Road.

7.8   Go around gate and pass upper parking lot.

7.9   RIGHT at kiosk into lower parking lot.

8.0   Arrive at starting point.

Route Directions for 21B *(double loop)*

Follow the route directions for 21A to mile 7.7, then continue:

7.7   RIGHT on Old Briones Road.

8.6   LEFT to stay on Old Briones Road.

9.3   RIGHT on Briones Crest Trail (pass Briones Peak again).

10.1   STRAIGHT on Table Top Trail; head for radio antennas.

10.8   RIGHT to stay on Table Top Trail.

10.9   STRAIGHT on Briones Crest Trail.

11.3   RIGHT on Crescent Ridge Trail (head past the archery range).

12.7   RIGHT on Homestead Valley Trail.

13.2   LEFT on Old Briones Road.

13.3   Go around gate and pass upper parking lot.

13.4   RIGHT at kiosk into lower parking lot.

13.5   Arrive at starting point.

22. LAFAYETTE-MORAGA REGIONAL TRAIL

Near Lafayette and Moraga

When suburbs grow so large that they connect town to town without any buffer of open land between them, one of the smartest things city planners can do is create spaces where people can get a little fresh air and sunshine—places protected from cars, traffic, and urban noise. The Lafayette-Moraga Trail is such a place, and it is used by more than half a million people per year.

It's not exactly a trip to the wilderness, but you will see plenty of squirrels along the trail—not plain old Bay Area gray squirrels, but cute and chubby red squirrels with shiny, rust-colored coats. I spotted some busily

ROUTE DETAILS

type of trail	paved bike path
difficulty	
total distance	15.4 miles
riding time	2 hours
elevation gain	550 feet

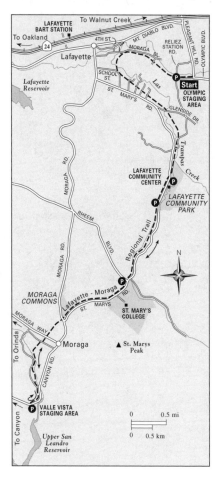

burying nuts in flower beds, their genetic instinct preparing them for the long, hard, snow-bound winter that will never come to sunny Moraga.

Also in the cute category, an entire pack of cub scouts cycled by me, dressed in their smart navy blue uniforms and tiny bicycle helmets. That's the kind of trail this is. A stretch of the old San Francisco-Sacramento Railroad, the path retains some of its railroad history with white crossing signs proudly displayed at junctions around Lafayette.

Unfortunately, Lafayette-Moraga Trail is intersected by several roads. Only one, St. Mary's Road, is likely to have much traffic. Beyond this crossing, you leave most of the neighborhoods behind and see less of St. Mary's Road (which parallels the trail up to this crossing). The trail passes St. Mary's College, which has a pretty white church tower set in the hillside and is surrounded by green playing fields. Shortly thereafter is Moraga Commons, a town park with a play area, restrooms, par course, and the like. A waterfall sculpture is located near a sign noting that Lafayette-Moraga Trail was opened in 1976 as one of America's first 500 rail trails. The trail's final stretch leads out to the country, ending at the Valle Vista Staging Area on Canyon Road, where you turn around and head back.

For more information, contact East Bay Regional Park District, 510/635-0135 or 510/562-7275; website: www.ebparks.org.

Driving Directions
From I-580 in Oakland, take Highway 24 east toward Walnut Creek. Go through the Caldecott Tunnel and take the Pleasant Hill Road exit south. Drive .7 miles to Olympic Boulevard and turn right. The parking lot is on the right in about 50 yards.

LAFAYETTE-MORAGA REGIONAL TRAIL

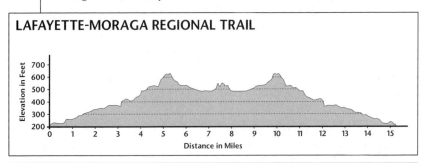

Route Directions for Lafayette-Moraga Regional Trail

0.0 Park at Olympic staging area. *Water is available along the trail.*

1.1 STRAIGHT at junction with Briones-to-Las-Trampas Trail.

3.3 Cross St. Mary's Road.

3.4 Lafayette Community Center. *Water is available.*

5.2 St. Mary's College campus.

6.0 Moraga Commons park. *Water is available.*

7.7 Valle Vista staging area. TURN AROUND.

15.4 Arrive at starting point.

23. STEWARTVILLE & RIDGE TRAIL LOOP

Black Diamond Mines Regional Preserve near Antioch

From 1860 to 1906, the Mount Diablo Coal Field was the largest coal mining district in California. Located in what is now Black Diamond Mines Regional Preserve, this productive coal field on the northern side of Mount Diablo prompted the digging of 12 major mines and the growth of five townships. Much of this mining history, and a large acreage of rolling grassland hills and chaparral-clad slopes, is preserved at Black Diamond Mines (925/757-2620).

ROUTE DETAILS

type of trail dirt road

difficulty

total distance 10.8 miles

riding time 2 hours

elevation gain 1,900 feet

This loop ride reveals some of the park's highlights and adds some heart-pumping, leg-burning exercise to the bargain. Start with a mind-expanding trip to the park visitor center, then ride level Railroad Bed Trail to Stewartville Trail. A .5-mile ascent brings you to a cattle gate at a high point. Pass through the gate and admire the deep, grassy valley below you. The good news is that you're going to ride into that pretty valley; the bad news is that you'll have to climb back out of it.

Don't miss two spurs off the loop: Upper Old Canyon Trail which leads steeply uphill to an overlook of the valley, and Tunnel Trail to Prospect Tunnel, an obvious gaping hole in the hillside. You can explore about 150 feet into the dark, cool mine shaft before you reach a steel gate. The shaft was driven in the 1860s by miners in search of coal or "black diamonds."

A mile past Tunnel Trail, make a sharp left turn on Ridge Trail, leaving the valley and beginning a steep, two-mile-long ascent. Ridge Trail rollercoasters along, dipping down occasionally but more often rising on very steep grades (the kind that may force you to walk your bike). The climb is eased by the sudden appearance of views to the north of Carquinez Strait, Suisun Bay, Pittsburg, and Antioch. Pause to enjoy the vistas while you catch your breath.

When at last Ridge Trail returns you to the gate at Stewartville Trail, consider a rest on the bench by the gate, where you can admire the rolling terrain you just explored. Then it's an easy 1.4 miles back to your car.

Because there is no technical single-track on this ride, it's tempting to bring beginning mountain bikers here. But unless they are very fit and ambitious, the many short but steep ascents will break their spirit. All riders should stay away from this park's trails when they are wet; the place is famous for its clay-like mud that can bring your wheels to a dead standstill, even on the downhills.

For more information, contact East Bay Regional Park District, 510/635-0135 or 510/562-7275; website: www.ebparks.org.

Stewartville & Ridge Trail Loop

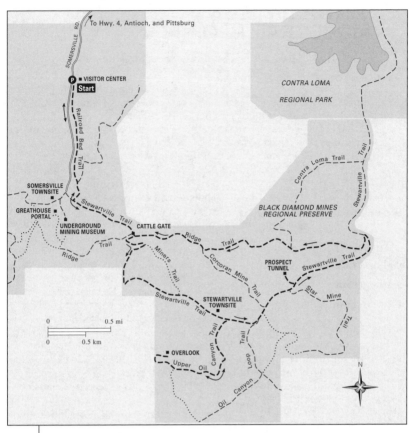

Driving Directions

From Highway 4 in Antioch, take the Somersville Road exit south. Drive three miles south on Somersville Road to the parking lot by the visitor center.

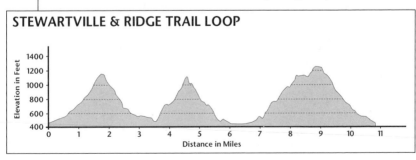

Route Directions for Stewartville & Ridge Trail Loop

0.0 Park by the visitor center on Somersville Road. Take Railroad Bed Trail from the southern end of the parking lot. *Water is available at the visitor center; supplies are available four miles away in Antioch.*

0.7 LEFT on Stewartville Trail.

1.4 Cattle gate and viewpoint. Go through gate, then RIGHT to stay on Stewartville Trail; steep descent.

1.8 RIGHT at junction with Miners Trail to stay on Stewartville Trail.

3.2 RIGHT on Upper Oil Canyon Trail.

4.4 Arrive at overlook. TURN AROUND.

5.6 RIGHT to continue on Stewartville Trail.

6.1 LEFT on Tunnel Trail. Park your bike and walk into the dark tunnel, then TURN AROUND.

6.4 LEFT to continue on Stewartville Trail.

7.3 LEFT (very sharp turn) on Ridge Trail; steep climb begins.

9.4 RIGHT on Stewartville Trail at cattle gate.

10.1 RIGHT on Railroad Bed Trail.

10.8 Arrive at starting point.

24. REDWOOD REGIONAL PARK LOOP

Oakland hills

They don't call this place Redwood Regional Park for nothing. The dark, shaggy-barked trees grow more than 100 feet tall and their shady canopy covers a vast expanse of the park. The redwoods are the second-generation offspring of the original trees that once towered over this canyon. Between 1840 and 1860, loggers felled these ancient giants to provide lumber for the growing cities of San Francisco and San Jose.

ROUTE DETAILS

type of trail — dirt road

difficulty —

total distance — 9.4 miles

riding time — 2 hours

elevation gain — 1,100 feet

The redwoods aren't the only prizes of Redwood Regional Park. The park is bordered by two high ridges to the east and west, both of which offer expansive views. This loop ride, a standard for East Bay mountain bikers, travels out the East Ridge and back on West Ridge. Although the ride is entirely on wide dirt roads, it still presents some technical challenges, particularly on a steep, rutted downhill on Canyon Trail and a steep uphill on West Ridge Trail. Strong beginners should be able to handle it, or at least walk their bikes if they can't.

From the Skyline Gate staging area, follow East Ridge Trail generally downhill for three miles in a two-steps-down, one-step-up fashion, rolling along small hills. Watch for long distance views of the reservoirs to the east. Turn right on Canyon Trail, drop steeply, then follow Stream Trail into the canyon to see up close some of the park's redwood stands. After a brief, level, out-and-back on Stream Trail, you'll face a hearty climb on West Ridge Trail. The first .75 mile is the worst (400-foot gain), but the trail continues to ascend moderately for almost three miles.

West Ridge Trail's final stretch passes by the newly built observatory at the Chabot Space and Science Center (worth a visit). You'll catch fine glimpses of Oakland and San Francisco Bay to the west; equally good is the

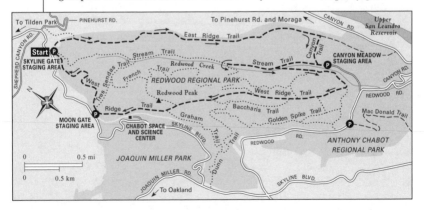

view to the east of looming Mount Diablo at 3,849 feet. The last mile is a delightfully easy cruise back to Skyline Gate through a shady forest of bay laurel, madrone, and Monterey pine.

For more information, contact East Bay Regional Park District, 510/635-0135 or 510/562-7275; website: www.ebparks.org.

Driving Directions

From I-580 in Oakland, take the 35th Avenue exit and turn north. Drive 2.4 miles (35th Avenue will become Redwood Road). Turn left on Skyline Boulevard and drive 3.7 miles to the Skyline Gate Staging Area, located at the intersection of Skyline and Pine Hills Drive. (Skyline Boulevard makes a sharp right turn after the first half mile.)

REDWOOD REGIONAL PARK LOOP

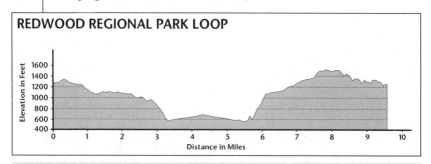

Route Directions for Redwood Regional Park Loop

0.0 Park at Skyline Gate staging area and take East Ridge Trail, the northern-most of three possible trails. *Water is available at the trailhead.*

2.9 RIGHT on Canyon Trail.

3.3 RIGHT on Stream Trail at Canyon Meadow Staging Area.

3.6 STRAIGHT at junction with Bridle Trail; you'll return to this intersection shortly.

4.2 End of bikes-allowed section of Stream Trail. TURN AROUND. *Stop at one of five picnic areas under the redwoods. Water is available.*

4.8 RIGHT on Bridle Trail upon return to previous junction.

5.0 RIGHT on West Ridge Trail; begin ascent to ridge.

6.3 RIGHT to stay on West Ridge Trail.

7.7 Chabot Space and Science Center.

9.4 Arrive at starting point.

25. MOUNT DIABLO

Blackhawk to Mount Diablo Summit

Almost everybody thinks about making the trip to 3,849-foot Mount Diablo from time to time. After all, you see it from just about everywhere in the Bay Area. It's not the tallest mountain around San Francisco Bay (Mount Hamilton near San Jose is 360 feet taller-see Ride 44, this chapter), but it has a way of making its presence known, looming in the background of the lives of millions of East Bay residents.

© ANN MARIE BROWN

Two cyclists pause for a break at Junction Ranger Station on the ascent up Mount Diablo.

ROUTE DETAILS

type of trail paved roads with moderate car traffic

difficulty 🥾🥾🥾🥾🥾

total distance 29.6 miles

riding time 4–5 hours

elevation gain 3,200 feet

Although most people travel to the summit of Mount Diablo by car, a better way to get there is by bike. Sure, it's a long grind with a nearly nonstop elevation gain, but this is what you live for, right? You haven't really experienced Diablo's Summit Road until you've ridden it on a bike. With every curve in the winding pavement, the views are constantly changing.

Two roads—North Gate and South Gate—travel up the mountain; they join at Summit Ranger station for the final 4.5 miles on Summit Road to the top. This ride follows South Gate Road from Blackhawk, elevation 738 feet; it's the easier of the two roads. Slightly easier, anyway. If you want to shorten this ride, just drive your car farther up the mountain road and start from one of the parking areas within the state park, like Curry Point or Rock City.

Pick a cool day (forget summer on this shadeless "devil's mountain") and be encouraged by the fact that water and rest stops are plentiful all the way up the mountain (most roadside picnic areas and campgrounds have water).

For more information, contact Mount Diablo State Park, 925/837-2525 or 925/837-0904; website: www.mdia.org.

Driving Directions

From the junction of I-680 and I-580 in Dublin, drive north on I-680 for five miles to the Crow Canyon Road exit. Drive east for four miles; Crow Canyon Road becomes Blackhawk Road at its junction with Tassajara Road. Park at or near Blackhawk Plaza shopping center and ride east on Blackhawk Road.

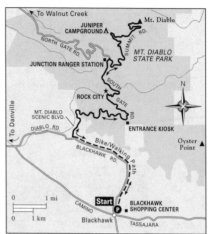

MOUNT DIABLO

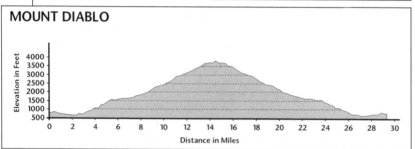

Route Directions for Mount Diablo

0.0 Park at or near Blackhawk Plaza shopping center and ride east on Blackhawk Road, then pick up the bike/walking path alongside the road. *Supplies are available at this shopping center.*

3.4 RIGHT on Mount Diablo Scenic Boulevard.

4.5 Mount Diablo State Park gate.

7.1 Entrance kiosk.

7.6 Rock City region of the park.

8.2 Rock City parking area (good alternate starting point).

8.8 Curry Point parking area.

10.3 RIGHT on Summit Road at Junction Ranger Station.

12.8 Juniper Campground.

14.8 Mount Diablo summit. TURN AROUND.

29.6 Arrive at starting point.

26. ROUND VALLEY REGIONAL PRESERVE

East of Walnut Creek and north of Livermore

If you ever start to feel like the East Bay is too crowded, too congested, and has too much concrete, take a trip a little farther east to the back side of Mount Diablo. Here on the far eastern edge of the San Francisco Bay Area are wide open spaces, spring wildflowers, and stately oak trees.

ROUTE DETAILS

type of trail   dirt road

difficulty

total distance   10.8 miles (or longer options)

riding time   1.5 hours

elevation gain   600 feet

You'll find all this and more at Round Valley Regional Preserve, the 2,000-acre home of nesting golden eagles, burrowing owls, chubby ground squirrels, and the endangered San Joaquin kit fox. The bike riding here is mellow and easy, unless of course you show up at midday in August, when it can be more than 100 degrees.

From the preserve staging area, the trail starts out with a long bridge over Marsh Creek. At the far side of the bridge, a right turn puts you on Miwok Trail. Immediately you face the only real hill of the day; the remaining miles of this ride are mostly level.

In .5 mile, the wide dirt road meets up with Round Valley Creek. If you've timed your trip for the wet season, the stream will run cool and clear alongside you for much of your ride. You'll notice the remains of old farming equipment along the dirt trail; this land was farmed by the Murphy family from 1873 until 1988, when it was donated to the East Bay Regional Park District (510/562-7275 or 510/635-0135; website: www.ebparks.org).

Stay on Miwok Trail through the entire length of the preserve, then turn right on Murphy's Meadow Trail. You'll loop back on the far side of Round Valley Creek. At a junction with Fox Tail Trail, follow Fox Tail Trail uphill for a short out-and-back excursion. Head for the top of the hill, where you'll find a wide view of rolling hills and vast, unpopulated parkland. What a fine spot for a picnic lunch.

Riders looking for more mileage can follow Miwok Trail out of the park, through a 1.6-mile stretch of Los Vaqueros Watershed, and into the east side of Morgan Territory Regional Preserve, where most trails are open to mountain bikes. Free maps available from the East Bay Regional Park District can get you where you want to go.

Driving Directions

From I-580 in Livermore, take the Vasco Road exit and drive north 13 miles. Turn left (west) on Camino Diablo Road and drive 3.5 miles. Where Camino Diablo ends, continue straight on Marsh Creek Road for 1.5 miles to the Round Valley parking area on the left.

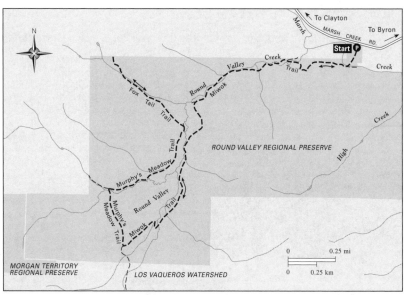

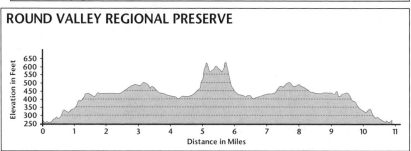

Route Directions for Round Valley Regional Preserve

0.0 Park at Round Valley staging area and ride across the bridge. *Supplies are available in Clayton, eight miles west.*

0.1 RIGHT on Miwok Trail at far side of bridge.

0.5 STRAIGHT at junction with trail on right.

2.8 RIGHT on Murphy's Meadow Trail. *Miwok Trail leaves the park here, travels through the Los Vaqueros Watershed and into Morgan Territory Regional Preserve, for more riding options.*

3.7 RIGHT to stay on Murphy's Meadow Trail.

4.6 LEFT on Fox Tail Trail.

5.4 End of Fox Tail Trail. TURN AROUND.

10.8 Arrive at starting point.

27. LAKE CHABOT LOOP

Lake Chabot and Anthony Chabot Regional Parks east of San Leandro

Lakeside trails are often level and somewhat predictable, but the trails around Lake Chabot never stop turning, twisting, climbing, and diving. You're either braking hard or pedaling hard the whole way. Still, with only 800 feet of elevation gain, the Lake Chabot Loop is suitable for all kinds of riders. The challenge of a few hills is compensated by the sheer fun of the ride. This is a good place to gain some experience on a mountain bike.

The popular bike trail around Lake Chabot is a mix of pavement, fire roads, and single-track.

ROUTE DETAILS

type of trail — dirt road and paved bike path

difficulty — ✂✂✂✂✂

total distance — 13.3 miles (or 9-mile, paved option)

riding time — 2 hours

elevation gain — 1,100 feet

You will have to put up with some irritating signs of civilization, though. In addition to the lake's busy marina and campground, you'll ride near a golf course and a shooting range. And if this is your first time here, you must pay careful attention to trail junctions. There are a ton of them.

An advantage to the prolific junctions is that Lake Chabot's trails can be customized according to your desires and abilities. The route described here combines the paved West and East Shore trails with several dirt fire roads for a 13.3-mile round-trip. Families with young children and skinny-tire riders will want to stick to pavement for a nine-mile out-and-back. The paved trails skirt the lake's edge, sometimes rising up along its steep walls, sometimes tracing a line just a few feet from the water.

Following the loop below, East Shore Trail's pavement ends 1.8 miles beyond the marina. Mountain bikers continue onward, walking their bikes over a bridge to connect with Honker Bay Trail (some use Live Oak Trail to make their loop; I prefer Honker Bay because it stays along the lakeshore).

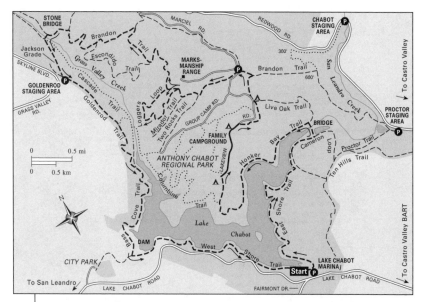

Take a trail map with you to negotiate the long stretch of Brandon Trail; it intersects annoyingly with what seems like a million other trails. Still, it offers some wide views of San Francisco Bay.

If you want to turn your bike ride into a day at the lake, Lake Chabot Marina (510/582-2198) has boats for rent, plus a small café that sells hot dogs and coffee. Lake Chabot is stocked with trout, bass, and catfish, and fishing prospects are quite good.

For more information, contact East Bay Regional Park District, 510/635-0135 or 510/562-7275; website: www.ebparks.org.

Driving Directions

From Oakland, drive east on I-580 and take the Dutton/Estudillo Avenue exit in San Leandro. Drive .5 mile, then turn left on Estudillo Avenue and drive .4 mile. Bear right at the "Y" with Lake Chabot Road and drive 2.5 miles to a T-junction. Turn left, then left again into the marina.

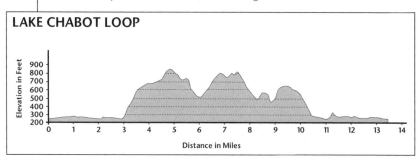

Route Directions for Lake Chabot Loop

0.0 Park at Lake Chabot Marina and head for the east side of the picnic area to the start of East Shore Trail. *Supplies are available at the marina store and café.* A trail map is posted on a signboard next to the marina café.

1.8 LEFT across narrow bridge at end of paved East Shore Trail; walk your bike.

1.9 LEFT on Honker Bay Trail.

3.5 Join paved campground road; ride through family campground on main road.

4.0 RIGHT on Towhee Trail.

4.8 LEFT on Brandon Trail (easy to miss—watch for it!).

4.9 Parking lot and restrooms; cross road and pick up Brandon Trail on other side.

5.5 LEFT on Logger's Loop Trail (or RIGHT to stay on Brandon Trail and save .9 mile).

6.6 Back on Brandon Trail.

8.4 LEFT and across stone bridge to LEFT on Jackson Grade to Goldenrod Trail.

8.8 Grass Valley Staging Area; stay on Goldenrod Trail

10.2 RIGHT on Bass Cove Trail.

11.5 LEFT on paved West Shore Trail.

13.3 Arrive at starting point.

28. PALOMARES ROAD

East of Hayward and Fremont

For a short stint of my life, I had the pleasure of living in the peaceful Sunol countryside, where on Sunday mornings I would awaken to the sounds of birds chirping and my roommate yelling, "Get up! Let's go ride Palomares Road."

Palomares Road is a peaceful country lane bordered by busy highways on both ends.

ROUTE DETAILS

type of trail paved roads with minimal car traffic

difficulty ▮▮▮▯▯

total distance 20.2 miles

riding time 1–2 hours

elevation gain 1,900 feet

And so we did, along with dozens of other East Bay cyclists, almost every Sunday, rain or shine. It was a happy habit that put some "country" into our urban lives.

The good news is that Palomares Road is still a peaceful country road, despite the fact that it's bordered by busy highways on both ends. It's perfect for a quick 20-mile training ride after work or on the weekends, and feels like a getaway even though it's very close to home for riders in the southeast Bay Area.

Some cyclists make a loop out of Palomares Road by riding Dublin Canyon Road to the north and Niles Canyon Road (Highway 84) to the south, then using Foothill Road as the east connector. I don't recommend it. These three roads were viable for cyclists a decade or so ago, but are now heavily trafficked almost 24 hours a day. Besides, who wants to ride on a freeway frontage road after spinning though Palomares Road's lovely forested scenery?

Palomares Road

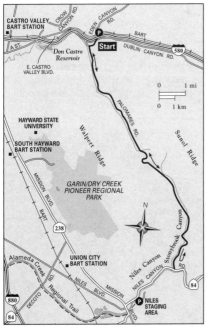

Palomares Road ascends from both ends; the high point is almost exactly in the middle. That means you get an invigorating climb and a fun descent in both directions. In between, you have many rolling curves and a chance to ride as fast as 40 mph on the downhills, if you so choose.

If you're more into savoring your rides than speeding through them, note that two wineries are now open on Palomares Road: Chouinard Winery (open weekends only; 510/582-9900) and Westover Vineyards (open daily; 510/885-1501).

Driving Directions

From Hayward, drive four miles east on I-580 and take the Eden Canyon Road/Palomares Road exit. Turn left, cross under the freeway, and park on the north side of the freeway in the dirt pullout (start of Eden Canyon Road).

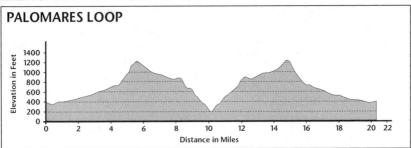

PALOMARES LOOP

Route Directions for Palomares Road

0.0 Park in the dirt pullout at the start of Eden Canyon Road, by the I-580 freeway overpass. Ride under the overpass and cross Dublin Canyon Road to access Palo Verde Road. *Supplies are available in Hayward or Dublin.*

0.4 LEFT on Palomares Road.

5.4 Summit of Palomares Road.

6.3 Chouinard Winery.

6.6 Westover Vineyards.

10.1 End of Palomares Road at Highway 84. TURN AROUND.

20.2 Arrive at starting point.

29. MORGAN TERRITORY ROAD

Livermore to Clayton

One of the finest roads in the East Bay crosses through the Black Hills north of Livermore and passes by the eastern flank of mighty Mount Diablo and neighboring North Peak. Morgan Territory Road, as it is known, leaves the shopping centers and I-580 freeway traffic far behind as it carves a narrow path through hillside grasslands and scenic oak woodlands. If the hustle and bustle of the East Bay has started to wear you down, you need a ride on Morgan Territory Road.

Morgan Territory Road is only one lane wide.

ROUTE DETAILS

type of trail paved roads with minimal car traffic

difficulty ▮▮▮▮▯

total distance 46.2 miles

riding time 3–4 hours

elevation gain 3,500 feet

As an out-and-back ride, this route from Livermore to Clayton has a good hill climb in both directions, so a stop in Clayton for lunch is recommended, and also perhaps a rest stop near the road's summit at elevation 2,100 feet, near Morgan Territory Regional Preserve. Your main concern is the weather—this kind of climbing in these sunny, exposed hills should be reserved for the cooler days of fall, winter, and spring.

Another concern is the narrowness of Morgan Territory Road; one car and one bike makes a crowd. Fortunately, cars are few and far between.

Although it seems sensible to make a loop out of this ride by returning from Clayton to Livermore on Marsh Creek Road and Vasco Road, a

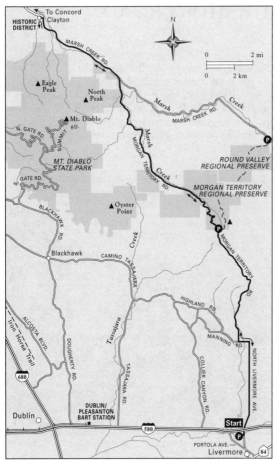

five-mile stretch of Vasco Road has been widened in recent years, making it as fast and hectic as a freeway. Intrepid riders may still want to make this loop, but be forewarned of the long hill climb on Vasco Road with cars peeling by you at 70 mph. Although the road's shoulder is wide, riding it is just plain stressful. An out-and-back on Morgan Territory Road is safer, more scenic, and far more relaxing.

For more information on the parks in this area, contact East Bay Regional Park District, 510/635-0135 or 510/562-7275; website: www.ebparks.org.

Driving Directions

From Livermore on I-580, take the North Livermore Avenue exit and park at the shopping center just south of I-580 on North Livermore Avenue.

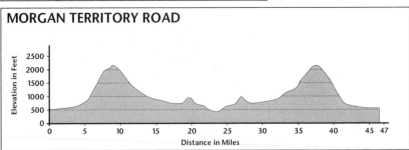

MORGAN TERRITORY ROAD

Route Directions for Morgan Territory Road

0.0 Park at the shopping center just south of I-580 on North Livermore Avenue and ride north, crossing under the freeway. Set your odometer on the north side of I-580. *Supplies are available in Livermore.*

3.5 LEFT on Manning Road.

4.0 RIGHT on Morgan Territory Road.

4.7 Road narrows to single lane.

9.5 Entrance to Morgan Territory Regional Preserve on right.

15.0 Road widens to two lanes.

18.7 LEFT on Marsh Creek Road.

22.7 LEFT on Marsh Creek Road (also called Clayton Road in Clayton).

23.2 Arrive in Clayton historic district. TURN AROUND. *Supplies are available in Clayton.*

46.2 Arrive at starting point.

30. ALAMEDA CREEK TRAIL

Pleasanton to Coyote Hills Regional Park

Alameda Creek, the largest stream in Alameda County, was once a valuable resource to the Ohlone Indians who settled along its banks. Today, Alameda Creek Trail follows the creek from the mouth of Niles Canyon in Fremont 12 miles westward to San Francisco Bay.

ROUTE DETAILS

type of trail	paved bike path
difficulty	🍼🍼🍼🍼
total distance	24 miles (or longer options)
riding time	2 hours
elevation gain	200 feet

The trail is actually two parallel trails on the south and north bank of the creek. The south side trail (paved) is for bikers, hikers, and runners, and the north side (unpaved) is for equestrians, too. The south side trail, described here, accesses Coyote Hills Regional Park, where more riding is available.

Everything is in place here to make your ride easy. Unlike some trails in the East Bay's impressive system of paved recreation paths, the Alameda Creek Trail is unique in that it is uninterrupted by street intersections, so you have 12 miles of worry-free riding in both directions. Mileage markers are installed along the trail, and water and restrooms are available at several points. Even when the afternoon westerly wind comes up from the bay, it will be at your back for the slightly uphill ride home.

Alameda Creek Trail passes under highway overpasses and alongside neighborhood backyards, so it isn't exactly a nature trail, although you will probably spot birds along the narrow-channeled creek. If you're clamoring for something more, well, natural, add on a ride in Coyote Hills Regional Park, a bayside park with an abundance of wildlife and fascinating Native American history. Skinny-tire riders are restricted to adding 3.5 paved miles

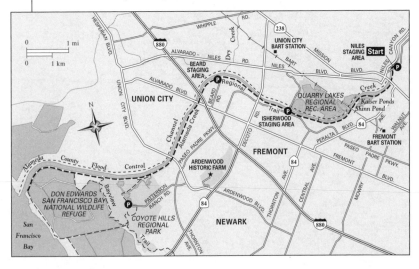

on the park's Bay View Trail, but mountain bikers can pedal around on the numerous dirt trails that roll up and down Coyote's rounded hills. Those who enjoy steep ups and fast downs should not miss Red Hill Trail, but the park has many other trail options for mountain bikers.

For more information, contact East Bay Regional Park District, 510/635-0135 or 510/562-7275; website: www.ebparks.org.

Driving Directions

From I-680 in Fremont, take the Mission Boulevard exit and drive west to Highway 84/Niles Canyon Road. Turn right, then right again on Old Canyon Road. The staging area is on the left.

ALAMEDA CREEK TRAIL

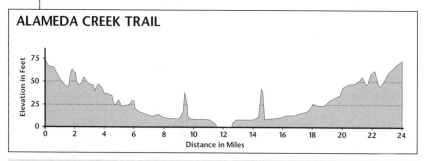

Route Directions for Alameda Creek Trail

0.0   Park at Niles staging area and follow the trail out of the parking lot. *Water and restrooms are available at the staging area and along the trail.*

1.4   Pass Kaiser and Shinn Ponds.

2.6   Bridge at end of Thornton Avenue.

3.5   Isherwood Staging Area.

4.3   Decoto Road.

5.4   End of Beard Road; Beard Staging Area.

6.1   I-880.

6.4   Alvarado Boulevard.

7.8   Newark Boulevard.

9.7   Sign at base of hill leading to Coyote Hills Regional Park.

12.0   Edge of San Francisco Bay. TURN AROUND. *Or, take the 50-foot connector trail from Alameda Creek Trail to the paved Bayview Trail in Coyote Hills Regional Park, adding on a 3.5-mile paved loop. Mountain bikers can add on several miles of dirt riding in the park.*

24.0   Arrive at starting point.

31. MONTARA MOUNTAIN

McNee Ranch State Park north of Half Moon Bay

You like a long, sustained hill climb and a lightning-fast descent? You get them both on this ride from the Pacific Ocean to the top of Montara Mountain, elevation 1,898 feet. Make sure your body has plenty of fuel and water for the 4.8-mile climb up, and wear your sturdiest helmet for the ride down.

ROUTE DETAILS

type of trail dirt road and deteriorating pavement

difficulty

total distance 9.6 miles

riding time 2 hours

elevation gain 2,000 feet

Aside from the heart- and leg-pumping work, there isn't much to think about on this ride, which has almost no intersections. Instead, you can focus on the views, which are downright spectacular on clear days. You ride with the ocean mostly at your back for the first 1.5 miles, heading deep into Montara Mountain's coastal canyon. Gradually the trail rises above the valleys and starts to show off glimpses of the blue Pacific. At the 2.2-mile mark, where two posts mark a side trail off-limits to bikes, the panorama opens wide, exposing the crashing surf and tall cliffs of Montara State Beach (650/726-8819) and Gray Whale Cove. From this point onward, every time you pause to catch your breath those sublime ocean vistas are waiting for you.

When at last you attain Montara Mountain's transmitter tower–littered summit, your view expands to include the north and east: Mount Tamalpais, the skyline of San Francisco, the famous sign on U.S. 101 proclaiming "South San Francisco the Industrial City," San Mateo Bridge, San Francisco Bay, plus Mount Diablo in the background. This is one of the most all-encompassing views possible in the Bay Area.

The trail's grade is fairly moderate all the way up except for one .5-mile stretch at 2.6 miles, which is *really* steep (it gains 500 feet in .5 mile). The

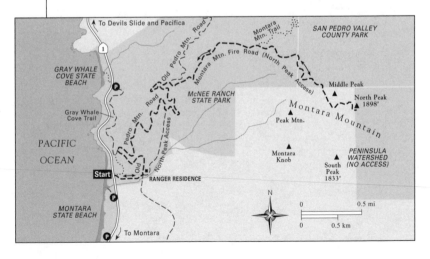

path's first 2.4 miles are a mix of deteriorating pavement, gravel, and dirt (often squeezed into single-track by encroaching pampas grass). You're riding on old San Pedro Mountain Road, which used to be the route from Montara to Pacifica before Highway 1 was built. The last 2.4 miles follow Montara Mountain Fire Road, a wide dirt road. Because of its rough surface, descending can be like riding on ball bearings; it's difficult to control your speed. Move your butt way back off your seat or you'll go down for sure. Guess how I know?

Driving Directions

From Half Moon Bay, drive north on Highway 1 for 10 miles to just north of Montara State Beach and the Chart House Restaurant and just south of Devil's Slide. The trailhead is marked by a yellow metal gate on the east side of the highway, with parking for about six cars. If this lot is full, park .2 mile farther south at Montara State Beach.

MONTARA MOUNTAIN

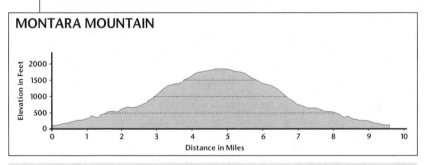

Route Directions for Montara Mountain

0.0   Park at McNee Ranch trailhead by the yellow metal gate. Begin riding on the wide road behind the gate (not the single-track trail). *Supplies are available in Montara, one mile south.*

0.2   LEFT at fork by ranger's house.

1.7   Dirt road merges in from the right.

2.2   Coastal viewpoint where hiker's trail leads west (signed as No Bikes).

2.4   RIGHT on dirt Montara Mountain Fire Road (deteriorating pavement veers to the left); prepare for brutal .5-mile climb.

3.5   Pass Montara Mountain Trail on left (hikers-only trail from San Pedro Valley County Park).

4.4   South Peak of Montara Mountain on left; continue straight.

4.8   Arrive at North Peak of Montara Mountain. TURN AROUND. *Climb up the rocky, short trail (about 20 feet) next to the communication towers for the best view of the day.*

9.6   Arrive at starting point.

32. SAWYER CAMP RECREATION TRAIL

Off I-280 near Hillsborough and Millbrae

Few bike trails are as well-loved and well-used as the Sawyer Camp Trail. This paved, car-free recreation trail is long enough so you can feel like you got some exercise riding it, easy enough so that even the most casual rider can try it, and surprisingly scenic as well. Its only drawback is its popularity: With so many people living nearby on the northern Peninsula, the trail is almost always packed with walkers, runners, in-line skaters, and baby strollers, in addition to bikers. No matter; just get here early to avoid the crowds, especially on weekends.

Cyclists share Sawyer Camp Trail's six mile length with joggers and other users.

© ANN MARIE BROWN

ROUTE DETAILS

type of trail — paved bike path

difficulty — ▮▯▯▯▯

total distance 12 miles

riding time 1 hour

elevation gain 250 feet

The trail travels the length of Lower Crystal Springs Reservoir, then leads through marshlands to southern San Andreas Lake, ending just beyond the lake's dam at Hillcrest Boulevard in Millbrae. Unlike many paved recreation trails, it isn't as straight as a stick; it twists and curves gracefully around the reservoir's shoreline. You have a good chance of seeing deer, raptors, herons, and egrets somewhere along the route.

The ride is an easy cruise; you probably won't even shift gears for the first 4.5 miles. The only noticeable hill is in the last stretch near San Andreas Lake's dam. Be sure to make a stop to see the Jepson laurel tree, 3.5 miles in and 25 feet off the trail (near a picnic area). More than 600 years

old and 55 feet tall, the tree is the old-est and largest living California laurel, named for botanist Willis Jepson.

Another of the trail's highlights is a plaque on a boulder at trail's end at Hillcrest Boulevard, which marks the spot where Captain Gaspar de Portolá made camp after his discovery of San Francisco Bay in 1769.

Riders looking for more mileage can connect this trail with a ride on Caña-da Road, two miles south of the Sawyer Camp Trailhead, which is good for rid-ing any time but especially good every Sunday, when four miles of its length are closed to cars. For more informa-tion on Cañada Road Bicycle Sunday, phone San Mateo County Parks and Recreation, 650/363-4020.

Driving Directions

From I-280 in San Mateo, take the Highway 92 exit west, then turn right (north) immediately on Highway 35. Drive .5 mile to Crystal Springs Road and the trail entrance.

SAWYER CAMP RECREATION TRAIL

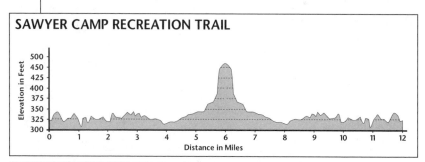

Route Directions for Sawyer Camp Recreation Trail

0.0 Park in the small parking lot by the trailhead, or alongside the road. Ride through the signed gate to enter the trail. *Water is available along the trail.*

3.5 Restrooms, drinking water, and picnic area by short path to Jepson laurel tree.

4.8 Beginning of hill climb.

5.1 Cross dam over San Andreas Lake.

6.0 Arrive at gate at Hillcrest Boulevard. TURN AROUND. *Note historic mark-er for Gaspar de Portolá's camp just past the gate.*

12.0 Arrive at starting point.

33. HALF MOON BAY BACK ROADS

South of Half Moon Bay

Many Bay Area residents complain that the coastal resort town of Half Moon Bay has left its "country" roots behind and become too much of a city. This loop ride on Half Moon Bay's back roads (with a mere 6.8-mile stretch on busy Highway 1) proves that there's still plenty of country left in this coastal town, you just have to know where to find it.

The ride begins at the Half Moon Bay firehouse at the junction of Main Street and Higgins Purisima Road. The toughest part is the first 100 yards, in which you must use impeccable judgment when crossing the stream of cars on Highway 1. With this accomplished, you face a quick, level jaunt south on the highway, followed by another careful crossing and a left turn on Tunitas Creek Road. Now you're in the country, and you'll face nothing but quiet roads and pastoral scenery for the rest of your ride.

The only serious hill appears at mile 19.8, when Purisima Creek Road becomes Higgins Purisima Road at a hairpin turn in the road. Here you'll

ROUTE DETAILS

type of trail paved roads with minimal car traffic

difficulty 🍶🍶🍶🍶🍶

total distance 24.1 miles

riding time 2 hours

elevation gain 1,500 feet

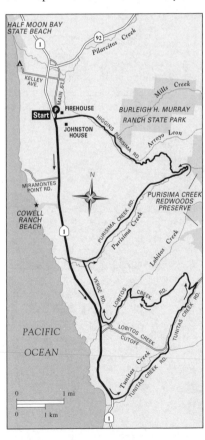

gain 400 feet in about two miles, then lose it again on your way back in to town. Otherwise, there's some climbing on Lobitos Creek Road, but it's nothing to complain about. The views of the remote coastal canyons will more than compensate.

Driving Directions

From Half Moon Bay at the junction of Highway 92 and Highway 1, head south on Highway 1 for 1.2 miles to Higgins Purisima Road (by the firehouse). Turn left and park along Main Street near the firehouse.

HALF MOON BAY BACK ROADS

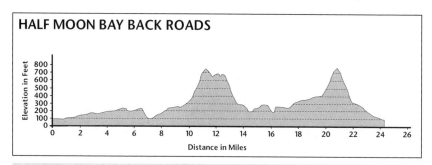

Route Directions for Half Moon Bay Back Roads

0.0 Park on the south end of Main Street in Half Moon Bay, near its junction with Higgins Purisima Road and Highway 1. Ride out the last few yards of Higgins Purisima Road and cross Highway 1 to head south. *Supplies are available on Main Street or Highway 1 in Half Moon Bay.*

1.9 Pass Cowell Ranch Beach turnoff.

6.8 LEFT on Tunitas Creek Road.

8.8 RIGHT at junction with Lobitos Creek Cutoff.

9.8 Enter redwoods.

10.4 LEFT on Lobitos Creek Road (a very sharp left turn).

14.6 RIGHT on Verde Road (parallels Highway 1 with nice views of the ocean).

16.2 RIGHT on Purisima Creek Road.

19.8 Pass entrance to Purisima Creek Redwoods Open Space Preserve at hairpin turn; road changes names to Higgins Purisima Road.

24.1 Arrive at starting point.

34. PURISIMA REDWOODS LOOP

Off Skyline Boulevard in Woodside

It might seem more sensible to start this loop ride from its lowest point, at the Purisima trailhead south of Half Moon Bay, so that you could climb uphill when you're fresh and save the downhill for the way home. But there's room for only a few cars at the Half Moon Bay trailhead, and these spaces are almost always filled. Unless you live in or near Half Moon Bay, it's not worth the drive to the trailhead only to discover there is no place to park.

ROUTE DETAILS

type of trail dirt road and single-track; paved road with moderate car traffic

difficulty ▮▮▮▯▯

total distance 10 miles

riding time 2–3 hours

elevation gain 1,600 feet

Instead, start this ride at the top of the loop, at the large Purisima parking lot on Skyline Boulevard near Woodside. Folks who live in San Francisco and the northern Peninsula will find that this trailhead is close enough that they can show up after work on the long days of summer and still have enough daylight to complete the ride.

"Summer" is a key word here, because the Whittemore Gulch section of this trail is closed to bikes during the rainy season. It's a beautiful single-track trail tunneling through a flower-filled Douglas fir forest, with lots of fun twists and tight turns. (You access it .8 mile from the trailhead, after a rather bumpy ride on North Ridge Trail, a dirt road.)

The upper section of Whittemore Gulch Trail provides long-distance views of the Half Moon Bay coast—or Half Moon Bay fog, depending on the weather. The trail keeps descending until at about two miles from the start, you've entered a deep, dark redwood canyon. The area was logged in the late 1800s, so these are second- and third-growth trees, but impressive nonetheless. The return leg of the loop is uphill on Purisima Creek Trail, a gradual but steady climb alongside a pretty stream and some very large redwoods, followed by a quick, two-mile stint on paved Skyline Boulevard.

If you must ride in the wet season, you can follow an alternate route in Purisima from the same trailhead: downhill on Harkins Ridge Trail and uphill on Purisima Creek Trail. The Midpeninsula Open Space District (650/691-1200; website: www.openspace.org) keeps these wide trails open no matter what the weather. There's no comparison, though; Whittemore Gulch is the trail to ride in this park.

Driving Directions

From San Francisco, drive south on I-280 for 19 miles to the Highway 92 west exit. Go west on Highway 92 for 2.7 miles, then turn left (south) on Highway 35 (Skyline Boulevard). Drive 4.3 miles to the Purisima Creek Redwoods Open Space Preserve parking area on the right, just past a small store.

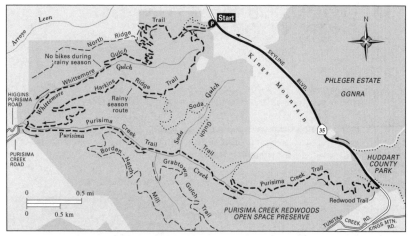

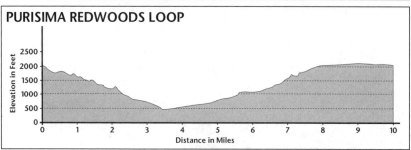

Route Directions for Purisima Redwoods Loop

0.0   Park at Purisima parking lot on Skyline Boulevard. Follow North Ridge Trail (dirt road) from the parking lot (not the hikers-only trail). *Supplies are available next door at the small store/deli.*

0.3   Straight at junction with Harkins Ridge Trail.

0.8   LEFT on Whittemore Gulch Trail.

1.4   LEFT to stay on Whittemore Gulch Trail.

2.8   Cross footbridge; trail widens and levels out.

3.7   STRAIGHT at junction with Harkins Ridge Trail. Cross wide bridge ahead.

3.8   LEFT on Purisima Creek Trail on far side of bridge.

4.8   STRAIGHT at junction with Borden Hatch Mill Trail.

5.1   STRAIGHT at junction with Grabtown Gulch Trail.

6.1   RIGHT at junction with Soda Gulch/Bay Area Ridge Trail.

7.8   RIGHT on Redwood Trail.

8.0   LEFT on Skyline Boulevard.

10.0   Arrive at starting point.

35. WOODSIDE TO SKYLINE SHORT LOOP

Woodside to Skylonda

The Woodside to Skyline Short Loop is as close to a perfect 20-mile training ride as you can get. It has a killer 3.4-mile hill (Old La Honda Road from Woodside to Skyline Boulevard) and just enough mileage to keep your heart rate up for an hour or two. Yet it's remarkably scenic, supplies plenty of convenient places to stop for fuel or rest, and offers a mix of wide bike lanes and less-traveled country roads. You'll have to put up with some traffic on Skyline Boulevard, but the payoff is worth it. (If you want more mileage and more hills in the Woodside area, see Ride 36 in this chapter.)

The historic Woodside Store (now a museum) is filled with local history.

ROUTE DETAILS

type of trail   paved roads with moderate car traffic

difficulty   🚴🚴🚴🚴🚴

total distance   20 miles

riding time   1.5–2 hours

elevation gain   2,200 feet

First, know that the tony community of Woodside is Bike Central. There isn't a more bike-friendly town anywhere in the Bay Area, a region filled with bike-friendly towns. And there isn't a more likely place to spot the most expensive bikes, the hottest gear, and the tautest leg muscles. It seems that people who can afford to live in Woodside have plenty of time for recreation and fitness. You can't hold it against them.

Whiskey Hill and Sand Hill Roads both have wide bike lanes that will get you through the busy Woodside corridor. Then you begin your epic climb on extremely narrow Old La Honda Road, a former logging toll road that today twists and turns through second- and third-growth redwoods. On any weekend day you'll find members of local

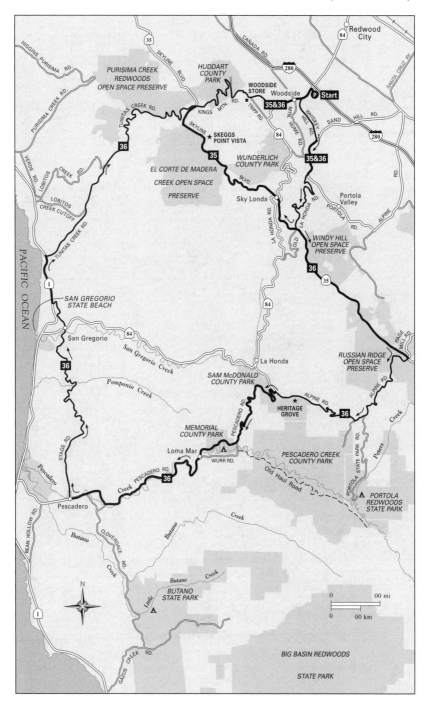

cycling clubs racing each other up this one-lane hill. Fortunately, few car drivers use Old La Honda Road except for those who live on it. It's so steep and narrow that at its high terminus on Skyline Boulevard it is signed "Downhill Bicycling Not Recommended."

The climb continues, more gradually now and with one 400-foot dip, as you cruise north on Skyline Boulevard. You can stop in Skylonda for a cool drink, or just continue onward to your big descent on Kings Mountain Road. Then it's back to Woodside, passing Huddart Park and the historic Woodside Store along the way. Stop in if it's open; the old store is now a museum with fascinating artifacts from the area's pioneer past.

Driving Directions
From I-280, take the Highway 84/Woodside exit and drive west for less than .25 mile to the Park and Ride lot.

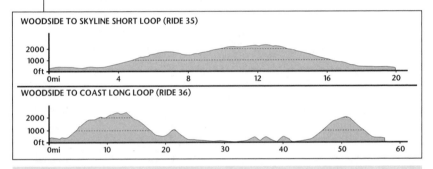

Route Directions for Woodside to Skyline Short Loop

0.0   Park at the Woodside Park and Ride lot. Ride west on Woodside Road (Highway 84). *Supplies are available in Woodside.*

0.5   LEFT on Whiskey Hill Road.

1.8   RIGHT on Sand Hill Road at Y-junction.

3.2   RIGHT on Old La Honda Road.

6.6   RIGHT on Skyline Boulevard.

8.1   Skylonda market and Alice's Restaurant at junction of Skyline and Highway 84. *Supplies are available.*

11.9   Skeggs Vista Point on right.

13.6   RIGHT on Kings Mountain Road.

16.5   Entrance to Huddart Park on left. *Water is available.*

17.7   LEFT at stop sign at Entrance Way.

17.9   Historic Woodside store at Tripp Road junction. *Stop in to the museum to see the local history exhibits.*

18.6   LEFT on Woodside Road (Highway 84).

19.4   Downtown Woodside. *Supplies are available.*

19.5   STRAIGHT at junction with Whiskey Hill Road (start of loop).

20.0   Arrive at starting point.

36. WOODSIDE TO COAST LONG LOOP

Woodside to Pescadero

A lot of hill climbing and a lot of scenery make up this all-day ride from Woodside to the coast. With 4,900 feet of elevation gain, it's not for the faint of heart. But for an epic cycling adventure in the San Francisco Bay Area, this loop can't be beat.

ROUTE DETAILS

type of trail  paved roads with moderate car traffic

difficulty 𝄞𝄞𝄞𝄞𝄞

total distance 57.1 miles

riding time 5-7 hours

elevation gain 4,900 feet

The ride's first 6.6 miles mimic those of the Woodside Short Loop, Ride 35 in this chapter. But where riders on the short loop head north on Skyline Boulevard, you'll head south, passing by Windy Hill and Russian Ridge Open Space Preserves while gaining another 500 feet, then turn west on Alpine Road. I hope your brakes are in good working order, because you're going to descend 2,000 feet in the next seven miles. Most of it is in open grasslands, but you also pass through a stretch of old-growth redwoods, called the Heritage Grove, in Alpine Road's last two miles. Lock up your bike and take a short walk through these magnificent trees.

With a left turn on Pescadero Road, you'll climb again over a steep grade for almost two miles, which seems like a terrible injustice. But then you drop again, this time all the way to sea level in the town of Pescadero. After a food and rest break in this small village, Old Stage Road and Highway 1 take you over comparatively easy terrain (two 300-foot climbs) to Tunitas Creek Road, where you begin your last major climb of the day. This nine-miler is one of the favorite training rides of cyclists on the coast. Why? Three reasons: The majority of it is in shady redwoods, the climb holds an average six percent grade (total 2,000-foot gain), and cars are a rarity. On nice weekends, the road is lined with dozens of cyclists.

Did I mention that the last six miles from Skyline Boulevard are all downhill back to your car? And a well-deserved downhill at that.

Driving Directions
From I-280, take the Highway 84/Woodside exit and drive west for less than .25 mile to the Park and Ride lot.

For trail map and elevation profile see pages 111–112 (Ride 35—Woodside to Skyline Short Loop).

A cycling club gathers on Skyline Boulevard after the climb from Woodside.

Route Directions for Woodside to Coast Long Loop

0.0   Park at the Woodside Park and Ride lot. Ride west on Woodside Road (Highway 84). *Supplies are available in Woodside.*

0.5   LEFT on Whiskey Hill Road.

1.8   RIGHT on Sand Hill Road at Y-junction.

3.2   RIGHT on Old La Honda Road.

6.6   LEFT on Skyline Boulevard. *Supplies are available 1.5 miles north (right) in La Honda.*

12.2   RIGHT on Alpine Road.

15.6   RIGHT to stay on Alpine Road.

15.9   RIGHT to stay on Alpine Road.

18.4   Small parking area and hiking trail at Heritage Grove.

19.7   LEFT on Pescadero Road.

20.2   Entrance to Sam McDonald County Park. *Water is available.*

24.1   Entrance to Memorial County Park. *Water is available.*

25.4   Loma Mar Store. *Supplies are available.*

31.5   RIGHT on Stage Road in Pescadero. *Supplies are available in Pescadero.*

38.7   Cross Highway 84 and stay on Stage Road. *Supplies are available at San Gregorio Store.*

39.8   RIGHT on Highway 1.

41.4   RIGHT on Tunitas Creek Road.

43.4   RIGHT at junction with Lobitos Creek Cutoff.

45.0   RIGHT at junction with Lobitos Creek Road.

50.5   Cross Skyline Boulevard and continue on Kings Mountain Road.

53.6   Entrance to Huddart Park on left. *Water is available.*

54.8   LEFT at stop sign at Entrance Way.

55.7   LEFT on Woodside Road (Highway 84).

56.5   Downtown Woodside. *Supplies are available.*

56.6   STRAIGHT at junction with Whiskey Hill Road.

57.1   Arrive at starting point.

37. STANFORD & PORTOLA VALLEY LOOP

Palo Alto to Portola Valley

This road ride is more urban than many others in this book, yet it covers some of the most bicycled territory in the Peninsula, the site of millions of "after work" or "in between classes" rides. The Loop, as it's known, is the kind of route where you'll find cyclists at any hour of any day, working off a little stress from their high-tech jobs or harried Stanford studies. If you choose to ride your mountain bike here, you can take off from the paved roads on to dirt trails in Arastradero Preserve and/or Windy Hill Open Space Preserve.

ROUTE DETAILS

type of trail paved roads with moderate car traffic

difficulty

total distance 18 miles

riding time 1.5 hours

elevation gain 750 feet

Cyclists start this ride from all over the Stanford and Palo Alto area; for convenience I've written it to begin at the Stanford Shopping Center. If you feel daunted by the first stint on busy Sand Hill Road's bike lane, fear not; you'll also ride a much quieter stretch on Portola Road and Alpine Road.

In addition, I've added to the traditional Loop a peaceful, two-mile, country-lane stretch on Arastradero Road, passing the grassy hills of Arastradero Preserve. This out-and-back begins at the historic Alpine Inn, formerly Rossotti's or "Zot's," reputed to be the oldest roadhouse in continuous operation in California. In the late 1800s, officials at Stanford tried to have the drinking and gambling establishment shut down, fearing its bad influence on students. They didn't succeed, and of course, the Alpine Inn has been a popular Stanford beer-and-burger hangout ever since.

When you ride through the pleasant, small town of Portola Valley, you might want to stop to see the little red Portola schoolhouse next to the town hall

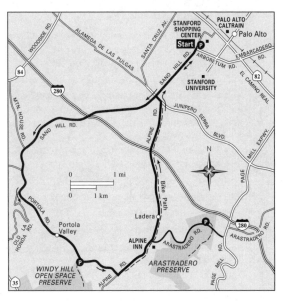

and library. Built in 1909, it now serves as an art gallery. The dirt trails of Windy Hill Open Space Preserve are also accessible from the roadside parking lot in Portola Valley (mile 7.6).

On the return leg on Alpine Road, you can opt to pick up the recreation trail that runs alongside the road, starting just past Los Trancos Road. The paved surface is a bit rough, however, so many cyclists stick to the wide shoulder of Alpine Road.

Driving Directions

From I-280 in Woodside, take the Sand Hill Road exit and drive east 2.8 miles to Arboretum Road and the Stanford Shopping Center.

STANFORD & PORTOLA VALLEY LOOP

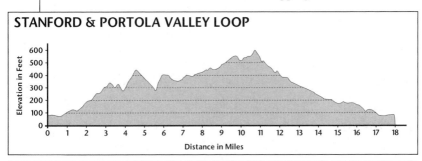

Route Directions for Stanford & Portola Valley Loop

0.0 Park at the Stanford Shopping Center near the junction of Arboretum Road and Sand Hill Road (near Nordstrom's). Ride west on the Sand Hill Road bike lane. *Supplies are available in Stanford Shopping Center.*

2.8 Cross under I-280.

5.1 Sand Hill Road becomes Portola Road (stay straight).

7.6 Parking area on right for Windy Hill Open Space Preserve in Portola Valley. *Mountain bikers can ride trails here.*

8.4 LEFT on Alpine Road. *Café and stores available at this junction.*

9.5 RIGHT on Arastradero Road; the Alpine Inn is immediately on the right. *Food and drinks are available at Alpine Inn.*

10.9 Arastradero Preserve on left (main entrance). *Mountain bikers can ride trails here.*

11.5 Arastradero Road ends at Page Mill Road. TURN AROUND.

13.5 RIGHT on Alpine Road (back at Alpine Inn).

15.3 Cross under I-280.

16.5 STRAIGHT at stoplight on to Santa Cruz Avenue.

16.6 RIGHT on Sand Hill Road.

18.0 Arrive at starting point.

38. PESCADERO & SAN GREGORIO LOOP

*San Mateo County coast
south of Half Moon Bay*

There's one rule about riding coastal Highway 1 south of Half Moon Bay: Ride south, not north, to avoid an often ferocious headwind. This loop around the town of Pescadero allows you to experience the best of Highway 1—heading in the direction of the prevailing winds, while riding on the ocean side of the highway in the safety of a mercifully wide shoulder. The return leg of the loop traces an inland route on mellow country lanes.

ROUTE DETAILS

type of trail   paved roads with moderate car traffic

difficulty   ▮▮▮▯▯

total distance   28.7 miles

riding time   2 hours

elevation gain   1,200 feet

Early morning or weekday rides are recommended to avoid potentially heavy beach traffic. This loop makes a great Sunday morning ride with an early start, with time allotted for coffee or breakfast stops in the charming towns of Pescadero and San Gregorio.

Although the mileage isn't high, three long, slow hills in the first six miles of Highway 1 will give you a workout. (Two more hills await on Stage Road, plus one on Cloverdale Road.)

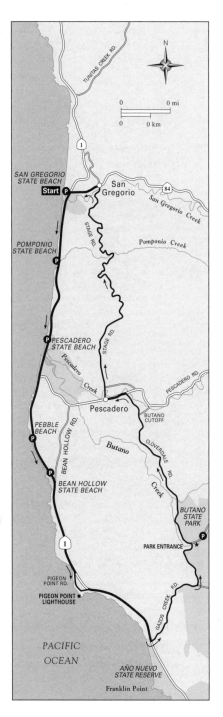

The coastal scenery on the first half of the loop is as good as it gets, with nearly nonstop views of the surging sea pounding against a rocky shoreline. A highlight is a visit to Pigeon Point Lighthouse, built in 1871 and now operated as a youth hostel. Lighthouse tours are usually available on weekends for a small fee, but you can always enjoy the views from the lighthouse grounds, and the windswept coast at neighboring Whaler's Cove.

Heading south from the lighthouse, you'll turn inland at Gazos Creek Road and enjoy a rolling ride through rural coastal hills. Pedaling north toward Pescadero, you'll pass by the entrance road to Butano State Park, a pretty redwood park with a campground and hiking trails. If you have energy to burn, it's worth a ride in for a look.

Pigeon Point Lighthouse, built in 1871, is one of the highlights of the Pescadero & San Gregorio Loop.

In the small town of Pescadero, historic Duarte's Restaurant is a favorite breakfast and lunch stop for cyclists, and two markets sell fresh-baked breads and other goodies. The ride concludes with a 7.2-mile stint on Stage Road, which before Highway 1 was built, was the only route from Pescadero to San Gregorio.

Driving Directions

From Highway 1 in Half Moon Bay, drive south for 13 miles to San Gregorio State Beach, just south of the junction with Highway 84. Park in the state beach parking lot.

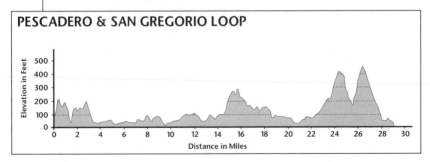

PESCADERO & SAN GREGORIO LOOP

Route Directions for Pescadero & San Gregorio Loop

0.0 Park at San Gregorio State Beach and turn right out of the lot, heading south on Highway 1. *Supplies are available in Half Moon Bay, 13 miles north on Highway 1, or in San Gregorio, .75 mile east on Highway 84.*

1.6 Pomponio State Beach.

3.5 Pescadero State Beach and Pescadero Marsh.

4.5 STRAIGHT at junction with Pescadero Road.

6.1 Pebble Beach.

7.0 Bean Hollow State Beach.

9.4 RIGHT on Pigeon Point Road; seaside riding on a quiet access road.

10.1 Pigeon Point Lighthouse. *Lighthouse tours are sometimes available on weekends.*

10.3 RIGHT on Highway 1.

12.5 LEFT on Gazos Creek Road. *Supplies are available at store 50 yards south on Highway 1.*

14.6 LEFT on Cloverdale Road.

15.8 Butano State Park turnoff on the right.

20.1 LEFT on Pescadero Road.

20.6 RIGHT on Stage Road. *Supplies are available in Pescadero (two blocks of shops).*

27.8 LEFT on La Honda Road. *Supplies are available at San Gregorio Store, straight ahead at intersection.*

28.5 LEFT on Highway 1.

28.7 Arrive at starting point.

39. OLD HAUL ROAD

Pescadero Creek County Park, Loma Mar

The Old Haul Road is an old logging route that runs for five miles between Pescadero Creek County Park and Portola Redwoods State Park. It tunnels through a thick forest of second-growth redwoods, providing a smooth dirt route that is ideal for beginning mountain bike riders. Built on a railroad

Mountain bikers can ride an easy out-and-back on Old Haul Road or a more strenuous loop.

© ANN MARIE BROWN

ROUTE DETAILS FOR RIDE 39A
(out-and-back)

type of trail	dirt road
difficulty	
total distance	10 miles
riding time	1 hour
elevation gain	500 feet

ROUTE DETAILS FOR RIDE 39B
(Old Haul Road and Alpine Road loop)

type of trail	dirt road and paved roads with minimal car traffic
difficulty	
total distance	17.6 miles
riding time	3 hours
elevation gain	2,100 feet

bed, it gains only 500 feet in elevation and has an easy grade in both directions. This makes the Old Haul Road a perfect choice for a carefree 10 miles of out-and-back riding.

On the Pescadero Creek County Park side, the trail starts by a small picnic area near the rushing creek gorge, then heads east. You'll see plenty of big stumps along the route—reminders of this forest's earlier state—and many tiny streams that run down the hillsides to empty into Pescadero Creek. The hard-packed dirt-and-gravel road is well signed and easy to follow the whole way. Your only concern is to watch out for equestrians and hikers, who also use this trail.

Those who want a more strenuous ride with greater variety can use the Old Haul Road to connect to paved Portola State Park Road and Alpine Road, home of the awe-inspiring Heritage Grove of old-growth redwoods. This loop features a long, slow climb of 900 feet over four miles on Portola State Park Road. It's followed by a long, fast descent on Alpine Road to the Heritage Grove.

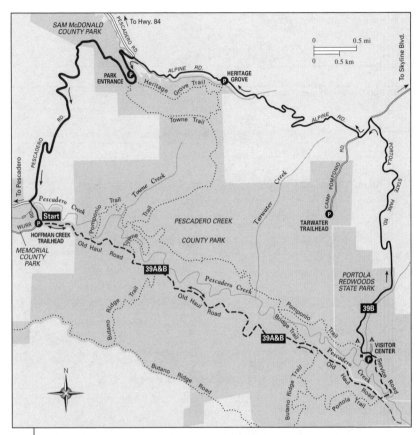

After enjoying the mighty trees, you face a second climb, this time with a steeper grade, as Pescadero Road ascends mercilessly for just under two miles. (Prepare to use your granny gear.) The last two miles are an easy downhill cruise back to your car. Although the roads on this loop are quite narrow, they get little traffic, so you won't have to worry much about cars.

For more information, contact San Mateo County Parks and Recreation, 650/363-4020, or Portola Redwoods State Park, 650/948-9098.

Driving Directions

From Highway 1 15 miles south of Half Moon Bay, drive east on Pescadero Road for 9.8 miles. Turn right at the second entrance to Wurr Road, .25 mile past the entrance to Memorial Park. Drive .25 mile to the Hoffman Creek Trailhead, where Old Haul Road begins. (Or, from I-280 at Woodside, take Highway 84 west for 13 miles to La Honda. Turn left on Pescadero Road and drive one mile, then bear right to stay on Pescadero Road. Continue 4.2 miles to Wurr Road on the left. Turn left and drive .25 mile to the trailhead.)

Old Haul Road

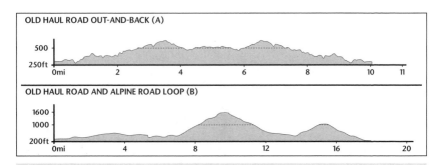

OLD HAUL ROAD OUT-AND-BACK (A)

OLD HAUL ROAD AND ALPINE ROAD LOOP (B)

Route Directions for 39A *(out-and-back)* for Old Haul Road

0.0   Park at the Wurr Road entrance to Pescadero Creek County Park. Begin riding at the entrance gate. *Supplies are available at the Loma Mar Store, 1.5 miles west on Pescadero Road.*

0.5   STRAIGHT at junction with Pomponio Trail.

1.1   STRAIGHT at junction with Towne Trail.

3.2   Reach high point in the trail and start to descend.

3.9   STRAIGHT at junction with Bridge Trail on left and Butano Ridge Trail on right.

5.0   Service road to Portola State Park on left and Portola Trail on right. TURN AROUND. *Water is available in the park.*

10.0   Arrive at starting point.

Route Directions for 39B *(Old Haul Road and Alpine Road loop)*

Follow directions for Ride 39A to mile 5.0, then continue:

5.0   LEFT at service road to Portola State Park; descend and continue past the gate on to paved road.

6.0   Portola State Park visitor center and restrooms on the left. *Water is available.*

6.4   Exit out of Portola State Park and follow Portola State Park Road.

9.3   LEFT on Alpine Road.

9.6   RIGHT to stay on Alpine Road.

12.1   Heritage Grove. *Take a short walk through these magnificent trees.*

13.3   LEFT on Pescadero Road.

13.8   Entrance to Sam McDonald County Park. *Water is available.*

17.4   LEFT on Wurr Road.

17.6   Arrive at starting point.

40. BIG BASIN & BOULDER CREEK LOOP

Santa Cruz Mountains and Big Basin Redwoods State Park

This road ride explores the ridges and forests of the Santa Cruz Mountains and includes a visit to California's first state park, Big Basin Redwoods. You'll see plenty of redwoods along the route, plus ridgeline forests of madrone and oak. Long climbs and descents are part of the package, and you'll have to put up with auto traffic on narrow, shoulderless roads. But it's worth it to complete this 43-mile epic trip through some of the South Bay's most remote countryside.

A shoulderless stretch of Highway 9 leads to Big Basin Redwoods State Park.

ROUTE DETAILS

type of trail paved roads with moderate car traffic

difficulty ▮▮▮▮▯

total distance 43 miles

riding time 3–4 hours

elevation gain 3,300 feet

The loop ride begins at Saratoga Gap at the junction of Highway 9 and Skyline Boulevard and heads southwest to Big Basin Redwoods State Park (831/338-8860 or 831/429-2851). A six-mile descent from Saratoga Gap at 2,634 feet to Waterman Gap at 1,267 feet is your warm-up for the day. Continuing straight on narrow, twisting Highway 236, you'll face a moderate up-and-down ride to state park headquarters. Lock up your bike at the parking lot and take the .5-mile walk on Redwood Trail, which shows off some of the park's largest and oldest redwoods, including the Mother of the Forest (329 feet tall) and the Santa Clara Tree (17 feet in diameter). Nothing compares to the humbling feeling of walking in the shadows of 2,000-year-old giants.

Back on your bike, you'll exit the park and continue south on Highway

Big Basin & Boulder Creek Loop

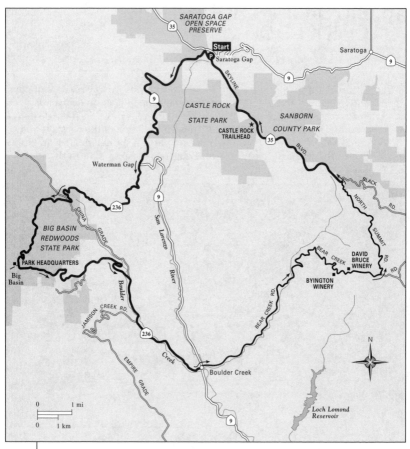

236, climbing briefly and then dropping down to the town of Boulder Creek. After a food and rest stop, and maybe a triple espresso, you face a strenuous climb from Boulder Creek (500 feet in elevation) to North Summit Road near Los Gatos (2,200 feet in elevation). You'll pass two wineries along the way. If you can somehow pull yourself through this unforgiving stretch, the remaining miles on narrow North Summit Road and Skyline Boulevard will seem relatively easy. Thankfully, the last two miles on Skyline Boulevard to your car at Saratoga Gap are actually downhill.

Driving Directions
From I-280 in Palo Alto, take Page Mill Road west for 8.9 miles to Skyline Boulevard (Highway 35). Turn left (south) on Skyline and drive 10.5 miles to the junction with Highway 9. The parking lot is on the left. Or, from Saratoga, take Highway 9 west for 7.5 miles to its junction with Skyline Boulevard (Highway 35).

BIG BASIN & BOULDER CREEK LOOP

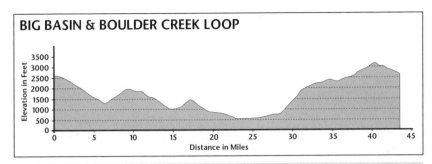

Route Directions for Big Basin & Boulder Creek Loop

0.0   Park at the large parking lot at the junction of Highway 9 and Highway 35. Ride west on Highway 9. *A vendor sells hot dogs and drinks in the parking lot on most weekends. Other supplies are available in Saratoga.*

1.8   Overlook point and restrooms on left.

6.1   RIGHT on Highway 236 at Waterman Gap.

10.8   STRAIGHT at junction with China Grade.

14.2   Big Basin Redwoods State Park headquarters. *Lock up your bike and take a hike on the .5-mile Redwood Trail from the main parking lot. Water, restrooms, and a small store are available (open most of the year).*

20.6   Pass golf course.

23.5   LEFT onto Highway 9 at stop sign. *Supplies are available in town of Boulder Creek.*

23.6   RIGHT on Bear Creek Road.

28.3   Begin major climb.

31.0   Byington Winery on right.

31.6   David Bruce Winery on left.

32.6   LEFT on North Summit Road (unsigned except for spray-painted word "Skyline" and arrow); end of major climb.

36.5   STRAIGHT at junction with Black Road; North Summit Road widens and becomes Skyline Boulevard.

40.4   Castle Rock State Park entrance.

43.0   Arrive at starting point.

41. SARATOGA GAP LOOP

Skyline Boulevard near Saratoga

When I was first getting into mountain biking, I met a pro rider on the trail who gave me one piece of advice: "If you want to learn how to handle single-track, ride Saratoga Gap Trail—often."

ROUTE DETAILS

type of trail	dirt road and single-track
difficulty	𝄃𝄃𝄃𝄃𝄃
total distance	12.9 miles
riding time	2–3 hours
elevation gain	1,600 feet

It was sage advice. I'm still not the world's greatest single-track rider (not even close), but I know where to go to sharpen my skills.

So does everyone else. This loop is one of the most popular in the South Bay, and for good reason. It starts at the busy junction of Highways 9 and 35, with easy access from most of Silicon Valley and the Peninsula, and carves its way through three separate parks and preserves: Saratoga Gap, Long Ridge, and Upper Stevens Creek.

The loop can be ridden in only one direction because one leg is open to uphill traffic only. If you can take your eyes off the six-foot space in front of your front tire, you'll find that the surrounding foothill scenery is lovely: open grassland ridges, fern-filled forests of handsome Douglas firs, wide views of wooded hillsides, and even a visit to a trickling creek in Stevens Canyon, which makes a perfect midloop rest stop.

Aside from the technical challenges of single-track on Saratoga Gap, Peters Creek, and Table Mountain trails, the only major difficulty on this ride is the long climb out on Charcoal Road, a 1.5-mile workout. But since it is preceded by a steep descent on Grizzly Flats Trail to Stevens Canyon, you are clearly forewarned that the uphill is coming. More than a few riders have been spotted walking their bikes here.

Note that this is a dry-season-only loop; many of the trails are closed during wet weather. Please don't ride them illegally.

For more information, contact Midpeninsula Regional Open Space District, 650/691-1200; website: www.openspace.org.

Driving Directions

From I-280 in Palo Alto, take Page Mill Road west for 8.9 miles to Skyline Boulevard (Highway 35). Turn left (south) on Skyline and drive 10.5 miles to the junction with Highway 9. The parking lot is on the left. Or, from Saratoga, take Highway 9 west for 7.5 miles to its junction with Skyline Boulevard (Highway 35).

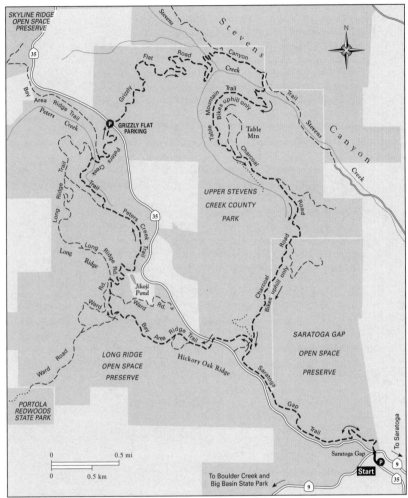

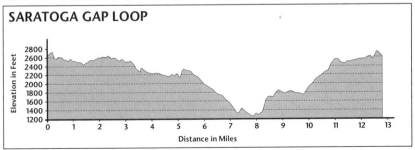

Route Directions for Saratoga Gap Loop

0.0 Park at the large parking lot at the junction of Highway 9 and Highway 35. Ride across Highway 9 carefully to access Saratoga Gap Trail. *A vendor sells hot dogs and drinks in the parking lot on most weekends. Other supplies are available in Saratoga.*

2.0 Single-track Saratoga Gap Trail ends at Highway 35; cross the highway and go RIGHT on Bay Area Ridge Trail.

3.2 RIGHT on single-track (signed for Grizzly Flat parking).

3.3 STRAIGHT at junction with Ward Road on left.

3.4 RIGHT on single-track Peters Creek Trail at major junction of Ward Road, Long Ridge Road, and Peters Creek Trail.

4.3 RIGHT to stay on Peters Creek Trail. Keep to right at next two forks to come out to Highway 35.

5.3 Cross Highway 35 and pick up Grizzly Flat Road on other side; steep and long descent.

7.8 Cross Stevens Creek.

8.0 RIGHT on Canyon Trail.

8.3 RIGHT on Table Mountain Trail (single-track signed "To Saratoga Gap").

9.5 RIGHT on Table Mountain Trail/Charcoal Road (wide road).

9.9 RIGHT on Charcoal Road; begin major hill climb.

10.4 RIGHT to stay on Charcoal Road.

11.2 LEFT at junction with Saratoga Gap Trail. *There are Miwok Indian grinding stones near this junction.*

12.9 Arrive at starting point.

42. SARATOGA TO MONTEBELLO ROAD SUMMIT

Saratoga to Montebello Ridge

The roads around Stevens Creek Reservoir and throughout Stevens Creek Canyon are well traveled by cyclists from the Silicon Valley every day of the week. The nearness of this pretty, tree-lined canyon to the hustle and bustle of Cupertino makes it perfect for after-work, lunchtime, and weekend rides.

ROUTE DETAILS FOR RIDE 42A
(paved out-and-back)

type of trail	paved roads with moderate car traffic
difficulty	🍶🍶🍶
total distance	21.2 miles
riding time	2 hours
elevation gain	2,000 feet

ROUTE DETAILS FOR RIDE 42B
(paved and dirt loop)

type of trail	dirt road and single-track; paved roads with moderate car traffic
difficulty	🍶🍶🍶🍶
total distance	27 miles
riding time	3 hours
elevation gain	2,300 feet

The two rides described here, one entirely paved and one a combination of pavement and dirt, are designed to allow for the most scenery with the least traffic. Both routes travel up Pierce Road from Saratoga through a mix of vineyards, red-tile-roofed mansions, and older farmhouses, then cruise through the foothills of Mount Eden Road and creekside Stevens Canyon Road to Montebello Road. Following this route, you've encountered two brief climbs already, but from here on out there's nothing but climbing on Montebello's increasingly narrow road. The road gains 1,500 feet over 4.3 miles, with grades occasionally as steep as 13 percent.

Achieving Montebello's high ridge is your reward, with its spreading views overlooking the Santa Clara Valley and a chance for wine tasting and a picnic at Ridge Winery (weekends only). The paved road continues a mile beyond Ridge Winery, but the views don't get much better. On the way back downhill,

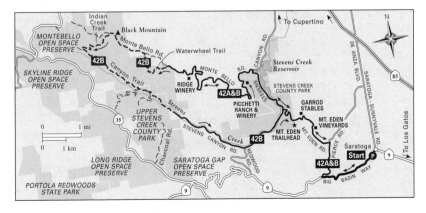

Saratoga to Montebello Road Summit

Bikes of all shapes and sizes are ridden to the summit of Montebello Road. © ANN MARIE BROWN

you may be able to stop at the Pichetti Ranch and Winery for some live music (Sunday only).

Mountain bikers have another option (Ride 42B). From Ridge Winery, continue up Montebello Road to the Waterwheel Creek Trail in Montebello Open Space Preserve, then follow that trail to the dirt section of Montebello Road. Shortly you're at the microwave-covered summit of 2,800-foot Black Mountain, the highest point on Montebello Ridge. Views are good in all directions, but the best view is to the west, as seen from near the 15-mph speed limit sign at an obvious outcrop of scattered rocks: Stevens Creek Canyon lies below you. Untrammeled grassland hills spread to the north and south along Skyline Ridge. The Pacific Ocean glimmers from afar. In springtime, the grassland wildflowers explode in a riot of colors.

The all-dirt downhill is exciting and fast; be careful not to mow over cyclists riding in the opposite direction. Indian Creek Trail drops 850 feet over 1.2 miles, then Canyon Trail descends almost as fast, adding a little single-track to the mix. Where the dirt ends you follow paved Stevens Canyon Road to Mount Eden Road, then retrace your tracks to Saratoga.

For more information, contact Midpeninsula Regional Open Space District, 650/691-1200; website: www.openspace.org.

Driving Directions
From San Jose, take Highway 17 south for six miles to the Highway 9 exit in Los Gatos. Take Highway 9 northwest 2.5 miles into Saratoga and park in downtown.

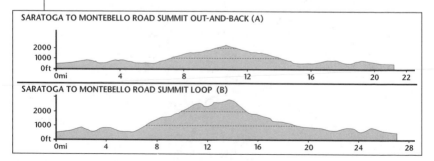

SARATOGA TO MONTEBELLO ROAD SUMMIT OUT-AND-BACK (A)

SARATOGA TO MONTEBELLO ROAD SUMMIT LOOP (B)

Route Directions Ride 42A *(paved out-and-back)* for Saratoga to Montebello Road Summit

0.0 Park in downtown Saratoga in any of the public parking lots one block off Highway 9. Ride west on Highway 9. *Supplies are available in town.*

1.6 RIGHT on Pierce Road (signed for Mountain Winery).

2.6 LEFT on Mount Eden Road.

3.1 Mount Eden Vineyards.

3.5 Garrod Farm Stables.

4.1 Mount Eden Trailhead on the left (no bikes).

4.9 STRAIGHT on Stevens Canyon Road at stop sign.

6.3 LEFT on Montebello Road.

6.8 Pichetti Ranch and Winery at Montebello Open Space Preserve (live music on Sunday).

8.3 Road narrows considerably.

10.6 Ridge Winery on the left. TURN AROUND. *Wine-tasting on weekends; restrooms and water are available.*

21.2 Arrive at starting point.

Route Directions Ride 42B *(paved and dirt loop)*

Follow Ride 12A to mile 10.6 (Ridge Winery), then continue up Montebello Road:

11.5 LEFT on Waterwheel Creek Trail (gated dirt trail).

12.9 LEFT on Montebello Road (dirt).

13.8 Summit of Black Mountain.

14.1 LEFT on Indian Creek Trail.

15.0 LEFT on Canyon Trail, stay left at next two junctions to stay on Canyon Trail.

18.5 Gate and start of Stevens Canyon Road.

20.4 LEFT to stay on Stevens Canyon Road.

22.1 RIGHT on Mount Eden Road.

27.0 Return to starting point.

43. COYOTE CREEK TRAIL

San Jose to Morgan Hill

Think San Jose and you probably think "industrial parks." It's true, San Jose has more than its share of these mammoth concrete complexes, but it also has peaceful farmlands, orchards, and gurgling creeks. The Coyote Creek Trail passes by all of it on its 14.7-mile length from Coyote Hellyer County Park south to Anderson Lake County Park. This makes a level, 29.4-mile round-trip on a paved recreation trail. If you simply want to crank out some level miles on your bike without worrying about cars or trail junctions, this is a good place to do it, and it's close to home for millions of Bay Area residents.

The trail begins at Coyote Hellyer County Park (408/225-0225), home of the only velodrome in Northern California. Bike races are usually held on Friday

ROUTE DETAILS

type of trail paved bike path

difficulty

total distance 29.4 miles

riding time 2–3 hours

elevation gain 400 feet

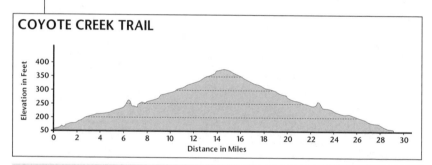

COYOTE CREEK TRAIL

Route Directions for Coyote Creek Trail

0.0   Park at the velodrome parking lot. The bike path begins by the restrooms. *Water is available at the park.*

0.4   Cottonwood Lake on the left.

0.8   Cross under U.S. 101.

3.0   LEFT at tricky intersection on far side of bridge.

5.5   Cross under U.S. 101.

6.8   Cross Metcalf Road to Coyote Ranch Road; go right to continue on path.

7.7   LEFT on Coyote Ranch Road, then RIGHT back on to path.

10.6   Cross Riverside Golf Course road.

14.0   Cross under U.S. 101.

14.7   Arrive at the ranger station for Anderson Lake County Park. TURN AROUND. *Water is available at the park.*

29.4   Arrive at starting point.

nights in summer. The open-air velodrome was built in 1962 as a training site for the Pan American Games.

In the trail's first half mile, you'll ride past small Cottonwood Lake on the left, a popular spot with shore fishermen. The lake, which was developed out of an old rock quarry, is stocked with rainbow trout. Shortly beyond it, the trail crosses under U.S. 101 to its east side. You'll cross the highway twice more along the route.

As you ride, ignore the numerous side bridges over Coyote Creek that access San Jose neighborhoods. Stay on the main path, which for a paved trail is a bit rough in places. You'll have to put up with the steady hum of road noise from U.S. 101 and Monterey Highway, which are never far away. But you'll also have the fine companionship of shady sycamores, cottonwoods, and live oaks along Coyote Creek, plus occasional scrub jays and ground squirrels. South of Metcalf Road, an equestrian trail parallels the paved trail, so you may see some horses, too.

The trail ends by the ranger station at Anderson Lake County Park, site of Santa Clara County's largest reservoir. You might want to lock up your bike here and take a walk on the one-mile, self-guided nature trail that runs to Malaguerra Avenue. It, too, follows Coyote Creek; a printed trail guide interprets its riparian habitat.

For more information, contact Santa Clara County Parks and Recreation Department, 408/356-2729 or 408/358-3741.

Driving Directions

From San Jose, drive four miles south on U.S. 101 and take the Hellyer Avenue exit. Drive .25 mile to the Coyote Hellyer County Park entrance. Just beyond the entrance kiosk, bear left at the fork and park at the velodrome parking lot.

44. MOUNT HAMILTON

Joseph D. Grant County Park, southeast of San Jose

The summit of Mount Hamilton at 4,209 feet is high enough so that on those rare winter days when snow falls in the Bay Area, it is gloriously crowned in white. It's the Bay Area's loftiest peak, and the highest you can drive to—or ride your bike to. It's also the home of Lick Observatory (visitor center, 408/274-5061), where astronomers from the University of California keep a watch on the stars. Constructed in 1887 by James Lick, the observatory was once famous for its 36-inch telescope, the world's largest at that time.

The ascent to Mount Hamilton's summit is challenging, but not impossibly so, thanks to the curving, twisting, switchbacking, steady 5- to 7-percent grade of Mount Hamilton Road. Beginning from Joseph D. Grant County Park (408/274-6121), you have 11.5 miles to gain 2,700 feet in elevation to the summit (this includes a 300-foot descent to Smith Creek, which you must regain).

Junctions are few and far between on this road, so you don't have route directions to worry about. Just follow the pavement uphill, through a landscape of grasslands, buckeyes, and mistletoe-draped oaks. In spring, the mountain is well known for its wildflower displays, and in autumn, the fall colors on the upper slopes can be delightful. As you ascend the mountain, you'll notice the foliage change: coulter pines with their big, heavy cones appear among the manzanita, plus leafy black oaks. It gets cooler the higher you go, and the views of Santa Clara Valley get better and better.

If you want to keep riding beyond the summit, help yourself. San Antonio Valley Road rolls, winds, and gradually descends until it changes names to Mines Road and eventually winds up in Livermore,

wild pig warning on Mount Hamilton Road near the observatory

© ANN MARIE BROWN

ROUTE DETAILS

type of trail   paved road with minimal car traffic

difficulty

total distance   23 miles (or longer options)

riding time   2 hours

elevation gain   2,700 feet

Mount Hamilton

45 miles later. Almost no cars travel this stretch of road, so it's all yours. If you happen to know someone in Livermore who will give you a ride back to Joseph Grant Park, you're in for a fine day.

Driving Directions

From I-680 in San Jose, take the Alum Rock Avenue exit and drive east 2.2 miles. Turn right on Mount Hamilton Road and drive 7.8 miles to the main entrance to Joseph D. Grant County Park on the right. Park in the county park lot (fee charged) or alongside the road in pullouts (no fee).

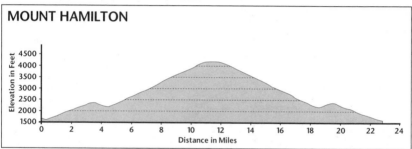

Route Directions for Mount Hamilton

0.0   Park near the entrance to Joseph D. Grant County Park and ride southeast on Mount Hamilton Road. *Water is available in the park campground; supplies are available eight miles north in San Jose.*

3.5   Twin Gates Trailhead and start of descent to Smith Creek. *Now or on the return trip, take a walk on Cañada de Pala Trail to see an abundance of blue-eyed grass, johnny jump-ups, brodiaea, shooting stars, and goldfields (springtime only).*

4.4   Smith Creek bridge.

5.6   STRAIGHT at junction with Kincaid Road on left.

10.9   RIGHT at Lick Observatory junction.

11.5   Arrive at main building and visitor area of observatory. TURN AROUND. *Water and snack machines are available when the visitor center is open, weekday afternoons and weekends 10 A.M. to 5 P.M. Public tours are available.*

23.0   Arrive at starting point.

45. GRANT RANCH LOOP

Joseph D. Grant County Park, southeast of San Jose

Joseph Grant County Park (408/274-6121), called "Grant Ranch" by the locals, lies due north of better known Henry Coe State Park, and it shares the same summer weather—hot as Hades. Plan your trip for the cooler months, preferably April or May when the grasslands are green and the slopes are gilded with wildflowers.

The old ranch roads at Joseph D. Grant County Park are lined with grasslands and oaks.

ROUTE DETAILS

type of trail dirt road

difficulty

total distance 10.9 or 12 miles

riding time 2 hours

elevation gain 1,600 feet

The park's trails are predominantly multiuse dirt roads that are used by mountain bikers more than anybody else. Almost every trail is an old ranch road, so if you are a single-track snob, you won't be happy here.

This challenging figure-eight loop trip takes you to the highest point in the park, Antler Point at 2,995 feet. The first two miles include some memorably steep uphill pitches, but the rest of the trip is more moderate. The ride starts at the Grant Lake Trailhead and follows Halls Valley Trail (open to bikes in the uphill direction only). The next 2.1 miles are the toughest of the ride, but as you gain elevation, you also gain surprising views of the South Bay's distant shimmering waters.

Where the trail tops out at Cañada de Pala Trail, turn left and enjoy an easier, more rolling grade. More views of the South Bay are seen to the northwest and Mount Hamilton shows up to the east. Look for abundant displays of spring wildflowers on this high, bald ridge.

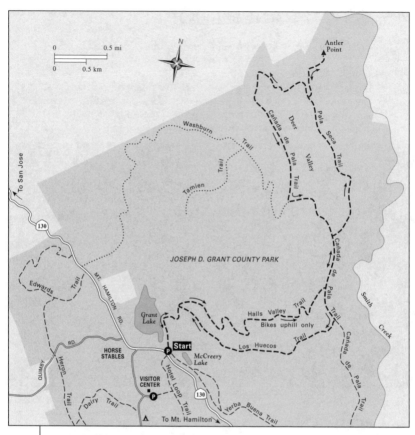

Your destination, Antler Point, is visible straight ahead, the highest hill around. Follow Pala Seca Trail through grasslands and occasional grazing bovines to Antler Point's spur trail. This grassy overlook supplies the day's best view of the South Bay, San Jose, Grant Park's rolling grasslands, and Lick Observatory on top of 4,209-foot Mount Hamilton.

For your return trip, loop back on Cañada de Pala Trail, enjoying more high views. You have some choices for the final leg: Los Huecos Trail (a very fast and steep downhill for a 10.9-mile loop) or Yerba Buena Trail (a more gentle downhill for a 12-mile loop). The latter will get you away from the biking crowds, but if you love screaming downhills, Los Huecos Trail is the only way to go.

Driving Directions

From I-680 in San Jose, take the Alum Rock Avenue exit and drive east 2.2 miles. Turn right on Mount Hamilton Road and drive 7.8 miles to the sign for Joseph D. Grant County Park on the right. Don't turn here; continue another 100 yards to the Grant Lake parking lot on the left.

GRANT RANCH LOOP

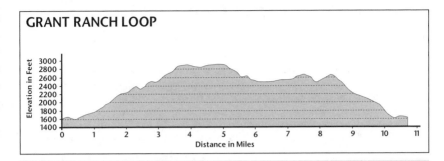

Route Directions for Grant Ranch Loop

0.0 Park at the Grant Lake parking area. Follow the trail to the left to Grant Lake. *Water is available at the park campground.*

0.3 RIGHT on connector trail to Halls Valley Trail.

0.6 Straight on Halls Valley Trail and begin steep climb.

2.7 LEFT on Cañada de Pala Trail.

3.1 RIGHT on Pala Seca Trail.

4.8 RIGHT on Antler Point Trail (walk your bike .2 mile uphill to this 2,995-foot viewpoint).

4.9 Arrive at Antler Point. TURN AROUND.

5.1 RIGHT at junction with Pala Seca Trail.

8.1 LEFT to stay on Cañada de Pala Trail.

8.5 RIGHT on Los Huecos Trail; begin fast, steep descent. *If you prefer a gentler descent, continue on Cañada de Pala Trail for 1.3 miles farther and turn right on Yerba Buena Trail; this gets you back to your car in a 12-mile round-trip.*

10.3 Straight to return to Grant Lake.

10.6 LEFT to return to parking lot.

10.9 Arrive at starting point.

46. MIDDLE RIDGE LOOP

Henry Coe State Park, east of Morgan Hill

The closest thing to a wilderness park in the South Bay area is Henry W. Coe State Park (408/779-2728; website: www.coepark.parks.ca.gov). This well known but little traveled state park is the second largest in California (the largest is Anza-Borrego Desert State Park near San Diego). Composed of tall ridges bisected by deep, steep ravines, the park is notoriously hilly. Its varied terrain includes grasslands, oaks, chaparral, pines, and mixed hardwoods.

© PETER KELLY

Henry Coe State Park provides a challenging single-track ride on the Middle Ridge Loop.

ROUTE DETAILS

type of trail dirt road and single-track

difficulty

total distance 10.8 miles

riding time 2 hours

elevation gain 2,100 feet

Henry Coe is so large—80,000 acres—and its terrain is so rugged that to see much of it, you need to pack your bike's panniers and plan to stay for a few days. But day visitors can tour the western part of the park on this 10.8-mile loop around Middle Ridge. The ride has some of the finest single-track to be found in the South Bay, but it also has some of the steepest fire road climbs. Come mentally and physically prepared for a workout; this park is not for beginners.

Pick a cool day for the ride, ideally in spring when Coe Park's wildflowers are blooming, or in autumn when the air is clear and cool. The park is extremely hot in summer, and its single-track trails are temporarily closed after winter rainstorms. Also in the rainy months, the wide Middle Fork of Coyote Creek at mile 7.2 may be more than a few feet deep and too dangerous to cross. Check with rangers before riding this loop after a period of rain.

The first leg of the ride follows Flat Frog Trail, a pleasant single-track that leads through a mixed woodland of ponderosa pines, black oaks, and

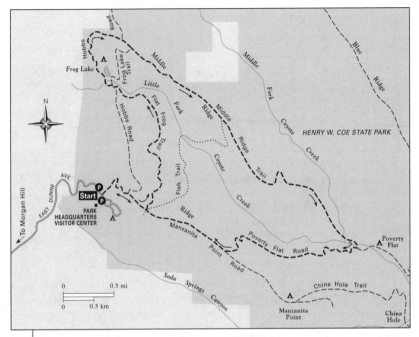

madrones. The trail connects with Hobbs Road just before Frog Lake; take the steep ranch road to the former cattle pond. (A backpacking camp is located nearby.) Tiny Frog Lake is spring-fed; it supports a few bass and bluegill. Frequently the surface of the water is completely covered with green algae. Cross Frog Lake's inlet and continue steeply uphill to Middle Ridge. The oak-dotted grasslands above Frog Lake support colorful wildflowers, which give you something to look at while you stop to catch your breath.

Once you reach Middle Ridge, look forward to a rollercoastering descent with many fine views of Coyote Creek canyon. Although Middle Ridge Trail initially leads through alternating grassy clearings and groves of pines and black oaks, it later enters a grove of giant, tree-sized manzanitas growing 15 feet tall. The trail loses 1,700 feet over 3.4 miles (with one short but steep uphill), and becomes more technical as it drops. In its final mile, it is downright treacherous—steep, loose, narrow, rocky, and rutted.

After crossing the Middle Fork of Coyote Creek, get ready to pay the price for all the fun you've had: You face a 1.8-mile climb on rocky Poverty Flat Road with a 1,400-foot elevation gain (12 percent average grade). Sometimes mountain biking is hell, and this is one of those times. When at least you reach Manzanita Point Road, the punishment is over, and you have an easy ride back to your car.

Driving Directions
From U.S. 101 in Morgan Hill, take the East Dunne Avenue exit and drive east for 13 miles to Henry W. Coe State Park headquarters.

MIDDLE RIDGE LOOP

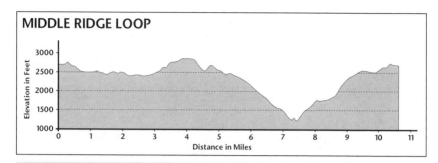

Route Directions for Middle Ridge Loop

0.0 Park at the lot near park headquarters. Follow paved Manzanita Point Road from near the headquarters building (pavement ends shortly). *Water is available at the trailhead; supplies are available in Morgan Hill.*

0.5 RIGHT to stay on Manzanita Point Road at junction with Hobbs Road.

0.7 LEFT on Flat Frog Trail.

2.9 RIGHT on Hobbs Road.

3.2 Frog Lake. Cross the dam and join trail to Middle Ridge (steep climb uphill).

3.8 RIGHT on Middle Ridge Trail; begin long, steep descent.

5.1 STRAIGHT on Middle Ridge Trail at junction with Fish Trail.

7.2 Cross Middle Fork of Coyote Creek at Poverty Flat.

7.3 RIGHT on Poverty Flat Road; begin long, steep climb out.

9.1 RIGHT on Manzanita Point Road.

10.3 LEFT to stay on Manzanita Point Road.

10.8 Arrive at starting point.

47. BERRY CREEK FALLS BIKE & HIKE (SKYLINE-TO-THE-SEA TRAIL)

Big Basin Redwoods State Park, south of Pescadero

You can see Berry Creek Falls the hard way, by hiking 5.5 hilly miles from park headquarters at Big Basin Redwoods State Park, or you can go see Berry Creek Falls the easy way, by riding your bike 5.8 nearly level miles from the coast near Davenport, then walking the last .6 mile.

ROUTE DETAILS

type of trail	dirt road and single-track
difficulty	∎∎ ⬡⬡⬡
total distance	11.6 miles (plus 1.2-mile hike)
riding time	2.5 hours
elevation gain	550 feet

The 70-foot falls are worth seeing no matter how you get there, but if you have children in tow, or if you aren't anywhere near the Boulder Creek entrance to the park, or if you'd just rather ride than walk, the bike route is a smart choice. Riders of almost any ability can handle the wide dirt road, and the trip begins and ends at an easy-access trailhead right on Highway 1.

The trail, which is the western section of the 38-mile-long Skyline-to-the-Sea Trail, used to be even easier to ride, but a series of heavy rains in the 1990s washed parts of it into Waddell Creek,

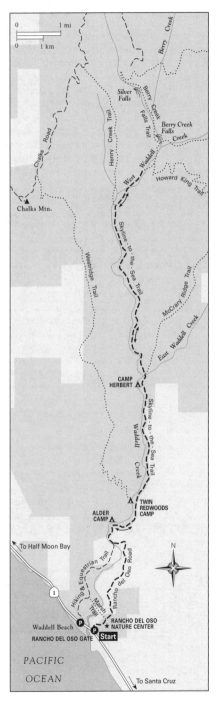

forcing one stretch to be rerouted as narrow single-track with a few ludicrously tight turns. The vast majority of riders simply walk their bikes through this 100-yard stretch.

The old ranch road begins by the highway, passes by Big Basin's Rancho de Oso visitor center and a few private farms, then enters the redwoods. The entire route parallels Waddell Creek until the final walk to the falls, where the trail follows Berry Creek. Several backpacking camps are located a few yards off the route, used mostly by hikers following the entire length of Skyline-to-the-Sea Trail.

Make sure you bring a bike lock so you can secure your wheels at the bike rack and take the 15-minute hike to the waterfall (bikes aren't allowed).

© ANN MARIE BROWN

An easy ride through the redwoods leads to beautiful Berry Creek Falls.

A bench on the viewing platform at Berry Creek Falls makes a perfect spot for lunch, if it isn't already in use by somebody else. Not surprisingly, this is a popular spot year-round. Plan a weekday trip if at all possible.

For more information, contact Big Basin Redwoods State Park at 831/338-8860 or 831/429-2851.

Driving Directions

From Half Moon Bay at the junction of Highway 92 and Highway 1, drive south on Highway 1 for 30 miles to the Rancho del Oso area of Big Basin Redwoods State Park (across from Waddell Beach, 7.5 miles north of Davenport). Park on the east side of the highway by the Rancho del Oso gate.

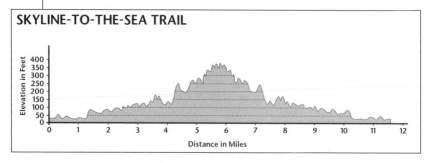

SKYLINE-TO-THE-SEA TRAIL

Elevation in Feet

Distance in Miles

Route Directions for Berry Creek Falls Bike & Hike (Skyline-to-the-Sea Trail)

0.0 Park at Rancho del Oso trailhead and ride into the parking lot and past the visitor center. *Supplies are available in Davenport, 7.5 miles south on Highway 1.*

0.4 Pass the Rancho del Oso nature center (open most weekends).

3.0 Trail washout creates tricky section with tight switchbacks. May have to walk your bike.

3.3 Crossing of Waddell Creek; follow the single-track trail to the right to a bridge if the stream is too high to cross.

5.8 Bike rack; TURN AROUND. *Lock up your bike and follow the hiking trail across the creek for .6 mile to Berry Creek Falls.*

11.6 Arrive at starting point.

CHAPTER 2

Mendocino and Wine Country

The Mendocino and Wine Country region encompasses a vast and diverse landscape from wave-swept beaches, rugged cliffs, and rolling sand dunes to vineyard-covered hills and valleys. Despite the technological advances of our modern 21st century, this area has retained its pastoral character more than perhaps anywhere else in California. Highway 1 winds up the rocky Pacific coast past seaside villages with population counts lower than their elevation—which is close to sea level. In much of the grassland hills east of the Sonoma and Mendocino coast, you're likely to see many more sheep or cows than people. The talk in the towns is about the crab harvest, or how many head of cattle are grazing in what plot of land, or whether or not grapes can grow in the coastal hills.

This peaceful, rural countryside makes for marvelous bicycling on country roads with little car traffic. For something more exciting, you can pedal the coastal highway itself, where rocky promontories, stately lighthouses, and sandy coves offer breathtaking panoramas. If you're clamoring for a fine meal or a bed-and-breakfast to ease you out of the saddle at the end of the day, the town of Mendocino with its charming shops and rugged headlands always welcomes visitors.

Bicyclists heading to the Mendocino coast to experience nature will find plenty of it here. The area is blessed with an abundance of parks. Within a few miles of Mendocino's town limits are three state parks where bicycling is permitted—Van Damme, Russian Gulch, and MacKerricher. Mountain bikers looking to cover more distance can choose from hundreds of dirt roads and trails in nearby Jackson State Forest.

Unforgettable too are the inland valleys, where U.S. 101 runs north from Santa Rosa to Wine Country. Most people think of Sonoma and Napa as Wine Country, but the wine-growing regions expand into several other valleys as well: Alexander Valley east of Geyserville, Dry Creek Valley west of Geyserville, and the Russian River Valley between Guerneville and Healdsburg. Even Mendocino County is now peppered with wineries in small towns like Boonville and Annapolis.

The town of Healdsburg is a bicycling haven in Wine Country. Its scenic, rural back roads are laced with tasting rooms. The local chamber of commerce happily supplies cyclists with area maps, and an annual Harvest Century Bicycle Tour is held each July. Fortunately, bicycling and wine tasting go together like, well, a bold merlot and French bread spread with Camembert. For a romantic date or even a relaxed family outing, the mostly level roads of the Wine Country valleys offer views of vineyards and picturesque farms, easy access to both world-famous and little-known tasting rooms, and celebrated cafés and gourmet grocery stores. If you like to eat, drink, and be merry, plus get a little exercise in the bargain, you'll enjoy this chapter's Wine Country bike rides.

For the best road riding in the more populated areas of Sonoma and Napa, avoid the "wine tourist" season, which is August to October. Instead, ride during the winter or in early spring, when the roads see much less traffic. One of the best bicycling months in Wine Country is February, when the mustard blooms beneath the grapevines and vineyards turn bright yellow.

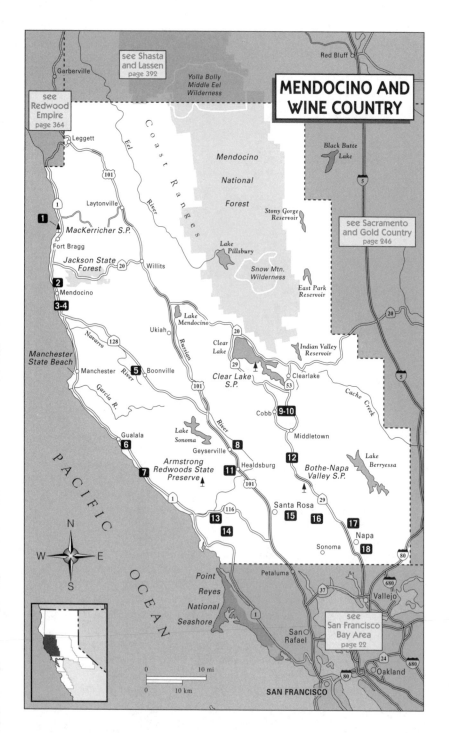

Garberville

Red Bluff

*Yolla Bolly
Middle Eel
Wilderness*

MENDOCINO AND
WINE COUNTRY

Leggett

*Black Butte
Lake*

101

1

Laytonville

Mendocino

National

Forest

*Stony Gorge
Reservoir*

1

MacKerricher S.P.

Fort Bragg

*Lake
Pillsbury*

*Jackson State
Forest*

20

Willits

*Snow Mtn.
Wilderness*

2

Mendocino

*East Park
Reservoir*

3-4

Navarro

128

*Lake
Mendocino*

Ukiah

20

*Clear
Lake*

*Indian Valley
Reservoir*

20

*Manchester
State Beach*

Russian

Manchester

River

5

Boonville

29

*Clear Lake
S.P.*

Clearlake

53

Cache Creek

Garcia R.

101

Cobb

9-10

Gualala

*Lake
Sonoma*

6

Middletown

*Lake
Berryessa*

8

Geyserville

12

7

*Armstrong
Redwoods State
Preserve*

Healdsburg

*Bothe-Napa
Valley S.P.*

11

101

1

116

13

Santa Rosa

29

14

15

16

17

Napa

Sonoma

18

80

Petaluma

Point

Reyes

37

Vallejo

National

Seashore

1

San
Rafael

24

680

N
W · E
S

P A C I F I C

O C E A N

80

Oakland

0   10 mi

0   10 km

SAN FRANCISCO

Coast Ranges

Eel River

Navarro River

CHAPTER 2
MENDOCINO AND WINE COUNTRY

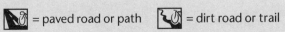

= paved road or path   = dirt road or trail

1. OLD HAUL ROAD/TEN MILE COASTAL TRAIL

MacKerricher State Park near Fort Bragg

First, the good news: Old Haul Road in MacKerricher State Park is one of the few trails near Mendocino where you can ride right alongside the ocean waves, enjoying miles of coastal scenery. It's a car-free, paved recreation trail, suitable for all kinds of riders and beach lovers.

ROUTE DETAILS

type of trail	 paved bike path
difficulty	▮ ▯▯▯▯
total distance	6.4 miles
riding time	.75 hour
elevation gain	250 feet

Now the bad news: Old Haul Road, also called the Ten Mile Coastal Trail, has suffered serious storm damage over the years and parts of it are completely washed away, replaced by millions of grains of blowing sand. State park managers have been hoping for funds to repair it, and also to fix an aged railroad trestle that connects Old Haul Road to Fort Bragg and beyond, but so far, they're still just hoping.

But that hasn't stopped bikers from using Old Haul Road, a historic railroad grade built in 1915 for transporting redwood logs to the mill in Fort Bragg. Bicyclists arrive in great numbers every sunny day and share the trail with hikers, baby strollers, dogs on leashes, and even some equestrians. Everybody has a good time.

A 3.2-mile oceanside section from Ward Avenue south to the closed-off railroad trestle over Pudding Creek in Fort Bragg allows uninterrupted riding. The first stretch passes by wide-open beaches, dunes, and coastline, then enters the main camping and day-use area of MacKerricher State Park. Here you might want to get off your bike and do some exploring around Laguna Point, where harbor seals and tidepools are plentiful along the rocky shore. South of the park the trail becomes somewhat less scenic; it passes behind the backs of seaside motels and provides occasional views of the Georgia-Pacific Lumber Company's smokestacks. Still, to the west, the open ocean is your constant companion—a symphony of white sand and wavy seas.

If you want to experience more of Old Haul Road, you can drive north on Highway 1 to just south of the Ten Mile River bridge, where the trail's north terminus is located. From here, you'll get a couple miles in the saddle before the pavement vanishes in the sand. This is the western edge of the 1,285-acre sand dune complex called Ten Mile Dunes, home to 12 threatened or endangered species, including the western snowy plover. If you wish to explore this area, head for the beach instead of walking on the fragile dunes.

The trail's entire length, including the section that must be walked, is seven miles one-way. Riding north from the Ward Avenue trailhead looks viable but isn't; the trail disappears into the sand in about 150 yards.

For more information, contact MacKerricher State Park at 707/937-5804 or 707/937-4296.

Driving Directions

From Mendocino, drive 13 miles north on Highway 1 to Ward Avenue (four miles north of Fort Bragg and one mile north of MacKerricher State Park). Turn left and drive .7 mile to the road's end at a small parking area.

OLD HAUL ROAD/TEN MILE COASTAL TRAIL

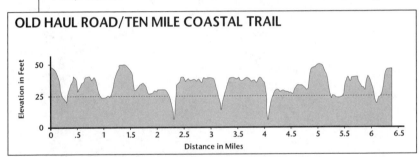

Route Directions for Old Haul Road/Ten Mile Coastal Trail

0.0 Park at the end of Ward Avenue at the sign for the recreation trail. Ride to your left (south). *Supplies are available in Fort Bragg.*

1.2 Gravel trail descends to main day-use area of MacKerricher State Park. *Lock up your bike and take a walk on the .5-mile Laguna Point Trail to see tide-pools and sea lions, or walk the trail along the perimeter of Lake Cleone for bird watching. Water is available at the campground.*

3.2 End of trail at closed Pudding Creek railroad trestle; TURN AROUND.

6.4 Arrive at starting point.

2. FERN CANYON TRAIL BIKE & HIKE

Russian Gulch State Park near Mendocino

The Fern Canyon Trail at Russian Gulch State Park is hardly long enough to be considered a bike trail, yet it is always popular with riders. Why? Because cycling on the forested, fern-lined Fern Canyon Trail is only one part of the adventure; part two comes when you lock up your bike at the paved trail's terminus and take a hike to Russian Gulch Falls, a gushing 36-foot waterfall that drops into a rocky fern grotto. The falls are framed by toppled tree trunks and hundreds of ferns in a lush, picturesque setting. After a good rain, Russian Gulch Falls really pours, but it is lovely to see even in the dry summer months.

Small riders may need some assistance on Russian Gulch's Fern Canyon Trail.

© ANN MARIE BROWN

ROUTE DETAILS

type of trail	paved bike path
difficulty	🍶🍶🍶🍶
total distance	3.2 miles (plus 3-mile hike)
riding time	1.5 hours
elevation gain	200 feet

The trail directions are a breeze. Just get on your bike and ride from the trailhead at the edge of the campground, following the smooth paved path 1.6 miles to a junction, where you'll find a few picnic tables and a bike rack. Here you must lock up your bike and continue on foot to the waterfall. Two trail choices will get you there: a short, .7-mile route accessing it from the north, or a longer, 2.3-mile route accessing it from the south. After viewing the falls, you can either return the way you came or hike the alternate trail back (for a 3-mile round-trip hike). Then it's back in the saddle and a quick return ride to the trailhead.

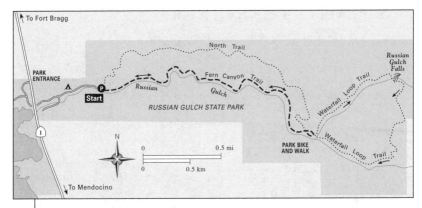

If you're planning a romantic weekend in Mendocino, this makes a fine morning or afternoon outing. It's also a great trip for families. For more information, contact Russian Gulch State Park at 707/937-5804 or 707/937-4296.

Driving Directions

From Mendocino, drive two miles north on Highway 1 to the entrance to Russian Gulch State Park on the left. Turn left, then left again immediately to reach the entrance kiosk. Continue past the kiosk and turn left again to cross under the highway. Drive through the campground to the Fern Canyon Trail parking area. (If the camp is closed for the winter, you must park near the recreation hall and ride through the campground.)

FERN CANYON TRAIL BIKE & HIKE

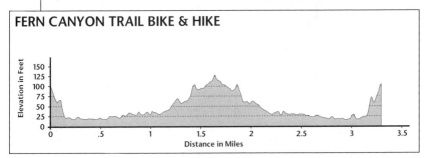

Route Directions for Fern Canyon Trail Bike & Hike

0.0   Park at the Fern Canyon Trail parking area, past the campground. *Supplies are available in Mendocino. Water is available at the park campground.*

1.6   Bike rack, picnic tables, and junction with Waterfall Loop Trail. TURN AROUND. *Lock up your bike and hike to the waterfall from here, via either a .7-mile trail or a 2.3-mile trail.*

3.2   Arrive at starting point.

3. FERN CANYON TRAIL

Van Damme State Park near Mendocino

It's a bit confusing: Within five miles of Mendocino are two Fern Canyon Trails. Both are paved bike trails, both were built on old logging roads, both are in state parks, and both carve their way through flora-rich canyons, paralleling streams.

ROUTE DETAILS FOR 3A
(paved route only)

type of trail paved bike path

difficulty

total distance 5 miles (plus optional 5-mile hike)

riding time .5 hour (plus 2 hours to hike)

elevation gain 250 feet

ROUTE DETAILS FOR 3B
(paved and dirt route)

type of trail dirt road and paved bike path

difficulty

total distance 7.4 miles

riding time 2 hours

elevation gain 450 feet

Here's the difference: The Fern Canyon Trail in Russian Gulch State Park has an optional add-on hike to a waterfall (see Ride 2 in this chapter). This Fern Canyon Trail, in Van Damme State Park (707/937-5804 or 707/937-0851), crosses Little River dozens of times, revealing spawning salmon and steelhead in the winter months. The trail also has an option for an add-on mountain bike ride or hike to a pygmy forest of miniature cypress and pine trees.

Both trails are worth experiencing. The Fern Canyon Trail in Van Damme State Park has one big catch, though. During the rainy season, its multiple bridges are removed, so you can't travel past the first mile. Generally you can count on the entire trail being open from April to October, but always phone the park before making a special trip. Storm damage in the 1990s closed the trail for extended periods, and if Mother Nature gets in the mood, it could happen again. One 50-yard-long washed-out stretch in the first mile serves as a reminder of these stormy days; most riders carry their bikes over the break in the pavement.

The first 2.5 miles are nearly level, curving through Little River's lush canyon lined with redwoods, firs, alders, berry bushes, and of course, the inevitable ferns—10 different kinds are found here. Where the pavement ends, two trails continue onward: a 2.5-mile, hikers-only trail (skinny-tire riders can lock up their bikes at the bike rack and hike this path) and a 1.2-mile dirt road that is open to mountain bikes. Both trails lead to the pygmy

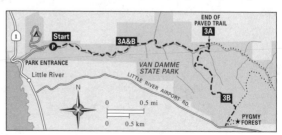

forest, where sandy, highly acidic soil has produced miniaturized flora. Mountain bikers, be prepared for a small climb to get there.

Driving Directions

From Mendocino, drive three miles south on Highway 1 to the entrance to Van Damme State Park on the left. Turn left and continue past the kiosk to the Fern Canyon Trail parking lot at the east end of the campground.

Van Damme State Park's Fern Canyon Trail

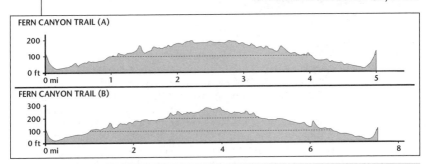

Route Directions for 3A *(paved route only)* for Fern Canyon Trail

0.0 Park at the east end of the campground in the signed Fern Canyon Trail parking area. *Supplies are available in Mendocino. Water is available at the park campground.*

0.4 Trail is washed out; road bikers will have to carry their bikes for 50 yards.

1.7 Pass the environmental campsites for hikers and bikers.

2.1 Fork in trail; take either route (they rejoin shortly).

2.5 Pavement ends. TURN AROUND. *You can lock up your bike and walk the hikers-only trail (on the left) 2.5 miles to the pygmy forest.*

Route Directions for 3B *(paved and dirt route)*

Follow directions for Ride 3A to the 2.5-mile mark, then continue:

2.5 Pavement ends; continue riding on dirt road to the right.

3.7 Arrive at pygmy forest. TURN AROUND. *Walk the footpath through the stunted trees.*

7.4 Arrive at starting point.

4. COMPTCHE LOOP

South of Mendocino

If you want to buy anything related to bikes in Mendocino, you have only one store to choose from: Catch-a-Canoe and Bicycles Too (707/937-0273). The people that run the place are old hands at suggesting rides for Mendocino visitors, and this loop (or one of several shorter variations of it) is one of their standards. If you didn't bring your bike to Mendocino, fear not: These same nice folks will rent you one.

ROUTE DETAILS

type of trail — paved roads with minimal car traffic

difficulty —

total distance 41.2 miles

riding time 3–4 hours

elevation gain 1,800 feet

The ride starts at Van Damme State Park (707/937-5804 or 707/937-0851) and heads up Little River Airport Road, with an optional stop at the park's pygmy forest at 3.2 miles. Here the pines and cypress trees grow only a few feet tall but are 50 to 100 years old. Their growth is stunted from the highly acidic, poorly drained soil.

After climbing some more, you gain a ridgeline 800 feet above the ocean, where Little River Road joins Comptche-Ukiah Road. A pleasant stretch of riding follows as you overlook inland canyons filled with miles of redwoods. The tiny town of Comptche, elevation 183 feet, is reached via two sustained descents punctuated by two level stretches. (One of the drops is almost four miles long; be glad you don't have to turn around and climb back up.) You and your wheels depart the dense forests and enter wide open pasturelands, dotted with herds of sheep and cows. Stop at the only store in Comptche, if it's open, to fuel up on snacks and drinks.

In the mid-19th century Comptche was a bustling lumber center, like most of the other towns in Mendocino County. Things are quieter now. Today, besides the store, the local post office is the main center of Comptche town life.

A scenic stretch on Flynn Creek Road leads to Highway 128 and Navarro River Redwoods State Park, which borders both sides of the highway. You'll face more car traffic from here to the end of the ride, but the scenery is worth it: The nearly level road curves through shady redwoods, paralleling the Navarro River. If it's a hot day, find yourself a cool pool to wade into (the best swimming holes are found in the two miles west of Dimmick Campground).

Before you know it, you're back at Highway 1, heading up the Navarro River grade to Navarro Point and then north through Albion and Little River to Van Damme State Park.

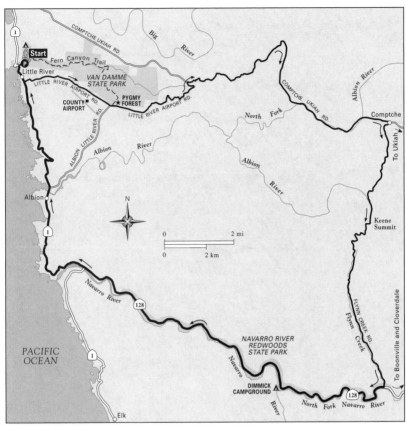

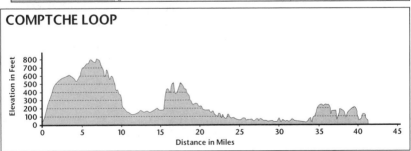

Driving Directions

From Mendocino, drive three miles south on Highway 1 to the entrance to Van Damme State Park on the left. Park in any of the park's day-use areas: either at the beach area on the west side of the highway or near the campground on the east side.

Route Directions for Comptche Loop

0.0   Park at one of the day-use areas at Van Damme State Park. Ride south on Highway 1. *Supplies are available in Mendocino, three miles north.*

0.5   LEFT on Little River Airport Road.

3.2   Pygmy forest on left. *Walk the raised wooden walkway through stunted trees and flora.*

6.6   RIGHT on Comptche-Ukiah Road.

15.4   Comptche. *Supplies are available.*

15.5   RIGHT on Flynn Creek Road.

22.9   RIGHT on Highway 128.

26.5   Dimmick Campground on the left. *Water is available. Swimming holes are found west of the campground.*

34.5   RIGHT on Highway 1.

41.2   Arrive at starting point.

5. BOONVILLE'S MOUNTAIN VIEW ROAD

Boonville to the Mendocino coast

There's more than one way to get to the Mendocino coast, and the best way I know is by bicycle from Boonville to Manchester on Mountain View Road. This is one of the great winding, twisting roads of Northern California—a former stagecoach route that is far too circuitous to encourage much car traffic. You will probably encounter deer instead, and quite possibly wild pigs.

ROUTE DETAILS

type of trail	paved roads with minimal car traffic
difficulty	🥾🥾🥾🥾🥾
total distance	50 miles
riding time	5 hours
elevation gain	5,600 feet

The ride is an out-and-back, with nearly equal amounts of climbing and descending in both directions. You could just as well start this trip at the coast, if you desire, and ride to Boonville and back. The road has not one summit but several, the highest of which are about 2,200 feet in elevation.

Begin with a steep, two-mile climb out of Boonville, passing the Boonville airport and redwood-filled Faulkner County Park, then prepare for a long, repeated series of "descend, climb, descend, climb." This goes on for the duration of the trip, as you curve in and out of one forested mile after another, until at mile 19.5 you make a final 5.5-mile descent down to Highway 1 and the coast. During this last drop, you exit the woodland and enjoy wide views of open pastureland and the glimmering ocean surface—provided it's not foggy. You'll have plenty of sheep for companions along this last stretch.

The road deposits you about midway between Point Arena and Manchester, so take your pick: You can head south a couple of miles to see the Point Arena Lighthouse or eat at one of the town's cafés, or head north a couple of miles to visit Manchester State Beach (the nearby KOA store sells snacks and drinks). Both of these short add-ons are basically level, especially when compared to what you've just ridden.

The ride back to Boonville is a surprisingly different experience. This

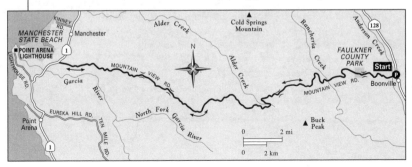

route serves as a great reminder that out-and-back rides are often as visually surprising as loops: Everything looks new heading in the opposite direction. Even the climbs are different: The first five miles heading up from the coast are the hardest, but a few miles later you get to enjoy a three-mile-long downhill stretch. Then it's more ups and downs all the way back to Boonville.

Understand that you need to be completely self-sufficient for this ride, because you won't find any 7-Elevens along Mountain View Road. Pack along a good repair kit and plenty of snacks. You can buy almost anything you need in Boonville, a small town best known for having its own language, called Boontling (it's one of the two recognized dialects of English in America). If you want a cup of coffee, ask for a "horn of zeese." The lingo was made up in the late 1880s, when outsiders started to infiltrate the remote town, as a way for the old-timers to talk among themselves.

After your ride, be sure to stop in at the Buckhorn Saloon (707/895-3369) in Boonville, where you can sit on a saddle-shaped barstool and partake in the Anderson Valley Brewing Company's fine ales, porters, stouts, and seasonal beers. After 50 miles in the saddle and more than 5,000 feet of climbing, you deserve it.

Driving Directions

From U.S. 101 just south of Ukiah, take Highway 253/Boonville Road west for 19 miles to Highway 128. Turn right (north) and drive one mile to Boonville. (Or, from Cloverdale, take Highway 128 north for 27 miles.)

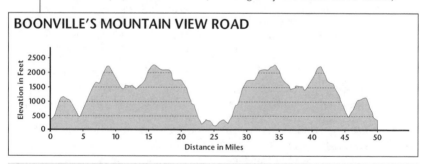

BOONVILLE'S MOUNTAIN VIEW ROAD

Route Directions for Boonville's Mountain View Road

0.0 Park in Boonville near the intersection of Highway 128 and Mountain View Road. *Supplies are available in Boonville.*

2.3 Faulkner County Park on the left; end of first climb.

25.0 Arrive at Highway 1. TURN AROUND. *Ride south three miles to Point Arena for supplies or to visit its lighthouse, or ride north 2.1 miles to Kinney Road and turn left for supplies at the KOA store and a visit to Manchester Beach State Park.*

50.0 Arrive at starting point.

6. GUALALA RIDGE & POINT ARENA LOOP

South of Mendocino

Today's suburban-looking Gualala Ridge used to be the stagecoach route from Gualala to Point Arena in the mid-1800s. Because this area is in Mendocino's well-known "banana belt" of warmer weather, much of the road is now lined with homes. It's a surprising sight on this fairly remote coast.

the final level, scenic miles to Point Arena Lighthouse

ROUTE DETAILS FOR 6A
(long loop)

type of trail paved roads with moderate car traffic

difficulty 🍶🍶🍶

total distance 40.3 miles

riding time 3–4 hours

elevation gain 1,600 feet

ROUTE DETAILS FOR 6B
(short loop)

type of trail paved roads with moderate car traffic

difficulty 🍶🍶

total distance 21.5 miles

riding time 1.5–2 hours

elevation gain 1,200 feet

Gualala Ridge is much drier than other ridges south of Mendocino; you won't find redwood forests here. The undeveloped areas are lined with madrones, manzanita, Douglas firs, and pines. Gaining the ridge requires a hefty 900-foot climb from Highway 1; the first mile will get your heart pumping. After that, the grade turns moderate and stays that way. Whether you choose the long loop (6A) or the short loop (6B), the descent to Highway 1 is fast and furious.

The long loop offers two unusual highlights along its stretch: Bowling Ball Beach and Point Arena Lighthouse. Bowling Ball Beach is accessed by a .5-mile walk from Schooner Gulch State Beach, four miles south of Point Arena. Its unusual formation of large, rounded rock outcroppings gives Bowling Ball Beach its name. The "bowling balls" are most visible during very low tides.

Point Arena Lighthouse is tied with Pigeon Point Lighthouse in San Mateo County as the tallest operating lighthouse on the

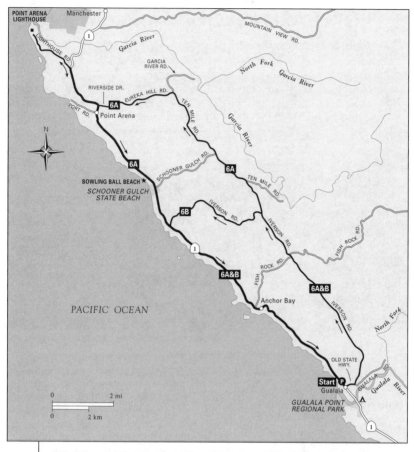

West Coast. It has been guiding ships since 1870, although the present structure was built after the original was destroyed in the 1906 earthquake. For a few bucks, you can climb the 145 steps to the top of the lighthouse tower, plus visit the adjacent visitor center to see a collection of fascinating old photos and maritime exhibits. And if you fall in love with the light-house and this area, as most people do, the cottages next door are available for overnight rental.

Although the short loop cuts off the lighthouse visit, you can always drive there, or ride there on another day by starting in downtown Point Arena. This makes an easy, pleasant 10-mile round-trip excursion.

Driving Directions

From Jenner at the junction of Highways 1 and 116, drive north on High-way 1 for 36 miles to Gualala. Old State Highway (Road 501A) begins on the south side of town.

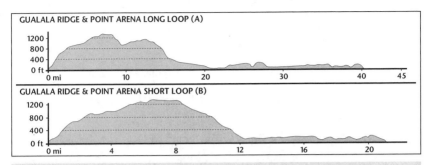

GUALALA RIDGE & POINT ARENA LONG LOOP (A)

GUALALA RIDGE & POINT ARENA SHORT LOOP (B)

Route Directions for Ride 6A *(long loop)* for Gualala Ridge & Point Arena Loop

0.0 Park in downtown Gualala and ride to the south side of town and the junction of Highway 1 and Old State Highway (Road 501A). *Supplies are available in Gualala.*

0.3 LEFT on Old Stage Road.

6.0 Old Stage Road changes to Iverson Road at Fish Rock Road junction.

8.0 RIGHT on Ten Mile Cutoff Road (Road 503A).

13.5 STRAIGHT at stop sign and junction with Eureka Hill Road.

16.5 Eureka Hill Road becomes Riverside Drive in Point Arena. *Supplies are available in Point Arena.*

16.6 RIGHT on Highway 1 (heading north).

18.4 LEFT on Lighthouse Road at Rollerville Junction. *Supplies are available.*

20.7 Entrance kiosk for Point Arena Lighthouse; fee required to enter.

21.1 Point Arena Lighthouse; TURN AROUND.

23.8 RIGHT on Highway 1 (heading south).

29.6 Schooner Gulch State Beach and Bowling Ball Beach on the right.

35.4 Village of Anchor Bay. *Supplies are available.*

40.3 Arrive at starting point.

Route Directions for Ride 6B *(short loop)*

Follow directions for Ride 6A to mile 8.0, then continue:

8.0 LEFT to stay on Iverson Road.

12.5 LEFT on Highway 1.

17.7 Village of Anchor Bay. *Supplies are available.*

21.5 Arrive at starting point.

7. ANNAPOLIS ROAD LOOP

Sonoma Coast near Sea Ranch

This pleasant road ride begins at the hamlet of Stewarts Point, once a thriving town located near the site of a busy shipping port at Fisherman's Bay. Today you won't find much in the neighborhood except a well-stocked general merchandise store and a post office.

historic Haupt Creek Bridge on Stewarts Point-Skaggs Springs Road near Annapolis

ROUTE DETAILS

type of trail — paved roads with minimal car traffic

difficulty — 🔋🔋🔋🔋🔋

total distance — 24 miles

riding time — 1.5–2 hours

elevation gain — 2,300 feet

You're on your own for most of this ride; there is little in the way of services for much of the route. Still, you're unlikely to need anything; the grades are mellow, traffic is light, and the scenery is sure to fill your senses. A few historic bridges make good photo opportunities; you might want to bring a camera.

The small town of Annapolis has two sights to its credit: its one-room schoolhouse, which has been restored by local volunteers, and the family-run Annapolis Winery (707/886-5460), which produces excellent sauvignon blanc, pinot noir, and gewürztraminer grapes. After many miles of no civilization, the "Wine Tasting Today" sign will take you by surprise. The tasting room is located just 50 feet off Annapolis Road and is open most days from noon to 5 P.M. If you visit in August, you can enjoy the fruits of their Gravenstein apple harvest, and even make your own juice in their apple press.

Beyond the winery, you'll start to see more homes of Annapolis residents, and as the road drops down toward the coast, you'll enter the community of Sea Ranch. Sea Ranch is well known for its architecture, a modern adaptation of the New England saltbox style. Designed to blend in with its coastal surroundings, this style was used to appease environmentalists who resisted the building of Sea Ranch. Also as part of the development agreement, the public is allowed access to four beaches in the Sea Ranch complex. You'll pass the signed turnoffs for Pebble Beach and Black Point Beach as you ride south back to Stewarts Point. Both are worth a look.

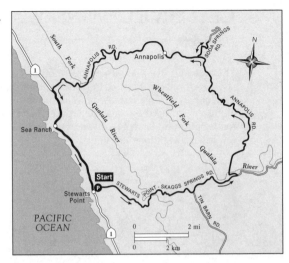

Driving Directions

From Jenner at the junction of Highways 1 and 116, drive north on Highway 1 for 25 miles to Stewarts Point (two miles south of Sea Ranch). Turn right on Stewarts Point-Skaggs Springs Road and park in the first available pullout.

ANNAPOLIS ROAD LOOP

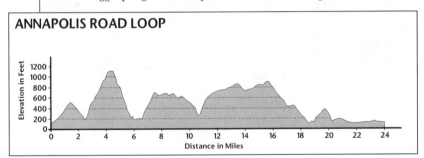

Route Directions for Annapolis Road Loop

0.0 Park at the pullout on the right side of Stewarts Point-Skaggs Springs Road, near its junction with Highway 1. *Supplies are available at Stewarts Point General Merchandise, or 11 miles north in Gualala.*

6.0 Historic Haupt Creek Bridge, originally erected in 1909 and moved here in 1937.

6.5 LEFT on Annapolis Road and cross bridge over Gualala River.

12.6 Pass Soda Springs Road on the right. Annapolis Winery is 50 feet down this road. *The winery is open most afternoons for tasting.*

13.4 Old Annapolis one-room schoolhouse.

14.5 Annapolis post office and a pay phone.

20.1 LEFT on Highway 1.

24.0 Arrive at starting point.

8. GEYSERVILLE WINERY LOOP

North of Santa Rosa

This ride tours the wine region surrounding Geyserville and Alexander Valley, one of the lesser visited of Northern California's grape-growing regions. The loop has a large number of junctions for its short mileage, so carry along a map and these suggested route directions. The abundant turns serve a purpose: They'll lead you past a half-dozen major wineries, plus a few interesting shops and sights.

The Geyserville Winery Loop is lined with grapevines.

© ANN MARIE BROWN

ROUTE DETAILS

type of trail paved roads with moderate car traffic

difficulty ▮▮ ♟♟♟

total distance 21.9 miles

riding time 1.5–2 hours

elevation gain 600 feet

One warning: Part of this ride follows Highway 128, where there is no shoulder, but thankfully not tons of traffic, either. Count on wide shoulders on the second half of the loop (west side of U.S. 101) and narrow to nonexistent shoulders on the first half. If you don't like this arrangement, just ride out and back on the loop's west side.

The roads are quite level, and the scenery seems to encourage malingering more than intense pedaling. Stop in Jimtown for a cup of coffee and some discussion about this year's grape crop, or at the Dry Creek General Store, established 1881, to find out about the history of this area. Do a little wine tasting at

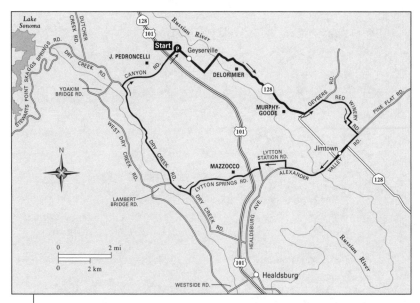

one, or all, of the wineries along the route. Even teetotalers will want to stop on Dry Creek Road at Timbercrest Farms, a retail establishment that sells dried fruits, nuts, and tomatoes.

Note that this area gets very hot in summer, so avoid midday riding then. Spring is the loveliest season, when the air is cool and the mustard blooms amid the myriad grapevines.

For more information, contact Healdsburg Chamber of Commerce, 800/648-9922 or 707/433-6935, website: www.healdsburg.org.

Driving Directions

From Santa Rosa, drive 25 miles north on U.S. 101 and take the Highway 128/Geyserville exit. Drive north on Geyserville Avenue for one mile and park in downtown Geyserville near the junction with Highway 128.

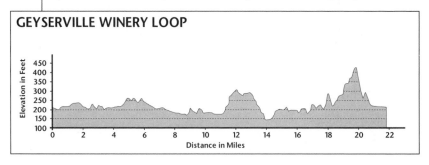

Route Directions for Geyserville Winery Loop

0.0 Park near junction of Geyserville Avenue and Highway 128 in down-town Geyserville. Ride east (right) on Highway 128. *Supplies are available in Geyserville.*

0.7 Cross bridge over Russian River.

0.9 RIGHT to stay on Highway 128.

1.9 De Lorimier Winery.

4.0 Murphy-Goode Winery.

4.5 LEFT on Geysers Road.

5.1 RIGHT on Red Winery Road.

7.4 RIGHT on Pine Flat Road.

7.8 STRAIGHT on Highway 128.

8.1 Pass through Jimtown. *Supplies are available.*

8.3 STRAIGHT on Alexander Valley Road. *Supplies are available at Alexander Valley Store and Bar.*

10.4 RIGHT on Lytton Station Road.

11.7 RIGHT on Lytton Springs Road.

11.9 Cross under U.S. 101.

12.6 Ridge and Lytton Springs Tasting Room.

13.2 Mazzocco Winery.

14.4 RIGHT on Dry Creek Road.

15.2 STRAIGHT at stop sign at Dry Creek General Store. *Supplies are available.*

15.3 Teldeschi Winery.

16.6 Timbercrest Farms (sells dried fruit).

18.0 Chateau Diana Winery.

18.8 RIGHT on Canyon Road.

19.7 J. Pedroncelli Winery.

20.9 Cross under U.S. 101.

21.0 RIGHT on Highway 128/Geyserville Avenue.

21.9 Arrive at starting point.

9. BOGGS LAKE LOOP

South of Clear Lake

The rolling hills south of Clear Lake are the setting for this loop ride, which affords expansive views of the region from several high points. Along the route are two highlights of radically different ilks: the Calpine Geysers geothermal facility and the Nature Conservancy's Boggs Lake Preserve.

ROUTE DETAILS

type of trail paved and dirt roads with minimal car traffic

difficulty

total distance 14.5 miles

riding time 1.5 hours

elevation gain 1,200 feet

At the geysers, billed as "the hottest spot in Wine Country," Calpine operates a working geothermal power plant, one of 19 in the area that is open to the public for tours with advance reservations. The free tour starts at the Calpine visitor center (866/439-7377, website: www.geysers.com) in Middletown. Visitors are then taken by bus to this or another working power plant.

At Boggs Lake you'll find a nature preserve filled with wildflowers, several rare and endangered species of plants, and prime bird watching. Over 150 species, including bald eagles, have been recorded in winter and spring.

When you reach the entrance to Boggs Lake at mile 7.2, lock up your bike and walk the one-mile loop along the lakeshore. Look for two unusual plants: bladderwort, with yellow blossoms that cover the surface of the lake in spring; and watershield, which lives beneath the water year-round except for two successive springtime days, when it pushes its reddish-purple blossoms above the water. On the first day it opens its blooms to receive pollen from other plants, then it pulls back into the lake. On the second day it protrudes from the lake once

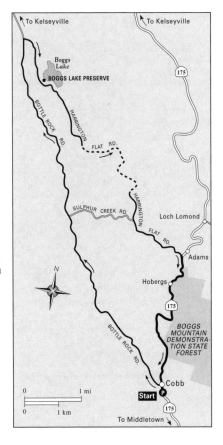

more, this time to disperse its own pollen before disappearing below the surface again, until next year.

The ride has only one significant climb on Bottle Rock Road, which lasts for two miles. Most of the route is suitable for a road bike except for a 1.5-mile stretch on Harrington Flat Road where the pavement turns to hard-packed dirt. If your road bike tires aren't too thin, you can probably get away with riding them. If you ride your mountain bike instead, this loop heads past the entrance to Boggs Mountain Demonstration State Forest at mile 13.4, where you can easily add on some miles if you wish. The forest features a cornucopia of single-track trails for mountain bikers.

Driving Directions

From Calistoga, take Highway 29 north for 17 miles to Middletown, then turn left on Highway 175 and drive eight miles to Cobb.

BOGGS LAKE LOOP

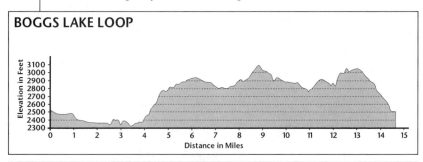

Route Directions for Boggs Lake Loop

0.0 Park in the lot by the post office and Cobb Village Inn on Highway 175. Ride north on Highway 175. *Supplies are available in Cobb.*

0.2 LEFT on Bottle Rock Road.

1.6 The Geysers geothermal facility on left.

3.5 Straight at junction with Sulphur Creek Road.

6.7 RIGHT on Harrington Flat Road.

7.2 Boggs Lake Preserve on left. *Lock up your bike and take a walk on one of the preserve's trails.*

8.6 Pavement ends.

10.1 Pavement begins again.

10.9 Straight at junction with Sulphur Creek Road.

12.0 RIGHT on Highway 175.

13.4 Entrance road to Boggs Mountain State Forest. *Many mountain biking possibilities here; see Ride 10 in this chapter.*

14.5 Arrive at starting point.

10. BOGGS MOUNTAIN DEMONSTRATION STATE FOREST

South of Clear Lake

No Northern California biking book would be complete without including Boggs Mountain Demonstration State Forest (707/928-4378), a mecca of legal, fun, single-track trails for mountain bikers. And yet, most mountain bikers would be hard-pressed to say where exactly Boggs Mountain is, and what exactly a demonstration state forest is.

ROUTE DETAILS

type of trail	dirt road and single-track
difficulty	
total distance	12.2 miles
riding time	2 hours
elevation gain	1,800 feet

To set the record straight, Boggs Mountain is about midway between Calistoga and Clear Lake. If you're in the northern Napa Valley or the southern Lake County area, you're close. If not, you face a long drive from everywhere, but luckily the state forest has a campground. And a demonstration state forest is a place where the California Department of Forestry experiments with forestry management techniques, including logging, so expect to see a few stumps among the tall trees growing here. At Boggs Mountain, the land managers also allow many kinds of recreation, including hunting. Given this, avoid the area during deer season (usually September).

The riding at Boggs Mountain is moderate, in terms of both technical and aerobic challenges. The terrain is mostly open woods and meadows at a 3,000-foot elevation, the hills are somewhat steep but always short, and other trail users are generally few and far between. As I said, Boggs is a bit *out there,* so come prepared for near solitude. The delightful scenery will keep you company, from forests of ponderosa pines, black oaks, and Douglas firs to blooming wildflowers and dogwoods in the spring.

riding through the autumn leaf litter at Boggs Mountain Demonstration State Forest

© ANN MARIE BROWN

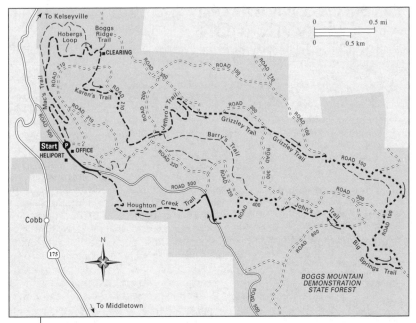

Maps of the state forest are generally available at the forestry office or heliport—near where you leave your car. Pick one up before you ride; there are a dizzying number of trails, dirt roads, and junctions here. If you get lost, just ride around as you please; every trail in this forest has something to offer. One trail not to be missed is Houghton Creek Trail, the final leg of this loop; it's a fern- and flower-lined single-track dream.

Driving Directions

From Calistoga, take Highway 29 north for 17 miles to Middletown, then turn left on Highway 175 and drive eight miles to Cobb. Continue one mile beyond Cobb and turn right on Road 500 (signed for State Fire Station). Drive .75 mile and park your car in the lot near the heliport and forestry office.

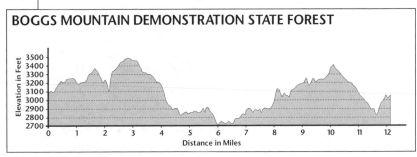

BOGGS MOUNTAIN DEMONSTRATION STATE FOREST

Route Directions for Boggs Mountain Demonstration State Forest

0.0   Park in the dirt lot by the forestry office and heliport. Follow Mac's Trail from the road alongside the parking lot. *Supplies are available in Cobb.*

0.8   RIGHT on Hobergs Loop Trail.

1.6   RIGHT on Boggs Ridge Trail (unsigned) to clearing with open view to southwest.

2.3   Junction with Road 210. Cross the road and pick up Karen's Trail.

3.0   RIGHT on Road 210, which soon narrows to single-track.

4.0   Junction with Road 200. Cross the road and pick up Jethro's Trail.

4.1   LEFT at junction with Barry's Trail (stay on Jethro's Trail).

4.8   RIGHT on Road 300.

5.3   LEFT on Grizzley Trail.

6.4   RIGHT on Road 100.

6.6   RIGHT on single-track Grizzley Trail.

7.1   RIGHT on Road 100.

7.2   Straight at junction of fire roads.

7.7   RIGHT on Big Springs Trail.

8.4   Cross fire road and pick up John's Trail (a few yards to the left on the fire road).

9.2   LEFT on Road 400. Stay left at next three junctions.

9.7   RIGHT on Road 400.

10.1 RIGHT on Road 500.

10.5 LEFT on Houghton Creek Trail (also called simply Creek Trail) at junction with Road 200 and Calso Camp.

11.4 Cross creek.

11.9 LEFT on Road 500.

12.2 Arrive at starting point.

11. HEALDSBURG WESTSIDE & EASTSIDE LOOP

West of Healdsburg

This is a classic winery road ride in the Russian River/Healdsburg area. Every day of the year you'll find cyclists on some part of this loop, which begins in downtown Healdsburg and passes dozens of wineries and tasting rooms. If you don't mind adding on a few miles on heavily trafficked River Road, you could easily start this ride in Guerneville as well.

a stop at Hop Kiln Winery on Westside Road

ROUTE DETAILS

type of trail paved roads with moderate car traffic

difficulty ▮▮▯▯▯

total distance 25.6 miles (or 20-mile option)

riding time 1.5–2 hours

elevation gain 700 feet

To put this ride in perspective, in the first six miles you pass seven wineries and tasting rooms. Although each of the loop's wineries is worth a visit, a highlight is Hop Kiln Winery (707/433-6491) at mile 6.1. Its much-photographed, three-towered hop barn is a designated historic site. Inside the barn is a well-stocked tasting room, with delicious mustards and other products for sale in addition to wines.

Another favorite is Foppiano Winery (707/433-7272) at mile 23.7, where you can lock up your bike and take a self-guided tour that starts at the tasting room and wends its way through vineyards to the Russian River. Foppiano's signature vintage is a petite sirah, which they have been making for 100 years.

If you want to learn about the history of California winemaking or see how wine is made, pay a visit to Rodney Strong Vineyard's Hospitality Center (mile 22.6), newly remodeled in 2002. This facility emphasizes visitor education along with its tasting and retail sales.

If in the course of this loop you have a few too many sips of wine (a forgivable error), you can cut the trip short by turning left on Wohler Road at 9.7 miles from the start. In one mile you'll cut over to Eastside Road, making a 20-mile roundtrip. You will still see many of this ride's highlights.

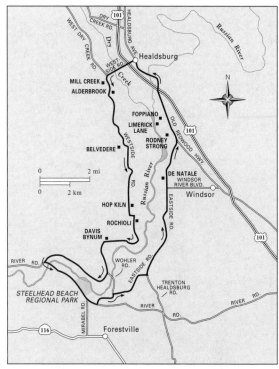

The loop begins and ends in the town of Healdsburg, a very bike-friendly town. The chamber of commerce (800/648-9922 or 707/433-6935, website: www.healdsburg.org), located at the junction of Healdsburg Avenue and Westside Road, provides handouts on bike rides and wineries. Within walking distance are many cafés and shops, plus two great bike stores.

Driving Directions

From Santa Rosa, drive 25 miles north on U.S. 101 and take the Westside Road/Guerneville exit in Healdsburg. Turn east toward downtown Healdsburg and park in one of the public parking lots.

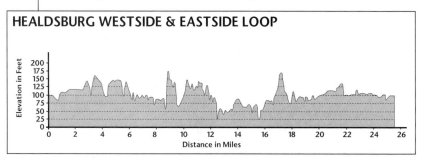

HEALDSBURG WESTSIDE & EASTSIDE LOOP

Route Directions for Healdsburg Westside & Eastside Loop

0.0   Park in downtown Healdsburg (near the junction of Healdsburg Avenue, Westside Road, and Redwood Highway) and ride west on Westside Road. *Supplies are available in Healdsburg.*

0.2   Cross under U.S. 101.

0.3   Alder Brook Tasting Room.

1.2   Mill Creek Tasting Room.

2.0   Armida Winery.

3.1   Rabbit Ridge Winery.

3.9   Belvedere Winery.

6.1   Hop Kiln Winery.

6.2   Rochioli Winery.

7.9   Davis Bynum Winery.

9.7   Wohler Road junction. *You could turn left here for a shortcut to Eastside Road and a 20-mile round-trip.*

10.7   Gary Farrell Vineyards.

12.5   LEFT to stay on Westside Road before bridge over Russian River.

12.6   LEFT on River Road (now looping back).

12.9   Berry's Market. *Supplies are available.*

14.7   Steelhead Beach Regional Park on left.

15.5   LEFT on Wohler Road.

16.1   RIGHT on Eastside Road.

17.3   LEFT at stop sign to stay on Eastside Road.

22.5   LEFT on Redwood Highway.

22.6   Rodney Strong Winery.

23.5   Limerick Lane Cellars on the left (half mile off the road).

23.7   Foppiano Winery.

24.1   Cross under U.S. 101.

24.9   Bridge over Russian River.

25.6   Arrive at starting point.

12. MOUNT ST. HELENA

North of Calistoga

The spectacular view from the top of Mount St. Helena makes the protracted ascent on its wide, exposed road completely worth the effort. For the best possible trip, pick a cool, clear day in late autumn, winter, or spring— forget the hot days of summer. Then pack along a picnic lunch, fill your water bottles to the brim, drive to the trailhead, and start climbing.

ROUTE DETAILS

type of trail 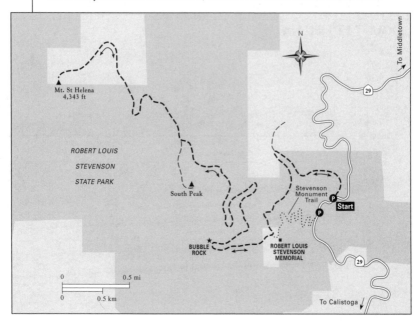 dirt road

difficulty

total distance 12 miles

riding time 2–3 hours

elevation gain 2,000 feet

You can turn off your brain for this ride, because it has only a few junctions along the entire route, and it's obvious which way to go. The dirt road's grade is fairly moderate, although unrelenting. You won't need your granny gear here, just some good aerobic endurance. And you don't have to wait until you reach the summit to reap visual rewards: You gain fine vistas of Napa Valley, the Vaca Mountains, Lake Berryessa, and the volcanic rock of the Palisades at several points along the road.

The ride starts out in a shady black oak forest, but all that changes after the first mile. Notice the terrain change as you climb: You're in big knob-cone pines, manzanita, and madrones by 1.5 miles, enjoying the open sunshine and views of the Napa Valley. Keep climbing. At a tight switchback at 1.6 miles you reach Bubble Rock, where rock climbers strut their stuff.

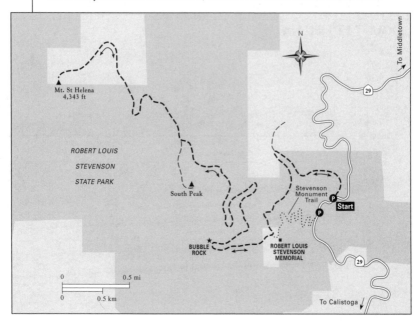

One major junction shows up at mile 4.0, along the ridgeline of Mount St. Helena. The road to the left leads to South Peak, a lesser summit at 4,003 feet. Continue straight for the mountain's higher northern summit, but not without first exclaiming over the vista from this point. This is your most expansive view so far.

Save your applause, because now you're only two miles from Mount St. Helena's summit at 4,343 feet. When you reach the top, pay no attention to the buildings and microwave equipment. Instead stroll around and take in the amazing 360-degree scene. There's Lake Berryessa and the Sierra Nevada to the east. To the southeast lies Mount Diablo, 60 miles away. Most impressive of all is the clear-day view of Mount Shasta to the north, nearly 200 miles distant. Often Mount Lassen is visible as well, with 7,056-foot Snow Mountain in the northern foreground. Pull out a map of Northern California, a pair of binoculars, and your picnic lunch.

You may notice some odd-shaped rocks under your feet on the northwest side of the wide summit. If you've ever visited Devils Postpile National Monument in the eastern Sierra, you'll recognize them; they're the five-sided tops of lava columns. Although Mount St. Helena is composed of volcanic rock, it's not a volcano. It's part of a large ancient lava flow.

For more information, contact Robert Louis Stevenson State Park, c/o Bothe-Napa Valley State Park, 707/ 942-4575 or 707/938-1519; website: www.napanet.net/~bothe.

Driving Directions

From Highway 29/128 in Calistoga, turn north on Highway 29 and drive eight miles to the gated Mount St. Helena trailhead.

MOUNT ST. HELENA

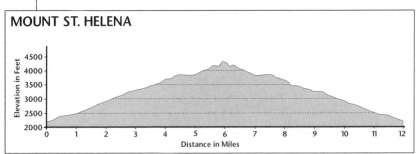

Route Directions for Mount St. Helena

0.0 Park in the pullouts alongside the gated road at the Mount St. Helena Trailhead. Start riding at the gate. *Supplies are available in Calistoga.*

0.7 LEFT at fork.

1.5 Pass the hikers-only Stevenson Monument Trail on left.

4.0 STRAIGHT at left turnoff for South Peak.

6.0 North Peak of Mount St. Helena, elevation 4,343 feet. TURN AROUND.

12.0 Arrive at starting point.

13. CAZADERO LOOP

West of Guerneville to the Sonoma Coast

Cazadero is not one of the most heavily visited towns in rural western Sonoma, nor is it one of the most populated, yet three separate roads lead to it: Old Cazadero Road, the Cazadero Highway, and Austin Creek Road. This loop trip follows narrow, winding Austin Creek Road to Cazadero on an old railroad grade that was once used to haul redwood logs to the nearby mills. Because of its origins, the road has a very gradual grade and is only one lane wide in many stretches (these were narrow-gauge trains).

ROUTE DETAILS

type of trail	paved roads with moderate car traffic
difficulty	🔋🔋🔋🔋🔋
total distance	38.2 miles
riding time	3–4 hours
elevation gain	2,000 feet

The road carves a path through dense groves of second- and third-growth redwoods, following picturesque Austin Creek the whole way. Enough homes line the road that you should expect auto traffic at any time, although you probably will encounter very little. If you tire of the somewhat rough paved surface of Austin Creek Road, you can cut over to much smoother Cazadero Highway, which parallels it, at mile 6.3. The two roads meet up again three miles later.

When you reach the bustling metropolis of Cazadero, you'll find a general store and a post office, and often a couple of dogs sleeping in the street. At one time this was a busy logging community, but Cazadero is now more famous for its annual heavy rainfall each winter.

Beyond the town you face a five-mile ascent on Fort Ross Road (1,300-foot climb), followed by a two-mile descent and another climb to a junction with Meyers Grade Road. The rest of the loop is a piece of cake, and if you are lucky enough to have clear weather, you'll enjoy ocean views as you descend to, and then ride alongside, Highway 1. From the top of Meyers Grade, the coastal view to the south expands to include Bodega Head, Tomales Bluff, and Point Reyes National Seashore. It is truly awe-inspiring.

When you reach the coast, take a short walk on the Vista Trail at the junction of Meyers Grade Road and Highway 1, or stop at one of the oceanview or riverview eateries in Jenner.

The final leg of this loop travels along busy Highway 116 back to Monte Rio, following the ever-scenic Russian River. Make a stop at Duncans Mills, which was once the site of a large lumber mill that processed the giant redwoods logged from these hills. Now it's a tiny village of shops and services.

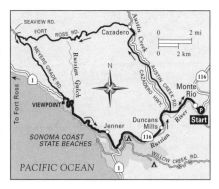

Driving Directions

From Santa Rosa, take Highway 12 five miles west to Sebastopol, then turn north on Highway 116 and drive 20 miles to Monte Rio (four miles west of Guerneville).

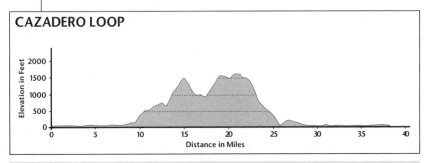

CAZADERO LOOP

Route Directions for Cazadero Loop

0.0 Park in Monte Rio near the junction of Highway 116 (River Road) and Bohemian Highway. Ride west on Highway 116. *Supplies are available in Monte Rio.*

2.7 RIGHT on Austin Creek Road.

6.3 STRAIGHT on Austin Creek Road at junction with Cazadero Highway.

9.3 LEFT on Cazadero Highway into Cazadero. *Supplies are available.*

9.7 LEFT on Fort Ross Road at junction with Old Cazadero Road and King Ridge Road; begin 5-mile climb.

15.3 Black Mountain Preserve on the left.

18.8 LEFT on Meyers Grade Road.

23.7 LEFT on Highway 1.

23.8 Vista Trail on the left. *Take a short walk on this Sonoma Coast State Beach overlook trail.*

28.5 Town of Jenner. *Supplies are available.*

30.0 LEFT on Highway 116.

33.8 Town of Duncans Mills. *Supplies are available.*

38.2 Arrive at starting point.

14. COLEMAN VALLEY LOOP

Occidental to Bodega Bay

Western Sonoma County is a land psychologically so far removed from anything to the south and east of it that it seems, well, like Shangri-la. You see a lot of sheep out here—happy-looking sheep. You'll see what I mean after you ride this loop.

Caution: bovine crossing on Coleman Valley Road.

ROUTE DETAILS

type of trail paved roads with minimal car traffic

difficulty 🍼🍼🍼🍼🍼

total distance 32.2 miles

riding time 2–3 hours

elevation gain 2,100 feet

The ride starts in the town of Occidental, a former railroad town now filled with quaint inns, good places to eat, and loads of charm. You can buy most anything you need here. From the center of town, take Coleman Valley Road west and uphill, gaining 500 feet in the first two miles to the ridgeline. Watch for the old Coleman Valley schoolhouse, built in 1864 and one of the oldest still standing in California.

After a long and glorious ridgeline ramble through bucolic meadows, followed by a fast and furious 900-foot descent to the coast (prepare to brake for cows or sheep crossing the road), you find yourself at Highway 1 across from Coleman Beach. Shake your head a few times to be sure the idyllic landscape you just experienced wasn't a beautiful dream. What you're about to ride isn't either—a couple of miles of seaside cruising with the waves breaking a few feet to your right.

When you reach the town of Bodega Bay, turn off on East Shore Road to cruise the perimeter of Bodega Harbor, a level, three-mile stretch that passes fishing boats and fish processing plants. Follow the road all the way to the tip of Bodega Head, then take the right fork to the west parking lot for a lovely ocean view, or climb up the Bodega Head Trail from there.

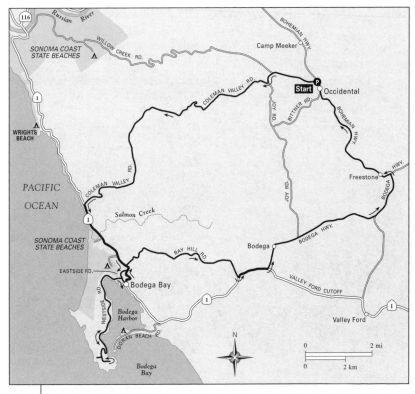

After enjoying the ocean air and salt spray, backtrack out of the harbor and take Bay Hill Road out of town. This peaceful eucalyptus-lined road climbs 600 feet from the coast, affording fine views of Bodega Bay over your right shoulder. Then it's downhill to Highway 1, and downhill some more to the town of Bodega. Of note: The town of Bodega, not Bodega Bay, was the setting for the Alfred Hitchcock movie *The Birds*. The old schoolhouse in the movie is located on Bodega Lane.

The last stretch follows Bodega Highway to Bohemian Highway and Freestone, where you might want to get a massage at Osmosis spa if your muscles are aching. If not, it's less than four miles back to your car in Occidental. Note that many riders opt to take Joy Road and Bittner Road back to Occidental (from just east of Bodega). Although these roads have less car traffic than the route suggested here, Joy Road includes a steep climb.

Driving Directions

From Santa Rosa, drive west on Highway 12 for five miles to Sebastopol. At the junction with Highway 116, continue straight on Bodega Highway for 5.7 miles, then turn right on Bohemian Highway. Drive 3.8 miles into the town of Occidental.

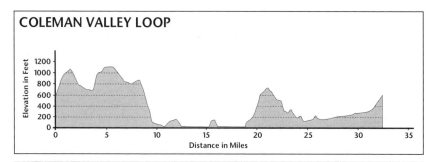

COLEMAN VALLEY LOOP

Route Directions for Coleman Valley Loop

0.0 Park in downtown Occidental near the intersection of Bohemian Highway and Coleman Valley Road. Ride west on Coleman Valley Road. *Supplies are available in town.*

1.8 RIGHT to stay on Coleman Valley Road.

10.1 LEFT on Highway 1 into Bodega Bay. *Supplies are available in town; water is available at campgrounds.*

12.4 RIGHT on East Shore Road.

12.5 RIGHT on West Shore Road. Ride out and back three miles along the edge of Bodega Harbor (road becomes Bay Flat Road). *Take the right fork to west parking lot for an ocean view and easy hike on Bodega Head Trail.*

15.5 Dead end at Bodega Head. TURN AROUND.

18.5 LEFT on East Shore Road.

18.6 LEFT on Highway 1.

18.7 RIGHT on Bay Hill Road (cross Highway 1 carefully).

22.6 LEFT on Highway 1.

23.5 LEFT on Bodega Highway.

24.0 Pass through town of Bodega. *Supplies are available.*

28.4 LEFT on Bohemian Highway.

28.7 Pass through town of Freestone. *Supplies are available.*

32.2 Arrive at starting point.

15. LEDSON MARSH & LAKE ILSANJO LOOP

Annadel State Park east of Santa Rosa

Annadel State Park (707/539-3911 or 707/938-1519) is a horsey kind of place. If you count the horse trailers in the parking lot, hoofprints all over the place, and horse manure along the trail, you might think more horses visit here than people.

grasslands and oaks near Lake Ilsanjo in Annadel State Park

ROUTE DETAILS

type of trail dirt roads and single-track

difficulty

total distance 14.2 miles

riding time 2–3 hours

elevation gain 1,400 feet

But Annadel is also a mountain biker's place. Not just the ranch roads but also most of the single-track at Annadel is open to bikes. That's convenient, because you need to cover a lot of ground to see Annadel's 5,000 acres, filled with woodlands, meadows, creeks, wildflowers, and even a 26-acre lake.

Pick up a park map at the ranger kiosk on your way in. Since 1997 Annadel's multiple trails have been undergoing reconstruction and repair in an effort to protect the park's delicate meadows, marshes, and archaeological sites. If you haven't ridden here in a few years, you'll notice a lot of changes.

This loop ride shows off two of Annadel's highlights: Ledson Marsh and Lake Ilsanjo. The riding is generally easy to moderate; the only difficulty is controlling your bike on some of the rocky trails and roads. Annadel is famous for its rocks. In the early 1900s the area was extensively quarried to provide cobblestone for the city of San Francisco.

The trip starts at the trailhead at the end of Channel Drive. Take the wide ranch road uphill through a dense and shady Douglas fir forest, with a few redwoods and bay laurels for variety. At 2.1 miles you'll head east on newly rebuilt, single-track South Burma Trail, connecting with Marsh Trail and

Ridge Trail to circle around Ledson Marsh. The marsh is popular with waterfowl and is a known habitat for the red-legged frog.

Next, you'll head west to loop back via Lake Ilsanjo. From the lake's earthen dam you gain the best views of blue water, tules, and paddling water birds. Curious about the origin of the lake's moniker? Ilsanjo is a combination of Ilsa and Joe, the names of the land's former owners.

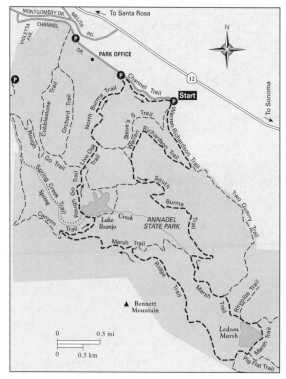

On the west side of Ilsanjo, head north on Rough Go, Live Oak, and North Burma Trails to connect to Channel Trail, which parallels the road you drove in on. Level Channel Trail heads back to the parking lot and your car.

Driving Directions

From U.S. 101 in Santa Rosa, take the Fairgrounds/Highway 12 exit. Highway 12 becomes Farmers Lane as it heads through downtown Santa Rosa. Turn right on Montgomery Drive and drive 2.7 miles (veering to the right), then turn right on Channel Drive. It's 2.2 miles to the end of the road and the parking lot.

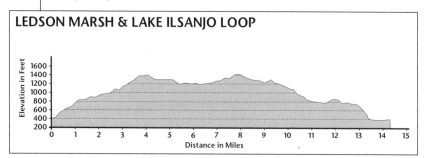

LEDSON MARSH & LAKE ILSANJO LOOP

Route Directions for Ledson Marsh & Lake Ilsanjo Loop

0.0 Park at the lot at the end of Channel Drive. Take wide Warren Richardson Trail uphill. *Supplies are available in Santa Rosa.*

0.8 RIGHT to stay on Warren Richardson Trail.

1.5 LEFT to stay on Warren Richardson Trail.

1.9 STRAIGHT to stay on Warren Richardson Trail.

2.1 LEFT on South Burma Trail (wonderful new single-track).

4.1 LEFT on Marsh Trail.

5.0 RIGHT to stay on Marsh Trail.

5.4 Ledson Marsh; trail circles around it to the left.

6.4 RIGHT on Ridge Trail.

9.1 LEFT on Marsh Trail.

10.6 RIGHT on Canyon Trail to Lake Ilsanjo.

11.2 LEFT at Lake Ilsanjo.

11.4 STRAIGHT on Rough Go Trail.

11.9 STRAIGHT on Live Oak Trail.

12.7 LEFT on North Burma Trail.

13.4 RIGHT on Channel Trail.

14.2 Arrive at starting point.

16. BALD MOUNTAIN LOOP

Sugarloaf Ridge State Park north of Sonoma

Although the grassy summit of Bald Mountain at 2,729 feet is the crowning glory of this loop trip in Sugarloaf Ridge State Park (707/833-5712 or 707/938-1519), each leg of the route presents its own rewards. This ride takes the most direct path to the summit, then loops back downhill on a roundabout tour of the park's varied terrain.

ROUTE DETAILS

type of trail　dirt road and paved bike path

difficulty

total distance　6.5 miles

riding time　1.5 hours

elevation gain　1,500 feet

The short mileage might make this ride seem easy, but keep in mind that you must gain 1,500 feet in less than three miles. The climb is made easier because it mostly follows Bald Mountain Trail, a paved service road. Hooray for pavement on a steep ascent.

The road begins in a hardwood forest but quickly climbs through slopes covered with ceanothus, manzanita, chemise, and toyon. The scented chaparral will take your attention away from the asphalt. At 2.4 miles, the pavement ends at a saddle and trail junction. The left fork leads to microwave-covered Red Mountain at 2,548 feet. You'll go right for Bald Mountain, now following a dirt fire road. The final half mile to the summit ascends grassy slopes with occasional outcrops of green serpentine. The dirt road curves around the north side of the mountain to meet Gray Pine Trail, the return of your loop. But first, take the short spur on the right to reach the 2,729-foot summit. It's bald indeed; not a single tree obstructs the sweeping view.

Two signs at the top identify all the neighboring landmarks, including Mount St. Helena, Mount Diablo, Bodega Bay, Mount Wittenberg in Point Reyes, Snow Mountain, Mount Tamalpais, the Golden Gate Bridge towers, Angel Island, and the Bay Bridge. Most impressive is the glimpse of the Sierra Nevada mountain range, 130 miles away. A posted quote from author Robert Louis Stevenson sums it up: "There are days in a life when thus to climb out of the lowlands seems like scaling heaven."

From the summit, wide Gray Pine Trail descends swiftly along a ridge. You're likely to have the least company on this side of the park, which is good because you'll need to concentrate on managing your downhill speed. A final stint on Meadow Trail is best ridden in springtime, when the trail's namesake meadow is littered with wildflowers: Douglas iris, California poppies, brodiaea, and blue-eyed grass. Often you'll spot deer grazing among them.

Driving Directions

From U.S. 101 in Santa Rosa, take the Fairgrounds/Highway 12 exit. Highway 12 becomes Farmers Lane as it heads through downtown Santa Rosa.

Bald Mountain Loop

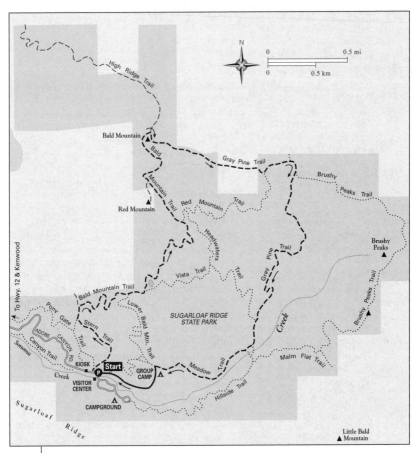

Continue on Highway 12 for 11 miles to Adobe Canyon Road and turn left. (Or, from Highway 12 in Sonoma, drive 11 miles north to Adobe Canyon Road, then turn right.) Drive 3.5 miles to the park entrance kiosk. Park in the lot about 100 yards past the kiosk, on the left.

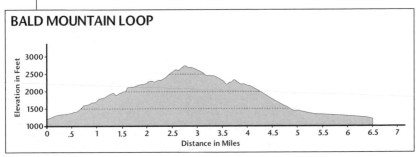

Route Directions for Bald Mountain Loop

0.0   Park in the lot 100 yards past the entrance kiosk. Pick up Stern Trail, a wide paved road, by the kiosk. *Supplies are available in Kenwood.*

0.5   RIGHT on Bald Mountain Trail.

2.4   RIGHT at junction with trail to Red Mountain; pavement ends.

2.8   RIGHT on Gray Pine Trail, but first walk up short right spur to summit to check out all the landmarks.

3.9   RIGHT to stay on Gray Pine Trail.

5.3   RIGHT on Meadow Trail.

6.2   LEFT through parking lot. Follow paved road.

6.5   Arrive at starting point.

17. YOUNTVILLE & SILVERADO TRAIL

Napa Valley

This wine country ramble takes you past dozens of wineries and vineyards on a five-mile stretch of the famous Silverado Trail, plus gives you a tour of the restaurants, inns, and shops of Yountville, one of Napa County's charming towns. Take along a bike lock so you can stop at some of the wineries along the route. This is not a ride for hurrying.

ROUTE DETAILS

type of trail	paved roads with moderate car traffic
difficulty	
total distance	18 miles
riding time	1.5–2 hours
elevation gain	500 feet

The riding is mostly level, and although car traffic can be dense on weekends, the shoulders are wide on the more heavily traveled roads. Be forewarned that you do have to ride on busy Highway 29 for just under a mile, but the wide shoulder should give you confidence through this congested stretch.

In addition to the 10 major wineries you'll pass (Robert Sinskey, Silverado, Pine Ridge, Stagg's Leap, Regusci, Chimney Rock, Clos du Val, Christina, Trefethen, and Trio) you'll also have the chance to visit two champagne makers: small S. Anderson on Yountville Cross Road, and giant Domain Chandon on California Drive. Technically their products must be called sparkling wine, not champagne, since their grapes are grown here in California, not in the Champagne region of France.

It's convenient to end your trip with a visit to Domaine Chandon (707/994-8844), located right across from where you parked your car. Nothing beats a little bubbly for celebrating a great ride in the Wine Country.

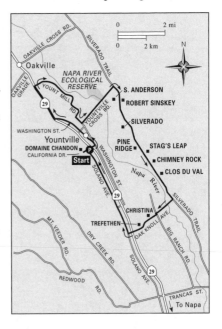

Driving Directions

From Napa, drive north on Highway 29 for nine miles to Yountville. Take the Yountville/Veterans Home exit, turn left on California Drive and cross under the highway. Park in the large gravel pullout on the left, next to the railroad tracks and across from the Veterans Home sign.

YOUNTVILLE & SILVERADO TRAIL

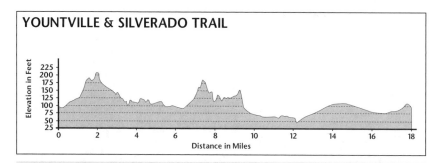

Route Directions for Yountville & Silverado Trail

0.0 Park at the junction of California Drive and Solano Avenue, in the gravel pull-out by the railroad tracks. Ride back under the highway on California Drive. *Supplies are available in Yountville.*

0.1 LEFT on Washington.

0.8 LEFT at Y to stay on Washington.

1.8 RIGHT on Hwy 29.

2.7 RIGHT on Yount Mill Road.

3.9 RIGHT to stay on Yount Mill.

5.0 LEFT on Yount Cross Road.

6.0 Napa River Ecological Reserve on left.

6.6 S. Anderson Champagne.

6.9 RIGHT on Silverado Trail (wide bike lane). *Robert Sinskey, Silverado, Pine Ridge, Stagg's Leap, Regusci, Chimney Rock, and Clos du Val wineries are found in the next four miles. Stop for tours and tasting wherever you please.*

11.5 RIGHT on Oak Knoll Avenue.

12.4 LEFT on Big Ranch Road, then immediate RIGHT to get back on Oak Knoll.

12.7 Christina Vineyards.

13.1 Trefethen Winery.

13.6 Cross Highway 29.

13.7 RIGHT on Solano Avenue.

15.8 Trio Vineyards.

17.1 Ride past your parked car and under the gates of Domaine Chandon.

17.5 Domaine Chandon Visitor Center. TURN AROUND.

18.0 Arrive at starting point.

18. SKYLINE WILDERNESS PARK

Napa Valley

The trailhead for Skyline "wilderness park" is located in an RV park packed with trailers, lawn chairs, and plastic flamingos. You can't access Skyline's fine trails without riding past the park's social hall and picnic areas, and through a corridor of chain-link fencing. (The latter passes by neighboring state hospital property.) It's an incongruous start to a nature-filled mountain bike ride.

ROUTE DETAILS

type of trail dirt road and single-track

difficulty

total distance 6.8 miles

riding time 1.5 hours

elevation gain 1,200 feet

Still, after a couple minutes of this strange meandering, you leave it all behind and enter the quiet, steep-walled canyon of Marie Creek. The loop's first leg follows a wide fire road uphill alongside the creek for two miles to Lake Marie, a long, narrow reservoir that is popular with bass fishermen. If you can look up while you're climbing, you'll notice striking cliff formations and caves among the dense forest of oaks, madrones, and bay laurel. Watch for the 100-year-old fig tree on the left at mile 1.3, near the junction with Bayleaf Trail. The enormous old tree still produces edible fruit.

At Lake Marie, cross over the lake's dam and turn right on Chaparral Trail. From here on out, the rest of your loop is single-track—and some of it is surprisingly technical, earning this brief ride its #3 rating for difficulty. (This park was once the site of the World Cup mountain bike race. If you ride here, you're in good company.)

Chaparral Trail climbs up a slick, rocky, steep stretch (I walked my bike here) to join Skyline Trail, a part of the Bay Area Ridge Trail. Narrow Skyline

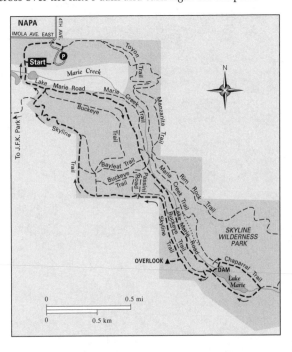

Trail follows the park's southwest ridge for 3.5 miles, offering good views of Napa Valley and San Pablo Bay. Watch for stretches of old stone walls amid the oak grasslands, and some fine examples of buckeye, live oak, and bay. This is lovely country. You'll note that Skyline Trail is well named: From a high overlook at 3.6 miles you can clearly make out the looming outline of Mount Tamalpais in Marin County. Looking north and west, you'll gain views of Mount Veeder and Sugarloaf Mountain.

The park has other single-track trails open to mountain bikes, so when you finish this ride, you can do more exploring. Just make sure you ride only on legal trails; the park is quite serious about enforcing this here.

For more information, contact Skyline Wilderness Park, 707/252-0481.

Driving Directions

From Highway 29 in Napa, turn east on Imola Avenue. Follow Imola Avenue four miles to its end at Fourth Avenue. Turn right into the park entrance.

SKYLINE WILDERNESS PARK

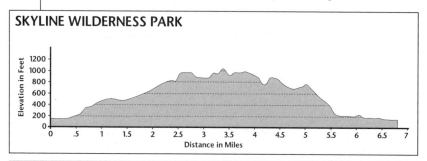

Route Directions for Skyline Wilderness Park

0.0 Park at the signed parking area for Skyline Wilderness Park ($5 fee). Follow the signs through the RV park to the actual trailhead. *Supplies are available in Napa.*

0.3 LEFT on Lake Marie Road.

2.3 LEFT across dam at Lake Marie.

2.4 RIGHT on Chaparral Trail (you may be walking and carrying your bike here).

2.9 RIGHT on Skyline Trail.

3.8 Indistinct trail to viewpoint leads right; take short trail to highest point on this ride.

4.4 Cross over Passini Road.

6.5 RIGHT to return to Lake Marie Road's start.

6.8 Arrive at starting point.

CHAPTER 3

Monterey and Big Sur

I t wouldn't be easy to choose the most spectacular stretch of California coastline, but if pressed, most beach connoisseurs would agree there is nothing quite as visually stunning as the 130 miles of cliffs, rocks, and waves that run from Davenport to San Simeon. Cyclists have been traveling this stretch of Highway 1 ever since the road was built in the 1930s. Along the way, they stop on top of 200-foot-high cliffs to admire the crashing surf, cross over concrete bridges spanning precipitous river gorges, and experience mile after mile of postcard-quality coastal scenery.

There is nothing to dislike here, from the mild climate to the wild landscape. Much of this area is isolated, undeveloped, and difficult to access, with high cliffs and few roads. Visiting this land means wandering along gravel beaches, watching sunsets over glimmering seas, and walking in the shadows of giant redwoods. South of Carmel, services are clustered in a few small towns: Big Sur, Lucia, Gorda, and San Simeon. In between is silence, solitude, and the sea.

In the midst of all this splendor, every winter and spring, like clockwork, a great natural spectacle occurs: gray whales pass by on their long migrations. Traveling from their summer home in Alaska's Bering Sea to their winter breeding grounds in Baja, then back again a few months later, they leave hundreds of frothy spouts and occasional glimpses of fins or tails as their calling cards. Any spot along the Monterey and Big Sur coastline is a good place to observe the more than 18,000 gray whales as they cruise by—but the bluffs of Andrew Molera State Park, open to mountain bikers, and the stretch of Highway 1 between Big Sur and Lucia, popular with road cyclists, are two of the better sighting areas. Whale watching is at its best from December to May, on days when the sea is flat and deep blue, with no wind or whitecaps.

Besides watching whales, there's much more to keep a bicyclist occupied in the Monterey and Big Sur region. To the north, mountain bikers cruise the trails of Wilder Ranch and Forest of Nisene Marks State Parks near Santa Cruz, or head for the more remote single-track of Soquel Demonstration State Forest and Fort Ord. To the south, they ride the dirt roads of Los Padres National Forest, including the spectacular trek up to Cone Peak Fire Lookout. Road cyclists have myriad coastal and inland routes to choose from in and around Monterey Bay, including the world-famous 17-Mile Drive with its ocean lookouts, golf courses, and mansions. And riders of all styles and abilities can pedal on the 14.5-mile Monterey Recreation Trail that runs from Marina to Pacific Grove, passing by highlights such as the Monterey Bay Aquarium and Cannery Row.

Whatever kind of riding you enjoy, you'll find the right trail in the Monterey and Big Sur region. Here at "the greatest meeting of land and sea" lies a world of bicycling opportunities.

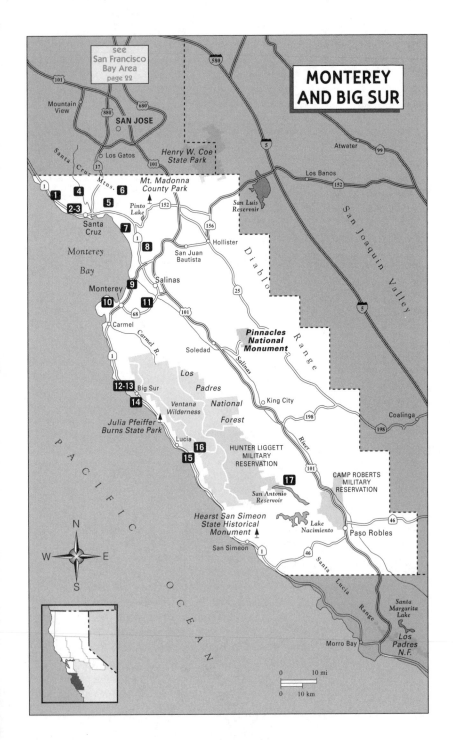

CHAPTER 3
MONTEREY AND BIG SUR

 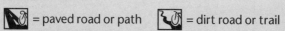
 = paved road or path   = dirt road or trail

1. DAVENPORT TO SANTA CRUZ LOOP

North of Santa Cruz

This loop road ride has a little bit of everything: coastal riding along Highway 1, a car-free recreation path along the beaches of Santa Cruz, and a hill climb workout on the forested backroads northeast of Santa Cruz.

ROUTE DETAILS

type of trail paved roads with moderate car traffic

difficulty

total distance 31.4 miles

riding time 3 hours

elevation gain 1,900 feet

You might want to start your ride with a hearty breakfast at the Davenport Cash Store. Then take off south on Highway 1, passing the entrance to Wilder Ranch State Park on your way to Santa Cruz. Once you're on the recreational trail that runs through Natural Bridges State Beach and alongside West Cliff Drive, you'll enjoy glorious coastside cruising with blue-water views. This is a popular path, though, so watch out for the usual gamut of baby strollers, in-line skaters, walkers, and the like. For some local color, stop at the Santa Cruz surfing museum in the old lighthouse building at mile 11.6. In the autumn and winter months, even brighter local color is found at Natural Bridges, where monarch butterflies nest in the eucalyptus trees.

Gear down for a climb up Bay Street and Empire Grade, passing by the entrance to the University of California, Santa Cruz. If you tire of the steady ascent, you can take a shortcut on Smith Grade at mile 19.3; otherwise, continue onward to Ice Cream Grade. This is a fun descent on a narrow, winding road. A left turn on Pine Flat Road brings you to Bonny Doon Winery (831/425-4518), where you can sample varietals and enjoy the view from the picnic area. Then check your brakes, because you're heading for a 10 percent downhill grade on Bonny Doon Road dropping down to Highway 1. One final northward mile brings you back to Davenport,

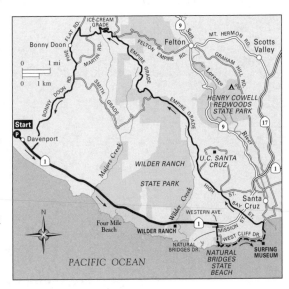

but you might choose to simply cross Highway 1 instead and head for the beach.

Note that although I describe the ride starting in the quaint coastal town of Davenport, you could just as easily join the loop from the University of California, Santa Cruz or downtown Santa Cruz.

Driving Directions

From Santa Cruz, drive north on Highway 1 for 11 miles to Davenport.

DAVENPORT TO SANTA CRUZ LOOP

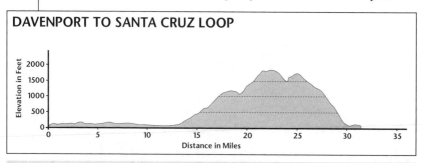

Route Directions for Davenport to Santa Cruz Loop

0.0 Park in downtown Davenport. Ride south on Highway 1. *Supplies are available in Davenport.*

7.0 Wilder Ranch State Park on the right. *Water is available.*

8.7 RIGHT on Western Drive.

8.8 RIGHT on Mission Street.

8.9 LEFT on Natural Bridges Drive.

9.2 STRAIGHT through gate into Natural Bridges State Beach (follow pavement). *Lock up your bike and walk the short trail to see the monarch butterflies from September to December.*

9.7 STRAIGHT on West Cliff Drive (exit Natural Bridges State Beach). Follow paved recreation trail alongside the road.

11.6 Surfing museum and Seal Rock on the right.

12.3 LEFT on Bay Street. Begin climb.

13.3 Cross Highway 1.

14.4 LEFT on High Street at entrance to the University of California, Santa Cruz; High Street becomes Empire Grade.

19.3 STRAIGHT at junction with Smith Grade on left. *Shortcut is possible by turning left here; it cuts off three miles.*

22.6 LEFT on Ice Cream Grade.

25.2 LEFT on Pine Flat Road at T-junction.

26.9 STRAIGHT on Bonny Doon Road; Bonny Doon Winery is on the left. *Wine tasting is available from 11 A.M. to 5 P.M. daily.*

30.4 RIGHT on Highway 1. *Or cross the highway and head for the beach on the other side of the railroad tracks.*

31.4 Arrive at starting point.

2. WILDER RANCH INLAND LOOP

Wilder Ranch State Park north of Santa Cruz

Wilder Ranch State Park's 5,100-acre north side is almost completely the domain of mountain bikers. The experience here is a lot like visiting a mountain bike park at the ski areas around Tahoe or Mammoth. Looking upward from the bottom of Wilder's coastal hills, dozens of bikers race toward you, each carving perfect S-turns on their descent down the slope. The park's 30 miles of trails seem to have been built with mountain biking in mind: They rollercoaster up and down with plenty of twists, turns, and a number of technical challenges, such as stream crossings and rock beds.

The inland trails at Wilder Ranch provide wide views of coast and hills.

ROUTE DETAILS

type of trail — dirt road and single-track

difficulty — 🍼🍼🍼🍼🍼

total distance — 9.1 miles (or 10.7 miles)

riding time — 2 hours

elevation gain — 800 feet

Not surprisingly, it's a popular place, but there's no reason to be intimidated by the crowds, even on sunny, busy weekends. The park is large enough to accommodate everybody. A major plus is the great view of Monterey Bay and the Pacific Ocean, visible from several high points in these coastal hills. You just have to be willing to climb a bit.

A wide range of possible loops exist at Wilder, but most start with an ascent on wide Wilder Ridge Trail. The loop outlined here is a solid intermediate ride with a good dose of single-track and some challenges to test your skills. The single-track begins at mile 1.2 mile where Wilder Ridge Loop Trail meanders around the open coastal hills through dozens of curves and turns. Next comes a stint on Zane Gray, with some steep uphill challenges, fol-

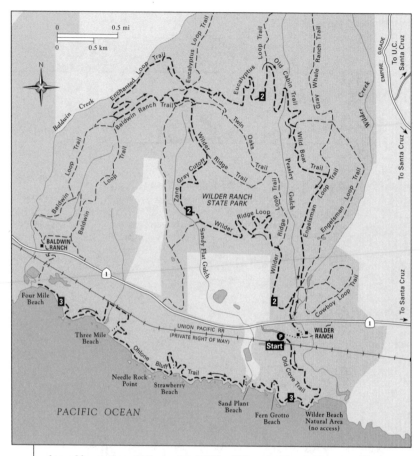

lowed by more uphill on wide Wilder Ridge Fire Road. Then you'll experience some fun single-track on Eucalyptus Loop and Old Cabin Trail, both which head steeply down, then up, a wooded gulch.

If you want to add a couple of more miles, tack on to this loop the 1.6-mile Enchanted Loop, which starts and ends at the rather confusing junction at mile 4.5. Its steep single-track and fire road pitches up and down through a dense redwood forest lined with sorrel and ferns along Baldwin Creek. This is what mountain biking was meant to be.

For more information, contact Wilder Ranch State Park at 831/423-9703 or 831/429-2851.

Driving Directions

From Santa Cruz, drive north on Highway 1 for four miles. Turn left into the entrance for Wilder Ranch State Park, then follow the park road to its end at the main parking area.

Wilder Ranch Inland Loop

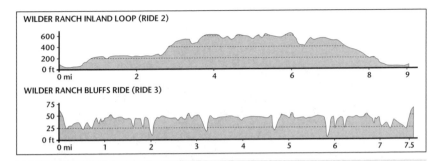

Route Directions for Wilder Ranch Inland Loop

0.0 Park at the main lot at Wilder Ranch. Walk your bike on the paved trail from the parking lot to the cultural preserve/ranch buildings. Walk past the buildings and picnic area, then ride your bike through the tunnel to the east side of Highway 1. *Supplies are available in Davenport to the north or Santa Cruz to the south.*

0.4 Hairpin LEFT on Wilder Ridge Fire Road.

1.2 LEFT on Wilder Ridge single-track.

3.0 RIGHT on Zane Gray single-track.

3.9 LEFT on Wilder Ridge Fire Road.

4.5 STRAIGHT on paved road toward Eucalyptus Loop at confusing junction. Or to add on 1.6 miles, turn left on Enchanted Loop, which will bring you back to this junction.

4.7 RIGHT on Eucalyptus Loop single-track.

5.9 RIGHT on connector to Old Cabin Trail.

7.0 RIGHT on fire road.

7.2 LEFT on Wild Boar Trail.

7.5 RIGHT on Engelsman Loop Trail.

8.7 STRAIGHT at junction with Wilder Ridge Fire Road. Ride past corrals, through tunnel, then walk bike through cultural center.

9.1 Arrive at starting point.

3. WILDER RANCH BLUFFS RIDE

Wilder Ranch State Park north of Santa Cruz

Old Cove Landing and Ohlone Bluff Trails are exactly the opposite of all other trails at Wilder Ranch State Park (831/423-9703 or 831/429-2851). These trails are coastal; the park's other trails are inland. These trails are almost completely level; the park's other trails are rollercoasting climbs and descents.

Old Cove Landing and Ohlone Bluff Trails trace the edge of oceanside cliffs at Wilder Ranch.

© ANN MARIE BROWN

ROUTE DETAILS

type of trail — dirt road and single-track

difficulty 🍶🍶🍶🍶🍶

total distance 7.6

riding time 1.5 hours

elevation gain 200 feet

For easy riding, a cruise on Old Cove Landing and Ohlone Bluff Trails is a great way to spend an afternoon at Wilder Ranch State Park. The trails reveal many surprises, including dramatic cliffs and sea arches, a seal rookery, windswept beaches, and a hidden fern cave.

Old Cove Landing Trail begins from the main parking lot to the right of the restrooms. Begin riding on a level ranch road through the park's agricultural preserve—nearly 900 acres of brussels sprout fields. The trail heads toward the coast, then turns right and parallels it. You're pedaling on top of sandstone and mudstone bluffs, the remains of an ancient marine terrace. In short order you'll pass a wooden platform overlooking Wilder Beach, a critical habitat area for the endangered snowy plover, followed by the trail's namesake, the old landing cove—a remarkably narrow inlet where small schooners pulled in and anchored to load lumber in the late 1800s.

Continuing onward, you'll cruise by a huge flat rock where harbor seals hang out, laying around in the sun to warm their flippers. At a wooden post marked as number 8, look down on Fern Grotto Beach, a small sandy cove. Tucked into its back wall is a shallow cave filled with sword and bracken ferns. A spur trail leads to it; you can carry your bike down and explore the cave if you please.

Beyond Fern Grotto Beach lie several more beaches. Accessing them, however, requires a little upper body strength. At Sand Plant Beach, a sign directs you down to the beach and across the sand. You'll have to carry your bike. Then follow another trail back up to the bluffs on the beach's south side. (The bluffs above Sand Plant Beach are private farming property; most of the year bikers are not permitted to ride through.)

Once you're back on the bluffs south of Sand Plant, the trail name changes to Ohlone Bluff Trail and travels 2.5 miles farther, past Strawberry Beach, Needle Rock, Three Mile Beach, and finally Four Mile Beach, a strip of sand well known for its clothing-optional tendencies. At Four Mile, the trail turns inland, crosses the railroad tracks, then passes through a tunnel under Highway 1 to connect to Baldwin Loop Trail on the east side of the park. Some riders connect to the inland trails this way, but the vast majority simply turn around and head back the way they came, enjoying the coastal scenery from the opposite perspective.

Driving Directions

From Santa Cruz, drive north on Highway 1 for four miles. Turn left into the entrance for Wilder Ranch State Park, then follow the park road to its end at the main parking area.

For trail map and elevation profile, see pages 205–206 (Ride 2—Wilder Ranch Inland Loop).

Route Directions for Wilder Ranch Bluffs Ride

0.0 Park at the main lot at Wilder Ranch. Take the signed Old Cove Landing Trail from the right side of the restrooms. *Supplies are available in Davenport to the north or Santa Cruz to the south.*

1.0 Fern Grotto Beach at marker 8.

1.3 Sand Plant Beach. Follow trail down to beach, across sand, and back up bluffs on other side (carry your bike).

1.9 Strawberry Beach.

2.6 Three Mile Beach

3.8 Four Mile Beach. TURN AROUND.

7.6 Arrive at starting point.

4. HENRY COWELL REDWOODS RAMBLE

Henry Cowell Redwoods State Park in Felton

Henry Cowell Redwoods State Park (831/335-4598 or 831/429-2851) is celebrated for its ancient groves of coast redwoods. It's famous for its Roaring Camp Railroad steam trains, which roar over tracks carving through the center of the park. And it's well known for the San Lorenzo River, which provides good swimming for park visitors in summer, and rushing waters for salmon and steelhead in winter.

Pipeline Road in Henry Cowell Redwoods meanders through dense forest.

ROUTE DETAILS

type of trail dirt road and paved bike path

difficulty 🍶🍶🍶🍶🍶

total distance 7.4 miles (or 9.7-mile option)

riding time 1.5 hours

elevation gain 850 feet

But while bicyclists may enjoy all these aspects of Henry Cowell Redwoods State Park, what they'll really like is Pipeline Road, a paved service road that travels the park's length. A few dirt roads branch off the paved route, giving mountain bikers a chance to see more of the park.

The initial, paved part of the ride travels through a forest of second- and third-growth redwoods, Douglas firs, and bay laurel, and passes by a railroad trestle crossing over the San Lorenzo River. (Don't be surprised if a steam train comes barreling through.) Although the river is only a few inches deep in summer, it can be 20 or 30 feet deep during winter rains.

The second mile of pavement climbs steeply to a ridgeline, from which

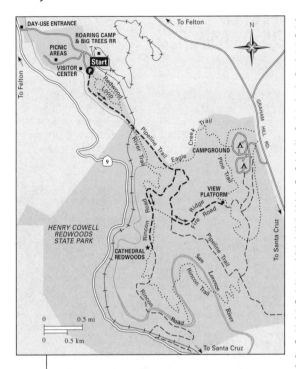

you can see all the way down the San Lorenzo River canyon to Monterey Bay and the Pacific Ocean. At a major junction of trails at mile 2.3, take Powder Mill Fire Road uphill (expect to encounter some annoying sandy patches where you'll lose traction) to a concrete observation deck. There you'll find a picnic table and water fountain, plus two surprising types of trees—knobcone pines and ponderosa pines. The latter, with its distinctive jigsaw-puzzle bark, usually is found at much higher elevations in places like the Sierra Nevada mountains. Walk up the observation deck's stairs and you'll have a somewhat obstructed view of Monterey Bay. (The trees have grown up since the deck was built.)

The park map makes it seem obvious to loop back from the observation deck by continuing on Ridge Fire Road, but this stretch is unrideable due to deep sand and foot-high stairsteps (drain bars). Instead, retrace your tire tracks down Powder Mill Road and Pipeline Road, then take Rincon Fire Road to Cathedral Redwoods, a peaceful grove of big trees. This is the suggested turnaround for this ride, but if you don't mind losing (and then having to regain) another 400 feet in elevation in the next half mile, you could continue down to the San Lorenzo River, where swimming holes abound in summer. Some riders choose to loop back on Highway 9 from this point, but the heavy traffic should discourage you. If you insist on doing so, you must carry your bike across the river, follow the service road for a half mile, then turn right on Highway 9 and ride three miles back to the park, for a 9.7-mile round-trip.

Driving Directions
From Santa Cruz at the junction of Highways 1 and 9, take Highway 9 north six miles to the right turnoff for Henry Cowell Redwoods State Park. Continue past the entrance kiosk to the visitor center and main parking lot.

HENRY COWELL REDWOODS RAMBLE

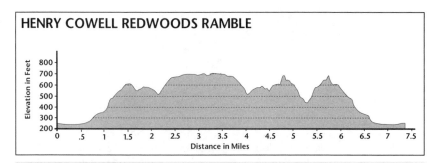

Route Directions for Henry Cowell Redwoods Ramble

0.0 Park at the main day-use lot, then follow the signs to the Redwood Grove and Nature Center. Take the paved road that leads to the right of the Nature Center to connect to Pipeline Road (behind the Nature Center). *Supplies are available in Felton. Water is available in the park.*

0.6 Pass railroad bridge over San Lorenzo River.

2.3 LEFT on Powder Mill Fire Road.

2.9 LEFT on Ridge Fire Road.

3.1 Observation deck. TURN AROUND. *Water is available.*

3.3 RIGHT on Powder Mill Fire Road.

3.9 RIGHT on Pipeline Road.

4.7 LEFT on Ridge Fire Road.

4.9 LEFT on Rincon Fire Road.

5.3 Cathedral Redwoods. TURN AROUND. *Or continue steeply downhill for .5 mile to swimming holes in the San Lorenzo River. See possible loop option in the route description above.*

5.7 RIGHT on Ridge Fire Road.

5.9 LEFT on Pipeline Road.

7.4 Arrive at starting point.

5. APTOS CREEK FIRE ROAD TO SAND POINT

Forest of Nisene Marks State Park east of Santa Cruz

Two major forces have shaped the land at Forest of Nisene Marks State Park (831/763-7063 or 831/429-2851): the railroad and unstable geology. Old-growth redwoods remained untouched in this steep and winding canyon for hundreds of years until the Loma Prieta Lumber Company came into ownership in 1881. Teaming up with Southern Pacific, they built a railroad along Aptos Creek and worked the land with trains, oxen, skid roads, inclines, horses, and as many men as they could hire, removing 140 million board feet of lumber over the course of 40 years. In 1922, when the loggers finally put their saws down, there were no trees left.

ROUTE DETAILS

type of trail   dirt road

difficulty   (4 for longer option)

total distance   13.8 miles (or 20.8-mile option)

riding time   3 hours

elevation gain   1,400 feet (or 2,400-foot option)

Luckily, Mother Nature has been busy in the last 80 years. Today the canyon is filled with second-growth redwoods and Douglas firs, and the higher ridges are lined with oaks, eucalyptus, and madrones.

Mother Nature was especially busy on October 17, 1989, when the park was the

epicenter of the famous Loma Prieta earthquake, which forcefully shook the entire San Francisco Bay Area. You'll ride past the earthquake epicenter on this out-and-back tour, which follows Aptos Creek Fire Road to Sand Point Overlook.

The ride is simple to follow, shaded all the way, and without a lot of technical challenges. The first 2.6 miles are inevitably the most crowded; the grade is so mellow here that even children can ride it. From George's Picnic Area, the hard-packed dirt road

taking a break alongside Aptos Creek

parallels Aptos Creek, climbing almost imperceptibly. After crossing a steel bridge and passing the earthquake epicenter area, the road's grade abruptly intensifies. You're entering a stretch known as the Molino Incline, which makes several hairpin turns as it ascends 660 feet in slightly over a mile. An incline railway just west of the road once lowered logs straight down the ridge to the mill on Aptos Creek. If you can make it to the "Top of the Incline" at 4.0 miles, the rest of the route seems easier. From the "Top of the Incline" to Santa Rosalia Mountain, Aptos Creek Fire Road follows the loggers' narrow-gauge logging railroad. It ascends more gently for the final three miles to Sand Point Overlook at 1,617 feet in elevation." The view from Sand Point is an open vista of Monterey Bay and the tree-filled canyons and ridges of the Santa Cruz Mountains. You'll probably share the overlook with a posse of other happy riders, especially on weekend afternoons.

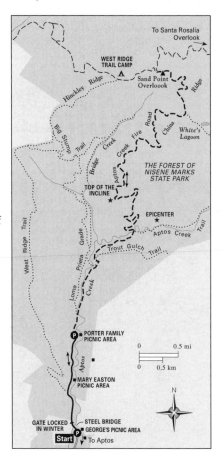

If you haven't had your fill of climbing, you can continue uphill from Sand Point; Aptos Creek Road continues another 3.5 miles to Santa Rosalia Overlook, elevation 2,529 feet. The trail section above Sand Point is known as "The Ladder" because it steepens, then levels out, then steepens, and so on. You'll even have a few downhills just before you reach Santa Rosalia Overlook, which is located at a wide clearing with blue-water views of Monterey Bay. This time you'll share the vista with less company.

Driving Directions

From Santa Cruz, drive south on Highway 1 for six miles to the Aptos/State Park Drive exit. Turn left at the exit, drive .25 mile, then turn right on Soquel Drive and drive .5 mile. Turn left on Aptos Creek Road and drive 1.8 miles to George's Picnic Area.

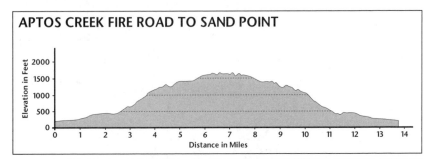

APTOS CREEK FIRE ROAD TO SAND POINT

Route Directions for Aptos Creek Fire Road to Sand Point

0.0 Park at George's Picnic Area. *Supplies are available in Aptos.*

2.6 Sign may be in place that reads "Epicenter Area, 7.1 Earthquake, 5:04 P.M., October 17, 1989." *A bike rack is located here. A hiking trail leads .5 mile from this sign to the exact epicenter.*

3.9 "Top of the Incline."

6.9 Arrive at Sand Point Overlook. TURN AROUND. *Or continue uphill 3.5 miles farther to Santa Rosalia Overlook; see route description above.*

13.8 Arrive at starting point.

6. SOQUEL DEMONSTRATION STATE FOREST

North of Santa Cruz

This ride in Soquel Demonstration State Forest (831/475-8643) is challenging, both in terms of elevation gain and the skills needed to ride its steep, technical single-track. But it's worth it. The state forest is in a remote area of the Santa Cruz Mountains on the northeast boundary of Forest of Nisene Marks State Park. The terrain is much like Nisene Marks—dense forests of redwoods, tan oaks, and madrones—but the trails are as different as can be, with miles of gnarly single-tracks that twist, turn, and pitch steeply up and down. This is the kind of trail that the true mountain biker lives for.

ROUTE DETAILS

type of trail dirt road and single-track; paved road with minimal car traffic

difficulty ▮▮▮▮◗

total distance 14.1 miles

riding time 3 hours

elevation gain 2,100 feet

The ride begins with a climb on paved Highland Way, following pretty Soquel Creek. Two right turns and more climbing on dirt roads bring you to the Santa Rosalia Overlook in Forest of Nisene Marks State Park. Enjoy the wide view of Monterey Bay from the clearing, then get ready for a long roller-coaster ride on single-track, heading back into the state forest. Ridge Trail pitches up and down steeply for 3.5 miles, supplying more ocean views at openings between the trees. Around the 8.3-mile mark the trail suddenly becomes too steep for anyone to ride. After pushing your bike for a 100-yard stretch, you'll follow Ridge Trail to the right as it becomes Sawpit Trail, one of the most amazing stretches of single-track in Northern California. It is a gross understatement to say that the next 1.2 miles are an extremely steep descent. (Lowering your seat is more than a good idea.) In addition, the trail is littered with every imaginable kind of obstacle, including redwood trees, ruts, hairpin turns, and

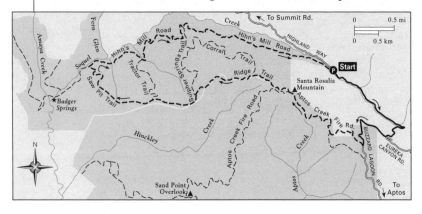

poison oak. If this trail doesn't scare the daylights out of you, you're going to have a ball.

The final stretch of the loop is a rather pedestrian climb on dirt Hihn's Mill Road back to your car. But after all the excitement you've had, you'll probably be relieved to ride on some plain old dirt road.

Driving Directions
From Santa Cruz, take Highway 17 north for 13 miles to the Summit Road exit. Drive southeast on Summit Road for five miles, where it becomes Highland Way. Continue on Highland Way for 4.7 more miles. A small sign by a bridge and a dirt road junction marks the parking area for Soquel Demonstration State Forest.

SOQUEL DEMONSTRATION STATE FOREST

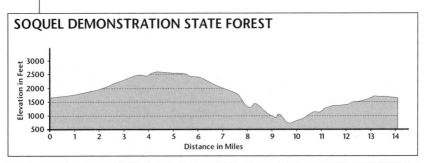

Route Directions for Soquel Demonstration State Forest

0.0   Park at Soquel Forest parking lot on Highland Way, then ride to your right (south) on paved Highland Way. *Supplies are available at the Summit Store on Summit Road.*

1.9   RIGHT on Buzzard Lagoon Road (dirt road).

2.9   RIGHT on Aptos Creek Fire Road.

4.1   Gate for Forest of Nisene Marks State Park.

5.1   RIGHT on single-track Ridge Trail at Santa Rosalia Overlook (wide, flat clearing with view of Monterey Bay). Stay LEFT on Ridge Trail at next three junctions.

7.4   Overlook point.

8.3   Impossible stretch; plan on walking.

8.5   RIGHT on Sawpit Trail (Ridge Trail simply turns right and becomes Sawpit Trail—not really a junction).

9.7   RIGHT on Hihn's Mill Road (dirt road).

14.1   Arrive at starting point.

7. SUNSET BEACH TO RIO DEL MAR

South of Santa Cruz

Despite their location between the bustling tourist towns of Santa Cruz and Monterey, the state beaches of Seacliff, Rio del Mar, Manresa, and Sunset have a remote feeling about them. The parks are set on high bluffs overlooking Monterey Bay and contain secluded groves of cypress and pine trees, grass-covered dunes, and long strands of white sand beaches. On the inland side, the beach parks are surrounded by green agricultural fields and small seaside villages.

ROUTE DETAILS

type of trail	paved roads with moderate car traffic
difficulty	
total distance	20.2 miles
riding time	2 hours
elevation gain	800 feet

This ride tours the four state beaches, starting at the southern end at Sunset State Beach (831/763-7062), a popular camping spot in the summer months. (If you're camping at Sunset, you can ride from your tent site and skip the first hill from the beach day-use area.) You could also begin this ride from any of the other beach parks

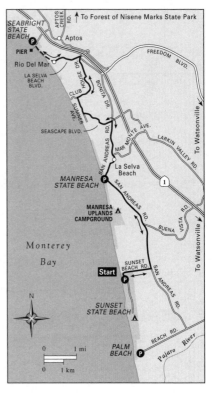

or campgrounds, or in the nearby towns of Aptos, Rio del Mar, Seascape, or La Selva. It's a take-your-pick deal.

This is a ride for dawdling, with many places to stop for supplies, and even more places to pause and enjoy the coastal scenery, maybe even plop down on a beach. Hills are few and far between, traffic is generally light, and bike lanes are wide. Don't forget your bike lock.

Among other highlights, you'll want to visit Seacliff State Beach's (831/685-6444) unusual pier, which is attached to a cement ship, the *Palo Alto*. The ship was constructed as a supply tanker for World War I but never saw active duty. After being towed to Santa Cruz, it served as a night club and amusement park for a brief period. Years of storms have taken their toll, and today the ship is reserved for the pelicans and seagulls. One end is moored to the wooden fishing pier that extends into Monterey Bay.

A biking/pedestrian path links Seacliff State Beach to Rio del Mar Beach, where Cafe Rio, a hip-looking seafood restaurant, is only a few feet from the sand. An espresso bar and sandwich deli is next door, and a small grocery store is on the same block. You'll also find restaurants and stores in Seascape.

For more information, contact Santa Cruz State Beach District, 831/429-2850.

Driving Directions
From Highway 1 south of Aptos, take the Buena Vista Drive exit and drive west 2.4 miles. Turn left on San Andreas Road, drive 1.3 miles and turn right on Sunset Beach Road. Follow the road 2.2 miles, past the park entrance kiosk to its end at the beach parking lot.

SUNSET BEACH TO RIO DEL MAR

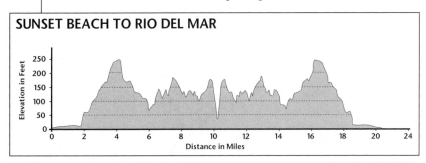

Route Directions for Sunset Beach to Rio Del Mar

0.0 Park at the beach day-use parking area at Sunset State Beach. Mileage begins at the parking lot restrooms. Ride uphill on the park road. *Supplies are available in Seascape, Rio Del Mar, and Aptos. Water is available at the trailhead.*

1.4 RIGHT at entrance kiosk.

2.2 LEFT on San Andreas Road (follow bike lane).

4.6 Manresa Uplands campground on left. *Water is available.*

5.3 Manresa State Beach on left. *Water is available.*

6.0 STRAIGHT at stop sign at Mar Monte Avenue.

6.8 LEFT on Seascape Boulevard.

7.5 Seascape Village shopping center. *Supplies are available.*

7.6 RIGHT on Sumner Avenue.

8.1 STRAIGHT at junction with Clubhouse.

9.3 LEFT on Rio del Mar Boulevard.

10.1 Rio del Mar Beach. TURN AROUND. *Supplies and a restaurant are available. Walk or ride your bike to the pier and concrete ship at neighboring Seacliff State Beach.*

20.2 Arrive at starting point.

8. ELKHORN SLOUGH LOOP

East of Moss Landing

The roads east of Moss Landing and surrounding the waters of Elkhorn Slough are immensely popular with road cyclists. The mostly level country thoroughfares see little traffic and allow the creation of several varied loops, with possible starting points in Pajaro, Prunedale, Moss Landing, or Castroville. This 21.8-mile loop starts at the visitor center at Elkhorn Slough National Estuarine Reserve (831-728-2822), a terrific place to take a short bird-watching walk, have a picnic, or get educated about the natural history of Elkhorn Slough.

ROUTE DETAILS

type of trail paved roads with minimal car traffic

difficulty 🔋🔋🔋🔋🔋

total distance 21.8 miles

riding time 2 hours

elevation gain 900 feet

The slough is the equivalent of a bed-and-breakfast for migrating birds on the Pacific Flyway. Here they find nourishment from the rich tidal waters and rest from their long journeys. The main channel of the slough winds inland nearly seven miles and encompasses 2,500 acres of marsh and tidal flats. This loop's final stretch on Elkhorn Road gives you the best look at the long, narrow channel. You won't even need binoculars to spot grebes, coots, ducks, geese, egrets, and herons as you ride.

The ride features only a few small hills, including one short-but-steep challenge leading up to Royal Oaks Park on Mahler Road. With its brief, mostly level mileage, this road ride can be enjoyed by cyclists of almost every ability. If you're in the mood, make a rest stop at Royal Oaks Park, a pretty spot lined with coast live oaks. You'll find water fountains, restrooms, and plenty of picnic spots in addition to softball fields and tennis courts.

Driving Directions

From Highway 1 at Moss Landing, turn east on Dolan Road (by

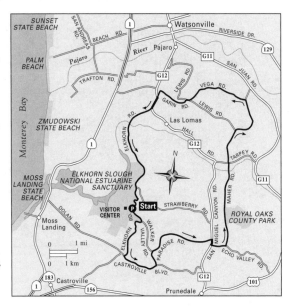

the power plant) and drive three miles. Turn left (north) on Elkhorn Road and drive 2.1 miles to Elkhorn Slough Reserve on the left.

ELKHORN SLOUGH LOOP

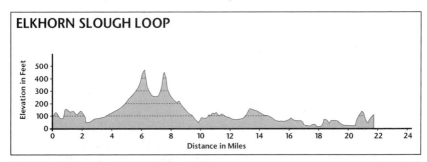

Route Directions for Elkhorn Slough Loop

0.0 Park at the visitor center parking lot at Elkhorn Slough, then ride out the entrance road to Elkhorn Road. If you arrive on Monday or Tuesday, when the visitor center is closed, park in one of the pullouts to the north along Elkhorn Road. *Supplies are available in Moss Landing, three miles west, or at Elkhorn Superette, 1.3 miles south on Elkhorn Road.*

0.1 RIGHT on Elkhorn Road.

1.3 Store on right. *Supplies are available.*

2.2 LEFT on Castroville Boulevard.

3.5 LEFT on Paradise Road.

6.4 RIGHT on San Miguel Canyon Road (Road G-12).

6.7 LEFT on Echo Valley Road.

7.1 LEFT on Mahler Road.

8.3 Royal Oaks County Park on right. *Water is available.*

10.1 LEFT on Tarpey Road, then immediate RIGHT on San Miguel Canyon Road.

12.6 LEFT on Vega Road.

14.9 RIGHT on Lewis Road.

15.1 LEFT on Garin Road.

16.5 LEFT on Elkhorn Road.

16.8 RIGHT to stay on Elkhorn Road.

19.2 Kirby Park access to Elkhorn Slough.

21.7 RIGHT into main entrance to Elkhorn Slough.

21.8 Arrive at starting point.

9. MONTEREY RECREATION TRAIL

Marina to Pacific Grove

Good news at the close of the 20th century: After 25 years of red-tape wrangling, a final link in the Monterey Peninsula Recreation Trail was built through Sand City, making the trail a "nearly complete" 14.5 miles of car-free riding (29 miles round-trip). Nearly complete? Well, close enough: There is a short stretch in which you follow bike lanes through Seaside's shopping center, but otherwise, you're largely free of the dreaded gas-guzzler, except for street and parking lot crossings.

a newly built stretch of the Monterey Recreation Trail

© ANN MARIE BROWN

ROUTE DETAILS

type of trail   paved bike path

difficulty

total distance   29 miles

riding time   2–3 hours

elevation gain   800 feet

Most people don't ride the entire trail, but it's nice to know it's an option. Obvious starting points are at the trail's north terminus in Marina and the trail's southwest terminus at Lover's Point Park in Pacific Grove. (Parking is difficult in Pacific Grove; the route directions below begin from the north end of the trail.) Many local riders begin midtrail at Laguna Grande Park in Seaside or a few blocks away at the aforementioned shopping center, where parking is free and easy.

The most congested trail section is the southwest end, where Cannery Row, Fisherman's Wharf, and the Monterey Bay Aquarium are located. The biggest obstacle there, besides the sheer number of walkers, bikers, joggers, and in-line skaters, are the four-wheeled, canopy-covered rental bikes that take up more than half the trail. Still, in between the bustling tourist areas are quiet stretches that belong only to you and the sea.

Monterey Recreation Trail

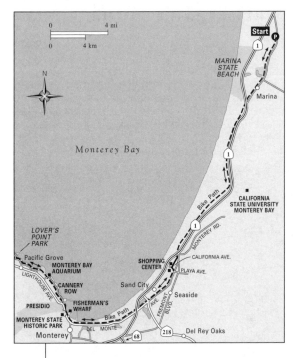

South of Cannery Row, the trail leads into the wealthy neighborhood of Pacific Grove, with its bed-and-breakfast hotels, restaurants, rugged, rocky coastline, and white sand beaches. This part of the trail is quintessential Monterey: Sea lions poke their heads out of the water, kayakers paddle by and wave, and sea otters float by on their backs munching on abalone. The trail ends near Lover's Point, an enchanting seaside park.

Not all of the trail is so lovely. The route through downtown Marina is commonplace at best, a stretch north of Sand City runs too close to noisy Highway 1, and the overall trail suffers from too many street intersections. But with this much car-free riding in beautiful Monterey, who's complaining?

For more information, contact the Transportation Agency for Monterey County, 831/755-8961, or Pacific Grove Recreation Department, 831/648-3130.

Driving Directions

To access the north end of the trail, from Highway 1 south of Moss Landing take the Marina/Del Monte Boulevard exit. Cross over to the east side of the highway; the trail begins at the junction of Del Monte Boulevard and Lapis Road, about 100 yards from Highway 1 (a dirt parking area is located there).

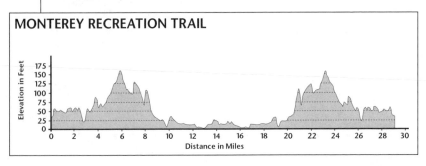

Route Directions for Monterey Recreation Trail

0.0 Park at the northern terminus of the trail at the junction of Del Monte Boulevard and Lapis Road in Marina. *Supplies are available all along the trail.*

2.7 Trail crosses Reservation Road in Marina and passes through downtown (trail parallels Del Monte Boulevard).

3.3 Trail crosses under Highway 1.

7.9 RIGHT then immediate LEFT where trail ends at California Avenue/Monterey Road junction; follow bike lane along California Avenue.

8.2 RIGHT on Playa Avenue (follow bike lane).

8.4 Bike trail resumes at end of Playa Avenue.

12.3 Fisherman's Wharf.

13.5 Monterey Bay Aquarium.

14.5 Lover's Point Park; TURN AROUND.

29.0 Arrive at starting point.

10. 17-MILE DRIVE

North of Carmel and south of Pacific Grove

One of the top reasons to ride your bike on the world-famous 17-Mile Drive is because it costs eight bucks to drive your car on it, but biking is free. Another reason is because it's gorgeous. Before cars became the normal mode of transportation, the 17-Mile Drive was navigated by horse-drawn carriages from Monterey's Hotel Del Monte. Tourists staying at the hotel in the late 1800s would be driven through Del Monte Forest and down to the same exquisite coastline that we see today, minus the sprawling golf courses (Pebble Beach Golf Links was opened in 1919).

The coastside leg of the 17-Mile Drive offers close-up views of the crashing surf.

ROUTE DETAILS

type of trail paved roads with moderate car traffic

difficulty 🚲🚲🚲🚲🚲

total distance 17.4 miles (or 15-mile option)

riding time 1.5–2 hours

elevation gain 900 feet

As you ride the 17-Mile Drive, you may wish for those days of carriages instead of cars, because in the summer tourist season this road is extremely congested. Although nobody drives the scenic route fast (after all, drivers want to get their money's worth), I don't recommend riding it in summer, except perhaps in the early morning on weekdays. I would especially avoid weekends and holidays. Some of the route follows shoulderless roads, and the vast majority of drivers are gawking at the scenery, not watching for cyclists.

The route described below begins at the Pacific Grove gate to the 17-Mile Drive. Two other gates also access the drive: the Highway 1 gate at the

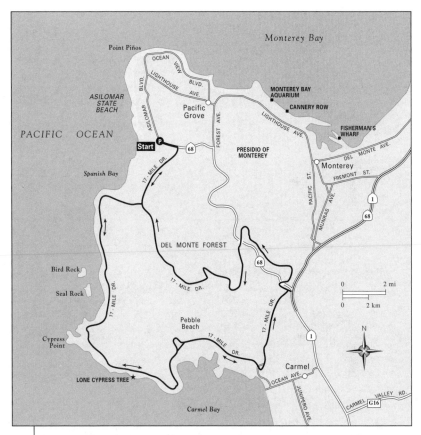

junction of Highway 1 and Highway 68, and the Carmel gate off Ocean Avenue in Carmel.

The 17-Mile Drive is signed like crazy, so there is no chance of getting lost, despite numerous turns. To orient yourself, you can pick up a full-color map at the entrance gate when you sign your liability waiver to bicycle the 17-Mile Drive. Many riders choose to ride the seven-mile coastal section of the drive as an out-and-back, rather than looping inland over several miles that are hilly and far less scenic—mostly suburban-looking homes and cypress forests. The coastal section is what everyone comes here for: ocean lookouts, impossibly green and fine-trimmed golf courses, showy mansions belonging to movie stars and the very wealthy, and the white sands and turquoise waters of Monterey Bay. If you opt for an out-and-back instead of the loop, turn around near mile 7.5 at Pebble Beach, before the route climbs uphill and heads inland. If you keep on the loop, mile 8.9 to 10.5 is a 1.6-mile uphill grind.

For more information, contact the Pacific Grove Chamber of Commerce, 831/373-3304.

Driving Directions

From the junction of Highway 1 and Highway 68 north of Carmel, take Highway 68 northwest to Pacific Grove. Highway 68 ends at the Pacific Grove gate to the 17-Mile Drive and the start of Sunset Drive. Parking is available on side streets off Sunset Drive or at Asilomar State Beach on Sunset Drive.

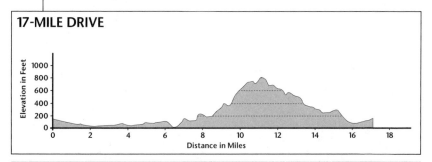

Route Directions for 17-Mile Drive

0.0 Park off Sunset Drive or near Asilomar State Beach in Pacific Grove. The mileage below begins at the junction of Sunset Drive and 17-Mile Drive. *Supplies are available at the small store on Sunset Drive near the 17-Mile Drive junction.*

0.2 Sign in at the 17-Mile Drive entrance gate.

1.1 RIGHT on Spanish Bay Road (17-Mile Drive).

3.5 Bird Rock and Seal Rock Picnic Area.

4.9 Cypress Point Lookout.

6.5 Ghost Tree and Pescadero Point.

6.8 RIGHT for Pebble Beach lodge, golf course, etc. *Supplies are available at Pebble Beach Market.*

7.5 RIGHT to exit Pebble Beach area (warning sign for cyclists: narrow road; no bike lane ahead). *Cyclists who would prefer to stick to the coastal side of the 17-Mile Drive should turn around here and head back.*

8.9 Start of climb.

10.5 Highway 1 entrance gate; cross Highway 68.

11.4 Shepherd's Knoll overlook.

12.7 Huckleberry Hill ocean view.

14.0 RIGHT then LEFT (follow signs).

14.8 RIGHT (follow signs).

15.0 Poppy Hills golf course, restaurant, bar.

16.1 RIGHT (follow signs).

16.7 RIGHT to return to Pacific Grove entrance gate.

17.4 Arrive at starting point.

11. FORT ORD LOOP

East of Monterey and west of Salinas

Fort Ord, an Army base dating back to 1917, has become a world-class recreation area for mountain bikers, hikers, horseback riders, and others of their ilk. The base, located just east of Monterey, was abandoned in 1994 and its management turned over to the Bureau of Land Management. The BLM maintains 7,200 acres of the old base for recreational use, including 50 miles of tight single-track and wide multiuse roads that wind through grassland hills, dense oaks, and coastal chaparral.

An interesting mix of single-track and fire roads runs through the grass-covered hills at Ford Ord.

ROUTE DETAILS

type of trail — dirt road and single-track

difficulty — 🍶🍶🍶

total distance 10.7 miles

riding time 1.5 hours

elevation gain 1,300 feet

That said, it's hard to figure out where to ride at Ford Ord. Trails meander all over the place, and on weekends, you see people riding all over the place. The best advice I got from a BLM recreation officer was "follow Toro Creek Road and then take any trail that doesn't look too steep." The best advice I got from local riders was "try anything; they're all good."

So here is the loop I assembled, containing a fair mix of single-track and wide road, some steep ups and steep downs, and a few places I wound up walking. Trails at Fort Ord are often sandy and dusty, especially late in the dry season, which can derail your chances at gaining traction. This got a bit irritating at times, but overall, I couldn't wipe the smile off my face. Two highlights: Skyline Trail, a

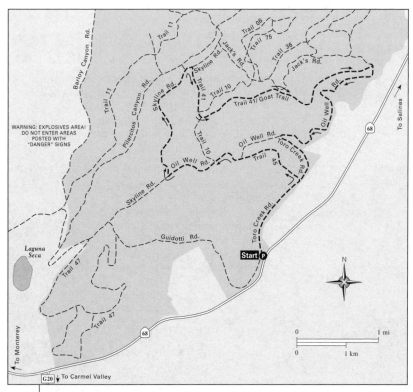

smooth ridgeline road, and Goat Trail, also known as Trail 41, a 2.8-mile dream of a single-track. It's smooth and rollercoastering, like a well-built trail at a mountain bike park.

Note that no matter how foggy the Monterey coast may be, it will probably be sunny here at Fort Ord. This means that summer riding can get quite hot. Think Southern California and you get a good idea of the landscape—few trees, lots of chaparral, and dry sandstone earth. Springtime is the optimal time to visit, when the wildflowers bloom and the grasses are green.

For more information, contact the Bureau of Land Management's Hollister Office, 831/630-5000 or 831/394-8314.

Driving Directions

From Highway 1 heading south in Marina, take the Marina/Reservation Road exit and drive east .25 mile. Turn right on Reservation Road and drive 8.8 miles. Turn right (west) on Highway 68 and drive three miles to the dirt parking area on the right.

Or, from Monterey at the junction of Highways 1 and 68, drive northeast on Highway 68 for 9.9 miles, past the entrance to Laguna Seca Recreation Area. Watch for the junction with San Benancio Road; the dirt parking area is 150 yards farther on the left.

FORT ORD LOOP

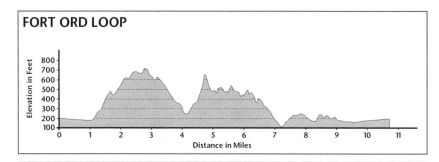

Route Directions for Fort Ord Loop

0.0 Park at the Fort Ord parking lot on Highway 68 and take the main trail from the lot. *Supplies are available in Monterey.*

0.1 RIGHT on Toro Creek Road.

0.9 LEFT on Trail 45 (steep climb uphill).

1.3 LEFT on Oil Well Road.

2.5 RIGHT on Skyline Road.

4.0 RIGHT on Trail 43 (climb on single-track).

4.6 LEFT on Trail 41/Goat Trail at major junction of trails.

7.4 RIGHT on Oil Well Road.

9.2 LEFT on Toro Creek Road.

10.6 LEFT at spur trail to parking lot.

10.7 Arrive at starting point.

12. ANDREW MOLERA RAMBLE

Andrew Molera State Park north of Big Sur

Mountain bikers can't make a loop out of the trails at Andrew Molera State Park (831/667-2315), and as a result, the park is largely underused by them, although it's quite popular with hikers. But this is one park where making a loop is irrelevant; the scenery is so grand that an out-and-back is just fine. You'll want to see the park's ocean views, wildflowers, and rollercoastering ridgelines more than once.

ROUTE DETAILS

type of trail 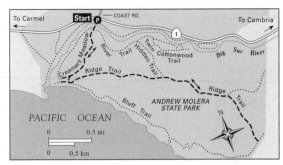 dirt road and single-track

difficulty

total distance 7 miles

riding time 1.5 hours

elevation gain 1,000 feet

The main pedaling is on Ridge Trail, an alternating wide and narrow ranch road that climbs quite steeply to a panoramic overlook. You access Ridge Trail by crossing a footbridge from the main parking lot, then following Beach Trail through Creamery Meadow. The level Beach Trail sees plenty of traffic from beachgoers, while steep Ridge Trail offers more solitude and a solid workout. Most of Ridge Trail is surrounded by low-growing chaparral, allowing open views of the ocean to the west and the chalky peak of Pico Blanco to the east. One surprising stretch enters an oak forest in a tangle of curving branches, followed by a short stint in redwoods. Ridge Trail ends at a bench with a fine view of the Pacific. (Hikers can loop back to the beach from here on Panorama Trail, but bikes are not permitted.)

Riding on Ridge Trail is a strenuous climb (10 percent grade) but has little in the way of technical challenges. That's convenient, because you'll want to keep your eyes on the coastal views and chaparral-covered headlands, not the trail. If you want to add more miles or more of a challenge to your day, you can combine this ride with Ride 13, the Old Coast Road, which begins across Highway 1 from this trailhead. Or consider an out-and-back on East Molera Trail, which runs from the east side of Highway 1 up into the coastal hills. A steep 1.5-mile climb will bring you to a small, secluded redwood grove. Pick up a park map at the entrance kiosk before you go.

Note that you won't be able to access any of Andrew Molera's coastside trails during the rainy season (usually November to March) without facing an ice-cold portage of the Big Sur River; the footbridge by the main parking lot is removed during the wet months. But for bikers, this is the best time to visit Andrew Molera. If you can stand taking off your shoes and socks and carrying your bike across a knee-high, 25-foot-wide river running over rounded rocks, you'll practically have the trails to yourself.

Driving Directions
From Carmel, drive 20 miles south on Highway 1 to the entrance to Andrew Molera State Park on the right (four miles north of Big Sur).

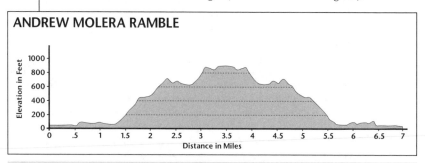

ANDREW MOLERA RAMBLE

Route Directions for Andrew Molera Ramble

0.0   Park at the main lot at Andrew Molera and walk your bike across the footbridge to access the trails. In winter, you may have to ford; see route description above. *Supplies are available in Big Sur, four miles south. Water is available at the trailhead.*

0.2   STRAIGHT on Beach Trail at junction with River Trail (confusing junction; head west toward the beach).

0.8   LEFT on Ridge Trail. Steep climb uphill.

0.9   LEFT to stay on Ridge Trail at junction with Bluffs Trail.

3.5   Bench at overlook point and junction of trails. TURN AROUND.

7.0   Arrive at starting point.

13. OLD COAST ROAD LOOP

North of Big Sur and south of Carmel

One of the most photographed icons of the Big Sur coast is the long, graceful span of the Bixby Bridge on Highway 1. But before that single-arch bridge was built in 1932, the thoroughfare that ran from Carmel to Big Sur was the Old Coast Road, which made a long arc inland before it could cross the deep gorge of Bixby Creek. That prebridge road still exists today, largely ignored by Highway 1 travelers but ideal for mountain bikers wanting to log some scenic miles.

To make a loop out of the Old Coast Road, it's best to start on its southern end by Andrew Molera State Park, where parking is ample. You follow the dirt-and-gravel Old Coast Road north, with no turns or junctions to concern yourself with until you come out at Highway 1 at the Bixby Bridge, 10.5 miles later. Then you ride south on Highway 1 to finish the loop, with the prevailing westerly winds at your back and the sparkling Pacific on your side of the road.

ROUTE DETAILS

type of trail   dirt road and paved road with moderate car traffic

difficulty

total distance   18.8 miles

riding time   3–4 hours

elevation gain   2,600 feet

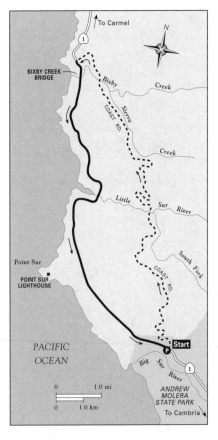

You will face a heck of a climb at the start of this ride, but the surface is hard-packed gravel and dirt, which at least bestows some traction. The road climbs for the first 2.5 miles, providing ocean views. Then it drops for two miles and climbs again, more steeply and on a much looser surface, for two miles. By about mile 6.5 you may be wishing you were driving this road instead of riding it, or maybe wishing you weren't here at all but just sitting on the beach in Big Sur. But suddenly, the road leaves the hot, dusty sunshine and makes a cool, three-mile descent through a redwood and fern forest. You may achieve mountain biking nirvana here.

After one more short climb at mile 9.5, you begin your descent to Highway 1, which is filled with the kind of scenery that makes Big Sur famous. Then it's a left turn on to the busy highway and 8.3 miles back to your car at Andrew Molera State Park. If it's a weekend, you might want to stop at Point Sur Lighthouse along the way for a tour. Or just head for the state park and its lovely beach, accessed by a .5-mile, level walk.

Driving Directions
From Carmel, drive 12 miles south on Highway 1 to the Bixby Bridge and the north end of Old Coast Road on the left. Take note of this junction, then continue another 8.5 miles south to the entrance to Andrew Molera State Park on the right, and the south end of Old Coast Road on the left.

OLD COAST ROAD LOOP

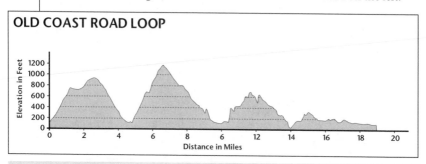

Route Directions for Old Coast Road Loop

0.0 Park at Andrew Molera State Park, then ride across Highway 1 to the start of Old Coast Road. *Supplies are available in Big Sur, four miles south.*

0.1 Start of Old Coast Road.

6.5 Summit and start of long descent in redwoods.

10.5 LEFT on Highway 1.

16.0 Right turnoff for Point Sur Lighthouse; weekend tours are available.

18.8 Arrive at starting point.

14. BIG SUR TO LUCIA

Big Sur coast

While it's true that thousands of cyclists ride coastal Highway 1 in its entirety every year, it's also true that many who do so admit that it's overrated. Common complaints include: too many cars, too narrow road shoulders, and too few chances to enjoy the spectacular coastside scenery because you're too worried about staying alive.

ROUTE DETAILS

type of trail	paved road with moderate car traffic
difficulty	
total distance	51 miles
riding time	5 hours
elevation gain	3,300 feet

Still, one stretch of the coastal highway that gets a big thumbs up from just about everybody is the 25 miles from Big Sur to Lucia. This area sees somewhat less traffic than other stretches of Highway 1 because the majority of drivers coming from the San Francisco Bay Area stop in Big Sur, and the majority of drivers coming from the Los Angeles area stop in San Simeon. This leaves a glorious length of coastline in between. By simple good fortune, this highway stretch has an adequate shoulder through its entire length (a rarity on Highway 1), and is not especially hilly. The coastal scenery is as good as it gets anywhere in California, with nonstop views of crashing waves and a dramatic, rocky shoreline. It is not uncommon to spot gray whales or dolphins swimming past, or sea otters frolicking in the kelp beds.

Chances are you'll start this ride from wherever you are staying in Big Sur, which is likely within a three-mile radius of Big Sur Station (.5 mile south of Pfeiffer Big Sur State Park and Big Sur Lodge). I describe this ride starting at Big Sur Station (831/667-2315), an ideal location for getting updated information about road and park conditions from the rangers there. The route directions below note some of the highlights of the

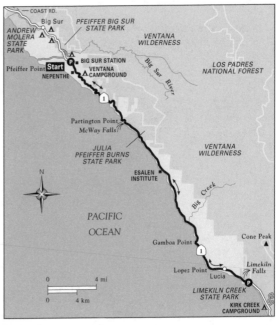

ride, which are numerous. Only one section is without services for any length, and that's the 13 miles from Julia Pfeiffer Burns State Park to Lucia Lodge. Otherwise, there are plenty of places to stop, relax, and enjoy the scenery. Bring a bike lock, plan to take a lot of breaks, and expect to eat well at the many restaurants and cafés along the route. There's no reason to hurry here; take your time and make a day of it.

Driving Directions

From Carmel, drive 25 miles south on Highway 1 to Big Sur. Continue south through town to Big Sur Station on the right, .5 mile south of Pfeiffer Big Sur State Park.

BIG SUR TO LUCIA

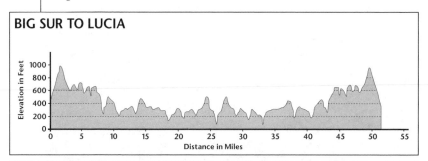

Route Directions for Big Sur to Lucia

- 0.0 Park at Big Sur Station, .5 mile south of Pfeiffer Big Sur State Park and Big Sur Lodge. Ride south on Highway 1. *Supplies are available to the north or south in Big Sur.*
- 1.1 Big Sur Bakery and Restaurant. *Supplies are available.*
- 1.8 Post Ranch Inn and Ventana Campground. *Supplies are available.*
- 2.4 Nepenthe Restaurant and Cafe Kevah. *Snacks and drinks are available. If you're ready for a meal, get the scallop and shrimp salad and sit outside on the deck at Nepenthe.*
- 2.7 Henry Miller Library. *Lock up your bike and take a look at the exhibits on this famous American writer, who spent many years living in Big Sur.*
- 3.3 Deetjen's Big Sur Inn.
- 5.6 Coast Gallery and Cafe. *Snacks and drinks are available.*
- 10.5 Julia Pfeiffer Burns State Park. *Lock up your bike and take the .5-mile walk to McWay Falls.*
- 23.6 Lucia Lodge, store, restaurant. *Supplies and meals are available; the restaurant's deck has a marvelous view.*
- 25.5 Limekiln State Park. TURN AROUND. *Lock up your bike and head for the beach, or hike the one-mile trail to the park's historic lime kilns or beautiful Limekiln Falls.*
- 51.0 Arrive at starting point.

15. NACIMIENTO-FERGUSSON ROAD TO THE MISSION

Big Sur coast to Jolon, west of King City

There's a marvelous country road that runs from Highway 1 south of Big Sur to Highway 101 near King City, and those who know of it wouldn't dream of heading inland any other way. That's Nacimiento-Fergusson Road, a narrow, winding, and twisting thoroughfare that climbs up from the Pacific Ocean to Nacimiento Summit, then drops down the east side to the grasslands and oaks of the Central Coast. Riding it out and back is challenging in both directions, certainly, but it's also filled with rewards.

a dizzying descent to Highway 1 and the coast on Nacimiento-Fergusson Road

ROUTE DETAILS

type of trail paved roads with minimal car traffic

difficulty 🚲🚲🚲🚲🚲

total distance 58.8 miles

riding time 5–6 hours

elevation gain 4,200 feet

The destination of this ride is Mission San Antonio de Padua (831/385-4478), founded in 1771 and the third of 21 missions began in California by Franciscan padres. San Antonio Mission is open to the public every day of the year, and Sunday mass is held weekly.

The mission has an unusual location: It sits in the middle of 170,000-acre Fort Hunter Liggett Military Reservation (831/386-3000), a land of rolling, oak-covered hills and extensive military operations. Because this is an active

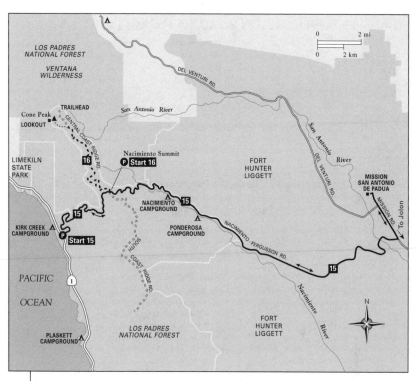

base, expect the unexpected on roads: gates, delays due to closures, the sudden appearance of jeeps and tanks, you name it. Military personnel are accustomed to bicyclists and are generally quite friendly and helpful, but you have to follow their rules.

The best season to take this ride is in spring when the wildflowers are blooming, or at least in the cooler months of year. The western miles of the ride travel through the wildlands of Los Padres National Forest and are completely without services, so you must be self-reliant for this trip. (You might be able to get water at one of two Forest Service campgrounds along the road.) As for the elevation gain, well, this isn't a ride for cyclists who don't like to climb. You'll gain 2,600 feet over seven miles from the ocean to Nacimiento Summit (mostly in the open sunshine), then lose 1,600 feet on the descent to the mission (mostly in a shady forest). Reversing it on the way back, your return trip is easier. Plus, the final downhill to the coast is one of the most breathtaking road rides in California. Check your brakes before you go.

Driving Directions

From Big Sur, drive 27 miles south on Highway 1 to Kirk Creek Campground and the left turnoff for Nacimiento-Fergusson Road. Park off the road (and out of the campground unless you're camping there).

NACIMIENTO-FERGUSSON ROAD TO THE MISSION

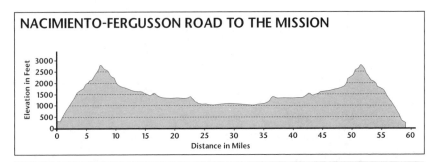

Route Directions for Nacimiento-Fergusson Road to the Mission

0.0 Park near the junction of Highway 1 and Nacimiento-Fergusson Road. *Supplies are available in Lucia, four miles north.*

7.0 Four-way junction with South Coast and Central Coast Ridge Roads.

10.8 Nacimiento Campground.

13.3 Ponderosa Campground. *Water is available when the campground is open.*

16.3 Enter Fort Hunter Liggett Military Reservation.

27.0 LEFT on Mission Road. *Supplies are available in Jolon, three miles to the right at this junction.*

29.4 Mission San Antonio de Padua. TURN AROUND. *A small shop is located in the mission and water is available.*

58.8 Arrive at starting point.

16. CONE PEAK LOOKOUT BIKE & HIKE

Los Padres National Forest south of Big Sur

The trip to Cone Peak Lookout is a must for campers staying at Kirk Creek or Plaskett Creek Campgrounds, or for anyone who wants to see some of the backcountry of the Big Sur coast. You can drive all the way to the 2.5-mile, hikers-only trail to the summit and lookout tower, but the route is far more enjoyable on a bike. With few cars and a steady but moderate grade, the 5.4-mile uphill from Nacimiento Summit is manageable for anyone in good cardiovascular shape. The dirt road presents no technical challenges, but provides many fine views of the inland ridges and valleys of the Ventana Wilderness, plus a few surprise looks at the Pacific Ocean—far, far, away. Some sections of the road are densely forested with madrones, oaks, and bay laurel.

view from an open clearing on the dirt road to Cone Peak

© ANN MARIE BROWN

ROUTE DETAILS

type of trail dirt road

difficulty 🍶🍶🍶🍶🍶

total distance 10.8 miles (plus 5-mile hike)

riding time 2 hours (plus 2-hour hike)

elevation gain 1,100 feet (bike ride only)

As you ride, keep your eyes open for the Cone Peak Lookout Trail on your left at mile 5.4, so you don't bypass it and continue uphill unnecessarily. It seems as if the road you're following would eventually reach the summit, but instead it ends at a Ventana Wilderness trailhead about a mile beyond Cone Peak Lookout's trailhead. Of course, if you're enjoying the ride and the wilderness vistas, you can pedal this last mile just for grins.

Make sure you bring a bike lock or are

prepared to stash your bike so you can hike the final 2.5 miles to the summit, which gains another 1,300 feet. This stretch on your feet feels much steeper than what you've just accomplished on your bike, but it's completely worth it. From the historic lookout tower, built on tinker-toy-style stilts in 1923, you can see as far as 100 miles on clear days. Perched at the lofty elevation of 5,155 feet, the tower looks down the west side of Cone Peak almost a vertical mile to the ocean.

The lookout is usually staffed in the summer and fall months. In case you are wondering, the staff person reaches the tower the same way you did—on foot via the 2.5-mile hiking trail. Supplies are brought in by helicopter.

For more information, contact the Monterey Ranger District of Los Padres National Forest, 831/385-5434.

Driving Directions
From Big Sur, drive 27 miles south on Highway 1 to Kirk Creek Campground and the left turnoff for Nacimiento-Fergusson Road. Turn left and drive seven miles (paved) to a four-way junction. Park off the road in the pullout.

For trail map, see page 237 (Ride 15—Nacimiento-Fergusson Road to the Mission).

CONE PEAK LOOKOUT

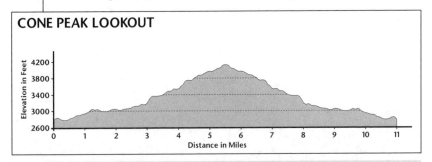

Route Directions for Cone Peak Lookout Bike & Hike

0.0 Park at Nacimiento Summit, at the junction of Nacimiento-Fergusson Road, South Coast Ridge Road, and Central Coast Ridge/Cone Peak Road. Ride north (left) on Cone Peak Road (dirt road 20S05). *Supplies are available at Lucia Lodge on Highway 1.*

3.7 Pass trail sign on left for trail to Vicente Flat.

3.9 Pass trail sign on right for San Antonio Trail.

4.0 Pass white marble outcroppings along road.

5.0 Ocean view at clearing.

5.4 Trail to Cone Peak Lookout on left (dirt road continues straight ahead but doesn't go to lookout tower). *Lock up your bike and hike 2.5 miles one-way to the lookout tower on the 5,155-foot summit.* TURN AROUND.

11.0 Arrive at starting point.

17. LAKE SAN ANTONIO LOOP

South of King City and north of Paso Robles

This hilly loop around Lake San Antonio presents a good workout combined with fetching views of the long, narrow lake and also nearby Lake Nacimiento. Both water bodies are county-owned reservoirs that are popular for waterskiing and fishing in summer, but largely deserted in the cooler seasons. Bicycling is best here from October to April, when there is little traffic on the roads and the air temperature is cool. Springtime displays of wildflowers and verdant grasslands in these sprawling hills are worth planning your trip around.

ROUTE DETAILS

type of trail	paved roads with moderate car traffic
difficulty	𝄞𝄞𝄞𝄞
total distance	53.2 miles
riding time	5 hours
elevation gain	2,200 feet

The ride starts at the marina on the north shore of Lake San Antonio. In addition to being the site of the annual Wildflower Triathlon in May and popular all summer for water sports, San Antonio is well known as a major habitat area for eagles, both bald and golden. The county parks department runs "Eagle Watch" boat tours in the winter months.

In any season, don't be surprised to see two unusual creatures along the roadways: wild turkeys and wild pigs. Both frequent the area.

Say good-bye to the water as you start your ride; you'll be heading out into the dry, grassy hills for a while. Ride back out the marina road, then turn right and follow Jolon Road east as it rolls up and down small hills. Almost back at U.S. 101, a right turn on Nacimiento Road takes you across the San Antonio River. You'll commence to climb soon, and continue to do so as you near the northeast edge of Lake Nacimiento. After a total four-mile ascent, enjoy a swooping descent to the hamlet of Bee Rock.

The next leg of the ride travels roughly parallel to Lake San Antonio's south shore. With 16 quiet miles of

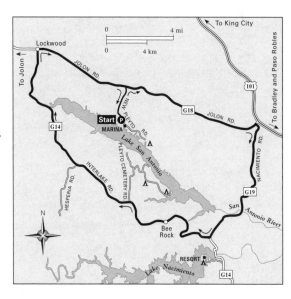

mostly level riding, you'll reach the town of Lockwood (store and café available), then make your final cruise back to the north shore. After all these miles, you might find yourself thinking that it's time for a swim.

For more information, contact Lake San Antonio Resort, 800/310-2313 or 805/472-2313; website: www.tcsn.net/lsar.

Driving Directions

From U.S. 101 north of Bradley, take the Jolon Road/G-18 exit west. Drive 8.7 miles west on Jolon Road (G-18) to New Pleyto Road. Turn left and drive five miles to Lake San Antonio's north shore and marina.

LAKE SAN ANTONIO LOOP

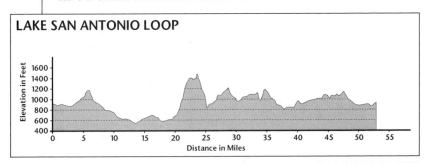

Route Directions for Lake San Antonio Loop

0.0   Park at the marina on the north shore of Lake San Antonio. Ride back out the way you drove in. *Supplies are available at the marina store.*

5.0   RIGHT on Jolon Road (G-18).

13.7   RIGHT on Lake Nacimiento Road (G-19) near U.S. 101.

18.7   Cross San Antonio River on steel bridge.

20.5   LEFT to stay on Lake Nacimiento Road just before the dam.

22.2   RIGHT on Interlake Road (G-14).

26.8   Hamlet of Bee Rock. *Supplies are available.*

42.2   RIGHT on Jolon Road (G-18) in town of Lockwood. *Supplies are available.*

48.2   RIGHT on New Pleyto Road to marina, store, and lake. TURN AROUND. *Supplies are available.*

53.2   Arrive at starting point.

CHAPTER 4

Sacramento and Gold Country

The Sierra Nevada foothills region surrounding the north-south corridor of Highway 49 is known as the Gold Country or the Mother Lode. It's the place where James Marshall discovered gold in January 1848, sparking a huge and frenzied migration westward. When it became known that a rich vein of gold ran from Mariposa to Downieville, the history of California was forever changed. Although other areas of California experienced their own Gold Rush, it was the Mother Lode that ultimately produced the richest deposits of ore.

Evidence of the area's mining past is obvious, from historic brick and wooden buildings to old bridges, mines, water ditches, and an abundance of antique shops. Many of the region's towns have barely changed since their heydays: Streets are just wide enough for two stagecoaches to pass, buildings are constructed of stones from local rivers and streams, and storefronts look like they're right out of a movie set. You can travel for many miles in the Gold Country without ever seeing a traffic light.

Rolling, low-elevation foothills studded with oaks and pines and roaring river canyons make up the landscape of the Gold Country. Hot weather is to be expected in summer, which means the roads and trails in this region are best for riding in the autumn, winter, and spring months.

Although the Gold Rush is long over, many of the area's towns have discovered there's gold to be found in the outdoor recreation industry, specifically mountain biking. The towns of Downieville and Nevada City have developed a tourism business centered around the sport. Bed-and-breakfasts, cafés, and outfitters cater to visiting mountain bikers, who test their suspensions on miles of dirt roads and rock-studded trails bordered by steep drop-offs into rugged river canyons. Road bikers aren't left out of the action; they can travel quiet back roads leading to gold boom-towns that have long since gone bust. There's a whole lot of California here just waiting to be rediscovered, preferably on two wheels that roll along wildflower-covered hills in springtime.

Also included in this region is the Central Valley, with its endless acres of cotton, orchards, and grazing lands, and its famous rivers: the Sacramento, American, and Feather, among others. Extending for hundreds of miles from these rivers are marshy wetlands that attract ducks and waterfowl. The Central Valley, which may seem like an empty wasteland to drivers on I-5 or Highway 99, is a place of critical refuge for millions of birds on the Pacific Flyway. From the seat of a bike, you can develop a new appreciation for this vast landscape of grasslands and waterways. Its relatively level roads offer fast and fun spinning for road cyclists.

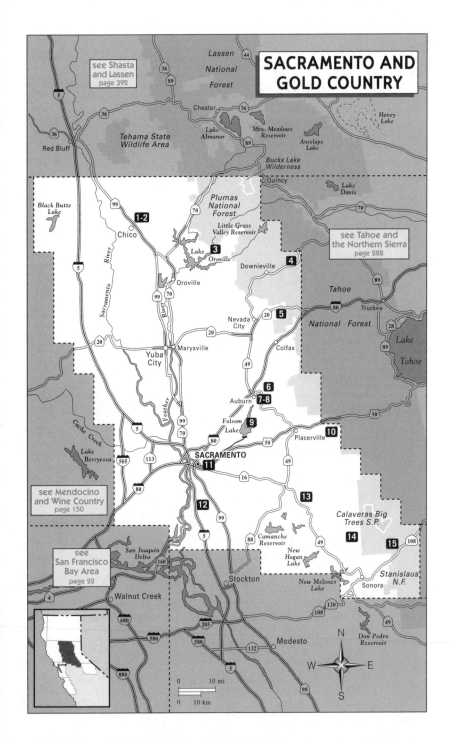

SACRAMENTO AND GOLD COUNTRY

see Shasta
and Lassen
page 392

Lassen

National

Forest

Chester

Honey
Lake

Red Bluff

Tehama State
Wildlife Area

Lake
Almanor

Mtn. Meadows
Reservoir

Antelope
Lake

Bucks Lake
Wilderness

Black Butte
Lake

Quincy

Lake
Davis

Plumas
National
Forest

Chico

1-2

Little Grass
Valley Reservoir

Lake
Oroville

3

Downieville

4

see Tahoe and
the Northern Sierra
page 288

Oroville

Tahoe

Nevada
City

5

National

Forest

Truckee

Marysville

Colfax

Lake

Yuba
City

49

Tahoe

6

Auburn

7-8

Folsom
Lake

9

Placerville

10

SACRAMENTO

Cache
Creek

11

Lake
Berryessa

see Mendocino
and Wine Country
page 150

16

13

Calaveras Big
Trees S.P.

12

14

see
San Francisco
Bay Area
page 22

San Joaquin
Delta

Camanche
Reservoir

New
Hogan
Lake

15

Stanislaus
N.F.

Walnut Creek

New Melones
Lake

Sonora

Stockton

Modesto

Don Pedro
Reservoir

N

W   E

S

0   10 mi

0   10 km

CHAPTER 4
SACRAMENTO AND GOLD COUNTRY

 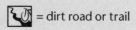
= paved road or path   = dirt road or trail

1. CHICO TO PARADISE LOOP

Chico to Paradise

Every April more than 3,000 bicyclists climb up Honey Run Road from Chico to Paradise. It's part of the annual Wildflower Century, a rite of passage for Chico-area cyclists.

ROUTE DETAILS

type of trail 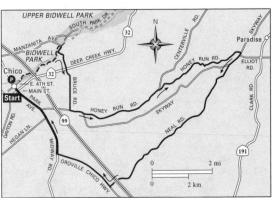 paved roads with moderate car traffic

difficulty

total distance 34 miles

riding time 3 hours

elevation gain 1,400 feet

Local riders use this as a regular workout ride, starting from a multitude of locations in downtown Chico. For simplicity, I describe the route starting from Main and East 4th Streets heading into Bidwell Park. A huge and well managed city park, Bidwell has plenty of water fountains, picnic tables, benches, and children's play areas. It is well-protected by shade trees: Oaks, maples, and sumacs line the route.

You'll follow Manzanita Avenue out of the park. Manzanita Avenue becomes traffic-intensive Bruce Road, which soon intersects the Skyway. The Skyway is your ticket to Honey Run Road, which is what you're here for. A twisting, winding snake of a road, Honey Run gets steeper and narrower as you climb (it gains 1,600 feet in six miles). As you ascend, you'll pass by a historic covered bridge over Butte Creek, known as America's only three-level covered bridge. You don't ride through it—the road crosses the creek on a more modern bridge just upstream. The climb is the steepest in its final four miles above Honey Run Covered Bridge, where the pavement narrows to one lane.

When you finally top out at the town of Paradise, you're on the Skyway again. Turn right and then shortly left on Neal Road. (Be very careful of fast traffic on the Skyway when making this tricky left turn.) Neal Road is mostly downhill all the way to Highway 99. Cross the highway and turn right on Chico-Oroville Highway, then turn right on Midway and ride back into Chico.

If you feel uncomfortable riding around car traffic, avoid this loop during commute hours.

Driving Directions

From Highway 32 heading east into Chico, stay on Highway 32 as it becomes

Nord Avenue, Walnut Street, and finally West 9th Street; turn left onto West 9th Sreet. Drive about 10 blocks on West 9th Street until you reach Main Street, then turn left. Turn right on East 4th Street and park.

CHICO TO PARADISE LOOP

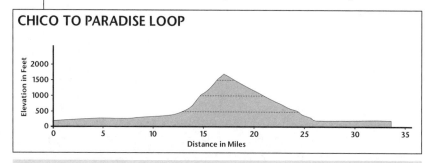

Route Directions for Chico to Paradise Loop

0.0   Park near East 4th and Main Streets in Chico. Ride east on East 4th Street into Bidwell Park. *Supplies are available in Chico. Water is available in Bidwell Park.*

0.3   Enter Bidwell Park and ride on South Park Drive (closed to cars).

3.3   RIGHT on Manzanita Avenue; the road becomes Bruce Road.

6.7   LEFT on the Skyway.

7.5   LEFT on Honey Run Road.

11.9   Covered bridge (veer RIGHT to stay on Honey Run Road). *Water is available.*

14.0   Road narrows to one lane.

17.5   RIGHT on the Skyway at end of Honey Run Road. *Supplies are available in Paradise.*

18.4   LEFT on Neal Road (be very cautious making this turn).

28.0   Cross Highway 99.

28.4   RIGHT on Chico-Oroville Highway.

31.4   RIGHT on Midway; Midway becomes Park Avenue (bike path parallels Midway for most of its length).

33.8   RIGHT on Main Street.

34.0   Arrive at starting point.

2. LOWER & UPPER BIDWELL PARK

Chico

The third largest city park in the United States includes a "wilderness" area that Chico locals call a miniature Grand Canyon. Grand it is. The 3,600-acre park encompasses both sides of Big Chico Creek canyon for five miles heading up into the foothills. This ride travels its length, providing an introduction to the area. If you like what you see, Bidwell Park has several other mountain biking trails, including a good amount of single-track. One of the many bike shops in town can point you on your way.

Lower Bidwell Park offers easy riding through plentiful shade trees, while Upper Park presents more challenges.

ROUTE DETAILS

type of trail — dirt and paved roads with minimal car traffic

difficulty — 🍼🍼

total distance — 17.6 miles (or shorter options)

riding time — 2 hours

elevation gain — 700 feet

This ride starts in Lower Bidwell Park with an easy cruise on pavement past tree-lined picnic areas, play areas, and water fountains. Shortly past Five Mile Recreation Area, you enter Upper Bidwell Park, which is a somewhat wilder version of the tame Lower Park. Note that dirt Upper Park Road is open to cars except for Sunday and Monday (your best choice for a ride). It's also closed to cars but open to bikes in the days following a rain.

Upper Park Road passes by tempting swimming holes at Alligator Hole, Bear Hole, Salmon Hole, and Brown's Hole. On warm days, bring a bike lock so you can access these Chico Creek pools. The road also travels past a series of basalt cliffs at Devil's Kitchen, which were formed over millions of years by the eroding action of the creek.

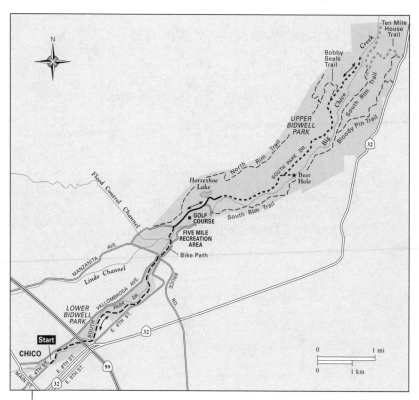

For more information, contact the Chico Parks and Recreation Department, 530/895-4972.

Driving Directions

From Highway 32 heading east into Chico, stay on Highway 32 as it becomes Nord Avenue, Walnut Street, and finally West 9th Street. Turn left on West 9th Street and drive about 10 blocks until you reach Main Street, then turn left. Turn right on East 4th Street and park.

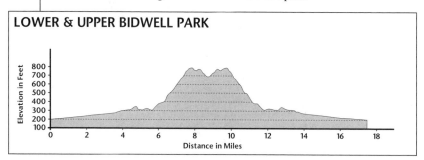

Route Directions for Lower & Upper Bidwell Park

0.0 Park at East 4th and Main Streets in Chico. Ride east on East 4th Street into Bidwell Park. *Supplies are available in Chico. Water is available in Bidwell Park.*

0.3 Enter Bidwell Park and ride on South Park Drive (closed to cars).

3.3 Cross Manzanita Avenue; stay on paved path.

3.5 Five Mile Recreation Area; bear RIGHT.

3.9 RIGHT on Wildwood Avenue. Cross the street and pick up bike path. Ride past Horseshoe Lake and Chico Rod and Gun Club.

4.7 Bike path ends at paved road and gate.

4.9 Road changes from pavement to gravel and dirt.

7.3 Devil's Kitchen parking area.

8.8 End of park road. TURN AROUND.

17.6 Arrive at starting point.

3. FEATHER FALLS

Plumas National Forest near Oroville

It's hard to believe the Feather Falls National Recreation Trail is open to mountain bikes. This loop trail is one of the finest hiking trails in Northern California, leading to a destination that is unsurpassed: Feather Falls, the sixth highest free-falling waterfall in the continental United States and the fourth highest in California.

ROUTE DETAILS

type of trail	dirt single-track
difficulty	
total distance	9.6 miles
riding time	2 hours
elevation gain	1,300 feet

The 640-foot waterfall is spectacular, and so is the trail that accesses it. Built as a loop, one side is shorter and steeper; the other side is longer and more level. Because it's a designated National Recreation Trail, the Feather Falls route is well maintained and has posted trail markers every half mile.

Bikes should take the longer side of the loop in both directions. It makes both the ascent and descent more manageable, and it will minimize your contact with hikers, who are the main trail users. Bikes are restricted to a 10-mph speed limit, which can be tough to maintain since the trail surface is smooth and has few technical challenges except for in its last half mile.

This is not a trail for hurrying. The northern Sierra foothills terrain shows off an incredible variety of plant life, including 17 species of trees: ponderosa pine, incense cedar, Douglas fir, black oak, canyon oak, madrone, bigleaf maple, white alder, bay, dogwood, digger pine, and more. They are joined by 20 kinds of shrubs, 11 types of vines, and 10 different ferns. Wildflower lovers should visit from March to May, when more than 180 species have been identified. That's also when the waterfall is usually at its peak flow.

From the trailhead, you reach the start of the loop in an easy quarter mile. Take the right fork (the longer way), and drop elevation for the next 1.5 miles to a bridge crossing over Frey Creek. Then parallel the creek and come out to a wide view of the Middle Fork Feather River canyon and Bald Rock Dome, a granite dome that rises 2,000 feet above the river.

At 4.3 miles you come to a wooden bench and trail junction where the two legs of the loop connect. They become

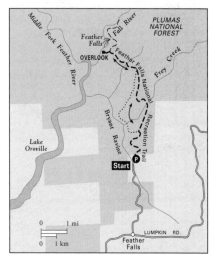

one for the final .5-mile ascent to Feather Falls' overlook. Be prepared to walk or stash your bike over the next stretch; some areas are quite treacherous. A couple of switchbacks bring you to a fenced viewpoint above the Middle Fork Feather River; in a few more pedal strokes, you're at the left turnoff for the falls overlook. Walk your bike along an elaborate series of short walkways that lead to a granite outcrop jutting into the middle of the canyon. From here you have a straight-on view of Feather Falls and the Fall River canyon—guaranteed to take your breath away.

For more information, contact the Feather River Ranger District of Plumas National Forest, 530/534-6500.

Driving Directions

From Highway 70 in Oroville, take the Oroville Dam Boulevard exit (Highway 162) and drive east 1.6 miles to Olive Highway/Highway 162. Turn right and drive 6.5 miles on Highway 162. Turn right on Forbestown Road and drive six miles. Turn left on Lumpkin Road and drive 11 miles. Turn left at the sign for Feather Falls and drive 1.6 miles to the trailhead.

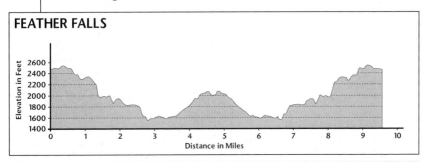

FEATHER FALLS

Route Directions for Feather Falls

0.0 Park at the Feather Falls Trailhead. *Supplies are available in the town of Feather Falls, four miles away. Water is available at the trailhead.*

0.2 RIGHT at fork at start of loop.

1.7 Bridge over Frey Creek.

4.3 RIGHT where two legs of the loop join.

4.6 LEFT at overlook turnoff.

4.8 Feather Falls overlook. TURN AROUND.

9.6 Arrive at starting point.

4. DOWNIEVILLE DOWNHILL

Gold Lakes Basin to Downieville

The little Gold Rush town of Downieville is now a mountain biker's town. Every shop, restaurant, and inn caters to the mountain biking tourist. And every weekend, downtown Downieville is filled with bikers milling around, usually splattered with mud or covered with dust, drinking cool drinks, and reviewing the day's adventures with their friends.

The town of Downieville is friendly to mountain bikers.

© ANN MARIE BROWN

ROUTE DETAILS

type of trail — dirt road and single-track

difficulty ▮▮▮▯▯

total distance 13.6 miles

riding time 2 hours

elevation gain 250 feet (4,200-foot loss)

Ninety-nine percent of them have just completed the Downieville Downhill, a world-famous one-way ride from Packer Saddle in the Gold Lakes Basin, elevation 7,100 feet, to Downieville, elevation 2,800 feet. You do the math.

There are several possible routes for the ride, but they all begin and end at the same spots. The route directions below follow the Butcher Ranch Trail and Third Divide Trail, since those trails are least vulnerable to erosion. (The Forest Service is greatly concerned about trail damage because so many thousands of people ride the Downieville Downhill each summer.) Even though the route is all downhill except for one short climb around mile 5.9, it is not by any means easy. The multiple miles of single-track will present plenty of challenges for intermediate to advanced riders: sharp turns, loose trail surfaces, steep drop-offs, jagged rocks, and the like. Beginners should sip a cappuccino back in Downieville and wait patiently for their friends.

Downieville Downhill

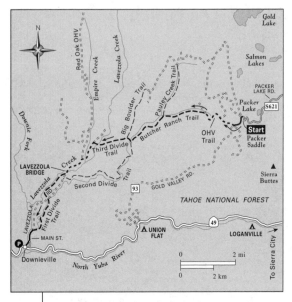

The biggest draw of this ride, besides the downhill single-track, is the incredible variety it provides. The scenery is spectacular: The trail passes meadows, crosses streams, and winds through wildflowers. At 7,100 feet the trail runs through old-growth red fir forests, but as the elevation drops the trees change to ponderosa pines and incense cedars. Try to go slow enough so you can enjoy this place, not just barrel through it.

The driving directions below are to Downieville, since most people leave their cars there; several tour operators in town will drop you off at the Packer Saddle trailhead, approximately 25 miles (45 minutes) from Downieville off Gold Lake Highway.

For more information on this ride, contact the Downieville Ranger District of Tahoe National Forest, 530/288-3231. For shuttle service to the trailhead, contact Yuba Expeditions, 530/289-3010, website: www.yuba expeditions.com, or Downieville Outfitters, 530/289-0155, website: www.downievilleoutfitters.com.

Driving Directions

From Nevada City, drive 45 miles northeast on Highway 49 to Downieville. (Or, from Truckee, drive 25 miles north on Highway 89, then turn west at Sierraville on Highway 49 and drive 35 miles to Downieville.) Numerous tour operators offer shuttle services from Downieville to the Packer Saddle trailhead.

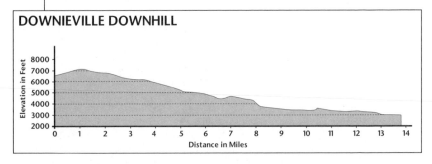

Route Directions for Downieville Downhill

0.0 Your shuttle driver will drop you off at Packer Saddle. Ride west down the paved road. *Supplies are available in Downieville or at Bassetts Station, five miles from Packer Saddle.*

0.5 RIGHT on paved road at Y-junction; the road soon turns to dirt.

1.2 LEFT on Butcher Ranch OHV Trail.

2.0 LEFT on Butcher Ranch single-track (where the road curves to the right).

3.8 LEFT at junction with Pauley Creek Trail on right.

5.7 Bridge crossing.

6.0 RIGHT on Third Divide Trail; begin smooth and fast section.

8.3 LEFT on Lavezzola Road. *If you are tired of single-track, you can ride this dirt road all the way back to Downieville instead of taking the single-track at mile 9.4.*

9.4 Cross bridge then turn RIGHT to enter the primitive campground. Pick up the dirt road which soon turns to single-track (the single-track goes left; this is First Divide Trail).

11.2 Cross Lavezzola Road and take the dirt road which changes to single-track and then widens again (this is still First Divide Trail).

12.7 LEFT on paved road. Cross bridge into Downieville.

13.7 Arrive at starting point.

5. PIONEER TRAIL

Off Highway 20 east of Nevada City

Pioneer Trail is the standard ride for mountain bikers seeking single-track in the Nevada City area. Like the Gold Rush town of Downieville, Nevada City has become a mecca for bikers, with enough trails in the area to keep

© ANN MARIE BROWN

Pioneer Trail's single-track weaves through the trees as it parallels Highway 20.

ROUTE DETAILS FOR 5A
(lower stretch only)

type of trail	dirt single-track
difficulty	
total distance	10 miles
riding time	2 hours
elevation gain	700 feet

ROUTE DETAILS FOR 5B
(lower and upper stretch)

type of trail	dirt road and single-track
difficulty	
total distance	20.6 or 30.2 miles
riding time	5 hours
elevation gain	1,800 feet

us riding on new territory for a long time. The word around town is that while mountain biking may have been born in Marin County, it has matured in Nevada County. A number of professional bike racers live and train in the area.

Pioneer Trail is a perfect pathway for an introduction to the region. Because Pioneer Trail starts at 3,500 feet in elevation and slowly cruises up to 5,000 feet, its first several miles are snow-free most of the year. The trail is as difficult as you want it to be, depending on how far you go. Most riders with some single-track experience can handle the first five miles of the trail. More advanced riders can enjoy up to 15 miles of single-track (one-way). Some bikers choose to leave cars at various points along Highway 20 and ride a one-way downhill shuttle trip, but the elevation gain is so gradual, you might as well ride out and back and get some exercise.

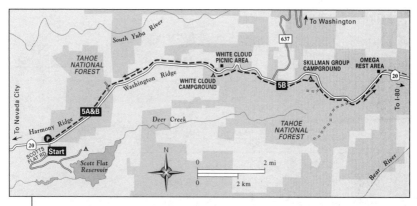

The trail consists of a lower and upper section. Both follow close to Highway 20, often in sight of the road, for their entire length. Lower Pioneer is less technical and easier to ride (Ride 5A), so start there and test your skills before moving on to Upper Pioneer (Ride 5B). The lower section runs from Harmony Ridge Market to White Cloud Picnic Area and Campground, a 10-mile round-trip with an extremely gradual 500-foot elevation change. The trail dips and rolls through the trees, crossing numerous driveways and dirt roads. Diamond-shaped markers on the trees keep you on the right path. Although the black oak and ponderosa pine forest is so dense that you don't gain any views, the beauty is in the journey here. This smooth trail is just plain fun to ride, with few technical challenges.

At White Cloud Picnic Area, the trail crosses the highway, enters White Cloud Campground, and becomes the more advanced upper trail (Ride 5B). The tread gets rockier and narrower until you reach Skillman Group Campground at mile 10.3. Some riders turn around here for a 20.6-mile round-trip; the intrepid continue onward to Omega Overlook and Rest Stop, another five miles east, for a 30.2-mile round-trip.

Highway 20's cool and shady campgrounds are popular destinations in the summer months. That means this trail sees a lot of use, especially on weekends.

For more information, contact the Nevada City Ranger District of Tahoe National Forest, 530/265-4531.

Driving Directions

From Nevada City at the junction of Highways 49 and 20, take Highway 20 east for five miles. Look for Harmony Ridge Market on the left (across from Scotts Flat Road); park in the rear area of the lot where it's signed for mountain bikers.

Pioneer Trail

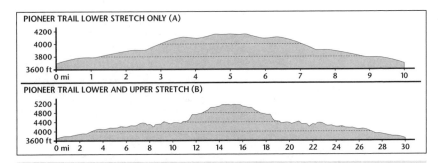

Route Directions for Ride 5A *(lower stretch only)* for Pioneer Trail

0.0 Park at Harmony Ridge Market. Trail is on the right side of the store (signed). *Supplies are available at the market.*

5.0 White Cloud Picnic Area. TURN AROUND. *Water is available across the street at the campground.*

10.0 Arrive at starting point.

Route Directions for Ride 5B *(lower and upper stretch)*

Follow directions for Ride 5A to mile 5.0, then continue:

5.0 White Cloud Picnic Area. Cross the highway and enter the campground. *Water is available.*

6.8 Trail veers sharply LEFT (follow trail markers).

10.3 Skillman Campground. *Water is available.*

15.1 Omega Overlook is across Highway 20 to the left. TURN AROUND.

30.2 Arrive at starting point.

6. FORESTHILL DIVIDE LOOP

Auburn State Recreation Area

At the trailhead for the Foresthill Divide Loop, I met a young rider who was trying to jump over a foot-high barricade—from a standstill position. He kept bouncing along on his bike, getting more and more air each time, trying to get high enough to clear that barricade. Then he flipped his bike around a full 180 degrees by using the same bouncing pogo-stick technique, his feet never leaving the pedals.

ROUTE DETAILS

type of trail   dirt road and single-track

difficulty

total distance   11.4 miles

riding time   1–2 hours

elevation gain   1,800 feet

If this was the kind of rider who traversed the Foresthill Divide Loop, I didn't want any part of it. But it turns out, even though this trail is frequently discussed in hushed tones around the bike shops of Auburn, Foresthill Divide is mostly smooth, well-built single-track. Compared to the rocky dirt roads in the area that are popular for mountain biking, this trail is quite easy to ride. Built by mountain bikers for mountain bikers, it was constructed so that the trail wouldn't erode easily. The path is single-track but not too narrow, its ups and downs are reasonably gradual, and its multiple swoops, turns, and curves are just plain fun. It's easy to get going pretty fast, but that's a mistake: You have a good chance of running into equestrians or hikers, who also use this trail.

Much of the trail runs through manzanita and black oak forest. In summer, this is by far the most comfortable trail in Auburn State Recreation Area (530/885-4527) because of its abundant shade. Look forward to canyon views and hilltop panoramas from the tops of several short climbs.

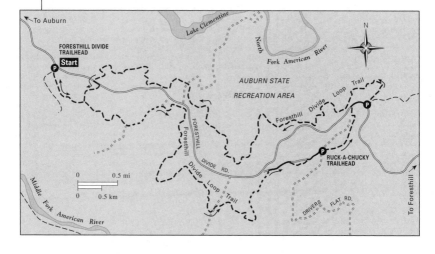

Foresthill Divide Loop

Although it crosses paths with some dirt roads and busy Foresthill Road, the route is well signed all the way. Foresthill Divide Loop can be ridden in either direction, and it makes little difference which way you choose. I've described a counterclockwise loop.

Driving Directions

From Sacramento, take I-80 east to Auburn and exit at Foresthill Road. Go right (east) on Foresthill Road. From its junction with Lincoln Way in Auburn, continue 4.6 miles on Foresthill Road to the trailhead on the right.

FORESTHILL DIVIDE LOOP

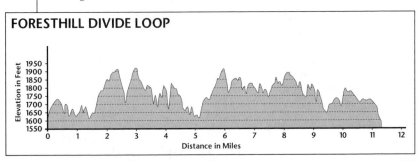

Route Directions for Foresthill Divide Loop

0.0　Park at the Foresthill Divide Trailhead. Take the left fork to start. *Supplies are available in Auburn.*

0.6　RIGHT at sign for Foresthill Divide Loop Trail.

1.0　LEFT on a dirt road.

1.5　Trail runs close to Foresthill Road.

3.3　LEFT on a dirt road, then immediate RIGHT on single-track.

3.8　LEFT on a dirt road.

4.4　RIGHT on paved road then immediate RIGHT on single-track.

4.9　Ruck-a-Chucky Trailhead parking area (Drivers Flat Road); ride across it and pick up trail.

5.6　Cross busy Foresthill Road carefully. Trail continues 70 yards to the right at parking area; veer left on trail.

9.0　Cross dirt road to Lake Clementine.

10.4　Cross busy Foresthill Road again. Trail continues 25 yards to the left.

10.8　RIGHT at junction (same junction you visited at mile 0.6).

11.4　Arrive at starting point.

7. LAKE CLEMENTINE LOOP

Auburn State Recreation Area

The Lake Clementine Loop strings together five different trails to form a classic Auburn ride, one that is a favorite among locals and visitors alike. You're either climbing or descending for every pedal stroke of this ride, which runs between two different forks of the American River: the Middle Fork and the North Fork.

One leg of the Lake Clementine Loop drops below the Foresthill Bridge over the American River canyon.

The first leg of the route is Stage-coach Trail, an old 1880s stagecoach route, which drops from Russell Road in Auburn down to the confluence of the North Fork and Middle Forks of the American River at the Old Foresthill Bridge. It's a fast descent on a well-worn dirt road—keep your speed below the posted 15 mph and enjoy the expansive views of the river canyon. At the bottom, cross the old bridge to connect with Lake Clementine Trail on the left. You'll climb upward toward the fancy "new" bridge, a marvel of mechanical engineering that looms 750 feet above this canyon.

The trail closely follows the edge of the North Fork, with some steep and scary drop-offs, until it reaches paved Lake Clementine Road. Next comes another nasty uphill (the pavement should help the ascent, but it doesn't feel like it) to Fuel Break Trail and finally Culvert Trail. Here the real fun, and a long-awaited downhill, begins. You ride through a dark, cool culvert under Foresthill Road, then connect to Confluence Trail at Mammoth Bar OHV Area. Confluence Trail is the most technically challenging trail of the day; it is extremely narrow and features exposed drop-offs, tree roots, and rocks galore. The path doesn't allow much room for error; a fall here means a 30-foot drop into the river.

If you make it through Confluence Trail, you're back at the Old Foresthill Bridge, and now all you have to do is climb back up Stagecoach to your car. Remember how fun it was to fly down? Now you'll see it from the opposite perspective.

If you aren't sure of your ability to handle this ride, you can cut it shorter by starting from the trailhead at the junction of Highway 49 and Old Foresthill Road by the American River (drive three miles southeast on

ROUTE DETAILS

type of trail — dirt road and single-track

difficulty — ▮▮▮▯▯

total distance — 11.2 miles (or 7.3-mile option)

riding time — 2 hours

elevation gain — 1,700 feet

Lake Clementine Loop

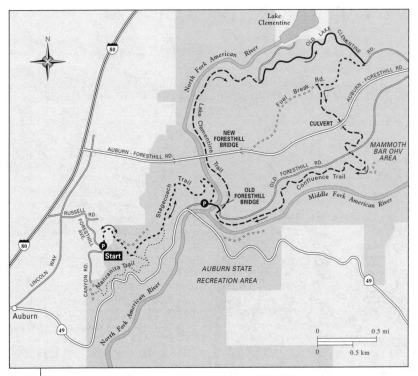

Highway 49 from Auburn). This will cut off the first steep descent from Russell Road and the ensuing climb back uphill at the end, dropping your mileage to 7.3 miles.

For more information, contact Auburn State Recreation Area, 530/885-4527.

Driving Directions

From Sacramento, take I-80 east to Auburn and exit at Russell Road. Drive southeast to the junction of Russell Road and Lincoln Way, then continue on Russell Road for .5 mile to a dirt parking area on the left (where Russell Road becomes Foresthill Road).

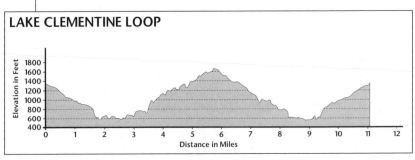

Route Directions for Lake Clementine Loop

0.0 Park at the Stagecoach Trail parking area on Russell Road. *Supplies are available in Auburn.*

1.8 RIGHT at fork.

2.0 LEFT on Old Foresthill Road/bridge where Stagecoach Trail ends.

2.1 LEFT on Lake Clementine Trail.

2.3 LEFT to stay alongside river.

3.9 RIGHT at gate at paved Lake Clementine Road.

5.3 RIGHT at gate, then follow trail on the right (Fuel Break Trail).

6.0 LEFT on Culvert Trail.

6.5 Go through culvert under Foresthill Road.

7.1 Cross Old Foresthill Road and enter Mammoth Bar OHV area; follow gravel road.

7.3 RIGHT at gate on to Confluence Trail.

9.2 LEFT at Old Foresthill Road/bridge.

9.3 RIGHT on Stagecoach Trail.

11.2 Arrive at starting point.

8. QUARRY ROAD TRAIL

Auburn State Recreation Area

Beginning mountain bikers can become easily discouraged in Auburn State Recreation Area (530/885-4527). From the novice's standpoint, the local trails climb with the average grade of a skyscraper. Their surfaces are rutted and rocky. The sun beats down upon them year-round. But still, the recreation area is wildly popular with mountain bikers. Every trailhead is filled with cars, and every car sports a bike rack. What's a wannabe to do?

ROUTE DETAILS

type of trail 🐴 dirt road

difficulty 🍶🍶🍶🍶🍶

total distance 10.8 miles

riding time 2 hours

elevation gain 1,200 feet

Head for Quarry Road Trail, which follows the south side of the canyon of the Middle Fork of the American River. The trail, really a wide road, starts near the confluence of the North and Middle Forks and runs for 5.4 miles to Maine Bar (spelled "Main Bar" on some maps). It's mostly level and smooth, with only three steep but short climbs over its entire distance. Quarry Road presents few technical challenges, except for the discipline it requires to keep your eyes on the trail instead of the beautiful American River flowing by. Do keep watch, however: Sections of the trail have washed out in winter storms and the drop-offs are severe.

One of Quarry Road's great charms is that it's a breeze to follow. It sticks to the river's edge for its entire distance and is frequently marked with small WST signs, which stand for Western States Trail (although technically this is the "alternate" Western States Trail, a lengthy equestrian trail). The few spur trails that intersect are all clearly signed No Bikes.

If it's a warm day, you'll have plenty of company in the first half mile, as sunbathers wander with their inner tubes in search of a good swimming hole. The level of solitude increases as you progress into the canyon. An old quarry, the trail's namesake, is the first notable landmark. The path gets slightly more technical (read: rocky) beyond the quarry.

Quarry Road continues, rolling up and down tiny hills, for several miles of uninterrupted riding and great vistas of the steep river canyon. The canyon's slopes are punctuated by a few digger pines—scraggly-looking conifers with gray-green needles—and some interesting rock outcrops. A few offshoot trails lead down to the river; take any of them if you wish to cool off.

After about four miles you'll leave the sunshine and the river views and head into dense oak and pine forest, where the trail narrows. You reach Maine Bar at 5.4 miles, where Maine Bar Trail takes off on the right and bikes are prohibited. Relax at the picnic table for a few minutes, then turn around and ride westward, enjoying the river canyon all over again.

Driving Directions

From Sacramento, take I-80 east to Auburn and exit at Highway 49 south. Head southeast through Auburn on Highway 49 for three miles. At the bottom of the canyon, where Highway 49 turns right and crosses a bridge over the river, set your odometer. In .4 mile, turn left on a dirt road (it's easy to miss). Quarry Road Trail is the gated dirt road by the parking area.

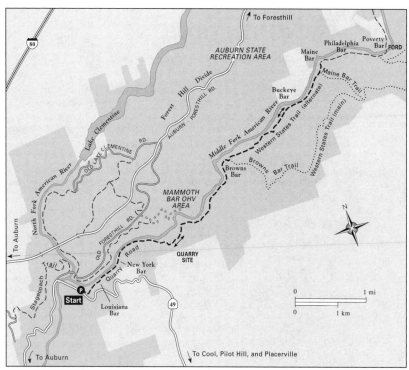

QUARRY ROAD TRAIL

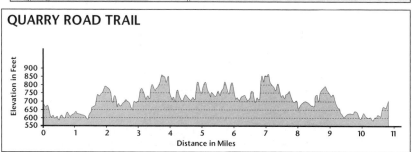

Route Directions for Quarry Road Trail

0.0 Park at the Quarry Road trailhead off Highway 49, just beyond the highway bridge over the river. *Supplies are available in Auburn.*

2.0 Mammoth Bar OHV area across the river.

3.3 Browns Bar Trail intersects on the right.

5.4 Maine Bar. TURN AROUND.

10.8 Arrive at starting point.

9. SALMON FALLS/ DARRINGTON TRAIL

South Fork of the American River near Folsom Lake

This is a classic Sierra foothills mountain bike ride with two names: Salmon Falls and Darrington. Most people call it the former, after a nearby waterfall on the South Fork of the American River, but its official, mapped name is the latter. If you live anywhere near Sacramento and you own a mountain bike, you've probably ridden this trail. If you haven't, you should. Strong, adventurous beginners can probably manage it as long as they are willing to walk some of the more technical sections, most of which happen to be in the first few miles of trail. Salmon Falls Trail starts out treacherous, but gets easier as it goes.

ROUTE DETAILS

type of trail   dirt road and single-track

difficulty   ▮▮▮▯▯

total distance   18.8 miles (plus shorter or longer options)

riding time   3–4 hours

elevation gain   2,000 feet

The trail meanders high above the South Fork of the American River just before the river empties into Folsom Lake. This is chaparral and rattlesnake country—hot and dry in the summer, but just right the rest of the year. The mostly wide single-track rolls along, offering expansive river canyon views. Name your pine trees as you ride: ponderosa, digger, and Jeffrey. Name your oak trees as you ride: valley, black, and Oregon. If it's summer, you'll wish there were a whole lot more of them—the reddish-colored earth lining the trail seems to reflect the heat of the sun.

Since Salmon Falls is an out-and-back, you can customize the route any way you wish. The best of the ride is over at about mile 7.5; this makes a good turnaround point if you don't need to refill your water bottles. If you do, continue to popular Peninsula Campground at mile 9.0 and slake your thirst. Some people opt to ride this trail as a one-way route with a car shuttle, leaving a second car at the camp area.

If you had so much fun on Salmon Falls/Darrington Trail that you're still hungering for more, try the nearby Sweetwater Trail, a similarly technical, out-and-back single-track. The trailhead is a quarter mile farther west on Salmon Falls Road (cross over the bridge) at the river access area on the right. The signed trail begins by the restrooms at the far west end of the parking lot.

For more information, contact Folsom Lake State Recreation Area, 916/988-0205.

Driving Directions

From Sacramento, take I-80 east to Auburn and exit at Highway 49 south. Head southeast through Auburn on Highway 49, then continue six miles through the town of Cool. Drive 3.3 miles past Cool on Highway 49, then turn right on Rattlesnake Bar Road. Turn left immediately on Salmon Falls Road and drive 6.1 miles to the trailhead on the right. There is additional parking 100 yards farther, across the highway bridge, in the pullouts on the right side of the road.

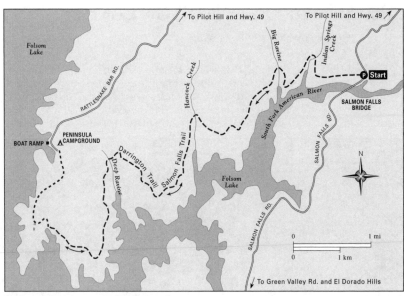

SALMON FALLS/DARRINGTON TRAIL

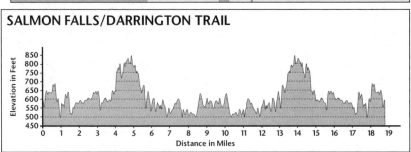

Route Directions for Salmon Falls/Darrington Trail

0.0 Park at the Darrington Trailhead. Take the lower, more obvious trail from the edge of the parking lot. *Supplies are available in Cool.*

1.0 LEFT on old road.

1.5 Road becomes single-track (veer RIGHT).

3.3 LEFT on jeep trail.

7.5 Optional turnaround point before climb begins (if you don't need water from Peninsula Campground).

8.0 STRAIGHT at four-way intersection of dirt roads.

8.9 Gate and paved road; follow the pavement to Peninsula Campground.

9.4 Peninsula Campground. TURN AROUND. *Water is available.*

18.8 Arrive at starting point.

10. SLY PARK'S JENKINSON LAKE

Pollock Pines east of Placerville

Sly Park Recreation Area (530/644-2545) is best known for family camping in its conifer-filled woods and fishing, swimming, and waterskiing in its blue waterway, Jenkinson Lake. It's the kind of place where Boy and Girl Scout troops go for a weekend and memories are made. It's also very popular with equestrians, who have access to a horse camp and a riding trail encircling the lake.

Pines and firs line the mountain biking and hiking trail at Jenkinson Lake.

© ANN MARIE BROWN

ROUTE DETAILS

type of trail dirt single-track

difficulty

total distance 7.4 miles

riding time 2 hours

elevation gain 600 feet

All this means it's surprising that mountain bikes are allowed here. But they are, and so far, conflicts have been rare. Make sure you pay attention to trail signs; in many spots, bikers and hikers take one fork and equestrians take another. Pay close attention or Mr. Ed may give you a swift kick in the rear (tire or otherwise).

The entire trail is a loop around the lake and a mix of single-track, double-track, and pavement. However, the best part of the trail is the first 3.7 miles (all single-track) on the lake's south shore. The rest of the loop has many confusing junctions amid a maze of campgrounds and picnic areas. I recommend riding out-and-back on the first 3.7 miles and not bothering with the whole loop, unless you enjoy riding through parking lots jammed with restrooms, barbecue grills, RVs, and campers.

From the lake's dam, the well signed single-track snakes and rolls through a wonderfully scented pine and fir forest. Watch out for narrow, twisting spots and some scary drop-offs. Lake views are quite pretty, especially early in the season when the lake is full.

An interesting highlight is the half-mile-long tunnel near the Hazel Creek Bridge, which was part of the original water system that formed Jenkinson Lake. Check out the museum in the main part of the park to learn more about it.

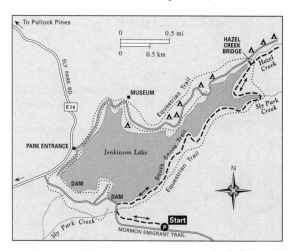

Driving Directions

From Placerville, drive 15 miles east on U.S. 50 to Pollock Pines. Exit on Sly Park Road and head south. In 4.4 miles you will pass the main entrance to Sly Park; continue beyond it for .5 mile to the left turnoff for Mormon Emigrant Trail. Turn left, cross the first dam and park off the road near the second dam. The trailhead is signed Southshore Hiking Trail on the southeast side of the second dam.

SLY PARK'S JENKINSON LAKE

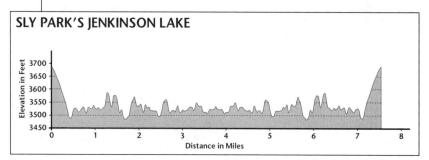

Route Directions for Sly Park's Jenkinson Lake

0.0 Park alongside the road near second dam and start riding on Southshore Hiking Trail. *Supplies are available at store across Sly Park Road from main park entrance.*

3.5 RIGHT just before the Hazel Creek bridge. Follow the trail uphill to see the long tunnel.

3.6 Backtrack to main trail and cross Hazel Creek bridge.

3.7 Arrive at Hazel Creek Campground. TURN AROUND. *Water is available.*

7.4 Arrive at starting point.

11. AMERICAN RIVER PARKWAY

Sacramento to Folsom Lake

The American River Parkway is one of the oldest and longest paved bike paths in the United States, a 32.8-mile trail leading all the way from Discovery Park in Sacramento to Folsom Lake. More than 500,000 people ride the trail each year. If you're in the mood, you can pedal the whole thing for 65.6 miles of paved recreation trail riding, with only a few slight rises for hills (Ride 11A).

Some sections are more scenic than others, however, so if it's your first trip, you might want to go straight to one of the best parts and ride westward from Beals Point at Folsom Lake (Ride 11B). To do so, start at the trail's eastern terminus. After leaving the Beals Point parking area (which can be an absolute zoo on summer weekends because of the lake's sandy beach and swimming areas), pick up the bike trail and ride to your left (west). Numbers painted on the trail's surface mark your mileage. You are starting at 32.8; the numbers drop as you ride west—31, 30, 29, etc.

Your first vistas are of Folsom Lake as you ride around its northwest edge on a wing of the huge, 340-foot Folsom Dam. The 18,000-acre reservoir was created in 1955 by building a main concrete dam on the American River, as well as several wing dams and dikes. Next you'll ride by a place you've heard about but never thought you'd visit: Folsom State Prison. Fortunately your surroundings quickly become less foreboding as you pedal through acres of grasslands with the American River at your side.

At three miles out, the river is dammed once again, this time by Nimbus Dam. You ride past Lake Natoma, which is smaller and quieter than Lake

ROUTE DETAILS FOR 11A

type of trail paved bike path

difficulty

total distance 65.6 miles (plus shorter options)

riding time 5 hours

elevation gain 450 feet

ROUTE DETAILS FOR 11B
(short and scenic option)

type of trail paved bike path

difficulty

total distance 20 miles (plus shorter options)

riding time 2 hours

elevation gain 250 feet

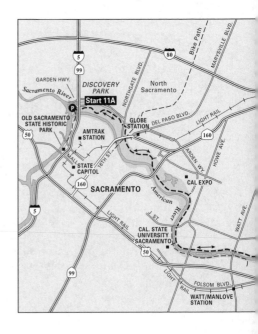

Folsom. Just beyond the highway bridge before Negro Bar is a high over-look looking down at the lake, with small boats floating by and people wading near the shore. A turnaround here, near mileage marker 29, will give you a 7.0-mile round-trip, perfect for families with small children. Or continue onward for another 6.5 miles to the Nimbus Fish Hatchery; a turnaround here makes a 20-mile round-trip. You will have a slight uphill on the way back to Folsom Lake, but it doesn't amount to much.

If you choose to start riding from downtown Sacramento instead, note that the trail's western terminus at Discovery Park isn't in the safest neigh-borhood. However, a one-mile spur trail runs from Discovery Park to touristy yet picturesque Old Sacramento, a much nicer area with shops, amenities, and parking. You could begin riding from there, or from two dozen other trailheads, including Sacramento State University, Goethe Park, and Nimbus Fish Hatchery. Restrooms, picnic tables, and water are available at numerous spots along the trail. Free maps of the American River Parkway and Sacra-mento's other paved bike trails are available at any bike shop in town.

Although the trail does cross a few major streets, this is remarkably peaceful pedaling in an extremely urban area. Birdwatching and berry picking are popular activities along the trail.

For more information, contact the American River Parkway Foundation, 916/456-7423, or Folsom Lake State Recreation Area, 916/988-0205.

Driving Directions
To reach the western terminus of the trail at Discovery Park: From I-5 in Sacramento, take the Richards Boulevard exit (or Garden Highway exit)

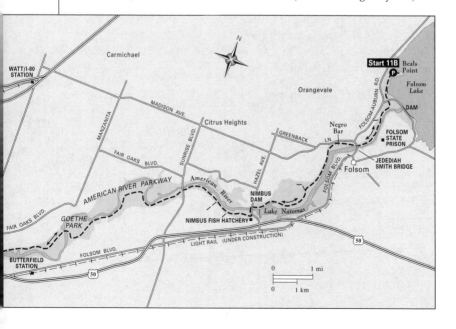

and follow the signs to Discovery Park on the west side of I-5. The bikeway begins at the park (underneath I-5).

To reach the eastern terminus of the trail at Folsom Lake: From I-80 in Sacramento, drive east for 15 miles and take the Douglas Road exit near Roseville. Drive east 5.3 miles on Douglas Road, then turn right on Auburn-Folsom Road and drive 1.7 miles. Turn left at the sign for Beals Point; you'll cross the bike path as you drive to the parking area.

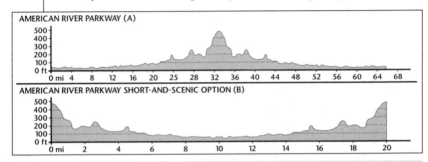

Route Directions for Ride 11A for American River Parkway

0.0 Park at the Discovery Park trailhead in Sacramento. The following are route directions for riding the entire trail west to east, although you could easily reverse the route or ride only a part of it. *Supplies are available in Sacramento; water is available at many points along the trail.*

2.8 STRAIGHT at junction (don't cross the river).

6.5 Cal Expo.

7.9 LEFT at junction (path crossing the river leads to Cal State Sacramento).

14.0 Goethe Park. Cross the river to the south side.

23.0 Nimbus Fish Hatchery and Hazel Avenue Bridge. Cross the river and pick up trail on the north side.

28.0 Jedediah Smith Bridge/Rainbow Bridge.

32.8 End of trail at Beals Point at Folsom Lake. TURN AROUND.

65.6 Arrive at starting point.

Route Directions for Ride 11B *(short-and-scenic option)*

0.0 Park at the Beals Point trailhead at Folsom Lake. See the trail description above for notes on traveling the trail from east to west.

12. SACRAMENTO RIVER DELTA

Southwest of Sacramento

It's flat out here. Flat as a pancake. Flat as a desktop. Flat as the fertile Sacramento River plains.

ROUTE DETAILS

type of trail 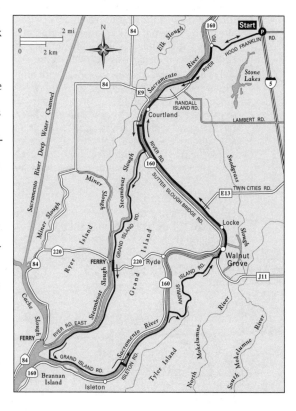 paved roads with moderate car traffic

difficulty 🍶🍶🍶🍶🍶

total distance 48.5 miles

riding time 3 hours

elevation gain 150 feet

If you just want to spin out some fast miles, there may be no better place to do it than around the Sacramento River Delta, where the pavement is smooth and hills are nonexistent. Only one element can slow you down and that's the wind, which comes up fairly consistently every afternoon. Those infamous Delta breezes that bring joy to the lives of local windsurfers can mean drudgery for cyclists. It's wise to avoid summer days when the Central Valley heats up; that's when the great wind machine along the waterways starts working hardest.

The Delta ride starts in the small town of Franklin and heads south along the Sacramento River, then circles back via four "islands:" Randall, Sutter, Grand, and Andrus. The islands, like dozens of others in the area, are manmade, created in the early 20th century by dredging the Delta wetlands and constructing the levees that we ride on today. Enterprising pioneers realized that if they could keep this swampy land high and dry, it would make rich soil for planting crops. And they were right. If you can, ride through this fertile region in the spring, when the area's walnut, apple, and pear orchards are in bloom.

Other highlights of the trip include good bird-watching opportunities at the Stone Lakes National Wildlife Refuge in the first stretch out of Franklin. Although the public can enter the refuge only on a few Saturdays each month, a wealth of bird life fills the surrounding skies year-round.

It's also a pleasure to ride past numerous old bridges and drawbridges across the Sacramento River and its sloughs. When automobiles became a common form of transportation in the early 20th century, more and more roads were constructed around the Delta. But with so many waterways to cross, the only options were building bridges or providing ferry service. In many places, standard bridges could not be built, as they would make it impossible for tall boats to pass through the shallow Delta waters. Drawbridges were the solution, and even today boaters in the Delta must pay careful attention to their schedule of openings and closings. If the bridgetender has gone home for the day, a tall boat may have to wait until the next day to pass.

On Grand Island Road, you'll get a look at the historic Grand Island Mansion, an Italian Renaissance–style villa (tours are available). The 58-room villa is the largest private estate in Northern California, and was built in 1917. It is available for rent for weddings and corporate events, and has been featured as a backdrop in many furniture and clothing catalogs. The ride also passes through the historic Chinese town of Locke, which was founded in 1915 after a fire broke out in the Chinese section of nearby Walnut Grove. Locke is listed on the National Registry of Historical Places as the only town in the United States built exclusively by the Chinese for the Chinese.

The ride follows narrow levee roads for almost its entire distance. Traffic can be heavy on Highway 160, but the rest of the roads should be fairly quiet. As you pedal alongside the blue, flat-water estuaries it's fun to think of the days when a few hundred paddlewheeler steamboats plied these waters, carrying passengers and goods from Sacramento to San Francisco, and announcing their arrival with steam-driven calliopes. One of these old ships, the five-story *Delta King*, now serves as a luxury hotel in Sacramento. It's an elegant relic of an almost forgotten time in California's history.

Driving Directions

From Sacramento, take I-5 south for 15 miles to the Hood-Franklin Road exit. Turn left (east) on Hood-Franklin Road and drive 1.2 miles to Franklin School, on the left.

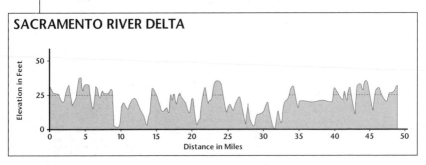

SACRAMENTO RIVER DELTA

Route Directions for Sacramento River Delta

0.0 Park near the Franklin School and ride west on Hood-Franklin Road. *Supplies are available in Sacramento or in towns along this ride.*

3.3 Town of Hood. *Supplies are available.*

3.6 LEFT on River Road (Highway 160).

5.5 RIGHT on Randall Island Road.

7.4 RIGHT on River Road (Highway 160).

7.6 Town of Courtland. *Supplies are available.*

8.9 LEFT on Sutter Slough Bridge Road (Highway 160) after bridge.

10.0 RIGHT on Grand Island Road after bridge.

16.0 STRAIGHT to stay on Grand Island Road.

24.5 RIGHT on Highway 160.

24.7 LEFT on Isleton Road.

28.0 RIGHT on Andrus Island Road.

32.7 RIGHT on bridge across slough; road becomes River Road.

33.0 Town of Walnut Grove. *Supplies are available.*

33.7 Town of Locke. *Supplies are available.*

40.0 STRAIGHT on Highway 160.

41.2 Town of Courtland. *Supplies are available.*

41.4 LEFT on Randall Island Road.

43.3 LEFT on Highway 160.

45.2 RIGHT on Hood-Franklin Road.

48.5 Arrive at starting point.

13. SUTTER CREEK & VOLCANO LOOP

North of Jackson

Sutter Creek's main thoroughfare is lined with antique shops, bed-and-breakfast inns, and restaurants. It's not quite what the gold miners must have imagined for the town back in the 1850s, but it's a charming place to spend a weekend and/or to use as a starting point for this loop ride in the Gold Country. The ride travels to the town of Volcano, which enjoyed a four-year stint as a gold boomtown from 1848 until 1852. The party ended when it was determined that the area was actually outside of the rich gold quartz belt. Today Volcano is a friendly town with a brewery and shops.

ROUTE DETAILS

type of trail — paved road with moderate car traffic

difficulty — 🍶🍶🍶

total distance — 28.2 miles (or 34.2-mile option)

riding time — 2.5–3 hours

elevation gain — 1,800 feet

From Sutter Creek's post office, ride east on Gopher Flat Road, which becomes Shake Ridge Road. After 12.7 pleasant miles, turn right on Rams Horn Grade. If you time your trip carefully and show up between mid-March and mid-April, you're in for a visual treat. On your left is Daffodil Hill (website: www.comspark.com/daffodil-hill), where you can feast your eyes on the spectacle of tens of thousands of daffodils and tulips blooming on the hillside. This extravaganza is the work of several generations of the McLaughlin family, who have been planting and caring for the bulbs for more than 100 years. Visitors are allowed to wander the planted hillsides. As many as 4,000 people show up per day on sunny weekends.

From Daffodil Hill it's a steep downhill through pine and oak forest into Volcano, elevation 2,053 feet. Spend some time enjoying the town, then head west on Sutter Creek Road. You'll have a fun, 12-mile descent alongside pretty Sutter Creek back to your starting point.

If you'd like to add on a few more miles, Indian Grinding Rock State Historic Park (209/296-7488) is three steep miles from Volcano. (Take Pine Grove-Volcano Road south from town.) This is California's only state park dedicated primarily to Native American culture. The surface of the eponymous limestone outcrop features more than 1,200 mortar holes (made by Miwok Indians grinding acorn meal) as well as petroglyphs. A campground is available here if you wish to turn this trip into an overnighter.

Driving Directions

From Stockton, take Highway 88/104 east for 45 miles to Highway 49, then turn north and drive 1.5 miles to Sutter Creek.

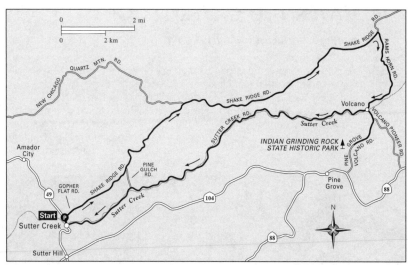

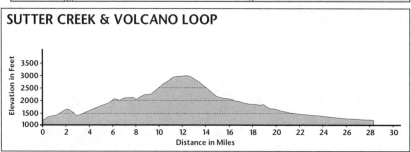

Route Directions for Sutter Creek & Volcano Loop

0.0 Park near the post office in Sutter Creek. Ride east on Gopher Flat Road, which becomes Shake Ridge Road. *Supplies are available in Sutter Creek.*

12.7 RIGHT on Rams Horn Grade; Daffodil Hill is on the left.

15.7 Town of Volcano. *Supplies are available. If you wish to add on six miles to your round-trip, ride out and back to Indian Grinding Rock State Park on Pine Grove-Volcano Road. Note that this is a steep descent to the park and a steep climb back out.*

15.8 STRAIGHT on Sutter Creek Road

27.8 RIGHT on Highway 49.

28.0 Arrive at starting point.

14. CAVERN TO CAVERN LOOP

Murphys, northeast of Angels Camp

The Cavern to Cavern Loop tours the rugged Sierra foothills and visits a few famous and forgotten Gold Rush towns, including Murphys, Calaveritas, and Sheep Ranch. Along the way you can opt to visit two unusual Gold Country attractions: California Caverns (209/736-2708, website: www.caverntours.com) and Mercer Caverns (209/728-2101, website: www.mercer-caverns.com), limestone caves that were first explored during the Gold Rush years. If it's a warm day, you'll be grateful for their cool, dark interiors.

© ANN MARIE BROWN

The historic Murphys Hotel is the start and finish of the Cavern to Cavern Loop through the Gold Country hills.

ROUTE DETAILS

type of trail — paved roads with moderate car traffic

difficulty 🥾🥾🥾🥾

total distance 39.7 miles

riding time 3–4 hours

elevation gain 3,800 feet

Begin your ride in Murphys, elevation 2,171 feet, named for the Murphy Brothers who struck gold here in 1848. Many historic stone structures stand in its tree-shaded downtown, including the Murphys Hotel which bears bullet scars from 150 years ago. North of Murphys, off Sheep Ranch Road, is Mercer Caverns. You can pay a few bucks for a 45-minute walking tour of the caves.

Next, follow San Domingo Road west to Dogtown Road through lovely oak forest and continue into the one-horse town of Calaveritas, elevation 1,040 feet, where you ride underneath an old railroad trestle. This is remote country compared to the busier Gold Country towns along Highways 4 and 49. Head east on Old Gulch Road and climb 1,000 feet to Michel Road and Mountain Ranch. A right turn takes you to California Caverns, a state historic landmark. Cave tours of varying lengths are available. (Skip this four-mile out-and-back if you're getting weary; there's more work ahead to finish out the loop.)

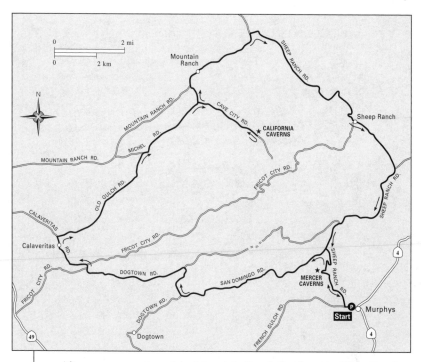

After your cavern tour, take Mountain Ranch Road east to Sheep Ranch Road and then head south to the hamlet of Sheep Ranch, which was once the site of gold mines operated by the Hearst family. It's now all but abandoned. The final southward run on Sheep Ranch Road back to Murphys can be murder if you're already tired; Sheep Ranch Road doles out four steep climbs and descents. Good thing there is an ample supply of tall, cool drinks waiting for you in Murphys.

Driving Directions

From Stockton, take Highway 4 east for 50 miles to Angels Camp. Continue east on Highway 4 for 9.5 more miles and take the Murphys Business District exit, which becomes Main Street.

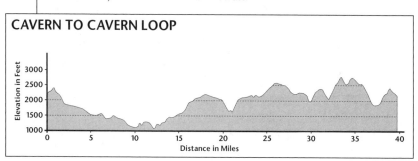

CAVERN TO CAVERN LOOP

Route Directions for Cavern to Cavern Loop

0.0   Park in Murphys near the junctions of Main Street and Sheep Ranch Road. Ride north on Sheep Ranch Road. *Supplies are available in Murphys.*

1.5   Road to Mercer Caverns on left. *Tour of the caverns available for a fee.*

2.1   LEFT on San Domingo Road.

7.2   RIGHT on Dogtown Road.

7.5   LEFT on Dogtown Road.

10.5   RIGHT on Calaveritas Road.

10.6   LEFT on Calaveritas Road.

12.5   RIGHT on Old Gulch Road.

16.6   RIGHT on Michel Road.

19.4   RIGHT on Cave City Road.

21.2   California Caverns. TURN AROUND. *Tour of the caverns available for a fee.*

23.0   RIGHT on Michel Road.

23.3   RIGHT on Mountain Ranch Road. *Supplies are available in Mountain Ranch.*

26.2   RIGHT on Sheep Ranch Road.

30.7   Sheep Ranch.

39.7   Arrive at starting point.

15. SUGAR PINE RAILWAY

West of Strawberry

The Sugar Pine Railway was named for the very large sugar pines that were harvested in this area and shipped along the railroad line from 1906 to 1965. A portion of that rail route, called the Strawberry Branch, is the basis for this trail along the sun-dappled Stanislaus River.

The old Sugar Pine railroad grade tunnels through dense forest alongside the Stanislaus River.

The trail starts at the river bridge near Fraser Flat Campground. Heading to your right (east), the dirt path starts out wide but eventually narrows to single-track. It's simple to follow; the path hugs the river and there are no turnoffs. Watch for an old wooden flume on the river's far side, known as the Philadelphia Ditch. Built in 1899 to supply gold miners with water to work their diggings, the flume is currently used by Pacific Gas and Electric Company to carry water and generate power from the Stanislaus River.

At 2.2 miles, the trail narrows considerably, turns away from the river, and heads uphill through meadows and forest. At 2.8 miles the single-track ends at a paved road, Old Strawberry Road. You can turn around here or ride into the town of Strawberry for lunch. To do so, turn left on the pavement. Ride one mile on Old Strawberry Road, then turn right on Strawberry Drive and come out to the Strawberry Inn. If you're not in the mood for a sit-down lunch, there's a grocery store across the street.

ROUTE DETAILS

type of trail	dirt road and single-track; paved road with minimal car traffic
difficulty	▮▮▯▯▯
total distance	8.6 miles (or 18.6-mile option)
riding time	1 hour
elevation gain	500 feet

If you enjoyed this stretch of trail, head over to Lyons Reservoir to pedal another piece of the old railroad grade. Drive seven miles west on Highway 108 to Lyons Reservoir Road, two miles east of Mi-Wuk Village. Turn right on Lyons Reservoir Road (open only from May to October) and drive 2.1 miles to the day-use area. Park and ride to your left on the gated dirt road. This trail is even easier, wider, and smoother than the Fraser Flat section of the rail trail. The path runs for five level miles to its end at a neighborhood on Middle Camp Road. A turnaround here will add 10 miles to your day.

Sugar Pine Railway

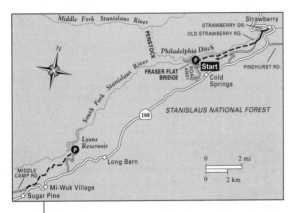

For more information, contact the Summit Ranger District of Stanislaus National Forest, 209/965-3434.

Driving Directions

From Sonora, drive east on Highway 108 for 30 miles to the Fraser Flat turnoff, nine miles east of Mi-Wuk Village and two miles west of Strawberry. (If you reach the Cold Springs Store, you've gone too far east.) Turn left on Forest Service Road 4N01, signed for Fraser Flat and Spring Gap. Drive 2.5 miles to the Fraser Flat Bridge.

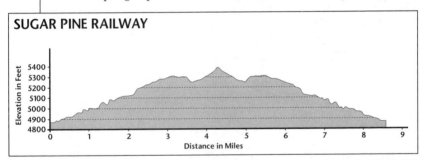

SUGAR PINE RAILWAY

Route Directions for Sugar Pine Railway

0.0 Park in the dirt pullout on the right, just before crossing the Fraser Flat Bridge. Ride on the trail heading upstream. *Supplies are available in Strawberry or Mi-Wuk Village.*

2.8 LEFT on Old Strawberry Road (paved).

3.7 RIGHT on Strawberry Drive.

4.3 Strawberry Inn. TURN AROUND.

8.6 Arrive at starting point. *Follow the route description above to drive to another trailhead for the rail trail at Lyons Reservoir, then add on another 10 miles round-trip.*

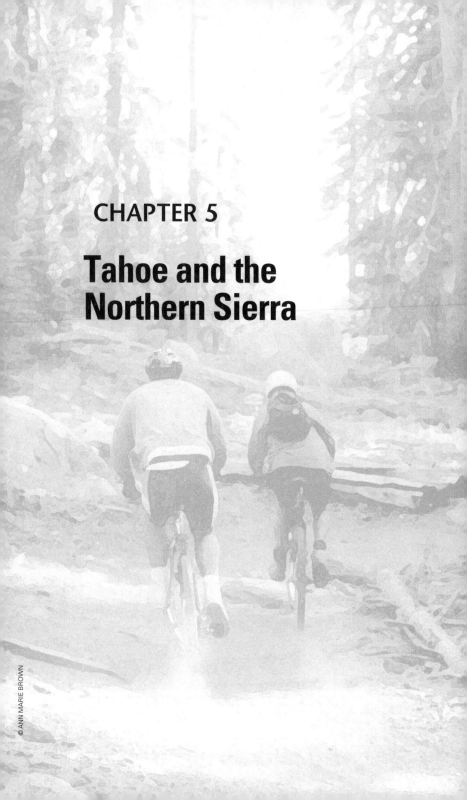

CHAPTER 5

Tahoe and the Northern Sierra

© ANN MARIE BROWN

For most visitors, the Tahoe region is clearly defined by its 22-mile-long, azure-blue lake—"a noble sheet of blue water lifted six thousand three hundred feet above the level of the sea, and walled in by a rim of snow-clad mountain peaks," in the eloquent words of Mark Twain. The 10th deepest lake in the world (1,645 feet at its deepest point) and with remarkable water clarity, it is among the most notable features in the landscape of North America.

Bicycling visitors to the Tahoe region will note two other outstanding features (besides the mammoth lake): rocks and hills. Whereas road cyclists will have to tackle only the latter, mountain bikers will frequently encounter both elements when riding through Tahoe's spectacular High Sierra scenery. In conjunction with the heart-pumping, high-elevation air, these obstacles make Tahoe well suited to riders seeking a challenge.

But that's not to say there aren't opportunities for the more casual rider. Tahoe is laced with paved bike paths, from the scenic Truckee River Trail that closely follows the rushing waters of the Truckee, to the more pedestrian West Shore Trail, which parallels busy Highway 89 from Tahoe City to Sugar Pine Point. Novice to intermediate mountain bike riders will find dirt trails to suit their abilities in the canyons of the lake's west shore. And for those who just want to coast downhill, not crank uphill, several Tahoe ski resorts operate their lifts in the summer so mountain bikers can be whisked to high summits, then cruise downhill on two wheels (see the list of Northern California Mountain Bike Parks in the Appendix).

The rides detailed in this chapter also encompass somewhat lesser-traveled regions surrounding Lake Tahoe, including Plumas County and the Gold Lakes Basin (north of Tahoe) and the Bridgeport area (southeast of Tahoe). Also included are four High Sierra passes between Tahoe and Yosemite; from north to south they are Echo Pass (U.S. 50), Carson Pass (Highway 88), Ebbetts Pass (Highway 4), and Sonora Pass (Highway 108). Carson and Ebbetts are two of the mountain passes featured in the annual Markleeville Death Ride, one of California's premier cycling events, which brings even expert riders to their knees with its staggering 16,000 feet of elevation change and 139 miles. Even if you'd never consider riding in a bike tour of this magnitude, it's worth showing up in July just to watch the spectacle.

The only disappointing fact about biking around Tahoe is that the season is so short. Snow can fall as early as mid-October, and the spring melt can hold off until June. Mountain bikers may find that even though trails may be snow-free as early as Memorial Day, they may be too wet to ride until mid- or late July.

Because of the brief season, thousands of riders take to the roads and trails of Tahoe each year in only a few months' time period. To avoid the crowds, the best time is usually September and October, when most of the summer visitors have gone home. And how fortunate, because that's when Tahoe's famous fall color show occurs. It's worth the wait.

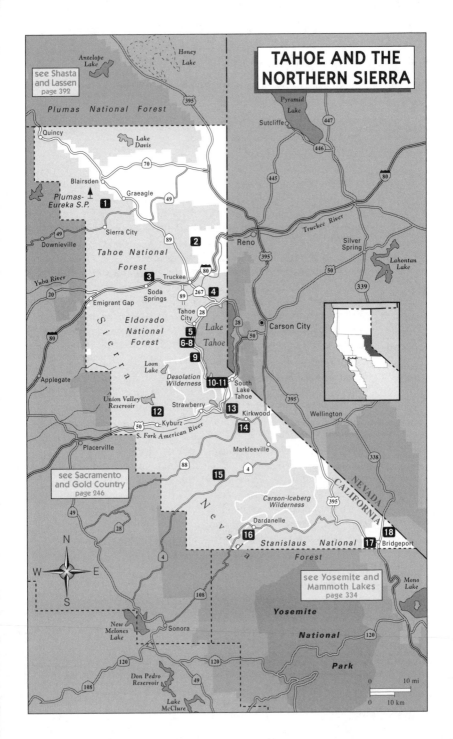

CHAPTER 5
TAHOE AND THE NORTHERN SIERRA

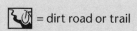 = paved road or path   = dirt road or trail

1. MILLS PEAK LOOKOUT

Gold Lakes Basin near Graeagle

The reward of any fire lookout ride is always the same: an impressive vista from a summit with a wide scope on the surrounding terrain. Although fire lookouts are a favorite destination of mountain bikers, by their nature they are rarely attained without a steep climb.

ROUTE DETAILS

type of trail — dirt road with minimal car traffic

difficulty

total distance — 6.6 miles (or 11.2-mile option)

riding time — 1–2 hours

elevation gain — 800 feet

Mills Peak Lookout in the Gold Lakes Basin is the exception. Perched on a rocky escarpment at 7,310 feet in elevation, the lookout offers an all-encompassing view of the Mohawk Valley and the Sierra Buttes to the south, but with a total climb of only 800 feet from the trailhead.

The well-graded dirt lookout road is open to cars and gets some traffic on summer weekends, so a weekday ride is preferable. It's virtually impossible to get lost as the road is marked with black arrows on orange signs nailed to trees (snowmobile markers).

The surface is only a little rocky and not technical at all, and although it's uphill all the way, the grade is quite moderate. This is a ride that strong beginners could accomplish.

And what a feeling of accomplishment when they reach the summit. The lookout tower itself is a square white cabin that was built in 1932. It is staffed somewhat inconsistently from July 4 to October 1 each year. Even if the tower is closed, you can check out the marvelous view from its base, which is almost as good as from the top.

On the ride back downhill, be sure to stop at

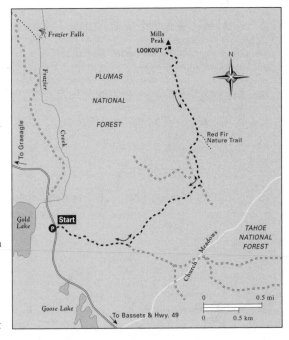

the Red Fir Nature Trail located 1.1 miles from the lookout (or 2.2 miles from Gold Lake Highway). Lock up your bike and take a short walk through the marvelous red fir forest, where the staghorn moss on the trees' large trunks gives an indication of the previous winter's snow level.

If when you return to your car you are still bounding with energy, ride north .5 mile on Gold Lake Highway and turn right at the sign for Frazier Falls. Ride 1.8 miles to the signed trailhead, then lock up your bike and take the .5-mile walk to the plunging 250-foot cataract. The round-trip ride to the Frazier Falls trailhead will add 4.6 nearly level miles to your ride, making an 11.2-mile day.

For more information, contact the Beckwourth Ranger District of Plumas National Forest, 530/836-2575.

Driving Directions

From Graeagle head south on Highway 89 for 1.5 miles, then turn right (west) on Gold Lake Highway, also signed as Lakes Basin Recreation Area. Drive seven miles to the sign for Mills Peak Lookout (.5 mile south of Gold Lake Campground). The lookout road is on the left; park in the gravel pullout on the right side of Gold Lake Highway, then ride across Gold Lake Highway to the start of the lookout road.

MILLS PEAK LOOKOUT

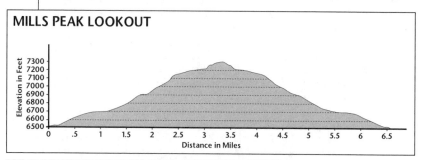

Route Directions for Mills Peak Lookout

0.0 Park in the pullout across Gold Lake Highway from the start of Mills Peak Lookout Road. *Water is available at Gold Lake Campground, .5 mile north on Gold Lake Highway.*

1.1 LEFT at fork.

2.2 Red Fir Nature Trail on the right. *Visit the big trees now or on your way back.*

3.3 Summit and lookout tower. TURN AROUND.

6.6 Arrive at starting point. *Add on an optional ride to Frazier Falls Trailhead and walk to the falls; see route description above.*

2. EMIGRANT TRAIL

North of Truckee near Stampede Reservoir

The Commemorative Overland Emigrant Trail is a 15-mile stretch of single-track that runs from Stampede Reservoir (the largest lake in the Tahoe area after Lake Tahoe itself) to Prosser Creek Reservoir (about one-fifth the size of Stampede). Both lakes are popular for fishing, boating, and camping, and now this trail has made them famous among the mountain biking crowd.

ROUTE DETAILS

type of trail — dirt single-track

difficulty — 🥾🥾🥾

total distance — 31.8 miles (or shorter options)

riding time — 4 hours

elevation gain — 2,000 feet

This is *the* ride to do around Lake Tahoe in the early summer because the area between Stampede and Prosser Reservoirs is typically snow-free a month before everywhere else near Tahoe. On a June weekend, the Emigrant Trail can be packed with riders who have been waiting all winter to get back on their bikes. Early summer is also the best time to visit the two reservoirs, because they are subject to severe drawdowns later in the year. By July and August, it gets quite dry and hot out here, and most of the bikers have moved on to somewhere cooler.

You can start the ride on either end; the elevation change is almost the same in both directions. Although the mileage is long for single-track, the grade consists of lots of gentle ups and downs through open pine and fir forests and meadows. Sage and mule's ears are common foliage.

If you've had some experience on single-track, you can ride pretty fast here; the only technical skill needed is the ability to balance on a narrow trail—the surface is generally smooth and hard packed. The main difficulty is that the trail is bisected by what seems like hundreds of roads and creekbeds. Fortunately there are signs everywhere, so it's hard to go wrong. You must ford a few streams on this ride; most of the creeks are too high and wide early in the summer to ride through. If the water is high in Prosser Creek at 8.2 miles, you will have to ride over to Highway 89 to cross it. This adds about a mile to your ride (included in the mileage below).

Many people ride this route as a shuttle, leaving one car at each end. That's one way to shorten the mileage, but the easier way is just to cut the ride short anywhere you please and turn around. Take your pick. Besides its two end points near Stampede and Prosser Reservoirs, the trail can also be accessed at Donner Camp Picnic Area on Highway 89, or along Old Reno Road out of Hobart Mills.

Note that this is called the "Commemorative" Overland Emigrant Trail because it's not exactly the real thing. Most of the actual trail taken by emigrants in the 1850s has been wiped out by roads and reservoirs; this trail parallels the original route.

For more information, contact the Truckee Ranger District of Tahoe National Forest, 530/587-3558.

Driving Directions

From Truckee, take I-80 east for seven miles and exit at Hirschdale/Stampede Reservoir. Cross under the freeway, then drive eight miles north on Stampede Road to Dog Valley Road. Turn left and drive 2.5 miles to the end of the pavement (past the turnoff for the boat ramp). A small parking area is on the left and the Emigrant Trail begins here.

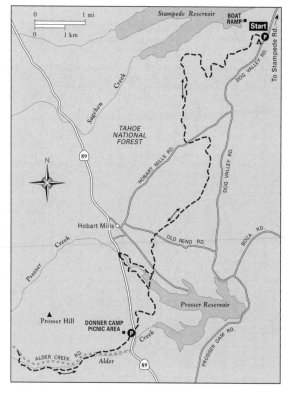

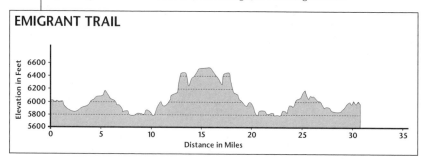

Route Directions for Emigrant Trail

0.0 Park at the Emigrant Trailhead at Stampede Reservoir. *Supplies are available in Truckee.*

0.2 LEFT (straight) toward Old Reno Road.

4.1 Cross paved road.

7.0 Cross old paved road.

7.4 Cross wooden bridge.

7.9 Cross paved road; view of Prosser Reservoir far off on the left.

8.1 RIGHT on dirt road, then immediate LEFT back on Emigrant Trail.

8.2 Prosser Creek Crossing on left (to be used only in low water late in the summer). If high water, go straight to Highway 89 where you can cross the creek on the highway.

8.8 LEFT on Highway 89 and across the bridge (walk your bike on left side of road).

8.9 LEFT on trail just past the guardrail.

9.6 Back on Emigrant Trail, which comes in from the left.

10.5 Cross paved road.

11.6 Donner Camp Parking area. Go RIGHT on pavement and cross Highway 89. *A short interpretive trail about the Donner Party is found here, plus picnic tables and restrooms.*

11.7 LEFT on trail before the dirt road.

12.5 Cross Alder Creek Road.

13.6 Cross Schussing Road; prepare to cross Alder Creek three times in the next mile.

15.9 Trail ends at a dirt road. TURN AROUND.

31.8 Arrive at starting point.

3. HOLE-IN-THE-GROUND TRAIL

Donner Pass west of Truckee

In 1998, Hole-in-the-Ground Trail was Tahoe's newly built, "secret" mountain biking loop. During the summer of 2001, more than 200 people rode this trail each weekend. More evidence that you can't keep a good trail secret.

Awe-inspiring vistas abound along Hole-in-the-Ground Trail.

© ANN MARIE BROWN

The trail's popularity is warranted. It visits two granite-bound swimming lakes (Sand Ridge and Lower Lola Montez) and doles out 10-plus miles of exciting single-track. Although you may see hikers and equestrians on sections of the loop, the main traffic will be other bikers. The ride is not for novices, and even intermediate riders will face technical challenges along the route. Plan for a long day unless you are very skilled at single-track riding.

Note that the loop can be ridden in either direction, and can also be started near the Soda Springs fire station. The trail signs are easier to discern if you ride it the way it's described here. Riding in this direction, you'll start with a steep climb up a dirt road and end with a couple miles of road riding. In between, you have lots of fun, technical single-track.

Starting at the Castle Peak Trailhead, one mile of rocky jeep road leads you to the Hole-in-the-Ground Trail. Nine miles of single-track follow. The first stretch includes a heart-pumping climb up Andesite Ridge, with awe-inspiring views of Castle Peak and Squaw Valley. Next comes a long 2.5-mile descent on a knife-thin ridge; try to keep your eye on your front wheel and not the stunning Sierra scenery. After more ups and downs, plus the two possible lake side trips, the route joins Lower Lola Montez Lake Trail and cruises downhill to the Soda

ROUTE DETAILS

type of trail dirt road and single-track; paved road with minimal car traffic

difficulty ♦♦♦♦◊

total distance 16.7 miles

riding time 3–4 hours

elevation gain 2,100 feet

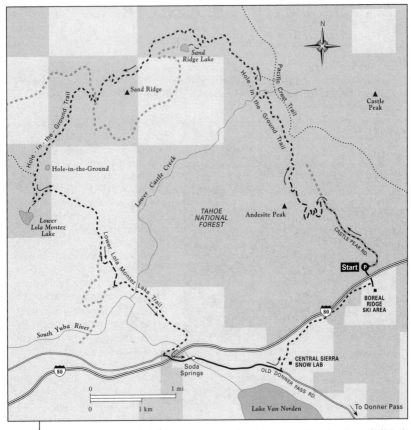

Springs fire station, then loops back on pavement. On the downhill Lola Montez section, please walk your bike through the steepest areas to prevent erosion.

So what's the hole in the ground? Nothing too exciting, just a grassy depression in the earth that fills up with snowmelt in early summer. You'll see it north of the spur to Lower Lola Montez Lake.

For more information, contact the Truckee Ranger District of Tahoe National Forest, 530/587-3558.

Driving Directions

From Soda Springs, drive three miles east on I-80 and take the Castle Peak/Boreal Ridge Road exit. Cross under the freeway and follow the pavement to its end at a metal gate, about 100 yards from I-80. Park alongside the road near the gate, but do not block it.

HOLE-IN-THE-GROUND TRAIL

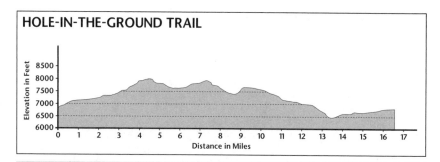

Route Directions for Hole-in-the-Ground Trail

0.0 Park at the end of the pavement on Castle Peak Road. *Supplies are available in Soda Springs, three miles west on I-80.*

0.1 RIGHT at unsigned fork in the jeep road.

0.5 LEFT at unsigned fork in the jeep road.

1.0 LEFT at junction with Hole-in-the-Ground Trail.

2.4 Top of the ridge and great views.

4.3 LEFT at trail junction.

5.4 .25-mile trail to Sand Ridge Lake on the left. *This lake is a great spot for a swim or a break.*

7.6 Dirt road crosses the trail. Stay straight on single-track.

9.7 .25-mile trail to Lower Lola Montez Lake on the right. *This lake is an even better spot for a swim or a break.*

10.1 Single-track becomes a wide jeep road, Lower Lola Montez Lake Trail. *Watch for signs to stay on trail, which alternates as single-track and wide road and passes through private property.*

12.8 Trail reaches pavement. Ride downhill past the fire station.

13.1 LEFT on Donner Pass Road and cross over I-80.

13.8 Soda Springs store. *Supplies are available.*

14.6 LEFT on dirt road signed for Central Sierra Snow Laboratories.

14.8 LEFT at fork.

15.8 Boreal Ridge Ski Resort parking lot. Ride across the lot and pick up Castle Peak/Boreal Ridge Road.

16.2 Take Castle Peak Road under I-80.

16.7 Arrive at starting point.

4. MARTIS PEAK LOOKOUT & WATSON LAKE

North of Lake Tahoe near Brockway Summit

This paved road ride to two wonderful Tahoe destinations can be split into two rides for those with less time or energy. The first leg is a 7.8-mile out-and-back ride to Martis Peak Fire Lookout, elevation 8,656 feet, one of the best overlook points in the Tahoe area. The second leg is a 13.2-mile out-and-back to Watson Lake, a shallow and popular swimming lake. The two legs of the ride are joined by a .6-mile stretch on Highway 267. If you ride the whole thing, you get a 22.2-mile day of fun and scenery. If you want to take it easy, skip the lookout tower ascent and just ride to Watson Lake, which has longer mileage but much less climbing.

rest stop at Watson Lake near Brockway Summit

© ANN MARIE BROWN

ROUTE DETAILS

type of trail paved roads with minimal car traffic

difficulty 🚴🚴🚴

total distance 22.2 miles (or 13.2-mile option)

riding time 2 hours

elevation gain 2,500 feet (or 1,200 feet)

On the Martis Peak ride the route is easy to follow, because you simply stay on the paved road and ignore the numerous junctions with dirt roads. You climb, climb, and climb some more, and after you've gained 1,500 feet in 3.9 miles, you're at the lookout. The tower is staffed by a Forest Service worker in summer and fall, who is happy to interpret for you the great view of Lake Tahoe and Carnelian Bay to the south, Boca and Stampede Reservoirs to the north, Donner Lake, Mount Tallac, the airport in Truckee, Twin Peaks, and so on. On clear days you can even see Mount Lassen, far, far away. The actual summit of Martis Peak is a quarter mile higher (accessible via a dirt trail), but the view is best from the fire lookout.

A speedy descent brings you back to the junction of the lookout road and

Highway 267. Cross the highway carefully, then ride south for .6 mile and turn west on Road 73, Mount Watson Road. A 500-foot elevation gain occurs in the first 1.5 miles from Highway 267, followed by a dip and another climb. Once you're on the ridgeline, the riding is easier and you gain some good views of Lake Tahoe through the trees. There are no turns until 5.9 miles from Highway 267, where you turn left at the orange spray-painted rock (Road 16N50). The lake is less than a mile away. Hope you brought your swimsuit.

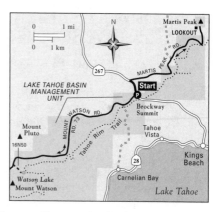

For more information, contact Lake Tahoe Basin Management Unit, 530/573-2600; website: www.r5.fs.fed.us/ltbmu.

Driving Directions

From Tahoe City, drive northeast on Highway 28 to Highway 267. Turn left on Highway 267 and drive 3.7 miles north. Just beyond Brockway Summit, turn right on Martis Peak Lookout Road.

MARTIS PEAK LOOKOUT & WATSON LAKE

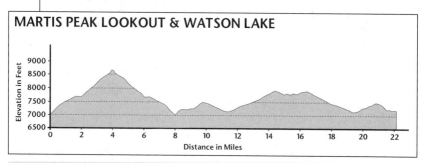

Route Directions for Martis Peak Lookout & Watson Lake

0.0   Park in any available pullout at the start of Martis Peak Lookout Road. *Supplies are available in Kings Beach or Tahoe Vista at Highway 89 and Highway 267.*

3.9   Martis Peak Lookout, elevation 8,756. TURN AROUND.

7.8   Cross Highway 267 and ride LEFT (south).

8.4   RIGHT on Road 73, Mount Watson Road.

14.3   LEFT at orange spray-painted rock (Road 16N50).

15.0   Watson Lake. TURN AROUND.

15.7   RIGHT back on to Road 73, Mount Watson Road.

21.6   Cross Highway 267 and ride LEFT (north).

22.2   RIGHT on Martis Peak Lookout Road. Arrive at starting point.

5. TRUCKEE RIVER RECREATION TRAIL

Tahoe City to Squaw Valley Ski Resort

Of the many paved bike paths in the Tahoe area, the Truckee River Trail is far and away the most scenic and well loved. On summer weekends, it can be difficult negotiating your way amidst all the other bikers, in-line skaters, walkers, and baby strollers on the trail. Nonetheless, whether you're a novice rider or Lance Armstrong you shouldn't miss this fun cruise. During peak vacation season, your best bet is to ride at the edges of the day—early in the morning or just before sunset—to avoid most of the trail traffic. On one beautiful September evening the trail was peaceful enough that I was able to spot a beaver swimming in the Truckee River, as well as dozens of Canada geese.

ROUTE DETAILS

type of trail paved bike path

difficulty

total distance 11.2 miles (plus longer options)

riding time 1 hour

elevation gain 150 feet

The route parallels Highway 89 north of Tahoe City, but it was ingeniously built so that much of its path is 15 to 20 feet below the highway embankment and within a few feet of the river. Because of this, the sight and sound of cars are no distraction and the river takes center stage.

The trail used to end at Alpine Meadows ski area but in 1999 was extended to run another mile to the entrance to Squaw Valley, crossing picturesque Midway Bridge along the way. Food and shops are available at both ski resorts. A common practice is to ride to the River Ranch Inn at the Alpine Meadows turnoff and have lunch on its riverside deck. In the summer, mountain bikers can ride to Squaw Valley and buy a ticket for the lifts; Squaw metamorphoses from a ski resort to a mountain bike park in the

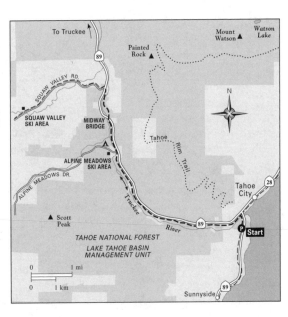

warm months of the year. Road bikers can also extend their trip at Squaw. A two-mile-long paved trail runs beside Squaw Valley Road, with views of the meadow and surrounding peaks.

After you return to the trailhead parking area in Tahoe City, you might want to check out the other paved trails that start there. North Shore Trail travels east to Dollar Hill (2.5 miles

Truckee River Recreation Trail is one of Lake Tahoe's most scenic pathways.

one-way, with access to Lake Forest Beach and Pomin Park). Or you can ride south on West Shore Trail (nine miles one-way to Sugar Pine Point). West Shore Trail, despite its terrific lakeshore views, has one major drawback: It crosses Highway 89 dozens of times. Use caution if you ride it.

For more information, contact Tahoe City Public Utility District, Parks and Recreation Department, 530/583-5544.

Driving Directions

From Tahoe City at the junction of Highways 89 and 28 drive .25 mile south on Highway 89 to the sign for the recreation trail parking area on the right. Turn right (west) and park.

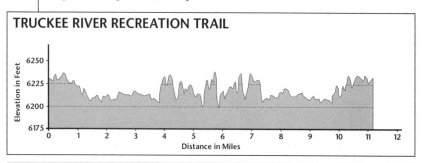

TRUCKEE RIVER RECREATION TRAIL

Route Directions for Truckee River Recreation Trail

0.0 Park at trailhead and ride across the wooden bridge, then turn LEFT. *Water is available at the trailhead; supplies are available in Tahoe City.*

4.5 Alpine Meadows ski area and River Ranch Inn. *Supplies are available.*

5.0 Cross scenic Midway Bridge.

5.6 Trail's end across from the entrance to Squaw Valley ski resort. TURN AROUND. *Supplies are available.*

11.2 Arrive at starting point. *You can add on more riding on other paved trails beginning from same trailhead; see route description.*

6. WARD CREEK & ALPINE MEADOWS LOOP

Southwest of Tahoe City

This is a great ride for when you want an aerobic workout without all the steep hills and rocky trails that Tahoe usually throws at mountain bikers. On this loop you ride enough miles to get away for a few hours and achieve an exercise high, but your nerves aren't jangled from trying to negotiate narrow single-track saddled with rocks, ruts, and steep drop-offs on both sides. This is a ride for stress-free spinning, perfect for a summer evening after work. Even strong beginners can handle the Ward Creek & Alpine Meadows Loop, as long as they have the fitness level to last for 15.7 miles. Completing this ride could be a real confidence builder.

Much of the trail travels through neighborhoods and the ski areas near Alpine Meadows, so the scenery isn't as spectacular as some other rides at Tahoe. You do gain some views of Lake Tahoe, the Truckee River, and the Paige Meadows area. If it's scenery you're after, hold out for the final six miles on the bike path alongside the Truckee River and heading south along Lake Tahoe's shore—those last miles are no disappointment. Note that this ride passes by the Tahoe Rim Trail's Twin Peaks Trailhead on Ward Creek Boulevard. For details on that trail, see Ride 7 in this chapter.

For more information, contact Lake Tahoe Basin Management Unit, 530/573-2600; website: www.r5.fs.fed.us/ltbmu.

ROUTE DETAILS

type of trail dirt road, paved roads with minimal car traffic, and paved bike path

difficulty 🍶🍶🍶🍶🍶

total distance 15.7 miles

riding time 2–3 hours

elevation gain 1,000 feet

Driving Directions

From Tahoe City, drive three miles south on Highway 89 to William Kent Campground, north of Pineland Drive.

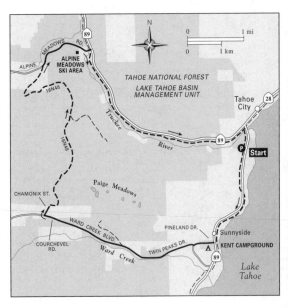

WARD CREEK & ALPINE MEADOWS LOOP

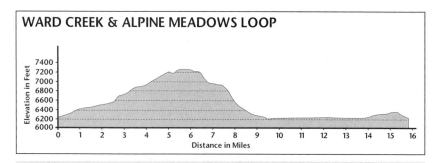

Route Directions for Ward Creek & Alpine Meadows Loop

0.0 Park near William Kent Campground and ride south on the Highway 89 bike trail. *Supplies are available in Tahoe City.*

0.2 RIGHT on Pineland Drive.

0.6 LEFT on Twin Peaks Drive at sign for Ward Valley; road becomes Ward Creek Boulevard and then Courchevel Road.

3.3 RIGHT on Chamonix Street; pavement soon turns to dirt road.

3.6 RIGHT on Road 16N48 (dirt).

4.7 Cross creek and pass road on right (stay left).

7.8 Steep descent and sharp turn to right.

8.2 Forest Service gate. Continue on paved road.

8.6 RIGHT on Alpine Meadows Road.

9.6 RIGHT on Highway 89. Ride the bike path alongside the highway.

13.3 RIGHT across bridge and into main parking area for Tahoe City bike paths. Head south on paved path that parallels Highway 89.

15.8 Arrive at starting point.

7. TWIN PEAKS & STANFORD ROCK LOOP

Southwest of Tahoe City

You'll want to have the lightest bike possible for this ride, because you're going to carry it—a lot. This is not a trail for bikers who are unhappy when pushing or carrying their wheels. Everyone does it on this loop. Most simply give up, stash their bikes, and hike, especially in the last mile to Twin Peaks summit.

ROUTE DETAILS

type of trail	dirt road and single-track; paved roads with minimal car traffic
difficulty	
total distance	16.4 miles
riding time	3–4 hours
elevation gain	2,500 feet

The adventure begins at William Kent Campground, a mere three miles south of Tahoe City. The first 2.3 miles are a warm-up on paved roads as you head out to the old Ward Creek Trailhead, now called the Twin Peaks Trailhead, an official part of the Tahoe Rim Trail. The next three miles are a gentle streamside ride on a smooth dirt road, which then narrows into the kind of single-track that provides fodder for sweet mountain biking dreams . . . until mile 5.8, when the trail moves away from Ward Creek. Those dreams may turn into nightmares.

Over the next 2.6 miles the trail gains 1,800 feet on a grade that is steeper than many hiking trails. Consider this: Since this trail was made a part of the Tahoe Rim Trail, it is much easier than it used to be. Extensive trail work was done in the late 1990s to lessen the grades and increase the mileage on this route. Thank heavens.

When at last you reach the summit of Twin Peaks, elevation 8,878 feet

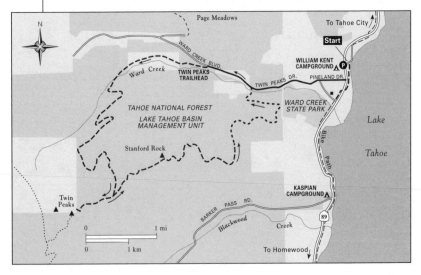

(*sans* mountain bike, if you're smart; you can leave it at the trail junction at mile 7.4), you'll understand why you put yourself through this: The views of Lake Tahoe and the Granite Chief Wilderness are stupendous. Congratulate yourself on a fine achievement.

You must backtrack one mile from Twin Peaks' summit before looping back via Stanford Rock. Although you might expect the way home to be all downhill, you have one more climb and a ridgeline ramble to reach Stanford Rock. Then before you know it you're back on paved Ward Creek Boulevard, nonchalantly riding through the suburban neighborhood as if nothing extraordinary just took place in your day. But you know that it did.

For more information, contact Lake Tahoe Basin Management Unit, 530/573-2600; website: www.r5.fs.fed.us/ltbmu.

Driving Directions

From Tahoe City, drive three miles south on Highway 89 to William Kent Campground, north of Pineland Drive.

TWIN PEAKS & STANFORD ROCK LOOP

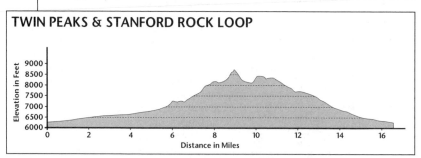

Route Directions for Twin Peaks & Stanford Rock Loop

- 0.0 Park near William Kent Campground and ride south on the Highway 89 bike trail. *Supplies are available in Tahoe City.*
- 0.2 RIGHT on Pineland Drive.
- 0.6 LEFT on Twin Peaks Drive at sign for Ward Valley; road becomes Ward Creek Boulevard.
- 2.3 LEFT at Twin Peaks Trailhead (gated dirt road). Follow the main road and ignore all turnoffs.
- 5.1 Dirt road ends and single-track begins at Ward Creek.
- 5.8 Steep climb begins.
- 7.4 RIGHT at road to Twin Peaks (it's advisable to stash your bike here; there's an 800-foot climb ahead over the next mile).
- 8.4 Summit of Twin Peaks, elevation 8,878 feet. TURN AROUND.
- 9.4 RIGHT to loop back via Stanford Rock.
- 14.8 RIGHT at Ward Creek Boulevard (paved).
- 16.4 Arrive at starting point.

8. BARKER PASS LOOP

Southwest of Tahoe City

For the lucky locals who live along the shores of Lake Tahoe, Barker Pass Road is a favored exercise ride. The road is used by cross-country skiers, cyclists, in-line skaters, skateboarders, and yes, cars. But cars are secondary. The sign at the road's junction with Highway 89 says "This is a multipurpose road: keep your speed down for driving"; for the most part, people do. The scenery is lovely on the way to Barker Pass: aspen groves in the canyons and old-growth firs as you rise up the pass. There's plenty to look at as you ride.

ROUTE DETAILS FOR 8A
(road ride only)

type of trail	paved roads with minimal car traffic
difficulty	🍼🍼🍼🍼🍼
total distance	10 miles
riding time	1–2 hours
elevation gain	1,300 feet

ROUTE DETAILS FOR 8B
(road and dirt loop)

type of trail	dirt and paved roads with minimal car traffic
difficulty	🍼🍼🍼🍼🍼
total distance	14.1 miles
riding time	2 hours
elevation gain	1,600 feet

The road is smooth pavement for the five miles from the off-highway vehicle area, allowing road cyclists a 10-mile out-and-back spin with a healthy 1,300-foot climb (Ride 8A). For the locals, it's a fast, convenient workout. Mountain bikers can continue on a loop, using the dirt road of Blackwood Canyon for the downhill (Ride 8B). (Some choose to ride the dirt road for the uphill and descend on pavement, but note that this is a much more challenging ride: The dirt road packs 1,300 feet of elevation gain into only three miles, while the pavement spreads it out over five miles. Plus there's the added difficulty of rough, rocky surface versus smooth asphalt. It all depends on what kind of ride you want.)

The ride described here goes uphill on paved Barker Pass Road to where the road turns to gravel at the popular Ellis Peak Trailhead. Riders on skinny tires who wish to add a hike to their day can do so by heading steeply uphill to Ellis Peak, 3.5 miles away. Even if you only climb one mile to the top of the ridge, the views are terrific. (Some mountain bikers attempt this trail, but they always wind up pushing their bikes. You'll see why in the first half mile.)

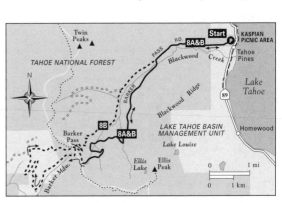

Mountain bikers keep riding where the pavement ends, following the now dirt Barker Pass Road for another half mile. A left turn on a dirt road near the Pacific Crest Trail junction takes you downhill to Barker Meadow and along Barker Creek. Where the road ends, turn right and climb steeply (ignore the numerous side roads and stay on the main road) until you return to dirt Barker Pass Road. From here it is 1.3 miles to the junction with Blackwood Canyon Road, where you make a fast descent back to your car. Much of Blackwood Canyon Road is rough, steep, and loose, so watch your speed. And be cautious of OHV users, who frequent this road, especially on weekends.

For more information, contact Lake Tahoe Basin Management Unit, 530/573-2600; website: www.r5.fs.fed.us/ltbmu.

Driving Directions

From Tahoe City, drive 4.2 miles south on Highway 89 to Forest Service Road 03, Barker Pass Road, at Kaspian Picnic Area. Turn right (west) and drive two miles to Blackwood Canyon OHV area. Turn right on the dirt road to the parking area.

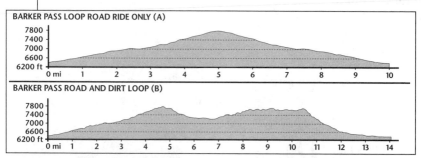

Route Directions for Ride 8A *(road ride only)* for Barker Pass Loop

0.0 Park at the Blackwood Canyon OHV parking area. Ride back out to paved Barker Pass Road and head right (west). *Supplies are available in Tahoe City.*

5.0 Pavement ends. TURN AROUND. *Add on an optional hike to Ellis Peak; see route description.*

10.0 Arrive at starting point.

Route Directions for Ride 8B *(road and dirt loop)*

Follow directions for Ride 8A to mile 5.0, then continue:

5.0 Pavement ends; continue riding on dirt road.

5.5 LEFT on wide road near the junction with Pacific Crest Trail.

7.5 RIGHT on wide road; ignore all possible junctions and keep climbing on the main road through two major switchbacks.

9.8 RIGHT on Barker Pass Road heading back to Barker Pass.

11.1 LEFT on Blackwood Canyon Road.

14.1 Arrive at starting point.

9. GENERAL CREEK LOOP & LOST LAKE

Sugar Pine Point State Park, west Tahoe

If you want to get the kids started on mountain biking, Sugar Pine Point State Park (530/525-7982 or 530/525-7232) is a great place to do it. By the same token, if you want to gain 1,400 feet on a challenging ride to a pretty alpine lake, Sugar Pine Point State Park is a great place to do that, too.

ROUTE DETAILS FOR 9A
(easy loop)

type of trail   dirt road

difficulty   ▮▯▯▯

total distance   4.7 miles (plus longer options)

riding time   1 hour

elevation gain   200 feet

ROUTE DETAILS FOR 9B
(Lost Lake out-and-back)

type of trail   dirt road and single-track

difficulty   ▮▮▮▯

total distance   13.8 miles

riding time   2.5–3 hours

elevation gain   1,400 feet

Two different rides, one trailhead—and it happens to be situated at one of Lake Tahoe's nicest state park campgrounds in woods filled with sugar pines. On a family camping trip, the kids can beg an adult to take them on the short loop while others saddle up for the bigger adventure to Lost Lake. Everyone will return to the campsite smiling.

Easy loop riders begin from campsite 149 in General Creek Campground. By heading straight past the first bridge, you ride the loop counterclockwise. The trail is very smooth dirt and sand, with plenty of room for both hikers and bikers and only one small hill right at the start. It runs through

General Creek Loop offers easy riding through sugar pines.

a thick forest of sugar pines, Jeffrey pines, lodgepole pines, and firs on the north side of General Creek and open meadows on the south side. One of the prettiest stretches is where the trail crosses over a marsh area and wooden bridge at mile 2.4; look for blooming corn lilies and wildflowers in the spring.

If after completing this short loop you want to do more easy riding, it's simple to connect to Lake Tahoe's West Shore bike path, which is paved. Just follow the park

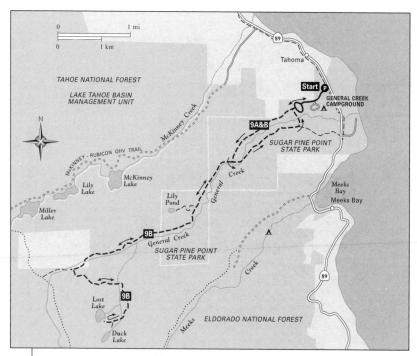

road out to Highway 89 and pick up the trail heading north. It crosses busy Highway 89 a few times, but it is almost completely level and leads to some interesting locations along the lakeshore. The trail extends all the way to Tahoe City, 10 miles north.

Those heading for Lost Lake (Ride 9B) will follow the same path from the campground for the first 2.4 miles, then continue straight instead of looping back. The trail starts out easy but soon narrows to single-track and runs over and around tree roots and boulders. Soon you will have to push or carry your bike, if not because of the obstacles then because of the loose, marble-like rock surface. (Think "bike hiking" and enjoy the upper-body workout.) After crossing General Creek, the single-track climbs mercilessly and then dead-ends into a jeep trail. Head left and climb (or push your bike through the rocks) to a high ridge, passing Duck Lake on your left on your way to Lost Lake, elevation 7,700 feet. Swimming, anyone? You deserve it.

Driving Directions

From Tahoe City, drive nine miles south on Highway 89 to the General Creek Campground entrance on the right.

General Creek Loop & Lost Lake

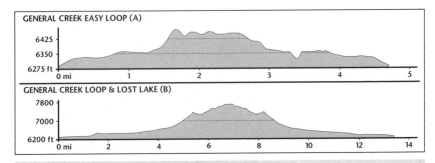

Route Directions for Ride 9A *(easy loop)* for General Creek Loop & Lost Lake

0.0 Park in the day-use parking area near the kiosk, then ride your bike on the park road. Stay to the right in the campground loop to access site 149 and the trail. (The mileage below begins at the day-use parking.) *Water is available in the campground; supplies are available on Highway 89.*

0.7 RIGHT on to trail at campsite 149.

0.9 STRAIGHT at junction with road on left (return of loop).

2.4 LEFT at junction to start loop return.

3.7 LEFT on bridge over General Creek.

3.8 RIGHT on trail.

4.0 Return to campsite 149.

4.7 Arrive at starting point. *You can continue riding by following the park road out to Highway 89, then heading north on the paved bike path.*

Route Directions for Ride 9B *(Lost Lake out-and-back)*

Follow directions for Ride 9A to mile 2.4, then continue:

2.4 STRAIGHT at junction.

2.9 LEFT at Lost Lake/Lily Pond junction; sections of this trail are not rideable so prepare to push your bike.

4.4 Cross General Creek; on far side, trail goes uphill next to the creek.

4.8 LEFT on jeep road to Lost Lake. Walk your bike through the boulders.

6.6 Duck Lake on the left. Continue past it.

6.9 Lost Lake. TURN AROUND.

13.8 Arrive at starting point.

10. FALLEN LEAF LAKE ROAD

South of Lake Tahoe on Fallen Leaf Lake

Fallen Leaf Lake Road is an honest-to-goodness road, complete with car traffic and speed limit signs, but it's as much like a paved recreation trail as any road could be. On summer days you'll find as many bikers and hikers on this lakeside route as automobiles. Due to the number of recreationists, plus the narrowness of the road, cars are forced to go slow, which makes the route safer for bikes than it would otherwise be. Still, I wouldn't recommend it for young children, or for bikers who are prone to attention deficits.

ROUTE DETAILS

type of trail paved road with moderate car traffic

difficulty 🚲🚲🚲🚲

total distance 11 miles

riding time 1 hour

elevation gain 600 feet

The road is an easy, level cruise that provides close-up views of large, 400-foot-deep Fallen Leaf Lake. In its final two miles, Fallen Leaf Lake Road is only 20 feet from the water's edge. Aside from the lake views, the ride's payoff is five miles out at a 100-foot cascade on Glen Alpine Creek, which roars with snowmelt into July. A half mile farther, the road dead-ends at the Glen Alpine Trailhead for the Desolation Wilderness, a trailhead so popular that often there isn't enough parking.

The first three miles pass by Fallen Leaf Campground and through a long stretch of forest. This may be the most peaceful part of the ride, before the road narrows to the width of one car and skirts the lakeshore, where a number of houses are located. You must watch for traffic entering and exiting driveways as you ride.

The final two lakeside miles bustle with activity from the houses, the Fallen Leaf Lake Store and Marina, the roadside waterfall, and the trailhead at Glen Alpine. But even with all the people sharing the narrow road, you still have plenty of chances to admire pretty Fallen Leaf Lake. Fortunately, on a bike, you are traveling at just the right speed to enjoy it.

For more information, contact Lake Tahoe Basin Management Unit, 530/573-2600; website: www.r5.fs.fed.us/ltbmu.

Driving Directions

From South Lake Tahoe at the northern junction of U.S. 50 and Highway 89, drive northwest on Highway 89 for three

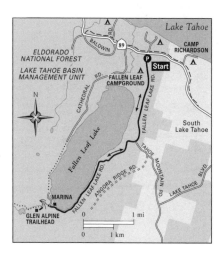

miles to the left turnoff for Fallen Leaf Lake (one mile past Camp Richardson Resort). Turn left on Fallen Leaf Lake Road and park in one of the dirt pullouts along the road.

FALLEN LEAF LAKE ROAD

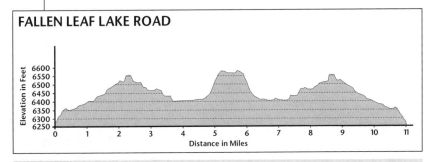

Route Directions for Fallen Leaf Lake Road

0.0   Park in the pullout at the start of Fallen Leaf Lake Road (near its junction with Highway 89) and start riding on the paved road. *Supplies are available one mile east at Camp Richardson, or farther east in South Lake Tahoe.*

0.5   Stay straight at right fork for Fallen Leaf Campground. *Water is available.*

4.4   Fallen Leaf Lake Store and Marina. *Supplies are available.*

4.8   LEFT at fork for Stanford High Sierra Camp.

5.0   Glen Alpine Creek waterfall.

5.5   End of the road at Glen Alpine trailhead. TURN AROUND.

11.0   Arrive at starting point.

11. ANGORA RIDGE LOOKOUT & LAKES

South of Lake Tahoe near Fallen Leaf Lake

This route to Angora Ridge Lookout and Angora Lakes is a fairly easy cruise on both paved and dirt roads to a high overlook of Lake Tahoe and two granite-bound lakes. You'll share much of the ride with some car traffic, but it's quite manageable because most drivers are going slow and enjoying the scenery (this isn't a through-road). If you're in the mood for an aerobic workout and some stellar scenery with no technical challenges, this is your ride.

ROUTE DETAILS

type of trail dirt and paved roads with minimal car traffic

difficulty

total distance 12 miles

riding time 1.5 hours

elevation gain 1,100 feet

The road starts out paved and then alternates as paved and dirt as it climbs gently to the top of Angora Ridge, elevation 7,290 feet. Views are good from the road, but walk a few feet to the fire lookout buildings to get the best perspective on Fallen Leaf Lake, 1,000 feet below you.

From the lookout, the road descends slightly to the parking area for Angora Lakes. The last mile to the lakes is on a car-free dirt trail, but the route is shared with a lot of hikers and dog walkers. You'll ride uphill to Lower Angora Lake, which has a few private homes on its edges, then proceed on level ground to more beautiful Upper Angora Lake, home to Angora Lakes Resort and its handful of picturesque cabins. (You must lock up your bike at the bike rack before entering the resort area.)

The upper lake at 7,280 feet is a perfectly bowl-shaped, glacial cirque lake, set in a pine and fir forest with lots of rounded rock boulders sprinkled around. Although it's nearly impossible to get a reservation to stay at one of Angora Lake's cabins, the resort owners are friendly to day-use visitors. They rent rowboats by the hour and run a small refreshment stand, pumping out lemonade by the gallon to thirsty bikers and hikers. A small sandy beach is popular for swimming and wading in summer.

For more information, contact Lake Tahoe Basin Management Unit, 530/573-2600; website: www.r5.fs.fed.us/ltbmu.

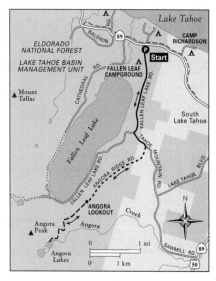

Driving Directions

From South Lake Tahoe at the northern junction of U.S. 50 and Highway 89, drive northwest on Highway 89 for three miles to the left turnoff for Fallen Leaf Lake (one mile past Camp Richardson Resort). Turn left on Fallen Leaf Lake Road and park in the dirt pullouts along the road.

ANGORA RIDGE LOOKOUT & LAKES

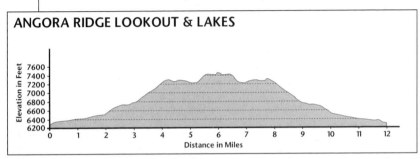

Route Directions for Angora Ridge Lookout & Lakes

0.0   Park in the pullout at the start of Fallen Leaf Lake Road (near its junction with Highway 89) and start riding on the paved road. *Supplies are available one mile east at Camp Richardson, or farther east in South Lake Tahoe.*

0.5   Stay straight at right fork for Fallen Leaf Campground. *Water is available.*

2.0   LEFT on paved Tahoe Mountain Road and head uphill.

2.4   RIGHT on Road 1214 (dirt Angora Ridge Road).

4.3   Angora Ridge Fire Lookout on right; great view of Fallen Leaf Lake.

5.4   Parking lot for lakes; ride across the lot.

5.5   Go past wooden markers and continue uphill on wide dirt trail.

5.8   Lower Angora Lake on left.

6.0   Upper Angora Lake; lock up your bike and walk the final steps to the lake. TURN AROUND.

12.0   Arrive at starting point.

12. BIG HILL LOOKOUT & WRIGHTS LAKE

Crystal Basin Recreation Area off U.S. 50

Few fire lookout towers have access roads that are paved all the way to the top, but the Big Hill Lookout does. This makes this road ride perfect for skinny tires or fat tires—an ideal trip that both kinds of riders can enjoy. In addition, the short climb to the lookout tower provides a healthy leg-and-lung workout in very little time and mileage. (It's like taking one of those Spinning classes at the gym.)

ROUTE DETAILS FOR 12A
(Big Hill Lookout only)

type of trail paved road with minimal car traffic

difficulty 🚴🚴🚴🚴🚴

total distance 7 miles

riding time 1 hour

elevation gain 700 feet

ROUTE DETAILS FOR 12B
(Big Hill Lookout & Wrights Lake)

type of trail paved road with minimal car traffic

difficulty 🚴🚴🚴🚴🚴

total distance 27 miles

riding time 3 hours

elevation gain 2,000 feet

Because this ride goes out and back in two directions from Ice House Campground, less hearty riders can climb to the lookout tower and call it a day (Ride 12A), while more ambitious types can continue on to Wrights Lake, adding on another 20 miles (Ride 12B).

From the start of Big Hill Lookout Road, one mile from the campground, the pavement ascends 700 feet over 2.5 miles. You'll be panting when you arrive at the summit, elevation 6,130 feet. The modern lookout, built in 1994 to replace the original 1933 building that burned down, has a neighboring heliport used for fast attacks on forest fires. (If the firefighters aren't busy, they might let you admire their shiny red helicopter.)

Oddly, the views from the top of Big Hill are of Union Valley Reservoir to the north and much smaller Wrights Lake to the east, but not of Ice House Reservoir directly below. One interesting bit of history: Big Hill Lookout was utilized during World War II for the protection of hot air balloons carrying fire bombs.

After admiring the view, enjoy the fast downhill coast back to Ice House Road, then cross it again and return to the fork just before the campground. Cyclists continuing on Ride 12B will

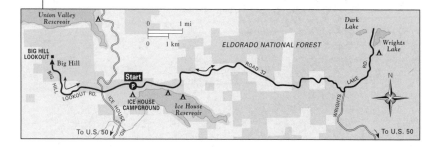

gain another 1,500 feet in elevation over the next 10 miles. The pavement rolls through mostly forested terrain to Wrights Lake Campground and the lake itself, which is ideal for swimming and fishing. The large, busy campground has a small visitor center that is staffed in summer.

For more information, contact the Pacific Ranger District of Eldorado National Forest, 530/644-6048 or 530/644-2349.

Driving Directions

From Pollock Pines, drive nine miles east on U.S. 50 and turn north on Ice House Road (Forest Service Road 3). Drive 10.5 miles to the right turnoff for Ice House Campground. Turn right, drive one mile and park in or near the campground (if you are not camping, do not park in designated campsites).

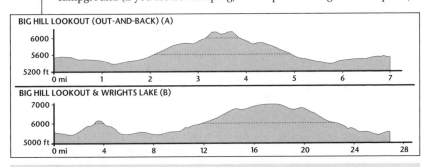

Route Directions for 12A *(Big Hill Lookout only)* for Big Hill Lookout & Wrights Lake

0.0   Park at Ice House Campground and ride back out the way you came in to Ice House Road. *Water is available at the campground; supplies are available at nearby Ice House Resort.*

1.0   Cross Ice House Road to the start of Road 11N58, Big Hill Lookout Road.

3.5   Big Hill Lookout. TURN AROUND.

7.0   Arrive at starting point.

Route Directions for 12B *(Big Hill Lookout & Wrights Lake)*

Follow directions for Ride 12A to mile 7.0, then continue:

7.0   LEFT at junction just before Ice House Campground (signed for Wrights Lake, Road 11N52).

8.7   LEFT on Forest Service Road 32.

14.9   LEFT on Wrights Lake Road.

17.0   Wrights Lake Campground and the lake. TURN AROUND. *Water is available at the campground.*

27.0   Arrive at starting point.

13. BIG MEADOW TO DARDANELLES & ROUND LAKES

South of South Lake Tahoe

In case you've been living in a cave for the past decade, the Tahoe Rim Trail is a 150-mile-long trail that runs along the mountain ridges surrounding Lake Tahoe, passing through two states and six counties. After years of hard work and political wrangling, it was completed in 2000. The entire trail is open to hikers and equestrians, with limited stretches open to mountain bikes.

ROUTE DETAILS

type of trail	dirt single-track
difficulty	▮▮▮◻◻
total distance	8.4 miles
riding time	2 hours
elevation gain	1,200 feet

One of the main access points for bikers is the Big Meadow Trailhead on Highway 89 south of South Lake Tahoe. From this major trailhead, riders can head north to Freel Meadows or Armstrong Pass, or south to Round Lake and Dardanelles Lake—all on single-track trails. This ride follows the latter route to both lakes for an 8.4-mile out-and-back. The mileage may be low, but the rid-

ing is fairly technical and challenging and the visual rewards are great. Don't forget your bathing suit for a dip in the two beautiful, but extremely different, lakes.

What makes them different is their geologic origins. Round Lake, which you'll visit first, is surrounded by stark-looking volcanic cliffs. Dardanelles Lake is a classic, glacially sculpted water body, surrounded by granite cliffs and boulders. As the crow flies, these two lakes are only about a mile apart, but they couldn't be more disparate—a clear example of the tremendous forces of fire and ice that have shaped the northern Sierra.

Don't be discouraged by the extremely rocky stretch of trail that takes off from Highway 89 right at the start. After the

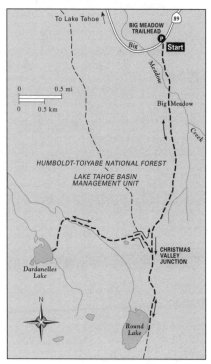

first half mile, the surface and grade improves markedly. Much of the trail is forested with giant red firs and sweet-smelling Jeffrey pines, except for a .25-mile stint through sunny Big Meadow. Both Round and Dardanelles Lakes are shallow enough for the water to warm up for swimming; I recommend a backstroke to the far shore of Dardanelles, where you'll find many small boulder islands.

For more information, contact Lake Tahoe Basin Management Unit, 530/573-2600; website: www.r5.fs.fed.us/ltbmu.

Driving Directions

From Meyers, drive south on Highway 89 for 6.5 miles to the Big Meadow Trailhead on the left side of the road.

BIG MEADOW TO DARDENALLES & ROUND LAKES

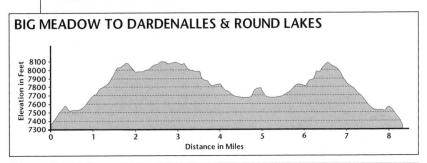

Route Directions for Big Meadow to Dardanelles & Round Lakes

0.0   Park at the Big Meadow Trailhead near the restrooms (bear left). The trail begins on the southwest side of the parking lot loop. *Supplies are available in Meyers or South Lake Tahoe.*

0.2   Cross Highway 89 and pick up the single-track by the signboard.

0.5   RIGHT at fork for Big Meadow.

1.9   Steep downhill stretch.

2.2   LEFT for Round Lake at Christmas Valley junction.

2.8   Round Lake. TURN AROUND.

3.4   LEFT at junction for Christmas Valley.

3.6   LEFT at trail to Dardanelles Lake.

4.8   Arrive at Dardanelles Lake. TURN AROUND.

6.0   RIGHT at junction.

6.2   LEFT at junction.

8.2   Cross Highway 89.

8.4   Arrive at starting point.

14. BURNSIDE LAKE ROAD

Hope Valley, south of South Lake Tahoe

For strong beginners, or intermediates looking for a moderate workout coupled with a fun destination, Burnside Lake Road offers a scenic and not-too-strenuous cruise through conifers and aspens to wide, shallow Burnside Lake, elevation 8,100 feet. The lake is good for trout fishing and better for swimming. On a hot day, you won't complain about the tules rimming its edges; you'll just drop your bike on the ground and wade in. Save some energy to take the short hike from the lake's edge to a high overlook of the Hot Springs Valley area.

ROUTE DETAILS

type of trail	dirt road with minimal car traffic
difficulty	
total distance	11.4 miles
riding time	2 hours
elevation gain	1,100 feet

The wide dirt road is open to cars, but because its only destination is the lake, it doesn't get much traffic. (On a beautiful September Saturday, we saw about 10 cars total; most were parked for firewood cutting.) The road has some washboard and is mildly rocky in places, but riding it doesn't require any technical skills. A gradual grade takes you uphill to the lake—it's just relentless enough to get you sweating. One short, steep stretch is covered in broken pavement, which produces better traction for the climb. As you ride, ignore the numerous possible side roads and stay on Road 019.

If possible, time your trip for October, when the aspens lining much of the route turn bright gold. Or take a ride in spring when the snow has melted but the road is not yet open to cars.

For more information, contact the Carson Ranger District of Humboldt-Toiyabe National Forest, 775/882-2766.

Driving Directions

From Meyers, drive south on Highway 89 for 11 miles to its junction with Highway 88. Immediately across Highway 88 is the start of a dirt road, with a large parking area and Hope Valley Wildlife Area information sign.

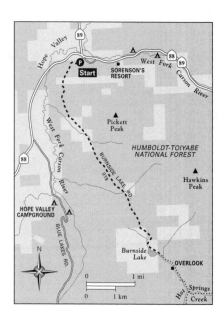

BURNSIDE LAKE ROAD

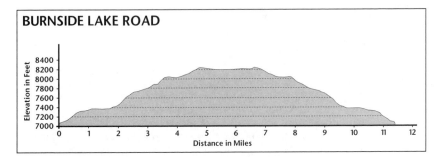

Route Directions for Burnside Lake Road

0.0 Park at junction of Burnside Lake Road and Highway 88 (across from Highway 89), by Hope Valley Wildlife Area signboard. Ride south on Burnside Lake Road (Forest Service Road 019). *Supplies are available at Sorenson's Resort, 1.2 miles east on Highway 88.*

2.6 Beautiful aspen grove.

2.9 RIGHT at fork to stay on Road 019.

5.5 LEFT at fork to stay on Road 019.

5.7 Burnside Lake. TURN AROUND. *Lock up your bike and take a .7-mile hike to an overlook 1,000-plus feet above Markleeville and Hot Springs Valley. The trail starts from the southeast end of the lake. Beyond a series of meadows and forest, you'll come out to the granite-lined overlook.*

11.4 Arrive at starting point.

15. BEAR VALLEY TO ALPINE LAKE

Off Highway 4 east of Arnold

Beautiful Alpine Lake on Highway 4 is the centerpiece of the Bear Valley Recreation Area. The granite-bound lake at elevation 7,300 feet is popular for trout fishing and has three Forest Service campgrounds near its lakeshore.

This paved trail runs between Alpine Lake and Highway 4.

ROUTE DETAILS

type of trail dirt single-track and paved bike path

difficulty

total distance 7 miles

riding time 1.5 hours

elevation gain 900 feet

This newly constructed single-track trail is the nonhighway route to Lake Alpine from Bear Valley, the big "town" in these parts. Although short, the trail includes a one-mile, heart-pumping climb. The trickiest part is finding the trail's start, which is just a few hundred feet east of Bear Valley on the south side Highway 4. I had to ride up and down the highway a few times before I spotted it (apparently it is sometimes signed, sometimes not).

The trail parallels Highway 4 at first, then heads away from the road and continues uphill. It meanders through the forest, then meets up with a portion of the historic Emigrant Trail pioneer route. After skirting the south side of Silvertip Campground, the trail turns into a wide gravel path that leads downhill toward Lake Alpine. A dirt road connects you to Lakeshore Trail, a paved bike trail that parallels the north shore of Lake Alpine. Lakeshore Trail runs smack in between the road and the lake, but the latter is so pretty with its rocky shoreline and shady pine forest that you won't even notice the nearby cars.

The riding is so pleasant on this trail that I recommend an out-and-back,

Bear Valley to Alpine Lake

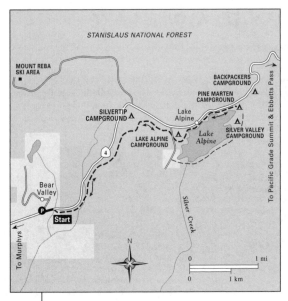

although you could easily turn this into a loop by heading back on Highway 4. Summer vacation traffic, especially on weekends, makes the loop option less appealing. You can also make a semi-loop by following the dirt trail and road on the back side of Lake Alpine (look for the trail at Pine Marten Campground), then returning on the single-track to Bear Valley.

For more information, contact the Calaveras Ranger District of Stanislaus National Forest, 209/795-1381.

Driving Directions
From Arnold, drive 29 miles east on Highway 4 to Bear Valley. Turn left on Bear Valley Road and park in any of the public parking areas near the shops.

BEAR VALLEY TO ALPINE LAKE

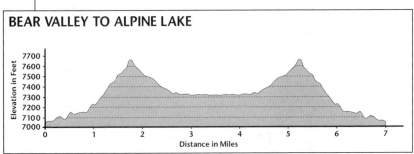

Route Directions for Bear Valley to Alpine Lake

0.0 Park at Bear Valley. Ride back out Bear Valley Road, turn left on Highway 4, and pick up the single-track on the right side of the road in about 75 yards. *Supplies are available in Bear Valley.*

1.8 Junction with Emigrant Trail

2.1 Silvertip Campground.

2.3 LEFT on dirt road.

2.5 RIGHT on paved bike path.

3.5 East end of Lake Alpine. TURN AROUND. *Or take one of possible loop options described above.*

7.0 Arrive at starting point.

16. SONORA PASS ROAD RIDE

Highway 108 from Dardanelle to U.S. 395

Some hard-core cyclists ride Tioga Pass, the mighty 9,945-foot pass in northern Yosemite with breathtaking glacial scenery and even more breathtaking high-elevation air. Equally hard-core cyclists ride 8,730-foot Ebbetts Pass, the impossibly narrow, winding, and steep mountain road that is part of the epic Markleeville Death Ride bike tour each July. But hard-core cyclists who qualify as true "cyclopaths" ride Sonora Pass—Highway 108, the steepest grade and most strenuous highway route across the Sierra Nevada.

ROUTE DETAILS FOR 16A
(Dardanelle to summit)

type of trail paved road with moderate car traffic

difficulty

total distance 29 miles

riding time 3–4 hours

elevation gain 3,900 feet

ROUTE DETAILS FOR 16B
(Dardanelle to U.S. 395)

type of trail paved road with moderate car traffic

difficulty

total distance 58 miles

riding time 7–8 hours

elevation gain 6,600 feet

The ride isn't for the faint of heart, or weak of quadriceps. From the traditional starting point at Dardanelle Resort, elevation 5,765 feet, to Sonora Pass, a mere 14.5 miles east, the route gains almost 4,000 feet, with grades as high as 26 percent. You'd think most cyclists would kiss the ground when they finally attain the Sonora Pass summit at 9,624 feet, but no . . . some just keep riding—all the way downhill to U.S. 395, doubling their distance. Having lost another 2,700 feet in elevation, riders have two choices: Turn around and ride back up the pass, or call their mommies to come pick them up.

Mere mortals are overwhelmed just driving Sonora Pass. The scenery is beyond spectacular—the granite and volcanic landscape is the sort of thing you'd hope to find after a week of backpacking in the Sierra. Since there's little or no shoulder on most of Highway 108, be wary of cars. Chances are good the drivers will be gawking at the scenery.

Driving Directions
From Sonora, drive 50 miles east on Highway 108 to Dardanelle Resort on the right side of the road (18 miles east of Strawberry).

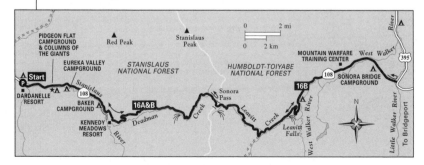

Sonora Pass Road Ride

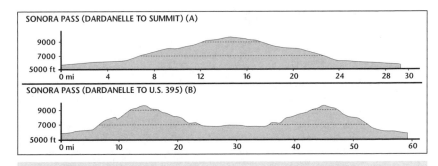

Route Directions for 16A *(Dardanelle to summit)* for Sonora Pass Road Ride

- 0.0 Park at or near Dardanelle Resort. *Supplies and lodging are available.*
- 2.0 Pidgeon Flat Campground and The Columns of the Giants Trailhead. *You'll be too tired to hike this short path on your way back, so go see this volcanic rock formation now. It's a mere .25-mile walk.*
- 3.0 Eureka Valley Campground. *Water is available.*
- 5.8 Baker Campground and turnoff for Kennedy Meadow. *Water is available.*
- 8.4 Vista point followed by more brutal climbing.
- 14.5 Sonora Pass summit, elevation 9,624 feet. TURN AROUND.
- 29.0 Arrive at starting point.

Route Directions for 16B *(Dardanelle to U.S. 395)*

Follow directions for Ride 16A to mile 14.5, then continue:

- 14.5 Sonora Pass summit, elevation 9,624 feet.
- 20.8 Leavitt Falls Vista. *Stop here for a view of the waterfall on Leavitt Creek and West Walker River Valley.*
- 22.5 Leavitt Meadows Campground. *Water is available.*
- 27.0 Sonora Bridge Campground. *Water is available.*
- 29.0 Highway 108 junction with U.S. 395. TURN AROUND.
- 58.0 Arrive at starting point.

17. BUCKEYE HOT SPRINGS

West of Bridgeport

A dip in a cold stream with hot springs bubbling up from its depths is the reward for this ride from U.S. 395 in Bridgeport. Even if you don't partake in the soothing waters, the view from this road as it ascends out of Bridgeport Valley is ample reward on its own.

ROUTE DETAILS FOR 17A
(hot springs out-and-back)

type of trail dirt road with minimal car traffic

difficulty

total distance 9.2 miles

riding time 2–3 hours

elevation gain 600 feet

ROUTE DETAILS FOR 17B
(loop with Twin Lakes Road)

type of trail 🐾 dirt and paved road with minimal car traffic

difficulty 🍶🍶🍶🍶

total distance 18.8 miles

riding time 4–5 hours

elevation gain 800 feet

The gravel surface of Buckeye Road provides good traction and the grade alternates between climbing and leveling out, giving you several chances to catch your breath. On the down side, the road is very narrow and has some frightening drop-offs. It is open to cars, although most drivers prefer to access the hot springs and neighboring Buckeye Campground via the paved Twin Lakes Road. Still, get far to the side if you hear a car coming on one of the tight, narrow curves.

The path is simple to follow—a straight course with no turnoffs. Initially the road climbs for one mile, then it levels as it travels through a piñon pine forest. Where the trees open up, you have stunning views of wide Bridgeport Valley and the jagged

peaks of the Sawtooth Range to the northeast. At 4.6 miles you reach the parking area for the hot springs. (There is no sign, but this spot is easy to identify by the cars parked there.) If you wish, lock up your bike or carry it downhill a few hundred feet to the stream, then take a dip in the undeveloped springs. Modest types might want to look around before they head to the stream:

The ride to Buckeye Hot Springs provides expansive views of Bridgeport Valley and far-off peaks in the Hoover Wilderness.

Occasional Buckeye Creek bathers have been spotted wearing only birthday suits. Know before you go.

Ride 17A returns to the starting point from here, but Ride 17B explores more of the area and makes a loop back on paved roads.

For more information, contact the Bridgeport Ranger District of Humboldt-Toiyabe National Forest, 760/932-7070.

Driving Directions

From Bridgeport, drive north on U.S. 395 for 3.8 miles. Turn left on gravel Buckeye Road, which is also signed for Buckeye Campground. Park in the large parking pullout alongside the start of the road.

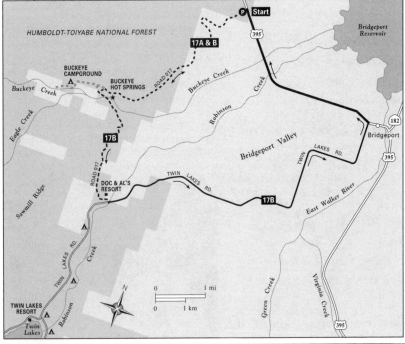

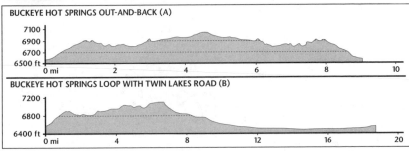

Route Directions for 17A *(hot springs out-and-back)* for Buckeye Hot Springs

0.0 Park at the start of Buckeye Road near its junction with U.S. 395. *Supplies are available in Bridgeport.*

1.0 First mile of climbing ends and road levels out.

1.4 Stay straight at two consecutive junctions.

2.2 Pass through a burned forest area; road climbs again.

2.8 Pass a Toiyabe National Forest sign.

3.0 Road levels out.

4.6 Buckeye Hot Springs parking area (an unsigned dirt parking area on the left side of the road). TURN AROUND. A hiking trail leads a few hundred feet down to the river and the hot springs. *Buckeye Campground is .5 mile farther; water is available.*

9.2 Arrive at starting point.

Route Directions for 17B *(loop with Twin Lakes Road)*

Follow directions for Ride 17A to mile 4.6, then continue:

4.6 Buckeye Hot Springs parking area.

4.8 LEFT at junction with fork to Buckeye Campground. *Water is available.*

7.8 Gravel road turns to pavement.

7.9 Doc and Al's Resort. *Supplies are available.*

8.0 LEFT on Twin Lakes Road (paved).

15.0 LEFT on U.S. 395 (wide shoulder).

18.8 Arrive at starting point.

18. MASONIC MOUNTAIN/ CHEMUNG MINE

Northeast of Bridgeport near Bridgeport Reservoir

This is a ride into Bridgeport's mining history. The Chemung Mine was one of a half-dozen profitable gold mines on the slopes of Masonic Mountain. Chemung Mine kept producing gold right up until the 1950s, when it was closed down. Many of its buildings still stand.

Early 20th-century mine buildings still stand along the slopes of Masonic Mountain.

ROUTE DETAILS

type of trail	dirt road with minimal car traffic
difficulty	🌢🌢🌢
total distance	10.4 miles
riding time	2–3 hours
elevation gain	1,600 feet

The route is simple to follow, as there are no turnoffs. Occasional cars drive this dirt road to visit the mine; stay alert for them. The road makes a moderate uphill climb through a somewhat desolate forest of piñon pines and western junipers, so don't expect any shade. When you reach the mine and stamp mill ruins, you'll note a lovely grove of aspens nearby, and a marvelous vista to the west of the Sawtooth Range. Views of the Sweetwater Mountains to the north are also good.

Take some time to explore around the six mine buildings and the machinery and debris left outside them. Walk around the site to get a feel for the excitement of the gold mining days. (Avoid entering the buildings; they are gradually decaying and falling down. Be especially cautious around the mine shafts themselves.)

For more information, contact the Bridgeport Ranger District of Humboldt-Toiyabe National Forest, 760/932-7070.

Driving Directions

From Bridgeport on U.S. 395, turn north on Highway 182 and drive 3.7 miles alongside Bridgeport Reservoir. Turn right on Forest Service Road 046, Masonic Road, which is just east of the reservoir's fishing access area. Park off the road in any available pullout.

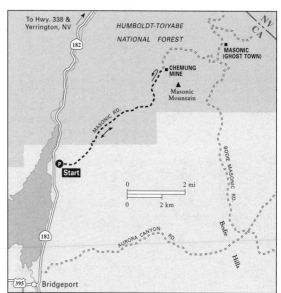

MASONIC MOUNTAIN/CHEMUNG MINE

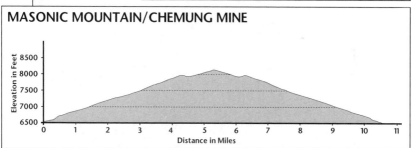

Route Directions for Masonic Mountain/Chemung Mine

0.0 Park alongside Masonic Road near its junction with Highway 182. *Supplies are available in Bridgeport, three miles south.*

1.3 Cattle guard; walk your bike.

1.6 Hairpin turn and a Toiyabe National Forest sign.

4.2 Road begins to level out; pass an old mine shaft from the neighboring Success Mine.

5.2 RIGHT to visit Chemung Mine buildings. TURN AROUND.

10.4 Arrive at starting point.

CHAPTER 6

Yosemite and Mammoth Lakes

*P*lunging waterfalls, stark granite, alpine lakes, pristine meadows, giant Sequoias, and raging rivers—you'll find them all in the Yosemite and Mammoth Lakes region, which encompasses not only world famous Yosemite National Park but also the popular recreation areas of Mammoth Lakes and the Eastern Sierra.

The centerpiece of this region, of course, is Yosemite National Park, a must-see on every traveler's itinerary. And what better way to see it than on two wheels, pedaling along the Yosemite Valley bike path? On a bicycle, you have wide open views of Yosemite Valley's famous waterfalls, three of which are among the tallest in the world, plus the towering granite of El Capitan, Half Dome, and Sentinel Rock. Those who seek more of a challenge can ride Glacier Point Road to its end at a vista that can only be described in superlatives. But then, almost everything about Yosemite inspires verbal extravagance.

As scenic as the national park itself are the resort areas just to the east, particularly Mammoth Lakes and June Lake on the U.S. 395 corridor. Best known for skiing and snowboarding in winter, the Eastern Sierra is also ideal for cycling in the warmer seasons. One of the greatest challenges for both road and mountain bikers is dealing with the thin air at this altitude, which ranges from 7,000 to 9,200 feet. Road and trail rides include easy loops near towns and more strenuous rides through alpine meadows, fir and pine forests, and sagebrush-covered plains.

Surrounding Mammoth and June Lakes, the lands of Inyo National Forest are suited for two-wheeled use. The area east of June Lake is dominated by the Mono Basin and Mono Lake, an ancient and majestic body of water covering 60 square miles. At more than 700,000 years old, Mono Lake is one of the oldest lakes in North America.

Just west of Mammoth Lakes is Devils Postpile National Monument, an 800-acre national park that preserves 60-foot-high basalt columns, remnants of an ancient lava flow, and breathtaking 101-foot Rainbow Falls. The road into the monument provides one of the most exciting bike rides on Northern California pavement, featuring a steep and fast descent on a narrow, twisty grade. Fortunately, a mandatory shuttle bus system minimizes auto traffic, making the road safer and more peaceful for cyclists.

Key to enjoying your experience in Yosemite and Mammoth is planning your visit for the least crowded months of the year. Summer is the busiest time and best avoided, especially in the national park. Springtime in Yosemite is ideal for viewing the valley's spectacular waterfalls. A visit before school lets out for the summer gives you a chance to see the valley without the masses.

Fall, too, is a fine time for cycling in and around Yosemite, and likewise, if there is a perfect time to visit the Eastern Sierra, it's in the transition between summer and winter. Autumn transforms the scenic canyons and pristine lakeshores into a wave of blazing color. Aspens, willows, and cottonwoods turn showy hues of orange, yellow, and red. The trees generally begin their color change early in September; peak viewing is usually in late September and early October. With an autumn show like this, why go to New England?

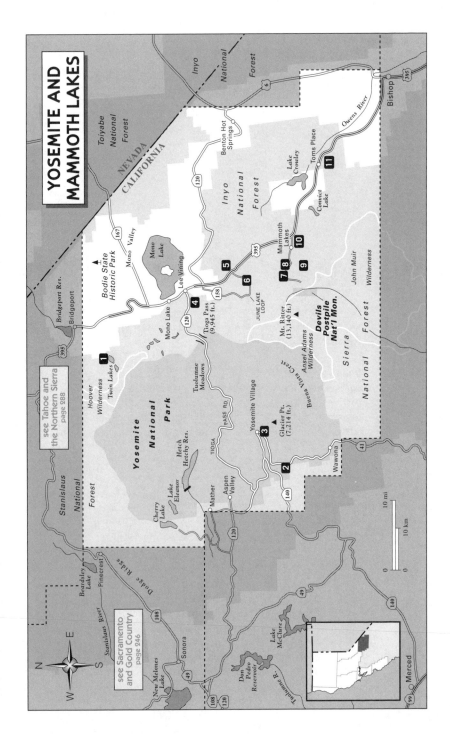

CHAPTER 6
YOSEMITE AND MAMMOTH LAKES

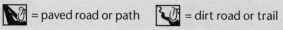
= paved road or path   = dirt road or trail

1. TWIN LAKES

West of Bridgeport

Bridgeport's Twin Lakes, elevation 7,100 feet, are a fine place for anglers to toss their lines in the water, gaze up at the jagged peaks of the Sawtooth Range, and forget their troubles for a while. The two scenic lakes are also just right for mountain bikers who want to string together a loop ride that circumnavigates the lakes, providing many unforgettable views of blue water and granite. The ride is mostly level and easy, leaving you free to focus on the glorious alpine scenery instead of the trail.

The Twin Lakes Loop combines dirt road, paved road, and single-track.

ROUTE DETAILS

type of trail dirt road and single-track; paved road with moderate car traffic

difficulty

total distance 8.3 miles (or longer options)

riding time 1.5 hours

elevation gain 400 feet

The ride takes off from Lower Twin Lakes Resort and immediately turns on to South Twin Road, skirting a few Forest Service campgrounds. Where the pavement ends, you follow a well-graded dirt road along the lakeshore, passing some summer homes and cabins. Soon the dirt road ends, too, and you follow a single-track trail for a short, technical stretch along the lake's edge, crossing Cattle Creek a few times. At the western end of Upper Twin Lake, the trail curves around Horse Creek. Follow the trail signs to cross a bridge over the creek and access the edge of a campground.

And what a campground it is. The peace and quiet of your lakeside ride is shattered upon entering Annett's Mono Village Resort, an absolute zoo of a vacation spot. The place is a miniature city, with a 300-site campground, cabins, motel rooms, a grocery store, marina, and the like. It will take you a few minutes to negotiate your way through this party scene and find your way back to paved Twin Lakes Road, where all is peaceful once more. Enjoy the final smooth miles on pavement back to your car at Lower Twin Lakes Resort.

If you want a longer ride, park in downtown Bridgeport and ride out Twin Lakes Road to the start of this loop. You'll add on 11 paved miles each way on a very moderate grade (only 600 feet of elevation gain). The ride travels through wide open pastures and grazing lands into Twin Lakes' canyon, and supplies excellent views of Sawtooth Ridge and Matterhorn Peak.

For more information, contact the Bridgeport Ranger District of Humboldt-Toiyabe National Forest, 760/932-7070.

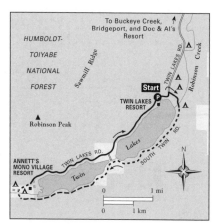

Driving Directions

From Lee Vining, drive north on U.S. 395 for 25 miles to Bridgeport. Turn left (west) on Twin Lakes Road and drive 11 miles to Twin Lakes Resort on the right (on Lower Twin Lake).

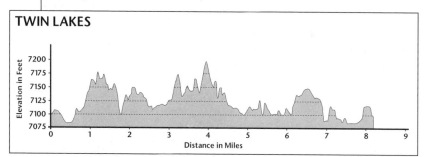

Route Directions for Twin Lakes

0.0 Park at Twin Lakes Resort, then backtrack .25 mile on Twin Lakes Road (head east) and turn right on South Twin Road. *Supplies are available at the store at Twin Lakes Resort.*

0.5 Paved road turns to dirt past the campgrounds.

2.6 RIGHT at junction. Ride downhill between the two Twin Lakes.

2.8 LEFT at junction to stay on southeast side of lakes.

3.3 Pick up single-track at end of dirt road.

4.0 Cross bridge to Annett's Mono Village Resort and campground. Ride through the maze of buildings to the entrance station (stay to the right, close to the lakeshore).

4.7 Back on Twin Lakes Road.

8.3 Arrive at starting point.

2. GLACIER POINT ROAD

Yosemite National Park

The view from Glacier Point—looking down 3,200 feet at Yosemite Valley and directly across at Half Dome and its granite neighbors, plus Vernal and Nevada Falls—is perhaps the most striking panorama of any in Yosemite National Park (209/372-0200), a place that does not lack outstanding views. Getting there on a bike instead of in a car only adds to the grandeur.

ROUTE DETAILS

type of trail paved road with moderate car traffic

difficulty

total distance 31.6 miles

riding time 3–4 hours

elevation gain 2,700 feet

The ride is less than ideal on summer weekends, however, when the park is overflowing with visitors, most of whom are driving around in cars. Weekdays are advisable, and early in the day is wise. The fewer cars you see on this often narrow, steep road, the more you'll be able to enjoy the world-class scenery.

From the start of Glacier Point Road you begin to climb immediately, with the sweet scent of bear clover (a small shrub also called mountain misery or kit-kit-dizzie) accompanying you. It lines the roadsides, forming a low-growing understory for the pines and firs. You won't see much but forest for the first several miles, so just focus on your climbing. If you need water, make a stop at Bridalveil Campground at 7.8 miles.

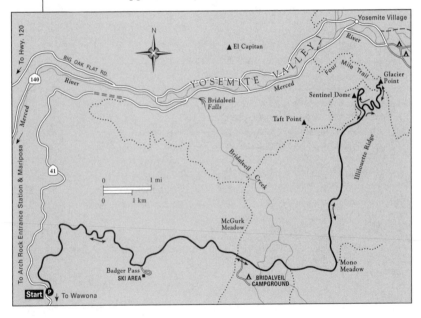

Beyond the camp turnoff, you start to get occasional peeks through the trees of the granite domes and summits ahead and to the south. Note the Taft Point and Sentinel Dome parking lot at mile 13.2; stop here for an easy hike on your return trip. The final two miles comprise a steep, circuitous descent to Glacier Point, passing Washburn Point overlook along the way. The vista from here is enough to make you fly right off the pavement, but hold on to your handlebars for the final stretch to Glacier Point's parking lot. Then lock up your bike and go enjoy the famous view (and maybe a hot dog from the snack stand) with everybody else.

For your return trip, the first two miles present a tough workout, but with the exception of one more short climb near Summit Meadow, you'll hardly pedal at all back down to Chinquapin.

Driving Directions

From Yosemite Valley, take the Highway 41/Wawona/Fresno turnoff (near Bridalveil Falls) and drive nine miles to the left turnoff for Glacier Point Road at Chinquapin Junction.

GLACIER POINT ROAD

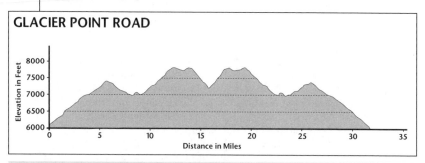

Route Directions for Glacier Point Road

0.0   Park at the small parking area at the junction of Wawona Road and Glacier Point Road (Chinquapin Junction). *Supplies are available in Yosemite Valley or Wawona.*

7.8   Turnoff for Bridalveil Campground on right. *Water is available.*

13.2   Trailhead for Taft Point and Sentinel Dome on left. *On your return trip, lock up your bike and take one or both hikes to these two panoramic overlooks (each hike is 2.2 miles round-trip).*

14.7   Washburn Point Overlook.

15.8   Glacier Point parking lot. TURN AROUND. *Lock up your bike and visit the overlook area and snack bar. Food and supplies are available.*

31.6   Arrive at starting point.

3. YOSEMITE VALLEY BIKE PATH

Yosemite National Park

It's congested, it's crowded, and it can be a zoo on summer weekends, but Yosemite Valley is still one of the greatest shows on earth. If you witness it from your bicycle seat rather than your car window, you'll see it in the best possible way.

ROUTE DETAILS

type of trail	paved bike path
difficulty	
total distance	8.2 miles
riding time	1 hour
elevation gain	450 feet

To optimize the experience, ride this trail as early in the morning as you can. Better yet, ride this trail before or after the summer vacation season (in April or May when the valley waterfalls are at their peak, or any time in fall or winter when there is no snow or ice on the ground).

Start your bike trip at Swinging Bridge picnic area on the south side of the valley. Head straight for the picturesque wooden bridge across the Merced River, then ride through the big meadow that faces Yosemite Falls. The drama begins immediately with the sight of this stunning waterfall and the immense granite walls that frame it.

At the Lower Yosemite Falls trailhead, make use of the bike rack and take the .25-mile hike to the falls. In early spring, the waterfall flows with such force that onlookers get showered with spray, even standing 50 yards away.

Steel yourself for the ride past the visitor center and through Yosemite Village, where the path gets very congested. Watch for stop signs at street intersections; cars are plentiful on the cross-streets, and they don't necessarily stop for bicyclists. Also, be cautious of other trail users, particularly pedestrians who are often completely oblivious.

Shortly beyond the Village is the right turnoff for Curry Village; ignore it and bear left to cross the Merced River two more times and pass through a peaceful area of pine forest, campgrounds, and no cars. Beyond the last of

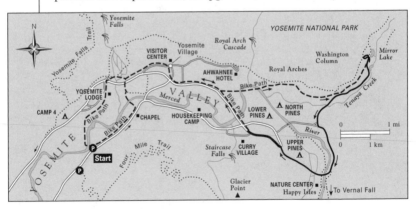

the campsites the bike trail turns right to head for Happy Isles and the east side of Curry Village; you go straight on the paved road to Mirror Lake. The road is closed to cars but open to Yosemite Valley's free shuttle buses, which pass by occasionally.

Here you meet the only hill of your ride. If you've rented your bike in Yosemite Village, you must park your bike at the rack and walk up the hill (for insurance reasons). If you're on your own bike, pedal away. At the top, take a moment to enjoy Mirror Lake, a large, shallow pool in Tenaya Creek, which varies in size from season to season. Most of the year, it's more of a meadow than a lake. Nonetheless, the view of Half Dome's 4,700-foot perpendicular face, seen from its base, is awe-inspiring.

For your return trip, you'll loop back via Happy Isles and Curry Village, then rejoin your previous path just before Yosemite Village.

For more information, contact Yosemite National Park, 209/372-0200.

Driving Directions

From the Arch Rock entrance station on Highway 140 in Yosemite Valley, drive east into the valley for 9.5 miles. Park in pullouts near the Four-Mile Trailhead (on the right), or at the Swinging Bridge picnic area just past this trailhead (on the left). The bike trail begins at the picnic area.

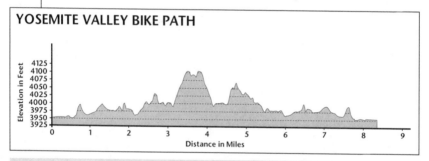

YOSEMITE VALLEY BIKE PATH

Elevation in Feet
4125
4100
4075
4050
4025
4000
3975
3950
3925

Distance in Miles

Route Directions for Yosemite Valley Bike Path

0.0   Park at the Four-Mile Trailhead or Swinging Bridge Picnic Area. *Supplies are available in Yosemite Village.*

0.9   Lower Yosemite Falls Trailhead. *Lock up your bike and take the .25-mile walk to the falls.*

1.5   Valley Visitor Center and Yosemite Village.

2.3   LEFT at fork (Curry Village to the right).

3.3   STRAIGHT for Mirror Lake at fork (Happy Isles and Curry Village to the right).

3.9   Mirror Lake. TURN AROUND.

4.5   LEFT toward Happy Isles; loop around Curry Village.

6.5   LEFT back to Yosemite Village.

8.2   Arrive at starting point.

4. MORAINES & MEADOWS

East of Tioga Pass and west of Lee Vining

The Moraines and Meadows Loop starts in an area burned by the Azusa Wildfire in 1999, but quickly leaves the blackened terrain and enters a world of alpine meadows and glacial moraines. The trail allows wide looks at giant-sized Mono Lake and neighboring Mono Craters, plus a visit to Upper and Lower Horse Meadows. A predominant manmade feature is also visible: the Los Angeles Aqueduct.

The ride begins with a 1.6-mile connector trail (Road 1N15) which seems to be heading straight for Mono Lake. But long before reaching the lakeshore (or U.S. 395), you turn right and begin a counterclock-

ROUTE DETAILS

type of trail	dirt road
difficulty	
total distance	11.3 miles
riding time	2 hours
elevation gain	1,200 feet

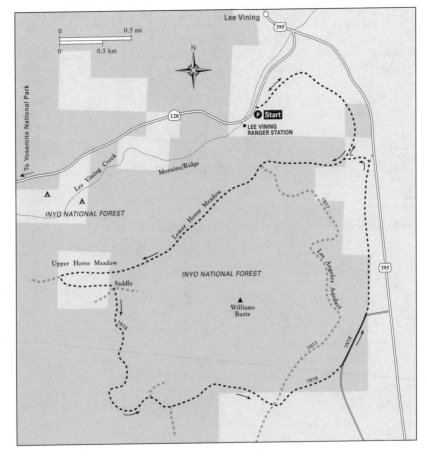

wise loop, circling Williams Butte (the hill that's on your left for much of the ride).

A three-mile climb to Lower and Upper Horse Meadows will get you huffing and puffing. The lower meadow is not lined with delicate shooting stars, but rather sagebrush, rabbit brush, and a mix of grasses. The upper meadow is a more traditional, grassy alpine meadow. Just beyond it, at a saddle, is the high point of the ride (mile 4.9). Views of the June Lake area to the south and its surrounding craggy peaks are outstanding.

From the saddle, take Forest Service Road 1N18 due left (south) and over the next four miles, enjoy losing all that elevation you've just gained. The final stretch of 1N18 crosses the Los Angeles Aqueduct road and then heads north, paralleling U.S. 395.

Note that this route is open to all-terrain vehicles. Although you probably won't encounter any on your ride, be alert for the high-pitched whine of their engines and get off the road if you hear one coming.

For more information, contact Mono Basin Scenic Area Visitor Center of Inyo National Forest, 760/647-3044.

Driving Directions
From the Tioga Pass entrance station to Yosemite on Highway 120, drive east for 11 miles to just beyond the Forest Service ranger station (three miles west of U.S. 395).

MORAINES & MEADOWS

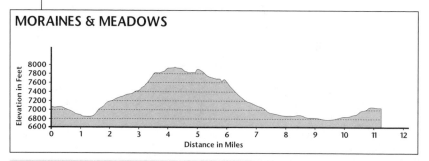

Route Directions for Moraines & Meadows

0.0   Park at the signed Moraines and Meadows Trailhead on Highway 120. Ride east on Highway 120 for a few yards and then turn off on Forest Service Road 1N15 (dirt). *Supplies are available three miles west in Lee Vining.*

1.6   RIGHT on 1N16 (Horse Meadows Road) at T-junction.

4.9   LEFT on 1N18 at saddle beyond Upper Horse Meadow.

7.1   STRAIGHT at junction with 1N17 (Aqueduct Road).

9.8   RIGHT on 1N15.

11.4   Arrive at starting point.

5. PANORAMA MOUNTAIN

Off U.S. 395 near June Lake

The Panorama Mountain Trail is a mountain bike route sanctioned by the Forest Service that consists of three consecutive loops on jeep roads and graded dirt roads. This is lonely sagebrush and big-sky country, where you probably aren't going to run into anybody else. Be entirely self-sufficient and carry plenty of water. The trail leads through sage and Jeffrey pines for the majority of the trip, with only occasional shade.

The sagebrush flats of Panorama Mountain Trail give way to the snow-capped Eastern Sierra.

© ANN MARIE BROWN

Because of the triple-loop formation, the number of junctions on this trail could drive you mad, but the Forest Service has very considerately signed the entire route. Just watch for their little brown signs and you'll be fine. Also, a few prominent landmarks will help guide you: U.S. 395, which is visible every time you climb a little; the Mono Craters, a chain of barren-looking volcanic vents poking up from the surrounding sagebrush plains; and the Aeolian Buttes, where the most recent volcanic activity in this area occurred perhaps only 600 years ago. The third of the three loops circles the buttes, and will take you up high enough so that you get surprising views of Mono Lake and its neighboring craters to the northeast, plus the snowcapped, granite mountains of the Eastern Sierra to the west. It's startling to see this juxtaposition of glacier-carved mountains and volcanic vents and tablelands all in one glance.

If you're new to riding in the Mammoth Lakes area, you may be a bit put off by the trail surface, even on these well-graded roads. The surface is a mix of pumice, gravel, and sand. You'll quickly learn to follow the line that looks the most hard-packed.

For more information, contact Mono

ROUTE DETAILS

type of trail   dirt road

difficulty

total distance   10.7 miles

riding time   2 hours

elevation gain   1,100 feet

Basin Scenic Area Visitor Center of Inyo National Forest, 760/647-3044.

Driving Directions

From the junction of U.S. 395 and Highway 158 (June Lake Junction), drive 150 yards north on U.S. 395 and turn right at the dirt road—1S35. Drive 100 yards down the road to the signed trailhead.

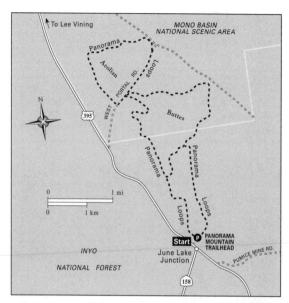

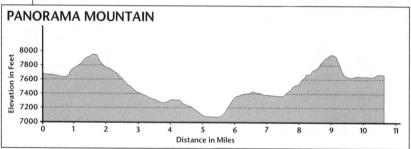

PANORAMA MOUNTAIN

Route Directions for Panorama Mountain

0.0 Park at the Panorama Mountain trailhead. *Supplies are available at June Lake Junction.*

0.0 This ride is a combination of three loops with more than 25 turns and numerous possible junctions. Follow the Forest Service's small brown signs along the trail. *Maps are available at the Mono Basin Scenic Area Visitor Center just north of Lee Vining on U.S. 395.*

10.7 Arrive at starting point.

6. JUNE LAKE LOOP RAMBLE

June Lake, north of Mammoth Lakes

Despite its name, this ride on the June Lake Loop is not a loop ride. The June Lake Loop is the main road through the June Lake area (Highway 158), but it's only a loop if you ride (or drive) a six-mile stretch on U.S. 395. It's much smarter, and more pleasurable, to ride the June Lake Loop as an out-and-back, and leave U.S. 395 to the giant tractor trailers hauling by at 70 miles per hour.

Granite peaks tower over the June Lake basin.

ROUTE DETAILS

type of trail paved road with moderate car traffic

difficulty 🍶🍶🍶🍶🍶

total distance 28.8 miles

riding time 2–3 hours

elevation gain 1,000 feet

Riding in this manner, you can plan on enjoying a couple of hours of some of the finest scenery in the eastern Sierra. You'll witness imposing granite peaks, the dancing leaves of aspen groves, and four sparkling, bright blue lakes. Because the route has many places to stop for supplies or breaks, this ride is well within the abilities of most cyclists. Traffic is as you might expect: heavier on summer weekends, lighter the rest of the time. The ride outlined here bypasses the main downtown area of June Lake and travels on the alternate Northshore Drive. This will spare you the company of a lot of automobiles.

Note that June Lake is virtually deserted after Labor Day (first Monday in September), making early fall a fine time to ride. In late September and early October the region's abundant aspens and cottonwoods don their golden headdresses for the annual autumnal dance.

The first 3.5 miles are all downhill or level and present pretty views of June Lake and Gull Lake. Then with a right turn near the June Mountain

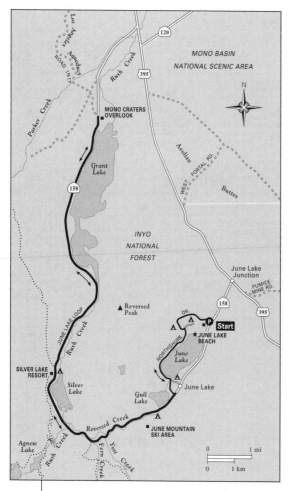

ski lifts you're on the official June Lake Loop. Traffic is busiest between miles 3.5 and 5.8 where numerous cabin resorts, shops, and private homes are located. There are dozens of places to stop for supplies along this stretch. You should certainly stop to admire granite Carson Peak, the predominant mountain towering over June Lake.

Beyond Silver Lake at mile 5.8, the road quiets down, but the wind may pick up in the next several miles as you near Grant Lake. You're leaving the shelter of granite peaks and entering wide open sagebrush plains. The road follows the shoreline of Grant Lake for more than three miles; this is the largest lake on the June Lake Loop.

A good turnaround point is mile 14.4 at the Mono Craters Viewpoint; it's only another 1.2 miles to the road's end at U.S. 395 (you've seen the best scenery already). At the viewpoint, you get a good look at the barren, pumice-covered volcanic cones called Mono Craters, which were created by a series of volcanic eruptions as recently as 600 years ago.

Good news for the return trip: The views of Carson Peak are even more tremendous from the opposite direction. And after climbing that hill from the ski resort back up Northshore Drive, you can treat yourself to a swim at June Lake's beach.

Driving Directions

From U.S. 395 at the Highway 203/Mammoth Lakes turnoff, drive 15 miles north on U.S. 395 to Highway 158, the southern turnoff for the June Lake Loop. Turn west on Highway 158 and drive .9 mile to Northshore Drive (signed for Oh! Ridge and Pinecliff). Turn right and park at the overlook area.

JUNE LAKE LOOP RAMBLE

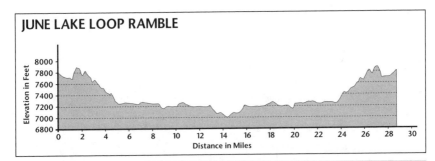

Route Directions for June Lake Loop Ramble

0.0   Park at the overlook at the corner of Northshore Drive and Highway 158. Ride north on Northshore Drive. *Supplies are available in downtown June Lake, or at the store at the corner of U.S. 395 and Highway 158.*

0.7   Turnoff for June Lake beach on left.

2.7   Turnoff to head into downtown on left.

3.5   RIGHT at junction of Northshore Drive and Highway 158 (June Lake Loop).

5.8   Silver Lake Resort on the left; Silver Lake on the right. *The resort store is the last place to stop for supplies until the return trip.*

9.5   Grant Lake on right.

14.4   Mono Craters Viewpoint. TURN AROUND.

28.8   Arrive at starting point.

7. DEVILS POSTPILE

Mammoth Lakes to Red's Meadow

If you want to earn the respect of all the hearty outdoors-types in Mammoth, ride your bike from Mammoth Mountain down into Devils Postpile. Eat lunch at the resort at Red's Meadow and then ride back up, up, up. Then go brag about it at one of the local watering holes.

ROUTE DETAILS

type of trail paved road with moderate car traffic

difficulty 🔋🔋🔋🔋🔋

total distance 19.6 miles

riding time 2–3 hours

elevation gain 1,500 feet

The paved road is narrow and has a 1,500-foot elevation change (down on the way in, up on the way back, with 1,000 feet of gain concentrated in a 2.5-mile stretch). Incredibly scenic throughout its entire length, the road delivers you to world-class destinations in Devils Postpile National Monument. Here's the best part: In summer, a mandatory shuttle bus system operates during daylight hours, so you'll encounter very few cars on the road. The winding, steep, sometimes one-lane road would not be rideable if it had the usual flow of national park traffic, so thank your lucky stars for the shuttle system. (Another plus to this system: Some riders coast downhill into Devils Postpile and then pay the shuttle bus to take them and their bikes back up the hill!)

The ride begins at Mammoth Mountain Ski Area, which is transformed into a mountain bike park in summer. You'll find a huge parking lot and opportunities to stock up on supplies. With a one-mile uphill to Minaret Vista, elevation 9,174 feet, you're at one of the finest viewpoints in the Sierra: a wide panorama of Mounts Ritter and Banner and the saw-toothed Minarets. Then you face a downward plunge into the forested canyon of Devils Postpile National Monument. Check your brakes before you go.

Once in the monument, you should plan on making a few stops. Stop at the ranger station and take the short walk to see the Devil's Postpile, a columnar basalt formation remaining from an ancient lava flow. Stop at the trailhead parking area just before Red's Meadow and take the one-mile walk to see 101-foot Rainbow Falls, one of the Sierra's most picture-perfect waterfalls. Then stop at Red's Meadow and eat a big, high-energy lunch, because you have 1,500 feet to gain back on the way uphill. You probably don't need to be reminded that the alpine air is quite thin at this elevation.

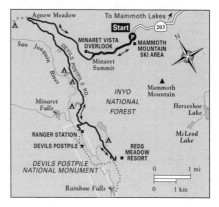

For more information, contact Devils Postpile National Monument, 760/934-2289, or the Mammoth Lakes Ranger District of Inyo National Forest, 760/924-5500.

Driving Directions

From U.S. 395 at Mammoth Lakes, take the Highway 203 turnoff and drive west for four miles, through the town of Mammoth Lakes, to the intersection of Highway 203 and Lake Mary Road. Turn right on Highway 203 (Minaret Road) and drive 4.5 miles to the main lodge area at Mammoth Mountain.

DEVILS POSTPILE

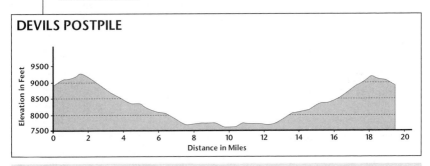

Route Directions for Devils Postpile

0.0   Park at Mammoth Mountain near the brass mammoth statue. Ride west on Highway 203. *Supplies are available at the mountain bike park and lodge.*

1.2   RIGHT at Minaret Vista Overlook; enjoy the view then TURN AROUND.

1.8   RIGHT on Highway 203/Devils Postpile Road; begin steep descent.

4.3   Agnews Meadows turnoff on right.

8.4   Devils Postpile Ranger Station turnoff on right. *Ride .3 mile to ranger station, lock up your bike, and hike .4 mile to the Devil's Postpile. Then continue riding on Devils Postpile Road.*

9.7   Rainbow Falls Trailhead on right. *Lock up your bike and take the one-mile hike to Rainbow Falls.*

9.8   Red's Meadow Resort on left. TURN AROUND. *Supplies are available.*

19.6   Arrive at starting point.

8. MOUNTAIN VIEW TRAIL

Mammoth Lakes

Mountain View Trail boasts 5.5 miles of single-track and jeep road, which winds its way from the Earthquake Fault overlook to Minaret Vista. It's a moderately challenging route through a dense forest of red firs, lodgepole pines, and Jeffrey pines; the route is packed with short-but-steep ups and downs, cambered turns, and plenty of loose and deep pumice. Keep watching for the brown Forest Service signs to keep you on track through several junctions.

ROUTE DETAILS

type of trail	dirt road and single-track
difficulty	
total distance	11 miles
riding time	2 hours
elevation gain	800 feet

Since you're starting at the Earthquake Fault parking area, you might as well take the short walk to see this phenomenon: a long, nearly straight fracture in hardened lava that is up to 60 feet in depth. Some scientists believe it was formed by a cooling volcanic fissure, while others claim it was caused by a small, local earthquake fault.

Ride back out the Earthquake Fault entrance road and pick up Mountain View Trail on the right 100 yards before Highway 203. Follow the trail uphill through big red firs to a nice view of Inyo Craters. After its first stint northward, the trail wends generally westward toward Minaret Vista, alternating as stretches of single-track and jeep road. Where the trees thin out, you gain good views of Mammoth Mountain. The forest changes from firs and big pines to the sturdier, high-elevation whitebark pines. They are smaller and somewhat stunted looking, but it's no surprise considering what they go through every winter at 9,100 feet.

Mountain View Trail ends at a dirt parking area on the entrance road to Minaret Vista. Turn right on the pavement to gain the Minaret Vista overlook, a fine reward for all your efforts. Here you'll gaze at the jagged outline of the Ritter Range to the west, with Mount Banner and Mount Ritter leading the pack of saw-toothed peaks, and the Inyo and White Mountains to the east.

Note that if this single-track has worn you out, you can take the easy route back to the Earthquake Fault parking lot by riding on paved Highway

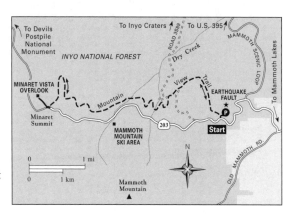

203 (Minaret Road). You'll cut a couple of miles off the round-trip, but more significantly, you'll be riding on smooth, descending pavement.

For more information, contact the Mammoth Lakes Ranger District of Inyo National Forest, 760/924-5500.

Driving Directions

From U.S. 395 at Mammoth Lakes, take the Highway 203 turnoff and drive west for four miles, through the town of Mammoth Lakes, to the intersection of Highway 203 and Lake Mary Road. Turn right on Highway 203 (Minaret Road) and drive 1.9 miles to the Earthquake Fault turnoff on the right.

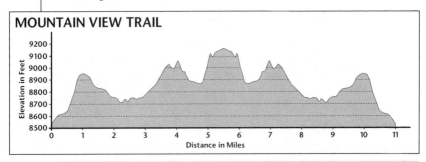

MOUNTAIN VIEW TRAIL

Route Directions for Mountain View Trail

0.0   Park at the Earthquake Fault parking lot, then ride back down the entrance road to the signed trail on the right, about 100 yards from Highway 203. (Watch for blue diamonds on the red fir trees and bike trail signs.) *Supplies are available in Mammoth.*

0.7   RIGHT at junction.

1.5   RIGHT at junction.

2.0   LEFT at junction with trail to Inyo Craters.

2.7   RIGHT then immediate LEFT at junction.

3.2   RIGHT at junction.

5.4   Dirt parking area. Turn right on pavement and ride uphill to Minaret Vista. TURN AROUND.

11.0 Arrive at starting point.

9. MAMMOTH LAKES BASIN & HORSESHOE LAKE

Mammoth Lakes

This is an easy cruise in the Mammoth Lakes area that tours the Lakes Basin and its five gorgeous, alpine lakes. Many visitor services are found along the way (cabin resorts, stores, restaurants, and more), but the area

is by no means overrun with commercialism. This is some of the eastern Sierra's most stunning, and most easily accessible, scenery.

If you're on a mountain bike, you'll be able to leave the cars and get off the pavement at the end of the ride and pedal the beautiful single-track loop around Horseshoe Lake. This trail is a great introduction to single-track riding. It is mostly level, presents no major obstacles, and is only 1.7 miles long.

Start your ride at the north end of Twin Lakes Road and pedal past the Lower Twin Lake and Tamarack Lodge, a cabin resort known for its award-winning restaurant. Ride south on Twin Lakes Road until it rejoins Lake Mary Road, then turn right. Take the long loop around the south side of Lake Mary, enjoying more picturesque lakeside scenery, then follow the spur road up to Lake George, the most fetching of the five lakes. At 9,200 feet in elevation, Lake George is deep

Crystal Crag dominates the granite peaks and deep blue lakes of the Mammoth Lakes Basin.

blue and lined with granite, but what sets it apart from its neighboring lakes is Crystal Crag, an exquisite chunk of rock that forms the lake's backdrop. If you have some free time, bring along a bike lock. Numerous short hikes can be taken from Lake George, including those to Crystal Lake, T.J. Lake, and Barrett Lake.

The final stretch of the ride passes lovely Lake Mamie and travels to the road's end at Horseshoe Lake. The white, sandy

ROUTE DETAILS

type of trail paved road with moderate car traffic (plus optional dirt single-track)

difficulty 🍶🍶🍶🍶

total distance 12.2 or 13.9 miles

riding time 1.5 hours

elevation gain 700 feet

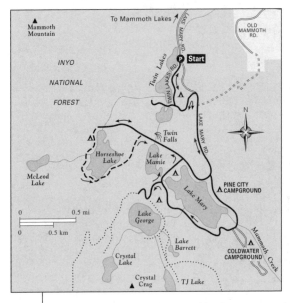

shores on the north shore of the lake are surrounded by dead trees, which met their end from carbon dioxide gas venting up through the soil, most likely from seismic action. If you're on a mountain bike, you can ride around the lake to the unaffected south side, which is lined with a thriving forest and plentiful wildflowers in midsummer.

Note that car traffic can be fairly heavy in the Mammoth Lakes Basin on summer weekends, although no one drives fast on these narrow, scenic roads. For the best experience, save your ride for the off-season or a weekday.

For more information, contact the Mammoth Lakes Ranger District of Inyo National Forest, 760/924-5500.

Driving Directions

From U.S. 395 at Mammoth Lakes, take the Highway 203 turnoff and drive west for four miles, through the town of Mammoth Lakes, to the intersection of Highway 203 and Lake Mary Road. Continue straight on Lake Mary Road for two miles, then bear right on Twin Lakes Road.

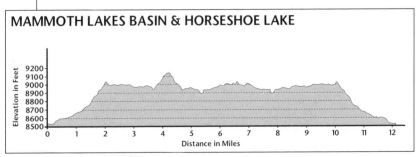

MAMMOTH LAKES BASIN & HORSESHOE LAKE

Route Directions for Mammoth Lakes Basin & Horseshoe Lake

0.0 Park at Twin Lakes in any of the day-use spots. The mileage below starts at the northern junction of Twin Lakes Road and Lake Mary Road. Ride south on Twin Lakes Road. *Supplies are available at Twin Lakes Store, Lake Mary Store, or Pokenobe Lodge.*

1.8 RIGHT on Lake Mary Road.

2.6 LEFT to loop around Lake Mary.

4.1 LEFT to Lake George.

4.4 Lake George. TURN AROUND. *Several short hikes are possible from here; see route description.*

4.7 LEFT to continue loop around Lake Mary.

5.0 LEFT on Lake Mary Road to Lake Mamie.

6.1 End of the road at Horseshoe Lake. TURN AROUND *Skinny-tire riders turn back now; mountain bikers can ride the 1.7-mile loop around Horseshoe Lake.*

13.9 Arrive at starting point (12.2 for skinny tires).

10. MAMMOTH CREEK PARK/ SHERWIN CREEK LOOP

Mammoth Lakes

Downtown Mammoth Lakes has one of the most scenic paved recreation trails in all of Northern California. It offers expansive views of the frequently snowcapped Sherwins, and a sense that you are far from the hustle and bustle of downtown Mammoth, even though you aren't.

ROUTE DETAILS

type of trail   dirt roads and paved bike path

difficulty

total distance   6.3 miles

riding time   1 hour

elevation gain   500 feet

This mostly dirt loop gives you a short taste of that paved trail, then turns off on to dirt roads. By bypassing the first turnoff, as described below, you'll ride a short out-and-back on the pavement to a spectacular mountain overlook atop a sage-covered hill. Enjoy the view from the trailside wooden benches, then glide back down to that first turnoff, go left, and begin the dirt stretch of the ride.

Well-maintained dirt road 3S09 follows the path of Mammoth Creek, passing by creekside aspen groves and offering great views of the surrounding mountains. (The best time to ride here is unquestionably in the fall, when the quaking aspens put on their fiery display.) After a right turn, a short but steep downhill, and a footbridge crossing the creek, you'll find a maze of dirt roads; just continue straight and uphill for .3 mile until you reach the wide, graded Sherwin Creek Road. Turn right and follow the road past a campground and day-use area. You'll face a slow, gradual climb to the east, inspired by a head-on view of Mammoth Mountain. Eventually the road changes from gravel to pavement. Turn right on Old Mammoth Road and head back to your starting point at the park.

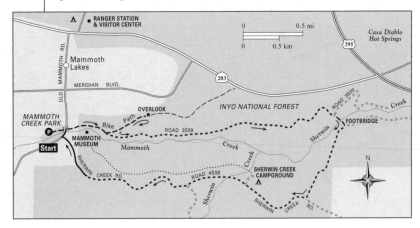

You may have to put up with some cars on Sherwin Creek Road; the dirt road extends east all the way to U.S. 395 and some people use it to access nearby hiking trails and a motocross track.

For more information, contact the Mammoth Lakes Ranger District of Inyo National Forest, 760/924-5500.

Driving Directions

From U.S. 395 at Mammoth Lakes, take the Highway 203 turnoff and drive west for 2.7 miles. Turn left on Old Mammoth Road and drive one mile to Mammoth Creek Park on the right.

MAMMOTH CREEK PARK/SHERWIN CREEK LOOP

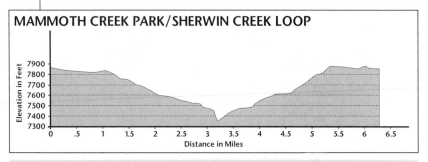

Route Directions for Mammoth Creek Park/Sherwin Creek Loop

0.0   Park at Mammoth Creek Park. Follow the paved trail from near the restrooms through the tunnel to the far side of Old Mammoth Road. *Supplies are available in Mammoth.*

0.5   Pass dirt road 3S09; note this junction.

0.9   Overlook of Sherwins on paved bike path. TURN AROUND.

1.3   LEFT at previous junction with 3S09.

2.6   RIGHT on dirt road that quickly narrows and drops downhill.

2.9   Cross footbridge. Continue STRAIGHT on other side of creek.

3.2   RIGHT on Sherwin Creek Road (4S08) at a major junction of graded roads.

5.9   RIGHT on Old Mammoth Road.

6.1   LEFT into Mammoth Creek Park.

6.3   Arrive at starting point.

11. LOWER ROCK CREEK

South of Tom's Place on U.S. 395

The single-track Lower Rock Creek Trail is more like two trails: the upper section, which is rideable by most mountain bikers with some single-track experience under their belt, and the lower section, which is extremely technical and for highly experienced (and gutsy) riders only. The trail varies greatly, consisting of rocky, narrow, and overgrown sections and less difficult, straight, and fast sections. The surface varies also: a mix of dirt, sand, loose gravel, and big and small rocks. This is a ride where you should expect the unexpected, from sharp turns and boulders lying in the middle of the path, to willows and other brushy vegetation crowding the trail, to the possibility of encountering hikers and anglers around every curve. A warning about controlling your speed: At Lower Rock Creek, the stories are legion of riders crashing into rocks after riding too fast around a blind turn. Exercise caution.

ROUTE DETAILS FOR RIDE 11A
(car shuttle trip)

type of trail	dirt single-track
difficulty	🌶🌶🌶🌶🌶
total distance	7.9 miles one-way with shuttle
riding time	1.5 hours
elevation gain	0 feet (2,000-foot loss)

ROUTE DETAILS FOR RIDE 11B
(loop with paved road)

type of trail	dirt single-track and paved road with moderate car traffic
difficulty	🌶🌶🌶🌶🌶
total distance	15.5 miles
riding time	2.5 hours
elevation gain	2,000 feet

If all of this starts to give you second thoughts once you've started riding, you can bail out at the first or second crossing of Rock Creek Road (mile 2.2 or 3.3), then ride back up the paved road to your starting point. Those who insist on continuing onward face the worst of the technical challenges beyond mile 3.5. There are no more bailouts beyond this point. Good luck.

Lower Rock Creek Trail's sandy single-track parallels the lush riparian environment of Lower Rock Creek.

© ANN MARIE BROWN

The trail loses 2,000 feet from top to bottom, so many ride it as a shuttle trip by leaving a car at both ends (Ride 11A). The other option is to ride back uphill on pavement (7.6 miles), which can be extremely hot on summer days and includes a nasty, steep stretch (Ride 11B). A third option would be to ride back uphill on the single-track, but darn near nobody attempts it. You'd carry your bike far too much of the time. Although the area around the start of this trail burned in a fire in August 2002, the trail itself was untouched. You'll leave all signs of the fire behind after the first couple miles.

If you've been riding around the Mammoth Lakes area prior to riding here, remember that you're not in Mammoth any more. Lower Rock Creek is in the arid, desert-like Owens Valley, quite a few miles from the nearest set of high mountain peaks. The sun is hot and unforgiving.

Still, the trail runs through Rock Creek's gorgeous stream canyon, which is surprisingly lush and filled with unusual geologic features, including columnar basalt like that found at nearby Devils Postpile National Monument. The entire ride follows the creek, often in the shade of aspens and Jeffrey pines (thankfully). This is a beautiful, pristine area, and it's a miracle that mountain bikers are allowed access to it. Let's all mind our manners and keep it that way.

For more information, contact the White Mountain Ranger District of Inyo National Forest, 760/873-2500.

Driving Directions

From U.S. 395 at the Highway 203/Mammoth Lakes turnoff, drive 15.5 miles south on U.S. 395 to Lower Rock Creek Road on the right, one mile south of Rock Creek Lakes Road. Turn right and park in the first available pullout. (To leave a shuttle vehicle at the southern end of the trail, continue south on U.S. 395 for 10.5 miles to the Paradise/Gorge Road exit. Turn right and drive three miles north on Lower Rock Creek Road to Paradise Resort; park across the road.)

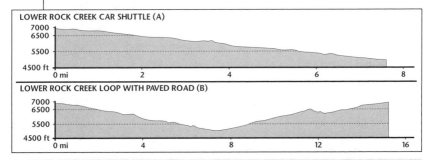

Route Directions for Ride 11A *(car shuttle trip)* for Lower Rock Creek

0.0 Park at the start of Lower Rock Creek Road near its northern junction with U.S. 395. The trail begins directly across from the Lower Rock Creek Recreation Area sign, about 150 feet from U.S. 395 on the south side of the road. *Supplies are available in Tom's Place, one mile north on U.S. 395.*

2.2 RIGHT on Lower Rock Creek Road and pick up the single-track on the far side of the bridge (in the small parking area).

3.3 Cross Lower Rock Creek Road; trail becomes much more technically challenging from here on out.

7.2 Single-track widens into dirt road.

7.9 End of trail at Lower Rock Creek Road and Paradise Resort. *Supplies are available. If you have a shuttle car waiting for you, you're finished.*

Route Directions for Ride 11B *(loop with paved road)*

Follow directions for Ride 11A to mile 7.9, then continue:

7.9 Ride north on paved Lower Rock Creek Road.

15.5 Arrive at starting point.

CHAPTER 7

Redwood Empire

*L*and of the tallest trees, dwelling place of the giants, the Redwood Empire is home to some of the largest remaining stands of old-growth sequoia sempervirens, or coast redwoods. These magnificent trees grow to more than 350 feet tall and live as long as 2,000 years, contributing to one of the most unique habitat areas in California, and in fact, the world.

These behemoth trees bring people to the Redwood Empire. Although the area boasts a rugged and beautiful coastline, quaint towns like Arcata and Trinidad, and wide, free-flowing rivers, the redwoods draw the visitors. Nowhere else in California can you gaze up at such an abundance of the world's tallest living things.

Although a redwood forest is considered to be a monosystem, many other plants live alongside the big trees, including ferns of all kinds, vine maples, huckleberry, salmonberry, and redwood sorrel. Visitors frequently say they get the feeling these woods are "alive;" in fact, they are more alive than almost any other place on earth. Per square inch of land surface, redwood forests have the greatest volume of living matter of any ecosystem in the world.

The Redwood Empire also features a wealth of wildlife, most notably its herds of giant Roosevelt elk. An adult male elk can weigh more than 1,000 pounds; their larger-than-life stature and huge antlers seem strangely appropriate among the giant redwoods. It's not uncommon to spot elk grazing while riding your bike on road or trail. Although they seem gentle, give them plenty of room.

Black bears also roam the redwood forests, searching for acorns and berries. Mountain lions and bobcat prefer the high grassland prairies, which are also good birding spots. The rivers and streams of the Redwood Empire, particularly the Smith and Klamath Rivers, are renowned for steelhead and salmon fishing.

No wonder these precious resources are preserved under the umbrella of Redwood National and State Parks, a co-managed park system that extends for 50 miles up the California coast and includes Redwood National Park, Jedediah Smith Redwoods State Park, Prairie Creek Redwoods State Park, and Del Norte Coast Redwoods State Park. More parks lie in the southern reaches of the Redwood Empire: Humboldt Redwoods and Sinkyone Wilderness State Parks, plus the Bureau of Land Management's King Range National Conservation Area. Clearly this is land worth protecting.

Although the area is infamous for rain, the summer months in the Redwood Empire are actually quite dry. The region receives an average of 69 inches of rain per year—almost six feet—but 90 percent of it occurs from November to March. Summer can be foggy, but this dense marine layer brings life-giving moisture to the giant redwoods, allowing them to grow to their lofty heights.

Always carry extra layers when cycling in the redwoods, since fog, wind, rain, and sunshine can be encountered all in one day, or in one bike ride. Also, consider wearing yellow-tinted sunglasses when riding in the deep shade of the big trees; most riders say they noticeably improve visibility.

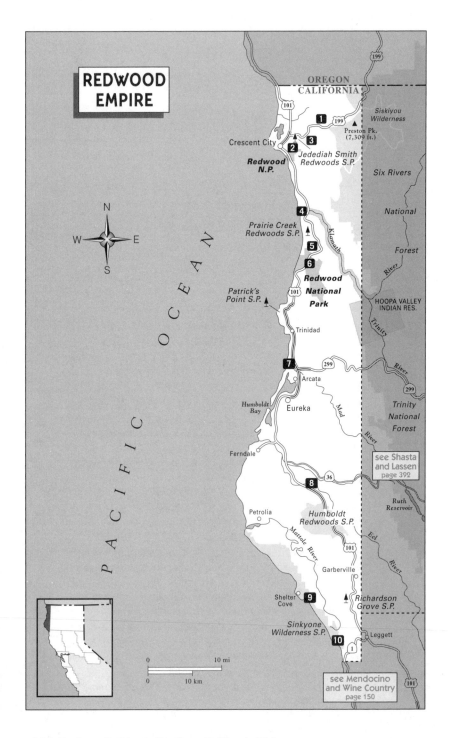

CHAPTER 7
REDWOOD EMPIRE

 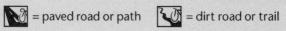
 = paved road or path   = dirt road or trail

1. GASQUET TOLL ROAD

Smith River National Recreation Area east of Crescent City

Gasquet (pronounced GAS-key) is one of the best small towns for outdoors enthusiasts in Northern California. Located on Highway 199 just a few miles east of the Redwood National and State Parks and right on the Wild and Scenic Smith River, Gasquet is the main supply point for visitors to the Smith River Recreation Area. It is home to a wonderful historic lodge and restaurant (Patrick Creek) and a throwback-to-the-'50s diner (She-she's). It's the kind of place where most of the talk centers around fishing (for steelhead, mostly).

cresting the high point on Gasquet Toll Road

ROUTE DETAILS

type of trail — dirt road and paved road with minimal car traffic

difficulty

total distance 25 miles

riding time 5 hours

elevation gain 2,100 feet

And it's also the start of the Gasquet Toll Road, a dirt road that in 1887 linked Crescent City with Waldo, Oregon. The road's owner, an enterprising Frenchman named Horace Gasquet, extracted a toll from stagecoach wagons on the route and made himself a wealthy man.

The road is open to cars, but you'll probably see only a handful on your ride. Today the road is purely for recreational use; it doesn't go anywhere. The surface is dirt and gravel, but it's not always hard-packed. In

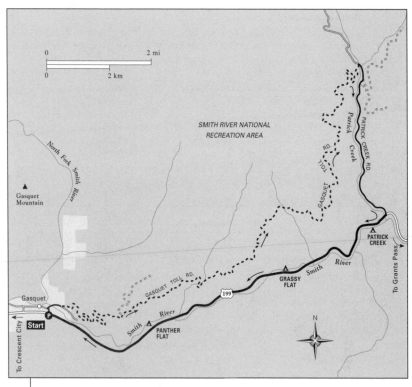

some areas, you'll experience minor technical challenges just from maintaining traction amid millions of small, loose rocks.

From Gasquet, the road climbs through mostly logged forests to higher, denser forests of madrone, cedar, manzanita, and toyon. By 9.0 miles, the highest point of the loop, you gain great views of the Siskiyou Range in Oregon, which is snow-covered much of the year. From the road's edge you can peer down at the scenic Smith River canyon far below.

After a two-mile downhill, at 11.5 miles you start to climb again. Finally the road junctions with Patrick Creek Road at a picnic area with percolation ponds left from mining days. The last 3.5 miles on dirt road parallel lovely Patrick Creek on a downhill grade and bring you out behind historic Patrick Creek Lodge (707/457-3323), a perfect stop for a meal or a drink.

To finish out the loop, you must ride the final 7.5 miles on busy Highway 199, but fortunately the road has wide shoulders and a fast, mostly downhill grade. Along the way, you might want to stop at the Botanical Trail sign on your side of the highway. Walk the .25-mile Darlingtonia Trail to see the unusual California pitcher plant, which traps insects and other small organisms in its cobra-like hood.

For more information, contact Smith River National Recreation Area, 707/457-3131.

Gasquet Toll Road

Driving Directions

From U.S. 101 north of Crescent City, turn east on U.S. 199 and drive 15 miles to Gasquet. Park near the junction of U.S. 199 and Middle Fork/Gasquet Road (the Smith River National Recreation Area visitor center is .25 mile farther east on U.S. 199).

GASQUET TOLL ROAD

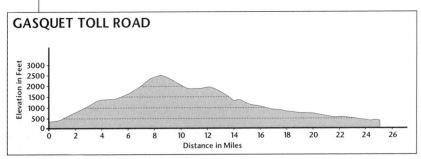

Route Directions for Gasquet Toll Road

0.0 Park in Gasquet. The mileage below starts at the junction of U.S. 199 and Middle Fork/Gasquet Road. Ride north on Middle Fork/Gasquet Road. *Supplies are available in Gasquet.*

0.2 RIGHT at fork, go past the Gasquet Memorial Bridge.

0.3 STRAIGHT (left fork) on North Fork Road.

0.6 RIGHT on Gasquet Toll Road. Pass the dump site; the road turns to gravel.

2.8 LEFT and head uphill at the fork.

3.0 RIGHT to stay on Gasquet Toll Road.

4.0 Road levels for next three miles.

4.9 Bridged creek crossing.

9.0 Highest stretch of the ride; great views of Siskiyou Mountains in Oregon.

14.0 RIGHT at fork with picnic area and percolation ponds; road becomes Patrick Creek Road.

14.4 STRAIGHT at junction.

15.0 Road surface turns to mixed pavement and gravel.

17.5 RIGHT on U.S. 199; Patrick Creek Lodge is on the right. *Supplies are available.*

21.6 Botanical Trail on the right. *Walk the .25-mile trail to see rare California pitcher plants.*

25.0 Arrive at starting point.

2. HOWLAND HILL ROAD

Jedediah Smith Redwoods State Park east of Crescent City

Howland Hill Road has one of the most incredible fern displays in the Redwood Empire, and for that reason alone you should take this easy bike ride. If that isn't enough to motivate you, consider that the ferns grow in the understory of one of the finest old-growth redwood groves in northwestern California. To ride here is to be wowed by the trees.

an enormous stump on Howland Hill Road

ROUTE DETAILS

type of trail   dirt road with minimal car traffic

difficulty

total distance   10.4 miles

riding time   1.5 hours

elevation gain   400 feet

One negative factor may plague your trip: You'll have to deal with some car traffic on Howland Hill Road, a dirt road that is open to passenger vehicles but closed to trailers and motor homes. In summer, the region gets the heaviest traffic. For the least amount of cars and the greatest chance of seeing the majestic redwoods in peace, visit between October and May.

The route directions are simple: Just ride up Howland Hill Road until about a mile beyond the Stout Grove, then turn back. The final mile, as you leave the big trees, provides some nice views of the Smith River. In one direction or the other, lock up your bike at the Stout Grove parking lot and walk its .5-mile trail through a particularly dense grove of redwoods. The Stout Tree is the largest among them, but when trees are this big, no single giant stands out much from the other giants.

If the Stout Grove has whetted your appetite for more hiking among the big trees, check out the Boy Scout Tree Trail at mile 1.9. This six-mile

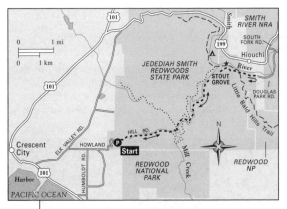

round-trip trail tunnels through another grove of immense redwoods and ends at a small waterfall.

For more information, contact Jedediah Smith Redwoods State Park, 707/464-6101 or 707/ 445-6547.

Driving Directions

From U.S. 101 in Crescent City, turn east on Elk Valley Road and drive 1.1 miles, then turn right on Howland Hill Road. Drive 1.8 miles to a road gate (signed for Stout Grove, 4.0 miles), where there are small pullouts on the left. The pavement turns to dirt and gravel.

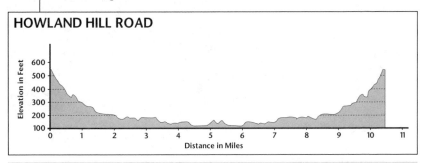

Route Directions for Howland Hill Road

0.0 Park in the pullouts 1.8 miles up Howland Hill Road, by the gate (usually open). *Supplies are available in Crescent City.*

1.9 Boy Scout Tree Trailhead.

2.7 Bridge crossing.

4.0 Stout Grove turnoff on the left. *Lock up your bike and take this short walk through the big trees.*

4.8 Little Bald Hills Trail on the right. *This trail is described in Ride 3 in this chapter.*

5.2 Dirt turns to pavement. TURN AROUND.

10.4 Arrive at starting point.

3. LITTLE BALD HILLS LOOP

Redwood National Park east of Crescent City

Check your calendar before you set out to ride the Little Bald Hills Trail. The trail is closed every winter from November to May to help prevent the spread of Port Orford cedar rot, a fungal disease that travels by spores which can be carried on muddy bike or car tires, hiking boots, and horse hooves. The disease has already taken out thousands of Port Orford cedars in Oregon and Northern California, and the National Park Service is determined to minimize its effects in Redwood National Park. If they can get the necessary funding, they plan to reroute a section of Little Bald Hills Trail to bypass an area that is already infected with the disease. Until that can happen, park rangers simply close the trail in winter and open it from June to October, when the ground is dry and there's no danger of spreading the cedar fungus. Fair enough.

descending through the redwoods on Little Bald Hills Loop

ROUTE DETAILS

type of trail dirt road and paved road with moderate car traffic

difficulty ▮▮▮▯▯

total distance 18 miles (or 19.6-mile option)

riding time 3.5–4 hours

elevation gain 1,900 feet

The loop follows South Fork Road alongside the clear, aqua-colored South Fork of the Smith River, climbing ever so slightly. A right turn on dirt Little Bald Hills Trail takes you uphill through several grueling switchbacks to high, grassy prairielands fringed by firs and pines. If you've been riding your bike around the nearby damp redwood forests, it's hard to believe how dry, and even sunny and hot, it can get up here.

From the ridgeline, the rocky and sometimes narrow old roadbed makes a 1,900-foot drop over 4.5 miles back to the land of big redwoods and Howland Hill Road. A right turn brings you back to South Fork Road in a flash; an optional side trip to the Stout Grove adds only 1.6 miles to your round-trip. Don't miss paying homage to these giants, including the 340-foot Stout Tree.

Even though the descent on Little Bald Hills Trail is fast and well

Little Bald Hills Loop

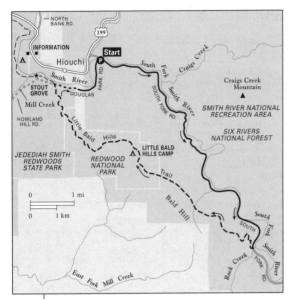

deserved, try to keep your speed down, especially if riding in springtime. The wildflowers that bloom in these hills' dry serpentine soils put on a remarkable show. Little Bald Hills Camp at mile 12.9 is also worth a look; the small backpacking camp sits on the site of the former Murphy Ranch, where in the late 1800s a hotel served travelers along this former mining route.

For more information, contact Redwood National Park, 707/464-6101.

Driving Directions

From U.S. 101 north of Crescent City, turn east on U.S. 199 and drive 6.8 miles to South Fork Road. Turn right and park in pullouts along the first half mile of road.

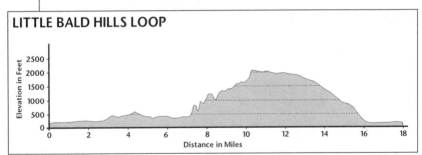

LITTLE BALD HILLS LOOP

Route Directions for Little Bald Hills Loop

0.0 Park in pullouts alongside South Fork Road near Tryon Bridge. Ride south on South Fork Road; the mileage below begins at Tryon Bridge. *Supplies are available in Hiouchi or Crescent City; water is available at the visitor center.*

7.3 RIGHT on dirt connector to Little Bald Hills Trail (just before Rock Creek Bridge; may be unsigned).

12.9 Little Bald Hills Camp turnoff; camp is 100 yards away. *Water is sometimes available.*

16.4 RIGHT on Howland Hill Road; gravel turns to pavement and road becomes Douglas Park Road. *Turn LEFT at this junction for 1.6-mile round-trip for optional side trip to Stout Grove of redwoods.*

18.0 Arrive at starting point.

4. COASTAL DRIVE

Redwood National Park near Klamath

The scenic Coastal Drive road is often missed by auto tourists traveling the Redwood National and State Parks because it's not particularly well marked at U.S. 101. On two trips here, I've shared the road with only a handful of other cars. This makes Coastal Drive a perfect thoroughfare for cyclists.

ROUTE DETAILS

type of trail	dirt and paved road with minimal car traffic
difficulty	
total distance	16.4 miles (or 30.4-mile option)
riding time	2.5 hours
elevation gain	800 feet

The road is a gravel and pavement mix, so mountain bikes are recommended, although some road bike tires could handle it. It begins near the small town of Klamath and heads west, winding through redwoods along the Klamath River's estuary and beyond to its mouth, before reaching the coastline and heading south. At mile 3.3 is an interesting historic site: Radar Station B-71, two concrete block buildings that were camouflaged during World War II to look like a farmhouse and barn. Shortly beyond, the High Bluff Picnic Area affords sweeping views of the ocean. Whales, sea lions, and pelicans are frequently seen.

This out-and-back ride is not without hills; a real doozy shows up around 1.9 miles as the road turns south. (This .5-mile stretch may require pushing your bike.) The remainder of the ride rollercoasters up and down with a gradual uphill to Coastal Drive's junction with Newton B. Drury Scenic Parkway. Ambitious riders can tack on another 14 miles out and back on the parkway to Prairie Creek Redwood State Park's visitor center. The road leads through beautiful redwood groves, but sees moderate to heavy tourist traffic.

Most riders are happy just to turn around and enjoy Coastal Drive's Pacific scenery one more time. You'll hardly pedal at all on the way back.

For more information, contact Redwood National Park, 707/464-6101.

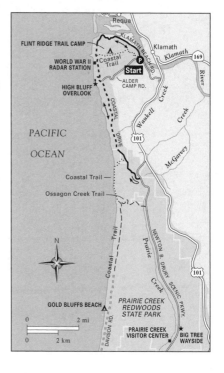

Driving Directions

From U.S. 101 at Klamath, drive south across the Klamath River and turn right on Klamath Beach Road/Coastal Drive. Drive two miles and park near the junction with Alder Camp Road (near the Flint Ridge Trail's east end).

COASTAL DRIVE

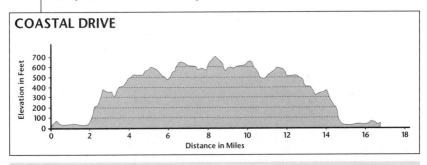

Route Directions for Coastal Drive

0.0 Park near junction of Klamath Beach Road and Alder Camp Road in pullouts alongside the road. *Supplies are available in Klamath.*

1.9 Beach at mouth of Klamath River and start of steep hill.

2.3 Flint Ridge Trail on left.

3.3 Radar Station B-71.

6.8 Overlook point.

8.2 End of Coastal Drive at junction with Newton B. Drury Scenic Parkway. TURN AROUND. *Or add on a 14-mile out-and-back on the parkway to Prairie Creek Redwood State Park's visitor center.*

16.4 Arrive at starting point.

5. GOLD BLUFFS & OSSAGON TRAIL LOOP

Prairie Creek Redwoods State Park near Orick

Prairie Creek Redwoods State Park is a shining jewel in the Redwood National and State Park system, which includes the national park itself and three state parks, all jointly managed. Prairie Creek's resident herd of Roosevelt elk and spectacular Fern Canyon area set it a cut above the other first-class parks in the neighborhood.

A Roosevelt elk crosses Davison Road on the Gold Bluffs & Ossagon Trail Loop.

© ANN MARIE BROWN

ROUTE DETAILS

type of trail	dirt roads and single-track; paved roads with moderate car traffic
difficulty	🍶🍶🍶🍶🍶
total distance	19 miles
riding time	4 hours
elevation gain	900 feet

But what bikers love best about Prairie Creek Redwoods State Park (707/464-6101 or 707/445-6547) is the Gold Bluffs and Ossagon Trail Loop, a 19-mile loop that serves up a terrific half-day adventure for intermediate-level riders. This ride has as much to offer as a half-dozen others combined: windswept beaches, up-close encounters with Roosevelt elk, hidden waterfalls, and giant redwoods.

Most riders start at the Prairie Creek Redwoods Visitor Center, but you could also start at Fern Canyon. The loop can be ridden in either direction, but if you prefer to climb on pavement and descend on dirt, follow the route directions below (counterclockwise). The first leg heads north on Newton B. Drury Scenic Parkway with a fairly wide shoulder and gentle uphill grade. The big redwoods lining this stretch are awe-inspiring; this is a road that every noncyclist should at least drive.

Gold Bluffs & Ossagon Trail Loop

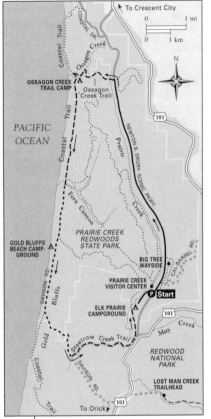

Watch for Ossagon Trail on the left, across from and just beyond the more obvious Hope Creek/Ten Taypo Trailhead. Next comes the single-track stretch of the loop. You might push your bike over the first steep quarter mile uphill, but then prepare for a fast descent of 700 feet in about a mile. (Please watch for hikers.) A set of railroad-tie stairsteps and a bridge over Ossagon Creek will slow you down and force you to dismount.

The trail leads to an alder thicket at the creek mouth, where you turn left and follow Coastal Trail south. The narrow path cuts through forest and opens out to a coastal prairie, the grazing grounds of Roosevelt elk. Give these animals a wide berth; although they seem gentle and disinterested in humans, you don't want to get on the bad side of a 1,000-pound creature with big antlers.

Following an inland route along the prairie's edge, you have a chance to see three 80-foot-tall, thinly streaming waterfalls that drop just a few feet off the trail, hidden in the forest. Listen for their sound and watch for their narrow spur trails. The best of the lot is Gold Dust Falls, found at 9.2 miles.

Where the trail deposits you at Fern Canyon parking area, lock up your bike and take the .25-mile walk into this incredible stream canyon with 40-foot-high fern-covered walls; it's like nothing you've seen anywhere else. Then follow gravel Davison Road alongside windswept Gold Bluffs Beach (watch for car traffic on the one-lane road and gravel dust in summer) to Steelrow Creek Trail, your ticket back to the park campground and visitor center.

Driving Directions

From Eureka, drive north on U.S. 101 for 41 miles to Orick. Continue north for five more miles, then take the Newton B. Drury Scenic Parkway exit and turn left. Follow the signs for one mile to the Prairie Creek Redwoods State Park Visitor Center. Drive past the entrance kiosk to the day-use parking area.

GOLD BLUFFS & OSSAGON TRAIL LOOP

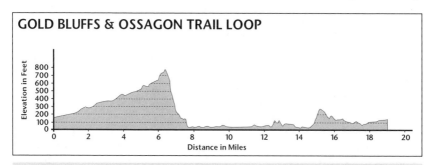

Route Directions for Gold Bluffs & Ossagon Trail Loop

- 0.0 Park in the day-use parking area near the visitor center. Ride back out the park road to Newton B. Drury Scenic Parkway and turn left; the mileage begins there. *Supplies are available in Orick; water is available at the trailhead.*

- 6.1 LEFT on Ossagon Trail; steep climb uphill.

- 7.8 LEFT on Coastal Trail.

- 8.7 LEFT at fork to stay on inland trail.

- 9.2 Gold Dust Falls (and two other waterfalls within .25 mile on either side). *The fall is hidden a few yards off the main trail in the forest; look for a spur trail leading to it.*

- 10.6 Fern Canyon parking area and trailhead. *Lock up your bike and hike the .5-mile trail into this amazing canyon.*

- 10.7 Follow gravel Davison Road past Gold Bluffs Beach and campground.

- 15.3 LEFT on Steelrow Creek Trail (previously named "Jogging Trail").

- 17.2 LEFT on Steelrow Creek Trail/Davison Trail

- 18.2 Trail's end at campground's trailer dump site. Follow park road straight ahead.

- 19.0 Arrive at starting point.

6. HOLTER RIDGE/LOST MAN CREEK LOOP

Redwood National Park near Orick

The Holter Ridge/Lost Man Creek Loop is a fickle trail. Each few miles, the nature of the ride changes so dramatically that it always takes you by surprise—even if you know it's coming. And therein lies the fun of this challenging ride.

ROUTE DETAILS

type of trail   dirt road and paved road with moderate car traffic

difficulty   𝄌𝄌𝄌𝄌𝄌

total distance   19.5 miles

riding time   4 hours

elevation gain   2,200 feet

The first 1.3 miles are almost perfectly level, paralleling gurgling Lost Man Creek. A couple of bridge crossings offer eye-opening peeks into the beautiful stream canyon. Centuries-old trees are everywhere you look, moss hangs from the alders, ferns grow to immense sizes. The trail is an old gravel roadbed, smooth as silk and often covered with fallen leaves and soft needles. The only obstacles are bright yellow and green banana slugs; try to avoid squashing them as they inch across the road.

Then abruptly, the old road starts to climb, and it does so on a brutal grade—1,400 feet in two miles. If you can't ride this grade, it's worth pushing your bike—don't bail out here. Once the trail gains Holter Ridge, the riding eases up again, with small, undulating ups and downs on a smooth gravel surface over seven miles.

Views of the coast are a fair compensation for the effort involved in getting up here at 2,300 feet above sea level. One final climb awaits around mile 10.0, but it's over in less than .5 mile.

Finally, paved Bald Hills Road descends from the ridgeline, passing the Lady Bird Johnson Grove (definitely worth a stop and a short hike) before making an

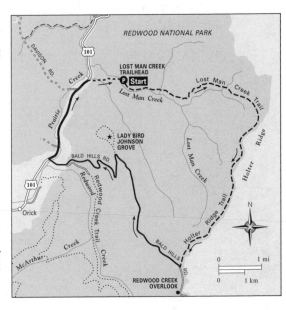

incredibly fast drop to U.S. 101. Both Bald Hills Road and the highway have substantial traffic, including tourists and logging trucks, so be very cautious. Two miles later, you're back at Lost Man Creek Road, pedaling the final level stretch to your car.

If you don't want to deal with auto traffic in the final miles of this peaceful nature ride, consider an out-and-back from the end of Holter Ridge Trail, near its junction with Bald Hills Road. The mileage is almost identical to the loop.

For more information, contact Redwood National Park, 707/464-6101.

Driving Directions
From U.S. 101 at Orick, drive north three miles to Lost Man Creek Road (on the right). Turn right and drive .9 mile to the end of the pavement, a picnic area, and trailhead.

HOLTER RIDGE/LOST MAN CREEK LOOP

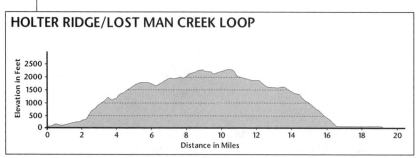

Route Directions for Holter Ridge/Lost Man Creek Loop

0.0 Park at Lost Man Creek Trailhead. *Supplies are available in Orick.*

1.3 Trail starts to climb steeply.

3.7 RIGHT on Holter Ridge Trail (trail simply curves to right).

10.2 RIGHT on paved Bald Hills Road. *Or turn left and ride .25 mile to the Redwood Creek Overlook and picnic area, a fine viewpoint on rare sunny days.*

13.8 Lady Bird Johnson Grove on your right. *Lock up your bike and walk the one-mile trail among the big trees.*

16.5 RIGHT on U.S. 101.

18.6 RIGHT on Lost Man Creek Road.

19.5 Arrive at starting point.

7. HAMMOND TRAIL

McKinleyville

The movement to convert abandoned railroad lines to multiuse trails for bicyclists, equestrians, and anyone else under nonmotorized power has gained a lot of momentum in California, which has thousands of miles of unused railroad track. The Hammond Trail is a proud example of this movement's success: It presents a safe and easy route from Arcata to McKinleyville, grand views of the coast and rural farmlands, beach access, and a ride through a historic railroad bridge that is closed to all motorized traffic. Two short sections of the trail follow quiet neighborhood streets, but the remainder is a paved, car-free recreation trail.

ROUTE DETAILS

type of trail paved bike path

difficulty 🍶🍶🍶🍶

total distance 13 miles

riding time 1 hour

elevation gain 400 feet

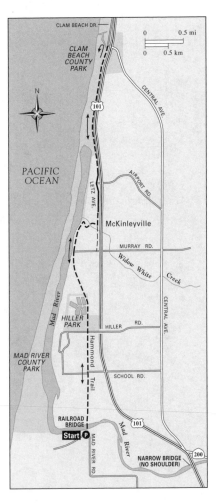

The trail begins at an old railroad bridge across the Mad River, a key piece of McKinleyville's history. The original bridge on this site was of the wooden covered variety, built in 1905. When it deteriorated, it was replaced by the existing steel truss bridge in 1941. It was used by the Hammond Lumber Company for its railroad until 1961.

Hammond Trail passes through the farmlands of Arcata Bottoms—a Northern California version of the English countryside with green fields and grazing cows and horses, then continues north through Hiller Park, a small community park. A stretch through dense coastal forest leads to Murray Road and a neighborhood of large, odd-looking houses built to resemble castles (some developer's imaginative idea). Beyond Murray

Road, bikers and horses split off from hikers and follow the trail on the west side of U.S. 101 (hikers cross an environmentally sensitive area over Widow White Creek). A .25-mile stretch on Letz Avenue connects to a vista point overlooking Trinidad Head to the north and the entire Mad River estuary. The trail's final stretch provides access to the brayed tan sands of Clam Beach.

For more information, contact Humboldt County Parks, 707/445-7651.

Driving Directions

From U.S. 101 in Eureka, drive north 10 miles to the north end of Arcata, then take the Giuntoli Lane exit and head left (west). Cross over the freeway, then turn right on to Heindon Road and drive .3 mile. Turn left on Miller Lane and drive .8 mile. Turn right on Mad River Road and drive 1.6 miles to an old steel railroad bridge.

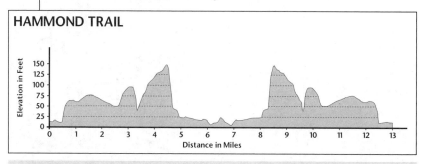

HAMMOND TRAIL

Elevation in Feet / Distance in Miles

Route Directions for Hammond Trail

0.0 Park at pullouts alongside old railroad bridge. *Supplies are available in Arcata.*

3.5 Murray Road and "castles;" bike trail splits from hiker trail to parallel U.S. 101.

6.5 End of trail at Clam Beach County Park and bridge over Strawberry Creek. TURN AROUND.

13.0 Arrive at starting point.

8. AVENUE OF THE GIANTS & MATTOLE ROAD

Humboldt Redwoods State Park north of Garberville

It's hard to resist a road with a name like Avenue of the Giants. It's even harder to resist when it's located in the third largest state park in California, Humboldt Redwoods State Park (707/946-2409; website: www.humboldtredwoods.org), where more than a third of 51,000 acres are ancient, old-growth redwood forests. And it's still harder to resist when you discover that the elevation gain along the entire out-and-back route is only 1,000 feet. Now if they would just block off the road to cars.

bicyclist enveloped by redwoods and ferns on Mattole Road

ROUTE DETAILS

type of trail paved roads with moderate car traffic

difficulty 🔦🔦

total distance 44.2 miles (or 16.2-mile option)

riding time 4 hours

elevation gain 1,000 feet

This bike ride follows the north end of the Avenue of the Giants, then takes a side trip to Mattole Road and Rockefeller Forest. Pick up a free Auto Tour pamphlet in the roadside boxes near the trailhead; nine numbered points are interpreted along the trail. The highlights range from the sublime 2.5-mile Newton B. Drury and Ralph W. Chaney Groves hiking trail (worth locking up your bike to explore) to the kitschy Immortal Tree, which survived lightning, the logger's axe, a forest fire, and the flood of 1964.

The best biking of the trip is found on narrow and less-traveled Mattole Road, which winds through the largest remaining ancient redwood forest in the world: 10,000-acre Rockefeller Forest. Once on this road a mother bear and cub lumbered across the pavement 100 feet ahead of me. This feels like primeval country.

If you want a shorter trip, try starting this ride at the end point, Humboldt Redwoods State Park visitor center, and riding the latter half of the route in reverse: Go north on Avenue of the Giants 4.5 miles to Founders Grove (stop and visit), then north another .3 mile to Mattole Road. Turn left on Mattole and ride 3.3 miles to the

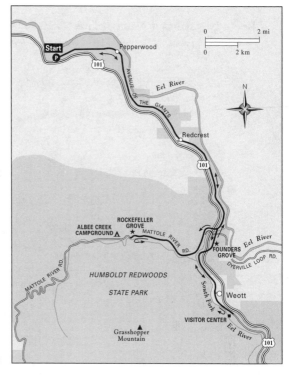

Big Trees Area (stop and visit). Round-trip mileage will be 16.2 miles, and it's almost all level.

Mountain bikers, if you're dying to get off the pavement, two popular dirt routes begin near the Big Trees Area on Mattole Road: the grueling 17-mile Grasshopper Peak Loop and somewhat less challenging 16-mile Peavine Road Loop.

Driving Directions

From Eureka, drive south on U.S. 101 for 30 miles to the Pepperwood/Avenue of the Giants exit.

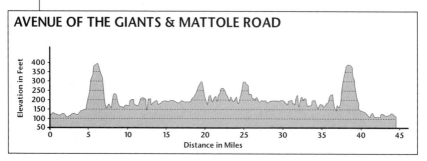

Route Directions for Avenue of the Giants & Mattole Road

0.0 Park in pullouts alongside the north end of Avenue of the Giants. *Supplies are available in Pepperwood.*

2.7 Newton B. Drury and Ralph W. Chaney Groves loop trail. *Lock up your bike and walk this 2.5-mile loop through the redwoods.*

5.1 Immortal Tree.

6.6 Village of Redcrest. *Supplies are available.*

8.5 Mahan Loop Trail. *Lock up your bike and walk this .6-mile loop through the redwoods.*

10.7 Dyerville Bar Overlook.

10.8 RIGHT on Mattole Road at signed Albee Creek Campground Road turnoff (Rockefeller Forest).

14.1 LEFT into Big Trees Area. TURN AROUND. *Lock up your bike and walk to the Giant Tree and Flat Iron Tree.*

17.4 RIGHT (south) on Avenue of the Giants.

17.7 Founders Grove on left. *Lock up your bike and walk the .5-mile trail around this grove; don't miss the Dyerville Giant.*

21.1 Village of Weott. *Supplies are available one block to the left.*

22.1 Humboldt Redwoods State Park visitor center. TURN AROUND.

44.2 Arrive at starting point.

9. CHEMISE MOUNTAIN

King Range Conservation Area, west of Garberville

They say that the Lost Coast has two seasons: six months of rain and six months of fog. Maybe so, but if you happen to ride the trail from Hidden Valley to Chemise Mountain on a rare sunny day (best chances in spring or fall), you'll be rewarded with a view that will knock your socks off—a wide panorama of the Yolla Bolly Mountains to the east, Sinkyone Wilderness and the Mendocino coast to the south, and King's Peak to the north.

ROUTE DETAILS

type of trail dirt road and single-track

difficulty

total distance 6.4 miles

riding time 1.5 hours

elevation gain 1,000 feet

Located in the King Range National Conservation Area (707/825-2300) region of the Lost Coast (north of Sinkyone Wilderness State Park), Chemise Mountain is lined with tan oaks and madrones that have replaced the majority of the Douglas firs, which were logged. Near Chemise Mountain's summit at 2,596 feet is chaparral, including manzanita and chemise (greasewood), from which the mountain gets its name.

This is a short ride, but a difficult one nonetheless. Chances are good you'll do some walking, especially in the first 1.5 miles of highly technical single-track and nearly a dozen tight uphill switchbacks. After that you gain a ridge, the grade eases up, and you are rewarded with sweeping views of the Pacific coast. One more mile and you're at the summit, enjoying the view if it's sunny. Then you backtrack one mile and loop back via pleasant Nadelos Campground and Chemise Mountain Road.

A highlight of the ride is lovely Hidden Valley. Its large meadow, which you ride past at mile 0.3, is frequently populated with grazing Roosevelt elk. They are "extras" relocated from the herd at Prairie Creek Redwoods State Park.

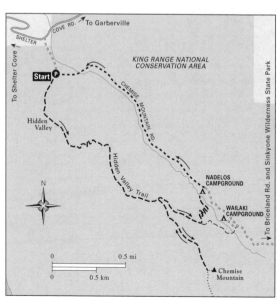

Driving Directions

From U.S. 101 at Garberville, take Redwood Drive three miles northeast to Redway, then take Briceland-Thorne Road west for 17.3 miles (it becomes Shelter Cove Road). Turn left on Chemise Mountain Road (dirt) and drive .25 mile to the Hidden Valley trailhead on the right.

CHEMISE MOUNTAIN

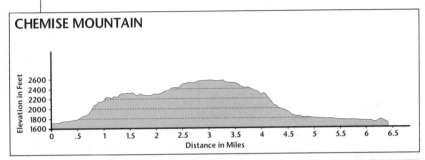

Route Directions for Chemise Mountain

0.0 Park at the Hidden Valley Trailhead. *Supplies are available in Garberville.*

0.3 Meadow with Roosevelt elk.

0.4 LEFT at junction.

0.5 LEFT at junction (steep switchbacks ahead).

2.0 RIGHT at junction. *If you're tired, stash your bike here and walk the last .5 mile to the summit.*

2.6 End of trail near summit of Chemise Mountain. TURN AROUND. *Leave your bike and walk the last 50 yards to the summit.*

3.2 RIGHT at previous junction.

3.8 LEFT at junction for Nadelos Campground.

4.8 LEFT on Chemise Mountain Road at campground.

6.4 Arrive at starting point.

10. HOTEL GULCH TRAIL

Sinkyone Wilderness State Park, west of Leggett

Highway 1 hugs the coast for almost the entire length of Northern California, allowing visitors easy access to glorious stretches of sea, sand, and surf. Except for one remote stretch: from north of Rockport to just south of Eureka, a land that has come to be called the Lost Coast.

ROUTE DETAILS

type of trail	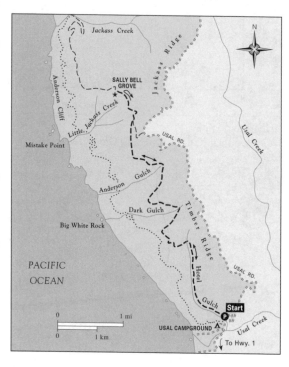 dirt road
difficulty	▮▮▮▯▯
total distance	12.6 miles
riding time	2.5 hours
elevation gain	2,400 feet

The Lost Coast may be remote, but it's not forgotten. One Saturday at an REI store in the Bay Area, I stood in the checkout line with three other customers and it surfaced that all four of us were heading separately to the Lost Coast. Lost? Hardly.

Still, this was late spring, which is the only "busy" season at the Lost Coast. From November to April, the area gets up to 80 inches of rain, which greatly reduces tourism (the area's dirt roads become impassable). In summer, the fog moves in. Autumn and spring are your best bets for a visit, and a chance to mountain bike the Hotel Gulch Trail at Sinkyone Wilderness State Park (707/986-7711).

The trail, an old logging road, travels the park's eastern ridgeline, not the coastline, although it does supply many fine views of the coast. From the north end of Usal Campground, Hotel Gulch Trail climbs 2.5 miles to the top of Timber Ridge at 1,200 feet, then descends for two miles, crossing Dark Gulch Creek and Anderson Gulch Creek. Although this area was heavily logged right up until the 1980s and the virgin trees are long gone, the landscape is dense with young forest and foliage. In a few hundred years, the big redwoods and firs will be back.

One more climb awaits around mile 5.0, shortly before the trail ends at a junction with Wheeler Road. There you turn left to visit the Sally Bell Grove of virgin redwoods. The grove was named for the last full-blooded Sinkyone Native American, a medicine woman who survived a massacre of her people.

Note that there is no piped water available at Usal Campground or anywhere near this trail. If you bring a purification system, you can filter water from the creek. Otherwise, fill your bottles in Westport or Leggett before you drive all the way out here.

Driving Directions

From Westport, drive north on Highway 1 for 13 miles (past Rockport) and turn left on County Road 431/Usal Road (may not be signed; look for the spot where Highway 1 turns inland at milepost 90.88). The road turns to dirt after 50 yards; drive six miles to Usal Campground, continue over the bridge, and turn left at the Hotel Gulch junction. (From Leggett, drive southwest on Highway 1 for 14.6 miles to County Road 431/Usal Road and turn right.)

HOTEL GULCH TRAIL

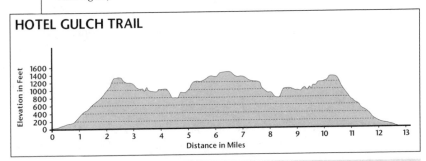

Route Directions for Hotel Gulch Trail

0.0 Park at the junction of Usal Road and Hotel Gulch Trail. *Supplies are available in Westport or Leggett.*

2.6 Summit of Timber Ridge.

5.8 LEFT at junction with Wheeler Road (end of Hotel Gulch Trail).

6.3 Sally Bell Grove. TURN AROUND. *Lock up your bike and wander among these old-growth redwoods.*

12.6 Arrive at starting point.

CHAPTER 8

Shasta and Lassen

*I*n the northeastern corner of California lies a part of the state where most people have never set foot. Ranging from the Oregon border south to Redding and from the Nevada border west through the Klamath Mountains, this northern interior is both the least populated and least visited region of the Golden State. Yet it is bestowed with some of California's most spectacular scenery: a landscape of rugged mountains, raging rivers in steep canyons, and vast expanses of sagebrush flats and pine- and fir-covered ridges. This is the land where osprey and eagles soar, and remnants of volcanoes sputter and fume.

Two national parks are found here, both celebrating the region's volcanic past: Lava Beds National Monument, with its 300 lava tube caves, vast volcanic cinder landscape, and western juniper forests; and Lassen Volcanic National Park, California's best example of recent geothermal activity. How recent? In May 1914, Lassen Peak began a seven-year stint of volcanic outbursts. Even today, visitors can witness volcanic action including seething hot springs, steaming volcanic vents, and boiling mud pots (springs filled with hot mud). One of the best ways to see the park is on the seat of a bike, by taking a long and strenuous ride on Lassen Park Road. The challenging climb is not for everybody, but for hearty riders it's a once-in-a-lifetime adventure.

Then there is the 2.1 million acres of Shasta-Trinity National Forest, dominated by mighty Mount Shasta, a dormant volcano whose summit attains the lofty height of 14,162 feet. At its base is Shasta Lake, the largest reservoir in California, which is part of another federally managed parkland: Whiskeytown-Shasta-Trinity National Recreation Area. Both Shasta and Whiskeytown Lakes offer mountain bikers some of the best single-track riding in the state. In fact, Whiskeytown was the site of one of the first official mountain bike races, the Whiskeytown Downhill, originally held in 1981.

Wildlife is plentiful in the northeast corner of the state. Black bear roam the mountainsides; herds of mule deer and pronghorn antelope migrate through the plains. Eagle Lake, the second largest natural lake in California, is one of the best spots in Northern California for bird watching. Lake Almanor near Chester has the largest summer population of ospreys in California. Paved recreation trails at these two lakes make them accessible to families and novice riders who are camping or visiting for the day.

A sense of history is also prevalent. Old gold mine sites, water ditches, and structures from the Gold Rush era can be explored on Whiskeytown Lake's trails. The Bizz Johnson Trail in Susanville is built on a circa 1900s railroad grade. Where cyclists ride today, thundering locomotives once rumbled through the canyon carrying heavy loads of logs and lumber.

The truth is, the only thing you won't find in northeast California is a crowd. And that may be the best reason of all to come here and ride your bike.

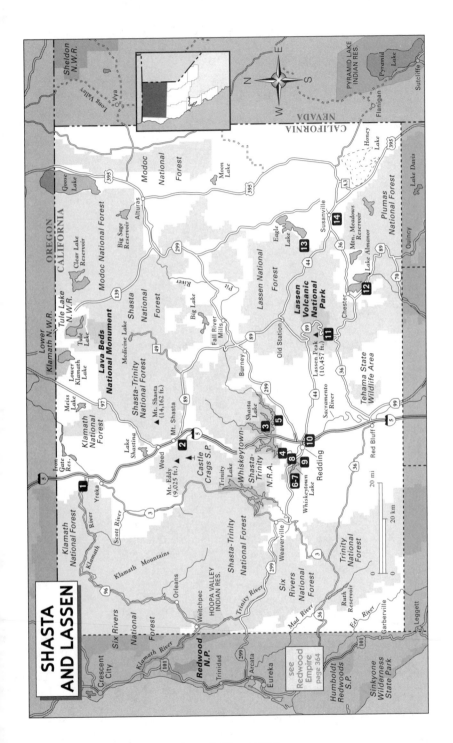

SHASTA
AND LASSEN

CHAPTER 8
SHASTA AND LASSEN

🏔 = paved road or path   🐾 = dirt road or trail

1. UPPER KLAMATH RIVER

North of Yreka

The Upper Klamath River ride is an out-and-back favored by rangers at Klamath National Forest. They suggest riding this 19-mile one-way route as a shuttle, with one car left at either end. You could do so, or follow my suggestion and simply ride out and back on the eastern 7.8 miles from the Ash Creek Bridge. Because the dirt road is quite level all the way—it ultimately loses only 500 feet during its 19-mile length—strong riders could take the entire trail out and back.

easy cruising alongside the rolling Klamath River

ROUTE DETAILS

type of trail	dirt road with minimal car traffic
difficulty	
total distance	15.6 miles (or longer/shorter options)
riding time	2–3 hours
elevation gain	800 feet

The ride follows an alternate route to Highway 96, the National Scenic Byway on the north side of the Klamath River. The "alternate" is an old stagecoach trail on the river's south side that was used by hard rock miners blasting for gold in the late 1800s. Today it's a gravel and dirt road seldom used by car drivers except those who own homes along the road. You'll have to put up with some washboard bumps, but otherwise, the riding is easy. Often the road pulls in quite close to the river; sometimes it will move away for a quarter mile or so. Highway 96 is usually visible on the river's north side, but barely noticeable with the roar of flowing water. In California, the 265-mile-long Klamath River is second only to Sacramento River in terms of the amount of water it empties into the Pacific.

The dirt road curves westward, into an arid landscape of rocky crags, juniper, chaparral, and oaks, which eventually changes to a more lush forest. Heading west on this road, the annual rainfall increases nearly one inch per mile, and this is reflected in the foliage. The turnaround point suggested, at mile 7.8, is at a high point with a nice view of the river.

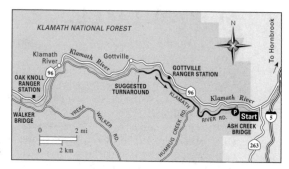

If you decide to ride the road's entire length, you'll find it is bookended by scenic bridges. Its eastern end is at the Ash Creek Bridge, built in 1901. Its western end is at the Walker Bridge, 19 miles to the west (the old stagecoach route continues past this point, but it becomes Walker Road). It might seem tempting to make a loop out of this ride by riding back on Highway 96, but that road is far too dangerous for bicyclists—it's busy, narrow, and with blind curves and no shoulder.

The Forest Service claims that this ride provides excellent chances of seeing great blue herons, muskrats, turtles, osprey, and so on, but the only creatures I saw were deer grazing on the petunias in the riverside cabin owners' yards.

For more information, contact Klamath National Forest Headquarters, 530/842-6131, or Scott River Ranger District, 530/468-5351.

Driving Directions

From Yreka on I-5, drive north for 10 miles to the Highway 96 exit. Drive southwest on Highway 96 for 2.1 miles to its junction with Highway 263, then continue on Highway 96 for 1.9 more miles to the Ash Creek Bridge on the left. Cross the bridge and park on its far side in pullouts.

UPPER KLAMATH RIVER

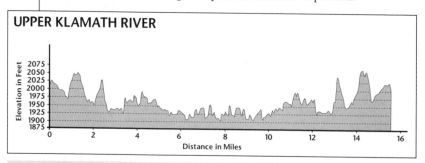

Route Directions for Upper Klamath River

0.0 Park across the Ash Creek Bridge on the south side of the river in dirt pullouts. *Supplies are available in Yreka.*

7.8 High point above the river. TURN AROUND.

15.6 Arrive at starting point.

2. SISKIYOU LAKE LOOP

West of Mount Shasta City

If you're vacationing at Shasta Lake and all the water-skiers and loud party boats are starting to wear you down, a trip to Lake Siskiyou could be the perfect antidote. Lake Siskiyou is one of the few reservoirs in California that was built specifically for quiet kinds of recreation; the lake speed limit is 10 mph. As a bonus, the water managers leave the lake level alone even when other lakes in the area are drawn down. Deep blue and full to the brim, Lake Siskiyou is a lake for scenery-lovers, surrounded by a thick conifer forest and with Mount Shasta holding court in the background.

ROUTE DETAILS

type of trail dirt and paved roads with minimal car traffic

difficulty ▮▮▯▯▯

total distance 10.3 miles

riding time 2 hours

elevation gain 200 feet

This loop around the lake's perimeter gives you an overview of the pretty lake. It starts from the beginning of North Shore Road, although you could add on a few miles by riding from downtown Mount Shasta. (Many riders on this loop are campers at Lake Siskiyou Campground, who start right from their tent sites.)

After the first mile on North Shore Drive, you reach the northern lakeshore. Several turnoffs on your left lead to dirt parking areas and shoreline access; take any of them to get an unobstructed lake and mountain view or just sit by the water. As you ride, North Shore Road gets rougher and rockier, especially beyond the 2.5-mile mark as you move out of sight of the lake—it goes from pavement to good gravel to worse gravel to rocky dirt track. The trickiest section is the crossing of the Sacramento River at mile 4.9, which is a 100-foot-wide field of rounded rocks and boulders, with or without a lot of water running over them. Because of this crossing, this ride is best taken in late summer or fall when the river level is down. The condition of the road is also better then—smoother and more tightly compacted.

Once across the river, the rest of the ride is easy. The dirt road quickly turns to pavement, and you'll pedal past the lake's campground and marina on your way back to your starting point. Watch for cars on the busier south

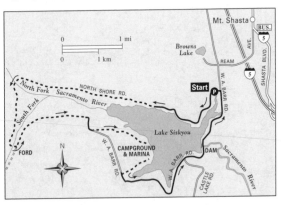

side of the lake. You might stop for a swim at the beach near the marina, or just pause along the way and enjoy the striking view of Mount Shasta.

For more information, contact Siskiyou Lake Campground and Marina, 530/926-2618.

Driving Directions
From Redding, drive north on I-5 for 60 miles to the town of Mount Shasta, then take the central Mount Shasta exit and turn left. Drive west over the overpass and drive one mile to W.A. Barr Road. Turn left and drive .7 mile to North Shore Road, where you turn right.

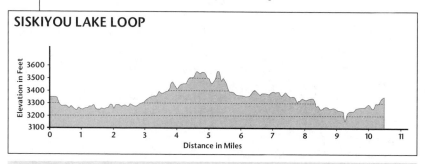

Route Directions for Siskiyou Lake Loop

- 0.0 Park in any of the pullouts on North Shore Drive near its junction with W.A. Barr Road. Ride west on North Shore Drive. *Supplies are available in Mount Shasta.*
- 1.5 Pavement turns to gravel.
- 2.5 Trail moves away from the lakeshore. Keep heading due west on the main road and ignore all turnoffs.
- 4.9 Crossing of Sacramento River.
- 5.0 LEFT on dirt road on far side of Sacramento River.
- 5.2 LEFT on paved W.A. Barr Road.
- 7.1 Siskiyou Lake Campground and Marina. *Water and supplies are available.*
- 10.3 Arrive at starting point.

3. WATERS GULCH & FISH LOOP

Shasta Lake, north of Redding

When you're ready for a technical single-track challenge, but not ready for long mileage or steep uphills that climb halfway to the stars, you're ready to ride on the Waters Gulch and Fish Loop Trails at Shasta Lake. The trails roll along with only short ups and downs but offer multiple lessons in technical riding, with plenty of bridges to cross, rocks strewn along your path, exposed tree roots, tight turns, and steep drop-offs into Shasta Lake. Better keep your eyes on the road.

ROUTE DETAILS

type of trail	dirt single-track
difficulty	▮▮▮▯▯
total distance	6.8 miles
riding time	1–1.5 hours
elevation gain	900 feet

Aside from the all-in-good-fun single-track, the surrounding forest of pines and oaks and the views of the Sacramento River arm of Shasta Lake are quite pretty. If you stop to stare at the bright blue lake surface, you might get lucky and see a golden eagle or an osprey go fishing. As you ride, oak leaves frequently get caught in your spokes, making a great shuffling sound as your wheels spin.

Waters Gulch and Fish Loop are separate but connecting loops. What ties them together is a .6-mile stretch on Packers Bay Road, which you drive in on. You can ride out and back on the single-track in both directions for a 6.8-mile round-trip, or, if you decide after the first leg that you've had enough of this path's technical challenges, you can return downhill on pavement for a four-mile round-trip.

Either way, start riding on Fish Loop, a short path around a small peninsula on Packers Bay. The trail gets narrower as manzanita bushes crowd in and brush your ankles. Fish Loop offers the best riding of the day and wonderful lake views, but it's over in only .7 mile. Too soon.

Go left where Fish Loop connects to Waters Gulch Trail and undulates up and down through more manzanita and dense oak forest. The trail moves away from the lake as it crosses the strip of land separating Packers Bay from Waters Gulch. As it nears the water again, the path becomes more technical and ascends more steeply. This is a good place to consider whether or not you will be comfortable returning downhill on this trail, or if you should loop back on pavement. Much of the upper part of Waters Gulch Trail has been heavily eroded and is quite rocky and narrow; the drop-off into a neighboring creek is nearly vertical. A couple of stairstep-style drops and an

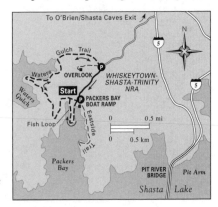

extremely tight, double switchback may give you pause. (I walked my bike here both uphill and downhill.) But shortly beyond the switchbacks, you're at the upper terminus of the trail, and probably feel disappointed (or perhaps lucky?) that it's over. Simply turn around and ride back or take the pavement downhill.

Remember that this is Shasta Lake, not Mount Shasta, so daytime temperatures in the summer months can be extreme. Plan your ride around the thermometer.

For more information, contact Shasta Lake Visitor Center, 530/275-1589, or Shasta-Trinity National Forest Headquarters, 530/244-2978.

single-track challenges on Waters Gulch Trail at Shasta Lake

Driving Directions

From I-5 at Redding, drive north for 15 miles and take the O'Brien/Shasta Caverns exit. Cross the freeway and get back on I-5 heading south. Drive one mile and take the Packers Bay exit. Drive 1.6 miles to the end of the road at the boat ramp.

WATERS GULCH & FISH LOOP

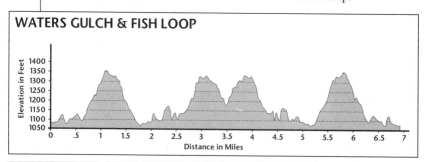

Route Directions for Waters Gulch & Fish Loop

- 0.0 Park at Packer's Bay boat ramp. Begin riding to the left at the Fish Loop Trailhead, which is 20 yards below a separate trailhead for Waters Gulch Trail. *Water is available at the trailhead.*
- 0.7 LEFT on Waters Gulch Trail.
- 3.1 Steep uphill with stairstep drops and tight switchbacks.
- 3.4 Upper trailhead parking area. TURN AROUND. *If you want to avoid the downhill single-track, follow the paved road downhill for a 4.0-mile round-trip.*
- 6.8 Arrive at starting point.

4. DRY FORK CREEK

Shasta Lake, north of Redding

The trail at Dry Fork Creek was built to assist anglers in accessing the good fishing areas near Shasta Dam, but it's become a favorite of mountain bikers. And no wonder—this is some sweet single-track. The only catch is that you can only ride it when the lake level is down about 15 feet or more at Shasta Dam, which isn't usually until midsummer. If the lake isn't down, part of the trail is under water.

Located on the west side of Lake Shasta's massive dam, Dry Fork Creek Trail skirts the shore of the lake.

ROUTE DETAILS

type of trail — dirt single-track

difficulty — ▮▮▮▯▯

total distance — 9.6 miles

riding time — 2 hours

elevation gain — 500 feet

This is not a trail for acrophobes. Almost five miles of single-track rise high above the lakeshore with some frighteningly steep drop-offs. Small rocks are abundant. The trail's width shrinks to less than 18 inches in places. If you're the kind of rider who gets psyched-out when you try to pick a line and follow it, you won't be happy here.

On the other hand, if narrow trails don't bother you at all, you'll love the sweeping views of Shasta Lake from this pathway. If it's a hot summer day, it's easy enough to jump in the lake; the trail curves its way in and out of small coves. You might even want to bring along your fishing rod and drop a line in the water. There are no trail junctions to worry about—just pure, unbridled riding. The first hill, right at the start of the ride, is the steepest of the day.

Note that rangers have plans to add more mountain biking and hiking trails around this area of Shasta Lake. By the year 2004, expect to see some new pathways along the west side of Shasta Dam.

Special note: Due to the tragic events of September 11, 2001, access to Shasta Dam is restricted as this book goes to press. In order to cross Shasta Dam to reach this trail, you must contact the Shasta Lake Visitor Center 48 hours before your arrival to obtain security clearance. How long this policy will be in effect is undecided.

For more information, contact Shasta Lake Visitor Center, 530/275-1589, or Shasta-Trinity National Forest Headquarters, 530/244-2978.

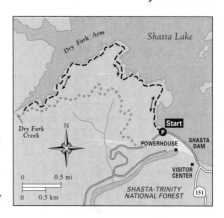

Driving Directions

From I-5 in Redding, drive north seven miles to Shasta Dam/Highway 151 exit. Drive west for seven miles to the dam, cross it, and park.

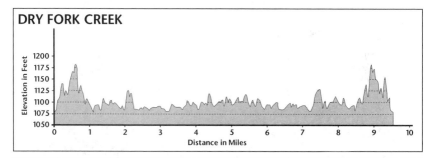

Route Directions for Dry Fork Creek

0.0 Park on the west side of Shasta Dam. The trail begins about 150 yards down the dirt road to the lake. *Water is available at the trailhead.*

4.8 End of single-track at junction with dirt road. TURN AROUND.

9.6 Arrive at starting point.

5. CLIKAPUDI

Shasta Lake, north of Redding

The name Clikapudi comes from the Wintu Native American word "klukupuda" which means "to kill." Fortunately it's a reference to a battle between the Wintu and local traders in the 1800s and does not reflect the difficulty of this trail's single-track.

ROUTE DETAILS

type of trail — dirt single-track

difficulty —

total distance — 9.7 miles

riding time — 2 hours

elevation gain — 400 feet

In fact, this single-track is downright manageable, even for people who don't have a lot of technical riding experience. The surface is smooth more than rocky, curves are graceful and not tight, and the main obstacles are hikers and horses, not rocks and tree roots. With only two short but challenging hills and a fair amount of shade from black oaks and conifers, this is a good trail to build your confidence on single-track. At the few difficult spots, simply dismount and walk.

It's also a good trail for a swim on a hot day, of which there are plenty in the summer months at Shasta Lake. Between miles 4.0 and 6.0 you'll find a couple of picnic tables and easy places to drop your bike and splash into the water.

For more information, contact Shasta Lake Visitor Center, 530/275-1589, or Shasta-Trinity National Forest Headquarters, 530/244-2978.

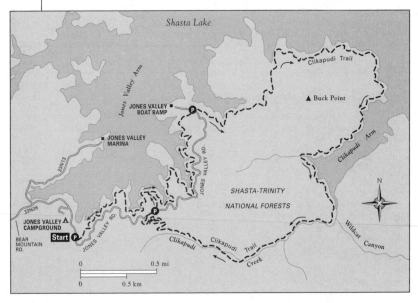

Driving Directions

From I-5 in Redding, take Highway 299 east for six miles to Bella Vista. Just past the small town, turn left on Dry Creek Road and drive 5.5 miles to a fork. Go right on Bear Mountain Road. Drive one mile and turn right on Jones Valley Road. Look for the pullout on the left in .4 mile (before the campground).

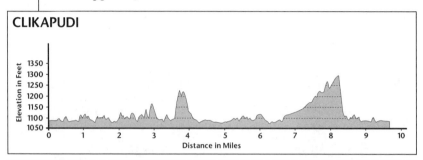

CLIKAPUDI

Route Directions for Clikapudi

0.0 Park at the trailhead on Jones Valley Road just before the campground. *Supplies are available at the store on Bear Mountain Road.*

1.3 STRAIGHT at junction with trail on right; this is your loop return.

2.9 Jones Valley parking area and boat ramp. *Water is available.*

3.7 LEFT at fork.

6.9 STRAIGHT on single-track at several junctions with jeep roads; watch for trail markers.

7.9 .25-mile switchbacking descent to pavement.

8.2 RIGHT on Jones Valley Road.

8.3 LEFT back on trail.

8.5 LEFT at junction (this is the junction you visited at mile 1.3).

9.7 Arrive at starting point.

6. OAK BOTTOM CHANNEL/ GREAT WATER DITCH

Whiskeytown Lake west of Redding

If you like riding on single-track and you like lakeside trails, the Oak Bottom Channel Trail is a perfect fit. It skirts the edge of Whiskeytown Lake, providing stunning blue-water views at almost every turn.

ROUTE DETAILS

type of trail	dirt single-track and paved road with minimal car traffic
difficulty	▐▐ ▯▯▯
total distance	6.6 miles (or 10.6-mile option)
riding time	1.5 hours
elevation gain	200 feet

The trail is also known as the Great Water Ditch (and is called that on some park maps), but it is signed on both ends as Oak Bottom Channel Trail. It is built on one of the area's many water ditches, which were part of the original irrigation system that developer Levi Tower built in the Gold Rush days to supply his hotel, farm, and mining operations.

The trail starts at Oak Bottom campground's access road and runs to the Carr Powerhouse, which is part of a huge water regulation system somewhat more complicated than Levi Tower's: The powerhouse diverts water from the Trinity River, stores it in Trinity Lake, sends it by tunnel to Whiskeytown Lake, then sends it to Keswick Reservoir and into the Sacramento River. All in an effort to keep the Central Valley from looking like a desert.

From the dirt pullout and trailhead along the Oak Bottom Camp access road, head downhill immediately for about 30 yards, then follow the single-track as it curves in and around the lakeshore. The trail runs between Whiskeytown Lake and Highway 299, so you are wowed by lake views the whole way. One section snakes through what may be the biggest manzanita bushes in all of Shasta-Trinity. The only minus is the road noise.

Where the trail ends at a paved road, follow the pavement to Carr Powerhouse Road, then cross Clear Creek and ride to the left to the Carr Powerhouse and picnic area.

To add four more miles to your ride, you can turn right after crossing Clear Creek (the road is pavement but soon turns to dirt, then single-track). After several steep uphill switchbacks,

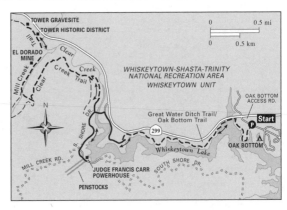

turn right, go straight at the next junction, then watch for a steep trail heading sharply downhill to the right. Now you're on Mill Creek Trail and will shortly reach the El Dorado Mine site. After examining the old mine buildings, continue on Mill Creek Trail past the ranger's house to the Tower Historic District and Tower Gravesite. Then return the way you came.

For more information, contact Whiskeytown National Recreation Area, 530/246-1225.

Driving Directions

From I-5 at Redding, take Highway 299 west for 13 miles (five miles west of the Whiskeytown Lake Visitor Information Center). Turn left at the sign for Oak Bottom Campground and Marina. Drive .2 mile on the Oak Bottom access road and park in the pullout on the right.

OAK BOTTOM CHANNEL/GREAT WATER DITCH

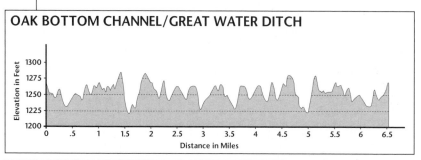

Route Directions for Oak Bottom Channel/Great Water Ditch

0.0 Park at the trailhead pullout near the top of Oak Bottom access road. *Supplies are available at the camp store at the end of the road.*

0.1 Right at fork (hikers take trail on left).

0.3 Trail comes out just below Highway 299.

1.5 Stairsteps by pumphouse and gate. Go around the gate and turn LEFT on dirt road, then in 25 yards, turn RIGHT back on trail alongside lake.

2.1 End of Oak Bottom Trail. Continue on pavement.

2.7 LEFT on Carr Powerhouse Road.

2.8 Cross Clear Creek and turn LEFT. *You can also opt to turn right and follow the service road to a single-track trail that switchbacks uphill and cuts over to Mill Creek Trail and El Dorado Mine (see description above).*

3.3 Judge Francis Carr Powerhouse and picnic area. TURN AROUND.

6.6 Arrive at starting point.

7. BOULDER CREEK LOOP

Whiskeytown Lake west of Redding

The Boulder Creek Loop is a classic Whiskeytown ride, with miles of technical single-track, a half-dozen creek crossings, and a couple of heartbreaking climbs. This is not a ride for beginners. The first 1.8 miles are the toughest aerobically (you gain 1,000 feet in this short stretch) but the next stint on Boulder Creek Trail's single-track is the toughest in terms of riding skills required.

ROUTE DETAILS

type of trail	dirt road and single-track
difficulty	
total distance	8.6 miles
riding time	2 hours
elevation gain	1,200 feet

Fortunately the first 1.8-mile hill climb is on a wide gravel and dirt road that is mostly shaded by oaks, pines, and madrones. After much grunting and huffing and puffing, you are rewarded with great views of Shasta Bally and Clear Creek Valley.

Next, single-track Boulder Creek Trail doles out a couple of small ups and downs before making its long drop into Boulder Creek valley. This 3.7-mile stretch is what makes this loop so favored among local mountain bikers. It's just plain fun (and challenging) to negotiate your way across the numerous running creeks and ride through dense, leafy, rocky woods. As the single-track progresses, it becomes increasingly more technical. The rocks seem to multiply exponentially.

Eventually the trail widens to a jeep road and meets up with South Shore Drive, where you cruise through a final three miles back to your car. Yes,

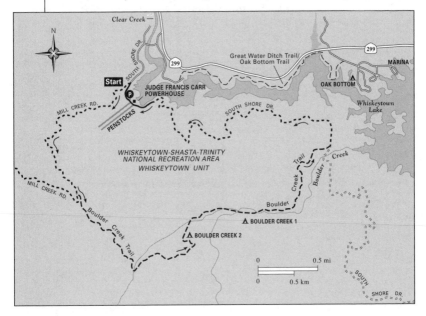

you have one more big hill to face, but it's nothing like that first one. You may see a few cars on this last dirt road stretch.

Note that if you want to turn this into an overnight trip, two hiker/biker camps are located along the Boulder Creek single-track. A permit from the visitor center is required. For more information, contact the Whiskeytown National Recreation Area, 530/246-1225.

Driving Directions
From I-5 at Redding, take Highway 299 west for 15 miles (7 miles west of the Whiskeytown Lake Visitor Information Center). Turn left at the sign for Judge Francis Carr Powerhouse and drive .5 mile to the picnic area.

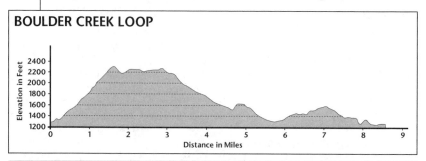

BOULDER CREEK LOOP

Route Directions for Boulder Creek Loop

0.0 Park at the picnic area by Carr Powerhouse, then ride back out the way you came in and turn left on Crystal Springs Road (gravel jeep road). *Supplies are available in Redding or at the Oak Bottom camp store.*

0.1 RIGHT at fork.

1.8 End of climb.

1.9 LEFT at junction with Boulder Creek Trail (single-track).

5.5 LEFT on South Shore Drive.

8.6 Arrive at starting point.

8. SOUTH FORK MOUNTAIN LOOKOUT

Whiskeytown Lake west of Redding

Whiskeytown is best known among mountain bikers for its miles of single-track. But every now and then, you aren't in the mood for single-track; you just want to put your climbing legs to work and get an aerobic workout, preferably with some great destination at the top of the hill.

ROUTE DETAILS

type of trail 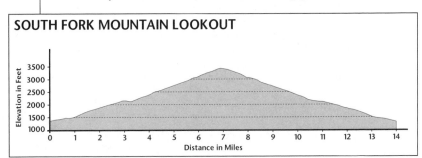 dirt road with minimal car traffic

difficulty

total distance   14 miles

riding time   3 hours

elevation gain   2,100 feet

Enter the South Fork Mountain Lookout Road ride. The dirt road, which is open to cars but doesn't see many, winds its way uphill over seven miles with a consistent, moderate grade, allowing you to gain 2,100 feet before you know it. A few level stretches will even give you a breather. There are no technical challenges to worry about except controlling your speed on the downhill return. Strong beginners can manage this ride, as long as they have the legs and lungs to grunt out a seven-mile, slow and sustained climb.

And the view from the top is worth it. From South Fork Mountain's Fire Lookout at 3,447 feet, you gaze down at Whiskeytown Lake directly south, the Trinity Mountains to the northwest, and the Sacramento River Valley and Mount Lassen to the east. Hang gliders are sometimes

SOUTH FORK MOUNTAIN LOOKOUT

Elevation in Feet / Distance in Miles

Route Directions for South Fork Mountain Lookout

0.0   Park at the visitor center and ride your bike carefully across Highway 299 to the start of South Fork Mountain Lookout Road (slightly east/right of the visitor center and often not signed). *Supplies are available in Redding or at the Oak Bottom camp store.*

0.2   LEFT at junction (gate is usually open).

6.3   LEFT at junction.

7.0   South Fork Lookout and other buildings on summit. TURN AROUND.

14.0   Arrive at starting point.

seen taking off near the summit.

The ride starts almost directly across Highway 299 from the Whiskeytown visitor center, on a road that starts out partially paved but soon turns to dirt. The few road junctions are obvious choices, so don't think at all—just head uphill.

Don't forget to pack along a picnic lunch for the summit. And if you're looking for an unusual adventure, try riding this road on a full moon night. Some bikers do so without even using a headlamp—the trail is that easy to follow.

For more information, contact Whiskeytown National Recreation Area, 530/246-1225.

Driving Directions
From I-5 at Redding, take Highway 299 west for eight miles. Turn left on John F. Kennedy Memorial Drive and park at the Whiskeytown Lake Visitor Information Center.

9. MOUNT SHASTA MINE LOOP

Whiskeytown Lake west of Redding

It's hard to believe that a ride this brief could kick so many butts. The mileage is ridiculously short and the overall elevation gain is minimal. It's just that a few sections have what you might call grades from Hades—straight up or down and as rocky as Yosemite Valley. Still, this is a favorite ride at Whiskeytown, and you're sure to have plenty of company on it. Just know that if you aren't a strong rider or sure of your technical skills, you'll be walking some of the time. A key is to ride the loop clockwise, not counterclockwise. This makes the hills a lot more manageable.

ROUTE DETAILS

type of trail dirt road and single-track

difficulty 🔋🔋🔋

total distance 3.1 miles

riding time 1 hour

elevation gain 500 feet

The old Mount Shasta Mine itself is visible from the loop, but sadly, all there is to see is a hole in the ground surrounded by a chain-link fence and an interpretive sign. Gaze at the hole and consider that this mine, which operated from 1897 to 1905, was the biggest gold producer in the entire Shasta mining district. It's strange to think of miners toiling away 100 years ago in a 465-foot-deep hole on land that today is our biking playground.

The loop begins with a steep .75-mile hill climb on a wide road to the top of Shasta Divide ridge, from which you'll gain high views of Whiskeytown Lake. Then it's a right turn on a menacing downhill single-track, which for many may be too steep to ride. Orofino Creek drops alongside the lower part of this stretch, creating pretty pools and waterfalls early in the year. At the bottom of the trail go right to reach the old mine site. Mountain bikers have made use of a large depression in the ground (probably an old slag pond) to create a spur trail for practicing a short but steep dip down, then up.

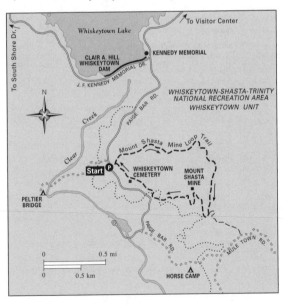

The last 1.2 miles from the mine back to the parking lot are the easiest—just fun, rollercoastering single-track through manzanita and pine forest. You'll pass by the Whiskeytown Cemetery, where you'll find some old gravesites worth viewing.

For more information, contact Whiskeytown National Recreation Area, 530/246-1225.

Driving Directions
From I-5 at Redding, take Highway 299 west for eight miles. Turn left on John F. Kennedy Memorial Drive (in front of the Whiskeytown Lake Visitor Information Center) and drive one mile, then turn left on Paige Bar Road and drive 1.2 miles to the dirt parking area on the left.

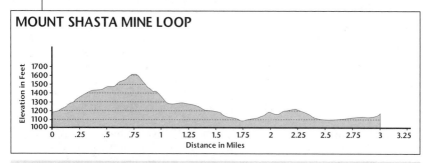

MOUNT SHASTA MINE LOOP

Route Directions for Mount Shasta Mine Loop

0.0 Park at the trailhead on Paige Bar Road. The trail (a dirt road) begins on the eastern end of the parking lot near the restrooms and between two big boulders. Go LEFT and uphill on the wide dirt road. *Supplies are available in Redding or at the Oak Bottom camp store.*

0.8 RIGHT on single-track trail (very steep downhill).

1.7 RIGHT on single-track at junction (it's a hard right turn).

1.9 Mount Shasta Mine on right.

2.6 RIGHT at junction, paralleling Paige Bar Road but not joining it, then immediately RIGHT again.

2.9 Pass by old Whiskeytown Cemetery.

3.1 LEFT to arrive at starting point.

10. SACRAMENTO RIVER TRAIL

Redding

If ever there was a perfect, easy trail for teaching someone how to ride a bike, or for taking a casual Sunday afternoon ride with a friend, the Sacramento River Trail is it. It takes you away from the hustle and bustle of downtown and offers plenty of good places to sit on a bench and watch the water roll by.

ROUTE DETAILS

type of trail	paved bike path
difficulty	
total distance	9.8 miles
riding time	1 hour
elevation gain	200 feet

Not surprisingly, the multiuse trail is popular with Redding locals, and you'll see plenty of dog walkers, anglers, baby strollers, and joggers in addition to dozens of squirrels and small flocks of quail. If you visit in mid-summer, you can pick a few handfuls of blackberries along the trail (careful, they stain your cycling gloves). If you time your trip for fall, you'll witness one of Redding's finest displays of autumn color.

The first mile of trail west from Riverside Drive is so tame and suburban-feeling, you'll be a little surprised when you suddenly enter wide-open foothill country. Here the paved trail seems out of place against the rugged landscape. At 2.5 miles, you reach a 418-foot-long, hiker and biker footbridge across the Sacramento River, just before Keswick Dam. A technological wonder, the bridge is considered to be environmentally safe because it is a concrete stress-ribbon, meaning it is supported by 200-plus steel cables in its concrete deck instead of pilings or piers dug into the riverbed.

Across the bridge the trail loops back on the river's north side. This side is steeper and has more tight curves, making it less popular with walkers and joggers. At a junction with the Diestlehorst Bridge that would lead back to the starting point, continue straight on a trail extension that runs into downtown Redding. The trail continues through Caldwell Park, across Market Street, and to the new Turtle Bay Museum. The trail bridge by the museum, scheduled to open in 2004, will be as architecturally stunning as the museum itself. Called Sundial Bridge, it will look like a boomerang with harp strings and function as a sundial. The floor of the span, built of frosted glass panels, will be lit up at night.

Note that in the near future

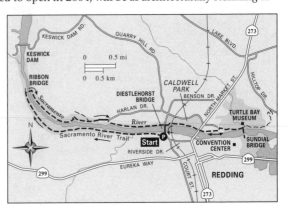

the Sacramento River Trail will connect to the nine-mile Sacramento River Rail Trail, an abandoned railbed that leads to Shasta Lake. The Bureau of Land Management and Shasta County are working together to make that happen.

For more information, contact City of Redding Community Services, 530/225-4512; website: www.ci.redding.ca.us; or the Redding Convention and Visitors Bureau, 530/225-4100.

Driving Directions

From I-5 at Redding, take Highway 299 west for two miles to its junction with Highway 273 heading north (North Market Street). Veer right on Highway 273, then turn left (west) on Riverside Drive. Don't cross over the river; go straight into the parking area at Riverside Park. Ride west on the bike trail from the parking area.

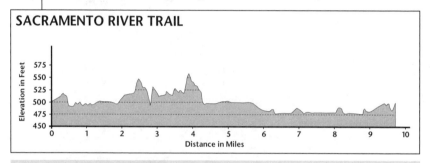

SACRAMENTO RIVER TRAIL

Route Directions for Sacramento River Trail

0.0 Park at Riverside Park and ride west on the bike trail. *Supplies are available in Redding; water is available at several points along the trail.*

2.5 Hiker and biker footbridge across the Sacramento River.

5.2 STRAIGHT at junction with Diestlehorst Bridge on right.

7.4 End of trail. TURN AROUND.

9.6 LEFT across Diestlehorst Bridge.

9.7 RIGHT on bike trail.

9.8 Arrive at starting point.

11. LASSEN PARK ROAD

Lassen Volcanic National Park east of Redding

Lassen Volcanic National Park is California's best example of recent geothermal activity. Before the 1980 eruption of Mount St. Helens in Washington, Lassen Peak was the most recently erupted volcano in the contiguous United States. It first blew its top in 1914; major volcanic outbursts continued for seven years. The park exhibits many present-day examples of geothermal action, including steaming sulphur vents, mud pots, and boiling springs. This out-and-back ride on the main park road gives you a close look at this strange and beautiful volcanic terrain.

ROUTE DETAILS

type of trail paved road with moderate car traffic

difficulty 🥾🥾🥾🥾🥾

total distance 55.8 miles

riding time 5 hours

elevation gain 4,350 feet

Because the ride follows the main park road, you will have to tolerate a great deal of car traffic, especially on summer weekends. The road has no shoulder and is quite narrow, so avoid riding at busy times. Weekday early mornings are best in summer. After Labor Day, when the park is largely deserted, is the ideal time to ride. The road is usually closed some time in October with the first snow and doesn't reopen until June. Although the season is short, the landscape of lakes, volcanic peaks, and red and white fir forest is breathtaking. This is one of the greatest road rides in Northern California.

The grade is a simple up-and-down in both directions. The first seven miles from Southwest Campground are a serious

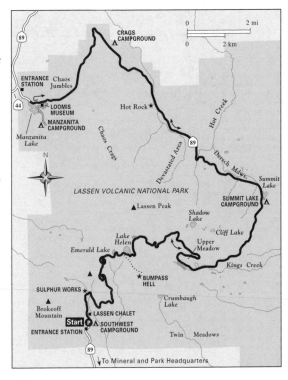

climb: You start at 6,800 feet in elevation and ascend to 8,500 feet at the Lassen Peak Trailhead area. Then you glide through the next 21 miles, dropping elevation to Manzanita Lake at 5,850 feet. After fueling up on snacks and drinks at the well-stocked Manzanita Camp Store and perhaps visiting the fascinating Loomis museum, you turn around and head back. The climb is gentler on the return, but those last seven miles drop like a rock back to Southwest Campground, with many extremely tight and narrow turns. Make sure you stop occasionally to give your brakes a rest; some of the drop-offs are severe and there's no room for error.

For more information, contact Lassen National Park at 530/595-4444; website: www.nps.gov/lavo.

Driving Directions

From I-5 in Red Bluff, drive east on Highway 36 for 45 miles. Turn north on Highway 89 and drive 4.5 miles to the park's southwest entrance station. Just beyond it is a large parking area on the right by Southwest Campground.

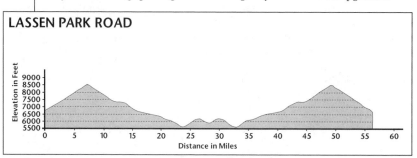

LASSEN PARK ROAD

Route Directions for Lassen Park Road

0.0 Park just past the entrance station near Southwest Campground. *Food is available at the Chalet. Supplies are available in Mineral, 10 miles south.*

0.1 Lassen Chalet. *Food and drinks are available.*

0.8 Sulphur Works on left. *Lock up your bike and take this .25-mile interpretive hike through the steaming fumaroles.*

5.7 Bumpass Hell Trailhead on right; Emerald Lake and Lake Helen on left. *Lock up your bike and take the three-mile Bumpass Hell hike to a larger and even more impressive geothermal area than Sulphur Works.*

6.8 Lassen Peak Trailhead on left.

16.4 Summit Lake Campground on right. *Water is available.*

27.9 Manzanita Lake area on left. TURN AROUND. *Supplies are available at the camp store .5 mile to the left; pay a visit to the nearby Loomis Museum to learn more about the park.*

55.8 Arrive at starting point.

12. LAKE ALMANOR RECREATION TRAIL

South of Chester and Lassen Volcanic National Park

The Lake Almanor Recreation Trail is a popular paved path for campers staying at the lake's five campgrounds. The lake, set at 4,500 feet in elevation, is one of the largest manmade lakes in California—13 miles long, six miles wide, and with 28,000 surface acres. It's well-known among anglers, who ply its waters for rainbow trout, brown trout, and Chinook salmon. It's also popular with water-skiers in summer.

low water at Lake Almanor at the end of the summer

© ANN MARIE BROWN

ROUTE DETAILS

type of trail	paved bike path
difficulty	🚲
total distance	19 miles
riding time	2 hours
elevation gain	600 feet

The recreation trail makes a perfect family bike trip, and its 19-mile round-trip length is long enough to make you feel like you got some exercise. Unfortunately the path follows the lakeshore for only a small portion of its length, but still it's quite pretty. Much of it runs through fragrant stands of pine, fir, and incense cedar, and passes meadows covered in wildflowers in spring and early summer. Interpretive signs are posted at several points along the trail, explaining the local flora and fauna. Keep your eyes out for osprey and bald eagles; they are frequently seen from the lake's west shore. Lake Almanor has the largest summer population of ospreys in California.

For more information, contact the Almanor Ranger District of Lassen National Forest, 530/258-2141.

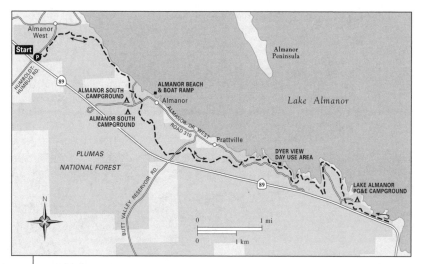

Driving Directions

From Chester, drive three miles west on Highway 36/89, then turn left (south) on Highway 89 and drive 4.3 miles. Turn left across from Humbug-Humboldt Road.

LAKE ALMANOR RECREATION TRAIL

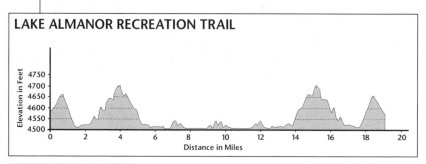

Route Directions for Lake Almanor Recreation Trail

0.0   Park at the northern trail access across Highway 89 from Humbug-Humboldt Road. *Supplies are available in Chester.*

2.5   Almanor North & South Campground and boat ramp. *Water is available.*

4.2   Jake's Lake, an ephemeral wetland that dries up by July.

5.4   Cross Butt Valley Reservoir Road.

6.5   Dyer View day-use area.

9.5   End of trail at Lake Almanor PG&E Campground. TURN AROUND.

19.0   Arrive at starting point.

13. EAGLE LAKE TRAIL

North of Susanville

Was Eagle Lake named for our national bird? Yes indeed. From the shores of Eagle Lake, bald eagles and osprey are commonly seen. On my bike ride I spotted both of those remarkable birds, plus white pelicans, western grebes, Canada geese, a great blue heron, a beaver, mule deer, and golden-mantled ground squirrels by the dozens. Eagle Lake is one of the best places to see wildlife in Northern California.

Be on the lookout for eagles and osprey on Eagle Lake's paved trail.

ROUTE DETAILS

type of trail	paved bike path
difficulty	🍶 🍶 🍶 🍶 🍶
total distance	10 miles
riding time	1 hour
elevation gain	100 feet

It's not surprising, considering a few facts: Eagle Lake is the second largest natural lake in California, after Lake Tahoe. Fed by natural, underwater springs, the lake is set in an enclosed basin with no natural outlets. As a result, its water is extremely alkaline. Only one species of trout can survive in it—the Eagle Lake rainbow trout. This fish is coveted for its size, fighting ability, and taste. Humans, as well as osprey and eagles, find them quite delicious.

Eagle Lake's paved recreation trail starts at Christie Campground near site number 12. The path stays right along the lake's south shore for the entire ride, curving in and out of pine forests and meadows, passing sandy beaches and offering nearly nonstop views of the water. Because the trail runs through several campgrounds, you have many chances for water breaks. At mile 4.0, you can stop at the marina store for snacks. Bike rentals are also available. A highlight along the trail is the wheelchair-accessible fishing area by the marina, which is also a prime bird-watching spot. Nearby Gallatin Beach is marked off for swimming.

The lake is set at 5,100 feet in elevation, so it's often cool and comfortable up here when the Susanville area is much warmer.

For more information, contact the Eagle Lake Ranger District of Lassen National Forest, 530/257-4188.

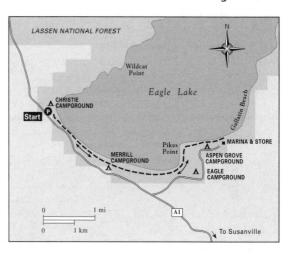

Driving Directions

From Susanville on Highway 36, drive west for three miles and then turn north on County Road A-1, Eagle Lake Road (next to the ranger station). Drive 14 miles to the lake, then follow the signs to Christie Campground.

EAGLE LAKE TRAIL

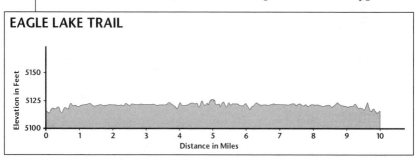

Route Directions for Eagle Lake Trail

0.0   Park outside Christie Campground at Eagle Lake and ride into the camp to site number 12 and the start of the trail. *Supplies are available in Susanville, 14 miles away.*

4.0   Gallatin Beach, marina and store. *Supplies are available.*

5.0   End of trail. TURN AROUND.

10.0 Arrive at starting point.

14. BIZZ JOHNSON TRAIL

Susanville, east of Red Bluff

The Bizz Johnson National Recreation Trail is one of the great success stories of the Rails-to-Trails movement in the United States. The longest rail trail in California, it follows the path of the Southern Pacific Railroad's Fernley and Lassen branch line between Susanville and Mason Station, four miles north of Westwood. Southern Pacific operated logging, freight, and passenger trains over the line from 1914 to 1955. Through the cooperative efforts of the Bureau of Land Management, U.S. Forest Service, and many community groups, the abandoned rail line is now a 25.4-mile-long trail for bikers, hikers, and horseback riders.

ROUTE DETAILS FOR RIDE 14A
(short out-and-back)

type of trail   dirt road

difficulty

total distance   13.4 miles

riding time   2 hours

elevation gain   500 feet

ROUTE DETAILS FOR RIDE 14B
(long loop)

type of trail   dirt road and paved road with moderate car traffic

difficulty

total distance   51 miles

riding time   5 hours

elevation gain   1,600 feet

The wide dirt-and-gravel road is ideal for mountain biking, whether you want a short and easy cruise along the scenic Susan River (Ride 14A), or a longer adventure riding the entire trail and then looping back on Highway 36 (Ride 14B). The route has a very easy 2- to 3-percent grade except for one short section, so you can spin out the miles fairly quickly. If you opt for the loop, be forewarned that the 15-mile stretch on Highway 36 gets substantial car traffic. (Bus service is available on some days if you want to ride the entire trail one-way; call the numbers below for details.)

The trail begins at the Susanville Railroad Depot and Museum, which is open daily including holidays. The first half mile runs through Susanville's neighborhoods, then reaches the Millerton Road trailhead and enters the scenic Susan River canyon. Both sides of the trail are lined with fascinating volcanic rocks; the pretty river flows mellifluously alongside. The trail passes through two old railroad tunnels (one 800 feet long and one 400 feet long and both extremely dark inside) and crosses nine scenic bridges. At the Devil's Corral trailhead at mile 6.7, riders following Ride 14A simply turn around and head back, enjoying the lovely river canyon all over again.

Beyond the Devil's Corral trailhead, the trail loses some of its scenic value. A detour takes you under Highway 36 with a short descent and climb. Then the trail moves farther from the river on a 6.2-mile stint to the Goumaz Trailhead. Mountain bikers who don't want to ride the whole route in a day can pack their panniers and spend the night at Goumaz's primitive campground (bring your own water). From there, it's another 5.1 miles to Westwood Junction, the highest point in the

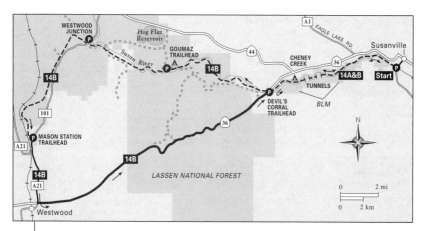

trail at 5,500 feet, and then a final 7.4 miles to Mason Station. The higher elevations in this last stretch are a major departure from the first arid miles of trail; Westwood Junction is ponderosa pine country (and snow country in winter).

To finish out the loop, ride four miles on county roads to Highway 36 and the small town of Westwood, where you'll find supplies and a 25-foot carved statue of Paul Bunyan, symbol of the Paul Bunyan Lumber Company. Then take Highway 36 east to Susanville.

So who was Bizz Johnson, anyway? A former California congressman who worked on this project and many other public works.

For more information, contact the Bureau of Land Management's Eagle Lake Field Office, 530/257-0456; website: www.ca.blm.gov/eagle-lake; or the Eagle Lake Ranger District of Lassen National Forest, 530/257-4188.

Driving Directions

From Highway 36 in Susanville, head east through town as the road becomes Main Street. At the first stoplight, turn right on South Weatherlow Street. Drive .4 mile to the railroad depot on the left.

one of two railroad tunnels on the historic Bizz Johnson Trail

Bizz Johnson Trail

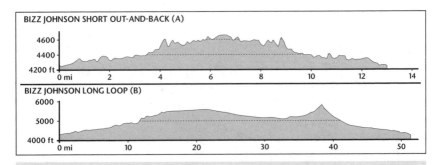

BIZZ JOHNSON SHORT OUT-AND-BACK (A)

BIZZ JOHNSON LONG LOOP (B)

Route Directions for Ride 14A *(short out-and-back)* for Bizz Johnson Trail

0.0   Park at the Susanville Railroad Depot. *Supplies are available in Susanville.*

0.5   Millerton Road Trailhead.

6.7   Devil's Corral Trailhead. TURN AROUND.

13.4   Arrive at starting point.

Route Directions for Ride 14B *(long loop)*

Follow directions for Ride 14A to mile 6.7, then continue:

12.9   Goumaz Trailhead and primitive campground.

18.0   Westwood Junction (trail's high point).

25.4   RIGHT on County Road 101 at Mason Station Trailhead (trail's terminus).

25.9   LEFT on County Road A-21.

29.0   LEFT on Highway 36 in town of Westwood. *Supplies are available .5 mile south of Highway 36 in town.*

44.4   RIGHT on Bizz Johnson Trail at Devil's Corral Trailhead (signed right turnoff from the highway).

51.0   Arrive at starting point.

Appendix

NORTHERN CALIFORNIA MOUNTAIN BIKE PARKS

The following downhill and cross-country ski resorts are transformed into mountain bike parks in summer. Mountain bikers pay a daily fee to ride all day on each park's trails. Most park fees include rides uphill on a chairlift or gondola, so if you choose your trails carefully, all you have to do is coast downhill.

Mt. Shasta Bike, Board, and Ski Park
104 Siskiyou Avenue
Mt. Shasta, CA 96067
530/926-8610 or 530/926-8686
website: www.skipark.com.

Mammoth Mountain Bike Park
P.O. Box 24
Mammoth Lakes, CA 93546
760/934-0606, 800/228-4947, or 800-MAMMOTH
website: www.mammothmountain.com.

Northstar-at-Tahoe
P.O. Box 129
Truckee, CA 96160
530/562-1010 or 800/GO-NORTH
website: www.northstarattahoe.com.

Squaw Valley USA
1960 Squaw Valley Road
Olympic Village, CA 96146
530/583-5585 or 800/545-4350
website: www.squaw.com.

Kirkwood Resort
P.O. Box 1
Kirkwood, CA 95646
209/258-6000 or 209/358-3000
website: www.kirkwood.com.

Bear Valley
P.O. Box 5120
Bear Valley, CA 95233
209/753-2834
website: www.bearvalleyxc.com.

Donner Ski Ranch
P.O. Box 66
19320 Donner Pass Road
Norden, CA 95724
530/426-3635
website: www.donnerskiranch.com.

Eagle Mountain
P.O. Box 1566
Nevada City, CA 95959
800/391-2254
website: www.eaglemtnresort.com.

NORTHERN CALIFORNIA BIKE SHOPS

San Francisco Bay Area

ALAMEDA

Alameda Bicycle, 1522 Park Street, Alameda; 510/522-0070; website: www.alamedabicycle.com.

Bicycles Alameda, 883 Island Drive, Alameda; 510/865-3400.

Cycle City, 1433 High Street, Alameda; 510/521-2872.

Stone's, 2320 Santa Clara Avenue, Alameda; 510/523-3264.

ALBANY

Solano Avenue Cyclery, 1554 Solano Avenue, Albany; 510/524-1094; website: www.solanoavenuecyclery.com.

ANTIOCH

Bikes for Life, 1344 Sunset Drive, Antioch; 925/754-8025.

APTOS

Aptos Bike Trail, 7556 Soquel Drive, Aptos; 831/688-8650.

BELMONT

California Sport & Cyclery, 1464 El Camino Real, Belmont; 650/593-8806.

BERKELEY

Mike's Bikes, 2133 University Avenue, Berkeley; 510/549-8350; website: www.mikesbicyclecenter.com.

Missing Link Bicycle Shop, 1988 Shattuck Avenue, Berkeley; 510/843-7471; website: www.missinglink.org.

Pacific Bicycle, 2701 College Avenue, Berkeley; 510/644-3751; website: www.pacbikeonline.com.

REI, 1338 San Pablo Avenue, Berkeley; 510/527-4140; website: www.rei.com.

Velo Sport, 1650 Martin Luther King Way, Berkeley; 510/849-0437.

BRENTWOOD

Brentwood Cyclery, Inc., 3901-A Walnut Boulevard, Brentwood; 925/634-5600.

BURLINGAME

Summit Bicycles, 1111 Burlingame Avenue, Burlingame; 650/343-8483; website: www.summitbicycles.com.

CAMPBELL

Performance Bike, 1646 South Bascom Avenue, Campbell; 408/559-0495.

Wheel Away Cycle Center, 402 East Hamilton Avenue, Campbell; 408/378-4636.

CASTRO VALLEY

Castro Valley Cyclery, 20515 Stanton Avenue, Castro Valley; 510/538-1878; website: www.cvcyclery.com.

Eden Bicycles, 3313 Village Drive, Castro Valley; 510/881-5000.

CONCORD

REI, 1975 Diamond Boulevard, Concord; 925/825-9400; website: www.rei.com.

CORTE MADERA

REI, 213 Corte Madera Town Center, Corte Madera; 415/927-1938; website: www.rei.com.

CUPERTINO

Cupertino Bike Shop, 10493 South De Anza Boulevard, Cupertino; 408/255-2217; website: www.cupertinobike.com.

Stan's Bicycles, 19685 Stevens Creek Boulevard, Cupertino; 408/996-1234; website: www.stansbikes.com.

DANVILLE

California Pedaler, 495 South Hartz Avenue, Danville; 925/820-0345; website: www.californiapedaler.com.

Pegasus Bicycle Works, 439 Rail Road Avenue, Danville; 925/362-2220; website: www.pegasusbicycleworks.com.

DUBLIN

Dublin Cyclery, 7001 Dublin Boulevard, Dublin; 925/828-8676; website: www.dublincyclery.com.

EL SOBRANTE

El Sobrante Schwinn Cyclery, 5057 El Portal Drive, El Sobrante; 510/223-3440.

The Pedaler, 3826 San Pablo Dam Road, El Sobrante; 510/222-3420.

FAIRFAX

Sunshine Bicycle Center, 737 Center Boulevard, Fairfax; 415/459-3334.

FREMONT

The Bicycle Garage, 37070 Fremont Boulevard, #106, Fremont; 510/795-9622.

Performance Bike, 39121 Fremont Boulevard, Fremont; 510/494-1466; website: www.performancebike.com.

REI, 43962 Fremont Boulevard, Fremont; 510/651-0305; website: www.rei.com.

Tri City Sporting Goods, 40900 Grimmer Boulevard, Fremont; 510/651-9600.

HALF MOON BAY

The Bike Works, 20 Stone Pine Center, Half Moon Bay; 650/726-6708.

Bicyclery, 101 Main Street, Suite B, Half Moon Bay; 650/726-6000.

HAYWARD

Cyclepath, 22510 Foothill Boulevard, Hayward; 510/881-5177.

LAFAYETTE

Hank and Frank Bicycles, 3377 Mt. Diablo Boulevard, Lafayette; 925/376-2453.

Sharp Bicycle, 969 Moraga Road, Lafayette; 925/284-9616.

LARKSPUR

Village Peddler, 1161 Magnolia Avenue, Larkspur; 415/461-3091.

LIVERMORE

Livermore Cyclery, 2288 First Street, Livermore; 925/455-8090; website: www.livermorecyclery.com.

Cal Bicycles, 2106 First Street, Livermore; 925/447-6666; website: www.calbicycles.com.

LOS ALTOS

The Bicycle Outfitter, 963 Fremont Avenue, Los Altos; 650/948-8092; website: www.bicycleoutfitter.com.

Chain Reaction Bicycles, 2310 Homestead Road, Los Altos; 408/735-8735; website: www.chainreaction.com.

LOS GATOS

Crossroads Bicycles, 217 North Santa Cruz Avenue, Los Gatos; 408/354-0555.

Los Gatos Cyclery, 652 North Santa Cruz Avenue, Los Gatos; 408/399-5099; website: www.losgatoscyclery.com.

Summit Bicycles, 111 East Main Street, Los Gatos; 408/399-9142; website: www.summitbicycles.com.

MARTINEZ

Martinez Cyclery, 4990 Pacheco Boulevard, Matinez; 925/228-9050; website: www.martinezcyclery.com.

MENLO PARK

Menlo Velo, 433 El Camino Real, Menlo Park; 650/327-5137.

MILL VALLEY

Mill Valley Cycleworks, 369 Miller Avenue, Mill Valley; 415/388-6774.

MILPITAS

Sun Bike Shop, 1549 Landess Avenue, Milpitas; 408/262-4360.

MOUNTAIN VIEW

Off Ramp, 2320 El Camino Real, Mountain View; 650/968-2974.

NOVATO

Bike Hut, 459 Entrada Drive, Novato; 415/883-2440.

Classcycle, 1531-B South Novato Boulevard, Novato; 415/897-3288; website: www.classcycle.com.

Pacific Bicycle, 132 Vintage Way, Suite F13, Novato; 415/892-9319; website: www.pacbikesandboards.com.

OAKLEY

Delta Freewheeler, 3831 Main Street, Oakley; 925/625-8200.

OAKLAND

A Round World Bike Shop, 2416 Telegraph Avenue, Oakland; 510/835-8763.

Cycle Sport, 3241 Grand Avenue, Oakland; 510/444-7900.

Wheels of Justice, 1969 Mountain Boulevard, Oakland; 510/339-6091.

Pioneer Bike Shop, 11 Rio Vista Avenue, Oakland; 510/658-8981.

PALO ALTO

Bike Connection, 2011 El Camino Real, Palo Alto; 650/424-8034; website: www.bikeconnection.net.

Garner's Pro Bikes, 63 Town & Country, Palo Alto; 650/327-6655.

Mike's Bikes, 2180 El Camino Real, Palo Alto; 650/493-8776; website: www.mikesbicyclecenter.com.

Palo Alto Bicycles, 171 University Avenue, Palo Alto; 650/328-7411; website: www.paloaltobicycles.com.

PETALUMA

The Bicycle Factory, 110 Kentucky Street, Petaluma; 707/763-7515.

Eastside Bicycles, 701 Sonoma Mountain Parkway, Suite B-6, Petaluma; 707/766-7501; website: www.eastsidecycles.com.

Petaluma Cyclery, 1080 Petaluma Boulevard North, Petaluma; 707/762-1990.

Sonoma Mountain Cyclery, 937 Lakeville Street, Petaluma; 707/773-3164.

PLEASANT HILL

Mike's Bikes, 1741 Contra Costa Boulevard, Pleasant Hill; 925/671-9127; website: www.mikesbicycles.com.

Pleasant Hill Cycles, 1494 Contra Costa Boulevard, Pleasant Hill; 925/676-2667.

PLEASANTON

Bicycles Pleasanton, 525 Main Street, Pleasanton; 925/461-0905.

Paquettes Bikes, 3506 Old Santa Rita Road, Pleasanton; 925/846-4788.

POINT REYES STATION

Cycle Analysis, Highway 1, Point Reyes Station; 415/663-9164.

REDWOOD CITY

Chain Reaction Bicycles, 1451 El Camino Real, Redwood City; 650/366-7130; website: www.chainreaction.com.

Garner's Pro Bike, 2755 El Camino Real, Redwood City; 650/366-2453.

Pacific Bicycle, 665 El Camino Real, Redwood City; 650/367-6094; website: www.pacbikeonline.com.

Performance Bike, 2535 El Camino Real, Redwood City; 650/365-9094; website: www.performancebike.com.

SAN ANSELMO

Caesar Cyclery, 29 San Anselmo Avenue, San Anselmo; 415/721-0805.

SAN BRUNO

Bike Route, 568 San Mateo Avenue, San Bruno; 650/873-9555.

SAN CARLOS

Broken Spoke, 782 Laurel Street, San Carlos; 650/594-9210.

REI, 1119 Industrial Boulevard, San Carlos; 650/508-2330; website: www.rei.com.

Velo Cyclo, 1316 El Camino Real, San Carlos; 650/591-2210.

SAN FRANCISCO

American Cyclery, 858 Stanyan Street, San Francisco; 415/876-4545.

Avenue Cyclery, 756 Stanyan Street, San Francisco; 415/387-3155; website: www.avenuecyclery.com.

Big Swingin' Cycles, 1122 Taraval Street, San Francisco; 415/661-2462; website: www.bigswingincycles.com.

City Cycle of San Francisco, 3001 Steiner Street, San Francisco; 415/346-2242; website: www.citycycle.com.

DD Cycles, 4049 Balboa Street, San Francisco; 415/752-7980.

Free Wheel Bike Shop, 980 Valencia Street, San Francisco; 415/643-9213.

Fresh Air Bicycles, 1943 Divisadero Boulevard, San Francisco; 415/563-4824.

Golden Gate Cyclery, 672 Stanyan Street, San Francisco; 415/379-3876.

Lombardi's Sports, 1600 Jackson Street, San Francisco; 415/771-0600; website: www.lombardissports.com.

Noe Valley Cyclery, 4193 24th Street, San Francisco; 415/647-0886.

Nomad Cyclery, 2555 Irving Street, San Francisco; 415/564-3568.

Ocean Cyclery, 1915 Ocean Avenue, San Francisco; 415/239-5004.

Pacific Bicycle, 1161 Sutter Street, San Francisco; 415/928-8466; website: www.pacbikeonline.com.

Pedal Revolution, 3085 21st Street, San Francisco; 415/641-1264.

Road Rage Bicycles, 1063 Folsom Street, San Francisco; 415/255-1351.

Roaring Mouse Cycles, 1352 Irving Street, San Francisco; 415/753-6272; website: www.roaringmousecycles.com.

Valencia Cyclery, 1077 Valencia Street, San Francisco; 415/550-6600.

Velo City, 638 Stanyan Street, San Francisco; 415/221-3499.

Vision Cyclery S.F., 772 Stanyan Street, San Francisco; 415/221-9766.

SAN JOSE

Calabazas Cyclery, 6140 Bollinger Road, San Jose; 408/366-2453; website: www.calabazas.com.

Campus Bicycles, 4724 Meridian Avenue, San Jose; 408/265-8112; website: www.campusbicycles.com.

Fast Bicycle, 2274 Alum Rock Avenue, San Jose; 408/251-9110; website: www.bike.com.

The Hyland Family's Bicycles, 1515 Meridian Avenue, San Jose; 408/269-2300; website: www.hylandbikes.com.

Pacific Bicycle, 1008 Blossom Hill Road, San Jose; 408/264-3570; website: www.pacbikeonline.com.

Reed's Cyclery, 3020 Alum Rock Avenue, San Jose; 408/926-1600; website: www.reedssportshop.com.

REI, 400 El Paseo de Saratoga Shopping Center, San Jose; 408/871-8765; website: www.rei.com.

Santa Teresa Bikes, 503 West Capitol Expressway, San Jose; 408/264-2453; website: www.fifthwave.com/stbikes.

Trail Head Cyclery, 14450 Union Avenue, San Jose; 408/369-9666; website: www.trailheadonline.com.

Willow Glen Bicycles, 1110 Willow Street, San Jose; 408/293-2606; website: www.willowglenbicycles.com.

SAN MATEO

Cyclepath, 1212 S. El Camino Real, San Mateo; 650/341-0922; website: www.cylepath.com.

Pacific Bicycle, 121 East 4th Avenue, San Mateo; 650/344-9702; website: www.pacificbikeonline.com.

Talbots Cyclery, 445 S. B Street, San Mateo; 650/342-0184.

SAN RAFAEL

Mike's Bicycle Center, 1601 Fourth Street, San Rafael; 415/454-3747; website: www.mikesbicyclecenter.com.

Performance Bike, 369 Third Street, San Rafael; 415/454-9063; website: www.performancebike.com.

SANTA CLARA

Calmar Cycles, 2236 El Camino Real, Santa Clara; 408/249-6907; website: www.calmarcycles.com.

The Off Ramp, 2369 El Camino Real, Santa Clara; 408/249-2848; website: www.offrampbicycles.com.

Shaws' Lightweight Cycles, 45 Washington Street, Santa Clara; 800/246-7881; website: www.shawscycles.com.

SARATOGA

Pacific Bicycle, 1821 Saratoga Avenue, Saratoga; 408/252-3600; website: www.pacbikeonline.com.

SAUSALITO

A Bicycle Odyssey, 1417 Bridgeway, Sausalito; 415/332-3050; website: www.abicycleodyssey.com.

Sausalito Cyclery, 1 Gate Six Road, Sausalito; 415/332-3200; website: www.mikesbicyclecenter.com.

SUNNYVALE

Walt's Cycles, 116 Carroll Street, Sunnyvale; 408/736-2630; website: www.waltscycles.com.

VALLEJO

Authorized Bicycles, 1220 Georgia Street, Vallejo; 707/648-1413.

WALNUT CREEK

Encina Bicycle, 2901 Ygnacio Valley Road, Walnut Creek; 925/944-9200; website: www.encinacycles.com.

Performance Bike, 1401 North Broadway, Walnut Creek; 925/937-7723.

Rivendell Bicycle Works, 2040 N. Main Street, Walnut Creek; 925/933-7304; website: www.rivendellbicycles.com.

Mendocino and Wine Country

CALISTOGA

Palisades Mountain Sport, 1330-V Gerrard Street, Calistoga; 707/942-9687; website: www.palisadesmountainsport.com.

CLOVERDALE

Cloverdale Cyclery, 125 North Cloverdale Boulevard, Cloverdale; 707/894-2841.

FORT BRAGG

Fort Bragg Cyclery, 579 South Franklin Street, Fort Bragg; 707/964-3509.

HEALDSBURG

Spoke Folk Cyclery, 201 Center Street, Healdsburg; 707/433-7171; website: www.spokefolk.com.

LAKEPORT

The Bicycle Rack, 302 North Main Street, Lakeport; 707/263-1200.

MENDOCINO

Catch-a-Canoe & Bicycles Too, 44850 Comptche-Ukiah Road, Mendocino; 707/937-0273; website: www.stanfordinn.com.

NAPA

Bicycle Madness, 2500 Jefferson, Napa; 707/253-2453.
Bicycle Trax, 796 Soscol Avenue, Napa; 707/258-8729.
Bicycle Works, 3335 Solano, Napa; 707/253-7000.

ROHNERT PARK

Adventure Bike Company, 1451 Southwest Boulevard, Rohnert Park; 707/794-8594.
Cambria Bicycle Emporium, 587 Rohnert Park Expressway, Rohnert Park; 707/206-9500; website: www.cambriabike.com.

SAINT HELENA

St. Helena Cyclery, 1156 Main Street, Saint Helena; 707/963-7736; website: www.sthelenacyclery.com.

SANTA ROSA

The Bike Peddler, 605 College Avenue, Santa Rosa; 707/571-2428; website: www.socobikes.com.
Dave's Bike Sport, 353 College Avenue, Santa Rosa; 707/528-3283; website: www.socobikes.com.
Nevin Cycles, 397 Aviation Boulevard, Suite B, Santa Rosa; 707/538-0253.
Rincon Cyclery, 4927 Sonoma Highway, Santa Rosa; 707/538-0868; website: www.rinconcyclery.com.
Santa Rosa Cyclery, 2300 Midway, Santa Rosa; 707/522-6232.

SONOMA

Goodtime Touring, 18503 Highway 12, Sonoma; 888/525-0453; website: www.goodtimetouring.com.

Sonoma Valley Cyclery, 20093 Broadway, Sonoma; 707/935-3377; website: www.sonomavalleycyclery.com.

UKIAH

Dave's Bike Shop, 846 South State Street, Ukiah; 707/462-3230.
Ukiah Schwinn Center, 178 East Gobbi Street, Ukiah; 707/462-2686.

WILLITS

The Bike Shop/Earthlab Energy Systems, 358 South Main Street, Willits; 707/459-3696.
Suncycles, 151 North Main Street, Willits; 707/459-2453.

WINDSOR

Windsor Bicycle Center, 9064 Brooks Road South, Windsor; 707/836-9111; website: www.windsorbicyclecenter.com.

Monterey and Big Sur

CAPITOLA

Cycle Works, 1203 41st Avenue, Capitola; 831/476-7092; website: www.jjbike.com.

CARMEL VALLEY

Bay Bikes at the Village, 10 East Carmel Valley Road, Carmel Valley; 831/659-2453.

GILROY

Sunshine Bicycle Shop, 311 First Street, Gilroy; 408/842-4889; website: www.sunshinebicycles.com.

HOLLISTER

Cherry Bike, 341 Tres Pinos Road Suite 106, Hollister; 831/636-0802; website: www.cherrybikes.net.

MONTEREY

Adventures by the Sea, 299 Cannery Row and 201 Alvarado Street, Monterey; 831/372-1807.
Aquarian Bicycles, 486 Washington Street, Monterey; 831/375-2144.
Bay Bikes, 640 Wave Street, Monterey; 831/646-9090.
Joselyn's Bike Shop, 398 East Franklin Street, Monterey; 831/649-8520.

PACIFIC GROVE

Winning Wheels, 223 15th Street, Pacific Grove; 831/375-4322.

SALINAS

Bobcat Bicycles, 141 Monterey Street, Salinas; 831/753-7433; website: www.bobcatbicycles.com.

SANTA CRUZ

Another Bike Shop, 2361 Mission Street, Santa Cruz; 831/427-2232; website: www.anotherbikeshop.com.
Armadillo Cyclery, 1211 Mission Street, Santa Cruz; 831/426-7299.
Bicycle Trip, 1127 Soquel Avenue, Santa Cruz; 831/427-2580.
The Bike Shop, 1325 Mission Street, Santa Cruz; 831/454-0909.
Family Cycling Center, 914 41st Avenue, Santa Cruz; 831/475-3883.
The Spokesman Bicycles, 231 Cathcart Street, Santa Cruz; 408/378-3408; website: www.spokesmanbicycles.com.
Sprockets, 1420 Mission Street, Santa Cruz; 831/426-7623; website: www.sprocketsbikes.com.

SCOTTS VALLEY

Scotts Valley Cycle Sport, 245 Mt. Hermon Road, Scotts Valley; 831/440-9070.

SEASIDE

Sports Center Bicycle, 1576 Del Monte Boulevard, Seaside; 831/899-1300.

WATSONVILLE

Trey's True Wheel, 1431 Main Street, Watsonville; 831/786-0200.

Sacramento and Gold Country

ANGELS CAMP

Mountain Pedaler, 352 South Main Street, Angels Camp; 209/736-0771.

AUBURN

Auburn Bike Works, 350 Grass Valley Highway, Auburn; 530/885-3861; website: www.auburnbikeworks.com.
The Bicycle Emporium, 483 Grass Valley Highway, Auburn; 530/823-2900; website: www.cambriabike.com.

CARMICHAEL

Bicycle Products of Carmichael, 5142 Arden Way, Carmichael; 916/488-5353; website: www.bicycleproducts.com.

CHICO

Campus Bicycles, 330 Main Street, Chico; 530/345-2081.
Chico Bike and Board, 845 Main Street, Chico; 530/343-5506.
Cyclesport, 222 West Second Street, Chico; 530/345-1910.

North Rim Adventure Sports, 178 East Second Street, Chico; 530/345-2453; website: www.northrimadventure.com.

North Valley Cycles, 2590 Cohasset Road, Chico; 530/343-0636.

Pullins Cyclery, 801 Main Street, Chico; 530/342-1055.

Sports Ltd., 240 Main Street, Chico; 530/894-1110.

Village Cycle, 1311 Mangrove Avenue, Chico; 530/342-2431.

CITRUS HEIGHTS

City Bicycle Works, 7885 Greenback Lane, Citrus Heights; 916/726-2453.

DAVIS

ASUCD Bike Barn, University of California Davis, 1 Shields Avenue, Davis; 530/752-2575.

B & L's Bike Shop, 610 Third Street, Davis; 530/756-3540; website: www.blbikeshop.com.

Freewheeler Bicycle Center, 703 Second Street, Davis; 530/758-5460.

Ken's Bike & Ski, 650 G Street, Davis; 530/758-3223.

Steve Larsen's Wheelworks, 247 F Street, Davis; 530/753-3118; website: www.stevelarsenswheelworks.com.

DOWNIEVILLE

Downieville Outfitters, 310 Main Street, Downieville; 530/289-0155; website: www.downievilleoutfitters.com.

Yuba Expeditions, P.O. Box 224, Downieville; 530/289-3010; website: www.yubaexpeditions.com

ELK GROVE

Laguna Bike Shop, 7701 Laguna Boulevard, Suite 400, Elk Grove; 916/691-3251.

FAIR OAKS

The Bike Shop, 4719 San Juan Avenue, Fair Oaks; 916/961-9646.

Bob's Cycle Center, 9920 Fair Oaks Boulevard, Fair Oaks; 916/961-6700.

Performance Bike, 5271 Sunrise Boulevard, Quail Point Shopping Center, Fair Oaks; 916/961-1488; website: www.performancebike.com.

River Rat Inc., 9840 Fair Oaks Boulevard, Fair Oaks; 916/966-6777; website: www.river-rat.com.

FOLSOM

Bicycles Plus, 705 Gold Lake Drive, Suite 320, Folsom; 916/355-8901; website: www.onlinecycling.com.

GRASS VALLEY

Mountain Recreation, 682-C Freeman Lane, Grass Valley; 530/477-8006.

Free Flight Sports, 153 South Auburn Street, Grass Valley; 530/272-7790; website: www.freeflightsports.com.

JACKSON

Jackson Family Sports, 225 East Highway 88, Jackson; 209/223-3890.

LINCOLN

Gold Country Bicycles, 150 G Street, Suite 104, Lincoln; 916/645-3753.

MODESTO

Valley Sporting Goods, 1700 McHenry Avenue, Suite D50, Modesto; 209/523-5681.
World of Wheels, 1544 Standiford, Modesto; 209/522-0804.

NEVADA CITY

Tour of Nevada City Bicycle Shop, 457 Sacramento Street, Nevada City; 530/265-2187; website: www.tourofnevadacity.com.

PARADISE

The Bicycle Shop, 6133 Skyway, Paradise; 530/872-9363.

PLACERVILLE

Golden Spoke Bike Shop, 679 Placerville Drive, Placerville; 530/626-8370.
Placerville Bike Shop, 1307 Broadway, Placerville; 530/622-3015.

RANCHO CORDOVA

Bicycle Products of Rancho Cordova, 12401 Folsom Boulevard, Rancho Cordova; 916/351-9066; website: www.bicycleproducts.com.

ROCKLIN

Sharp Bicycles, 6840 Five Star Boulevard, Rocklin; 916/630-8894.

ROSEVILLE

Bob's Cycle Center, 378 North Sunrise Boulevard, Roseville; 916/784-2255.
Sierra Outfitters, 1850 Douglas Boulevard, Roseville; 916/782-7500; website: www.sierraoutfitters.com.

SACRAMENTO

American River Bicycle, 9203 Folsom Boulevard and 256 Florin Road, Sacramento; 916/427-6199; website: www.americanriverbikes.com.
The Bicycle Business, 3077 Freeport Boulevard, Sacramento; 916/442-5246.
City Bicycle Works, 2419 K Street, Sacramento; 916/447-7730; website: www.citybikeworks.com.
Natomas Bike Shop, 3291 Truxel Road, Sacramento; 916/641-8640.
Performance Bicycle Shop, 5271 Sunrise Boulevard, Sacramento; 916/961-1488; website: www.performancebike.com.
Rest Stop Bike Accessories, 3230 Folsom Boulevard, Sacramento; 916/453-1870.

Sierra Outfitters, 2100 Arden Way #172, Sacramento; 916/922-7500; website: www.sierraoutfitters.com.

SONORA

JT Cycles, 55 South Washington Street, Sonora; 209/536-9882.
Sonora Cyclery, 13867 Mono Way, Sonora; 209/532-6800.

STOCKTON

Delta Cyclery, 6555 Pacific Avenue, Stockton; 209/951-5665.

VACAVILLE

Bicycle Products of Vacaville, 617 Elmira Road, Vacaville; 707/447-6399; website: www.bicycleproducts.com.
Ray's Cycles, 400 Main Street, Vacaville; 707/448-1911.

WOODLAND

Foy's Bike Shop, 352 West Main Street and 421 Pioneer Avenue, Woodland; 530/661-0900; website: www.blbikeshop.com.
Main Street Cyclery, 1041 Main Street, Woodland; 530/661-6800; website: www.mainstreetcyclery.com.

YUBA CITY

Twin Cities Bike and Repair, 980 Gray Avenue, Yuba City; 530/673-8409.
Vans Bicycle Center, 622 Gray Avenue, Yuba City; 530/674-0179.

Tahoe and the Northern Sierra

BEAR VALLEY

Bear Valley Adventure Company, 1 Bear Valley Road, Bear Valley; 209/753-2834; website: www.bearvalleyxc.com.

HOMEWOOD

Tahoe Gear, 5095 W. Lake Boulevard, Homewood; 530/525-5233.

HOPE VALLEY

Hope Valley Outdoor Center, 14655 Highway 88, Hope Valley; 530/694-2266.

KINGS BEACH

Tahoe Bike and Ski, 8499 N. Lake Boulevard, Kings Beach; 530/546-7437.

KIRKWOOD

Kirkwood Resort Adventure Center, 1377 Kirkwood Meadows Drive, Kirkwood; 209/258-7218; website: www.kirkwood.com.

NORTHSTAR

Northsport at Northstar, Highway 267 at Northstar Drive, Northstar; 530/562-2268; website: www.skinorthstar.com.

OLYMPIC VALLEY

Squaw Valley Sport Shop, Squaw Valley Mall, Olympic Valley; 530/583-3356.

SODA SPRINGS

Java Summit Sports, 21501 Donner Pass Road, Suite 19, Soda Springs; 530/426-3567.

SOUTH LAKE TAHOE

Lakeview Sports, 3131 Harrison Avenue, South Lake Tahoe; 530/544-0183; website: www.tahoesports.com.

Sierra Cycle Works, 3430 Lake Tahoe Boulevard, South Lake Tahoe; 530/541-7505.

South Shore Bikes, 1132 Ski Run Boulevard, South Lake Tahoe; 530/541-1549.

Tahoe Bike and Ski, 2277 Lake Tahoe Boulevard, South Lake Tahoe; 530/544-8060; website: www.tahoebikeandski.com.

TAHOE CITY

Alpenglow Sports, 415 North Lake Boulevard, Tahoe City; 530/583-6917.

The Back Country, 255 North Lake Boulevard, Tahoe City; 530/581-5861; website: www.thebackcountry.net.

Cyclepaths, 1785 West Lake Boulevard, Tahoe City; 800/780-BIKE; website: www.cyclepaths.com.

Olympic Bike Shop, 620 North Lake Boulevard, Tahoe City; 530/581-2500.

TRUCKEE

The Back Country, 11429 Donner Pass Road, Truckee; 530/582-0909.

Paco's Truckee Bike & Ski, 11200 Donner Pass Road #6, Truckee; 530/587-5561; website: www.pacosbikeandski.com.

Yosemite and Mammoth Lakes

BISHOP

Bikes of Bishop, 651 N. Main Street, Bishop; 760/872-3829.

FRESNO

Cyclo-path Fresno, 6459 N. Blackstone, Fresno; 559/432-2990.
Tri Sport, 132 W. Nees Avenue, Suite 111, Fresno; 559/432-0800.

MADERA

Sierra Cycle Works, 1501 Howard Road, Madera; 559/674-3315.

MAMMOTH LAKES

Footloose Sports, 3043 Main Street, Mammoth Lakes; 760/934-2400; website: www.footloosesports.com.

Mammoth Mountain Bike Shop, 1 Minaret Road, Mammoth Lakes; 800/228-4947; website: www.mammothmtn.com.

Mammoth Sporting Goods, 1 Sierra Center Mall, Old Mammoth Road, Mammoth Lakes; 760/934-3239; website: www.mammoth sportinggoods.com.

Sandy's Ski and Sport, 3499 Main Street, Mammoth Lakes; 760/934-7518.

MERCED

Kevins Bikes, 60 W. Olive Avenue, Merced; 209/722-2228.

Redwood Empire

ARCATA

Life Cycle, 1593 G Street, Arcata; 707/822-7755.

New Outdoor Store, 876 G Street, Arcata; 707/822-0321; website: www.pacific-outfitters.com.

CRESCENT CITY

Back Country Bicycles, 1331 Northcrest Drive, Crescent City; 707/465-3995.

Escape Hatch Sport and Cycle, 960 Third Street, Crescent City; 707/464-2614.

EUREKA

Henderson Center Bicycles, 2811 F Street, Eureka; 707/443-9861.

Pro Sport Center, 508 Myrtle Avenue, Eureka; 707/443-6328; website: www.pacific-outfitters.com.

Sport & Cycle, 1621 Broadway Street, Eureka; 707/444-9274.

Shasta and Lassen

CHESTER

Bodfish Bicycles, 152 Main Street, Chester; 530/258-2338.

MOUNT SHASTA

The Fifth Season, 300 North Mount Shasta Boulevard, Mount Shasta; 530/926-3606.

House of Ski and Board, 316 Chestnut Street, Mount Shasta; 530/926-1303.

Fast Wheels Bike Shop, 233 Main Street, Red Bluff; 530/529-1388.

Bikes Etc., 2400 Athens Avenue, Redding; 530/244-1954.

The Bike Shop, 3331 Bechelli Lane, Redding; 530/223-1205; website: www.thebikeshop.cc.

Chain Gang Bike Shop, 1180 Industrial Street, Redding; 530/223-3400; website: www.chaingangbikeshop.com.

Redding Sports Limited, 950 Hilltop Drive, Redding; 530/221-7333.

Sports Cottage, 2665 Park Marina Drive, Redding; 530/241-3115; website: www.sportscottage.com.

Village Cycle, 3090 Bechelli Lane, Redding; 530/223-2320; website: www.villagecycle.net.

INDEX

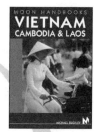

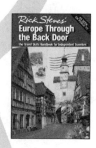

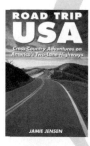